D1523991

Uncircumscribe

Uncircumscribed Mind

Reading Milton Deeply

Montante Family Library
D'Youville College

Edited by
Charles W. Durham and
Kristin A. Pruitt

SUP

Selinsgrove: Susquehanna University Press

©2008 by Rosemont Publishing & Printing Corp.

All rights reserved. Authorization to photocopy items for internal or personal use, or the internal or personal use of specific clients, is granted by the copyright owner, provided that a base fee of $10.00, plus eight cents per page, per copy is paid directly to the Copyright Clearance Center, 222 Rosewood Drive, Danvers, Massachusetts 01923. [978-1-57591-116-8/08 $10.00 + 8¢ pp, pc.]

Other than as indicated in the foregoing, this book may not be reproduced, in whole or in part, in any form (except as permitted by Sections 107 and 108 of the U.S. Copyright Law, and except for brief quotes appearing in reviews in the public press).

Associated University Presses
2010 Eastpark Boulevard
Cranbury, NJ 08512

The paper used in this publication meets the requirements of the American National Standard for Permanence of Paper for Printed Library Materials Z39.48–1984.

Library of Congress Cataloging-in-Publication Data

Uncircumscribed mind : reading Milton deeply / edited by Charles W. Durham and Kristin A. Pruitt.
    p. cm.
  Includes index.
  ISBN 978-1-57591-116-8 (alk. paper)
1. Milton, John, 1608-1674—Criticism and interpretation. 2. Milton, John, 1608-1674—Influence. I. Durham, Charles W. II. Pruitt, Kristin A., 1945-

PR3588.U63 2008
821'.4—dc22
                                2007020071

PRINTED IN THE UNITED STATES OF AMERICA

PR 3588
.U63
2008

To Annabel Patterson,
whose wit and wisdom delight and enlighten

FEB 15 2008

Contents

Acknowledgments

F̲OR SIGNIFICANT AND VARIED CONTRIBUTIONS TO THE SUCCESS OF THE 2003 Conference on John Milton, we wish to thank Kevin Donovan, John Shawcross, and Donald McDonough; the Middle Tennessee State University Department of English and the Virginia Peck Foundation for moral and financial support; and conference participants for their part in this spirited scholarly exchange; colleagues and friends at MTSU and Christian Brothers University who encourage our projects; Janie, Eliote, Carrie, Andrew, and Candice, ever our advocates; and most especially the contributors to this collection for "reading Milton deeply."

Uncircumscribed Mind

Introduction

THE TITLE OF THIS COLLECTION PAYS HOMAGE TO TWO YOUTHFUL PRO-
nouncements by John Milton. In "Prolusion 3," "Against Scholastic
Philosophy," the Cambridge student addresses his "collegiate audience"
(604).[1] After a scathing attack against "the so-called subtle doctors,"
Milton exhorts his listeners: "But your mind should not consent to be
limited and circumscribed by the earth's boundaries, but should range
beyond the confines of the world. Let it reach the summit of knowledge and learn to know itself and at the same time to know those
blessed minds and intelligences with whom hereafter it will enter into
eternal fellowship." In another academic piece, "At a Vacation Exercise
in the College," Milton acknowledges his preference for "some graver
subject" that also appears prophetic in terms of his mature poetic
works:

> Yet I would rather, if I were to choose,
> Thy service in some graver subject use,
> Such as may make thee search thy coffers round,
> Before thou clothe my fancy in fit sound.
> Such where the deep transported mind may soar
> Above the wheeling poles, and at Heav'n's door
> Look in.
>
> (29–35)

That Milton encourages his readers to "range" freely in their search
for knowledge with a "deep transported mind" and that he expresses
his personal choice of subject suggest that he may well have wished to
be a model for those who approach his works. And the sixteen essays
that comprise this collection represent how challenging, stimulating,
and far ranging are the efforts to read Milton critically and deeply. The
essays' subjects and approaches are purposefully diverse, suggesting
the variety of topics that engage contemporary readers of Milton's po-

etry and prose, but there are, nonetheless, relationships between and among them. Many focus on *A Mask Presented at Ludlow Castle, Paradise Lost,* and *Samson Agonistes,* albeit from distinctive perspectives. A number view the poetry and prose through the lens of seventeenth-century controversies, movements, and events. Several use Milton's prose works, like *Christian Doctrine* or the divorce tracts, to illuminate his poetry. In thematic terms, the first six essays deal with the issue of evil, the next two deal with the world of Milton's masque and the many worlds of his epic *Paradise Lost,* four examine influence—Milton's use of his sources or his impact on later writers—and the final four focus on Milton's later works, one on Milton's "brief epic" *Paradise Regained* and three on *Samson Agonistes,* all suggesting the ambiguity of Milton's treatment of trial and temptation.

In the opening essay in this collection, "Milton and the Problems of Evil: A Preemptive Modernism?" Annabel Patterson seeks to consider her topic "with a twenty-first-century design that does not do violence to Milton's late seventeenth-century mental technology." Suggesting that the "recent revival of Evil in the political vocabulary is regressive, archaic, and bad for thought," Patterson focuses on four problems of evil: (1) the problem of responsibility; (2) whether it is possible to distinguish between natural and moral evils; (3) whether it is necessary "to posit an Adversary figure in the cosmos to account" for evil; and (4) whether we can determine the source of evil and the significance of "writing a *narrative* of its genesis," as Milton does in *Paradise Lost,* a narrative suffused with "undecidability." Patterson contends: "he dealt with the seam between the Adversary and the Tempter narrative by marking the seam *as* narrative, as a matter of chronology, with the first part of the poem dedicated to Satan as Adversary, the second half to Satan as Tempter. Yet . . . everything he did to his inherited materials rather served to display the problems inherent in them than to resolve them," thus anticipating "the sense of ineptitude that Kant so brilliantly discerned in the Western myths of the origins of evil." Aligning Daniel Defoe's *The Political History of the Devil* with Milton's *Paradise Lost* demonstrates "what was *thinkable* in the early modern period, as distinct from the truly modern period."

In "'Not Without Dust and Heat': Alchemy and *Areopagitica*," Glenn Sucich argues that "[t]he influence of alchemy on Milton's prose and poetry has been grossly underestimated." During the seventeenth century, alchemy was commonly viewed as a censurable practice associated with black magic and therefore a means of understanding the

origin of evil in the world. Similarly, Milton's views on the subject are
often regarded as negative. To the contrary, Sucich proposes "a more
affirmative and constructive relation between the discourse of alchemy
and Milton's thought," focusing specifically on *Areopagitica*'s use of "alchemical imagery and ideas" relating to the concepts of "reduction to
first principles, digestion, and sublimation. These processes, which
were all integral to the theory and practice of early modern alchemy,
shape Milton's overarching attempt to transform Parliament's decision
regarding the Licensing Act of 1643. They also inform Milton's efforts
to promote spiritual health and moral integrity in individuals that he
deems crucial to the welfare of the English commonwealth." Thus,
alchemy "provided Milton a powerful metaphor for the pursuit of . . .
excellence that, in *Areopagitica*, is engendered by reading" as well as a
foundation upon which "to build his argument against prepublication
licensing."

William Shullenberger, in "Circe's Best Boy," analyzes *A Mask Presented at Ludlow Castle* as an initiatory ritual, occurring in a "liminal" or
threshold zone, "a boundary space for transition and transformation"
and staging "the fifteen-year old Alice Egerton's passage from girlhood
to womanhood." Within the masque, Comus serves as the Lady's ritual
antagonist, a "'mock bridegroom' figure to threaten and tempt the
Lady." He serves, then, as a seventeenth-century embodiment of satanic evil. Moreover, "[s]ince this initiation performs itself in the specific social setting of Caroline England, by means of the masque, a
genre of social drama favored by its ruling class, we can see in Comus's
ritual aggression against the lady a self-dramatization of the aristocratic excesses that Milton intends to critique and reform." Shullenberger traces Comus's origins as "bastard son of the transformative sex
goddess Circe and the Greco-Roman god of ecstatic release, Bacchus,
or Dionysus. This means double trouble for those who encounter
him." Circe, "the dominant parental influence on Comus," is also a
substantive "latent influence" in the *Mask* itself. Shullenberger claims
that "Comus never had it so good as when he was Circe's baby boy.
Bereft of her, he tries to recapitulate the luscious sensual fullness of his
infancy. He can never get enough of what he imagines Nature, in
Circe's place, has to offer." From a Lacanian perspective, "Comus plies
his illusions and champions moral dissolution to restore the maternal
enclosure and to replicate the dream world of oneness with the
mother." In closing, Shullenberger contends that, "[h]aving dramatically confronted, identified, and repudiated Comus's regressive trajec-

tory of desire, which conceals beneath the pretense of self-gratification a dynamic of despairing self-consumption, the Lady returns to her home as Milton's triumphant exemplar of the autonomous ethical self of progressive Reformation culture."

In another essay concerned with manifestations of evil and satanic figures, Bryan Adams Hampton, in "Infernal Preaching: Participation, God's Name, and the Great Prophesying Movement in the Demonic Council Scene of *Paradise Lost*," presents the council scene "within the context of preaching." And although many seventeenth-century preachers saw themselves as "'incarnations' or embodiments of Christ acting in and speaking to the world," Hampton cautions that Milton might well be skeptical of such a view. He argues: "As Milton the 'Church-outed' poet-preacher well knew, these angelic preachers have their demonic counterparts not only in Hell, but also on earth. The task before us, Milton repeatedly charges in his anticlerical prose tracts, is to discern true preachers from false and dissembling ones. We find a picture of the latter in book 2 of *Paradise Lost*. The dynamics of the demonic council scene are reminiscent of the 'Great Prophesying Movement' of the late sixteenth and early seventeenth centuries, where a panel of Puritan ministers gathered to deliver a series of sermons on the same 'text': the Name of God." According to Hampton, "the restless demons play language games that attempt to 'unsay' the name of God," a salvo that "is also a metaphysical assault on God's essence" and the role of the Son. "Rather than fulfilling what promises to be a proliferation of meaning through the freedom of individual reading," Hampton seeks "to show that their language games paradoxically inscribe them within a calculus of sameness, and a 'form of life' whose performance is characterized by aggression and violence, manipulation and self-interest."

From an earlier chronological but later narrative perspective in *Paradise Lost*, Pitt Harding, in "'Strange point and new!': Satan's Challenge to Nascent Christianity," examines Satan's response to the exaltation of the Son in book 5, an event that Milton "accord[s] absolute temporal priority" through his use of Scripture. Harding asserts that "[b]y disputing the Son's priority . . . Satan embodies an ancient skepticism regarding what became a central tenet of Christian faith, one so firmly established in orthodoxy as to be practically invisible: the doctrine of the Son's preexistence. At the chronologically earliest point in a narrative that thrives on disclosing ever-earlier points of origin, Satan ignites a conflict over the very idea of origins. In effect, he disputes the

firstness of the epic's first 'first.' " The implications of Satan's challenge "may be said to re-enact a drama recorded in some of the earliest Christian texts" and to "[embody] resistance to some of those texts' interpretive strategies." Harding also points out that Satan represents "the hostile disbelief that Paul encountered." In Acts 13:45, "the apostle propounds a reading of Hebrew Scripture that provokes a reaction not unlike that of Satan," who is "fraught / With envy" (*Paradise Lost*, 5.661–62) at the exaltation of the Son.

Jamie H. Ferguson similarly focuses on Satan and theological conflicts, in this case distinctions between the Roman Catholic and Protestant understanding of the Eucharist, in "Satan's Supper: Language and Sacrament in *Paradise Lost*." Ferguson believes that Eve's disobedience results in "a fall into language, which the poem presents as an inherently unstable medium. This view of language is illuminated by Milton's comments, in *De Doctrina Christiana*, on another kind of token, the Eucharist." Ferguson claims that "Satan's temptation of Eve in book 9 alludes suggestively to what Milton called the 'Missa Papistica,' " as "Satan ministers the fruit to Eve in terms that recall the specific form of communion Milton attributes to Roman doctrine in the *De Doctrina*: Satan tempts Eve with ascension to the rank of goddess through ingestion of an object whose intrinsic character he consistently emphasizes." Moreover, Ferguson states, antanaclasis, "repetition of the same word in different senses," allows Satan to suggest "that words—the words associated with obedience to God and words in general—bear no necessary relation to any particular referents. . . . Allusions to the Roman Mass in and around the Temptation-sequence suggest a parallel between this conception of language and Milton's discussion, in *De Doctrina*, of the sheer indeterminacy of the eucharistic sign independent of its recipient." According to Ferguson, "the period's intense doctrinal polemics concerning the status of the Eucharist provide an important source of comparative insight into the period's abiding preoccupation with defining the nature of language."

Using Samuel Johnson's critique of Milton's masque as a springboard to her consideration of aesthetics and form in "Transforming the 'Corporal Rinde': The Songs of Milton's *A Mask Presented at Ludlow Castle*," Eliza Fisher Laskowski, like Shullenberger, deals with boundaries—but of a different sort. She suggests that "Milton's songs are another layer through which he interrogates the larger theological issues of body and soul." The world of the masque, as revealed through the thematic emphases of its songs, is a complicated one, "where the bodied and bodiless, the mortal, immortal, and divine are repeatedly juxtaposed and evaluated. In this world, the relationship of body to spirit is unfixed, a continuum rather than a rigid distinction." Laskowski concludes that

> [t]hough Dr. Johnson essentially dismissed their poetic value, the songs of Milton's masque become a keystone for not only understanding Milton's generic expansion, but also for aligning the implications of the masque more closely with the poet's mature works. . . . The complicated tangle of the bodied and the bodiless, the illusion of the spiritual represented as the temporal and the temporal as the spiritual, the questionable nature of transcendence from without, not from within, all these problems are interwoven through five seemingly straightforward musical moments within the masque. Along the banks of the Severn, in the woods beyond Ludlow Castle, bodies and souls do not seem to exist in rigid distinction; the boundaries between them are as quick and liquid as the waters of the neighboring river.

In "Milton's Other Worlds," Lara Dodds's epigraph, "in such abundance lies our choice" (*Paradise Lost*, 9.620), serves as a touchstone for her examination of "the controversy surrounding the plurality of worlds" in *Paradise Lost* that, she proposes, "provides Milton with a vocabulary for expressing the conditions and consequences of . . . choice." Similarly, "the poem also depends on the reader's simultaneous perception of multiple worlds that must be understood as both separate and coexistent." Like Shullenberger and Laskowski, Dodds reflects on boundaries. As she says, Milton's "worlds include the separate spaces of Heaven, Hell, and Earth, and extend to worlds that are bounded in other ways: fallen and unfallen; male and female; mortal and angelic; past, present, and future." Dodds discusses the seventeenth-century controversy regarding the plurality of worlds fanned by astronomical discoveries of the past century and Milton's incorporation of "the perspectives of both the enthusiastic advocate for the 'new science' and the skeptical traditionalist whose books were among Milton's sources for astronomical knowledge." Focusing on book 8, "which brings together a dialogue about the spatial arrangement of the physical world (or worlds) with a dialogue concerning the social arrangement of the human world," Dodds claims that "Adam's two conversations with Raphael . . . may be seen as working through [the] transformation from a vertical hierarchy to the recognition of horizontal differentiation."

In the first of several essays examining influence and how Milton's story of the Fall is impacted by earlier works or affects later ones, William Walker contends in "Reassessing Milton's Republicanism: History, Machiavelli, and *Paradise Lost*" that although Milton's epic is "now widely seen to reflect the republican tradition of political thought that so strongly informed it," this view has not been unchallenged: "Some Miltonists and historians of political thought have . . . questioned the going argument for the classical and Machiavellian credentials of Milton's republicanism in particular and English republicanism at large." For Walker, "[a] much more complicated and problematic picture of mid-seventeenth-century English political thought is emerging from this scholarship, and it is to such a picture that I propose to add some details, not so much by observing the religious dimensions of Milton's republicanism as by observing how the religious dimension of his thinking *conflicts* with many of the tenets of the classical and Machiavellian republicanism with which he has been aligned." Focusing on classical sources, Machiavelli's *Discourses* and *The Prince*, and Michael's account of human history in books 11 and 12 of *Paradise Lost*, Walker documents Milton's differences from his earlier sources "when it comes to the importance of Roman political, social, and military history, the importance of the history of Israel, the nature of the human subject that experiences history, the causes of this experience, the overall shape of this experience, and its meaning and value." According to Walker, "a comprehensive definition of [republicanism] must include an account of the way its principal figures think about history. In light of such a definition of republicanism and the way in which Milton represents history in *Paradise Lost*, it is clear that in this poem Milton not only departs from but openly repudiates a major dimension of republican political thought."

The literary influence on Milton of "our sage and serious poet Spenser" (*Areopagitica*, 728) has long been a subject of critical interest, and in "The 'Legend of Holinesse' and the Fall of Man: Spenser's *Faerie Queene* 1 as Milton's Original for *Paradise Lost* 9 and 10," Christopher Bond, while detailing obvious differences "of character and structure" between the two epics, maintains the existence of "a broader conceptual debt to Spenser in the structure and characterization of *Paradise Lost*" and provides evidence for "the importance of book 1 of *The Faerie Queen*—'The Legend of the Knight of the Red Crosse or of Holinesse'—to a reading of the later books of *Paradise Lost*." In particular, Bond examines "two levels of heroism: one fallible, human, engaged and supplicant, and the other more perfect, less human, detached and interventionist" in both *Faerie Queene* and *Paradise Lost*, suggesting that "[t]he extent to which Milton uses elements of the Knight as a prototype for Adam is perhaps most apparent in the extraordinary emotional range displayed by both characters in the course of their degradation and redemption." Bond also sees similarities between Spenser's composite Una/Duessa figure, "positive and negative types of femininity," and Milton's Eve. Finally, Bond reveals how, in both epics, "sexual lapses by flawed Everyman-figures prompt the intervention of the poems' more perfect, elevated heroes, and the interventions of Arthur and the Son serve to emphasize the fallibility of the more human characters." A comparison of these interventions "demonstrates the theological distinctions that Milton drew between himself and his precursor in terms of the kinds of mercy and grace represented by Arthur and the Son, and of the models of Christian redemption and education represented by Red Crosse and Adam."

Milton *as* influence is the topic of Anthony Welch's "Losing Paradise in Dryden's *State of Innocence*." In opening, Welch queries, "Why did Dryden set out in the early 1670s to write an opera based on *Paradise Lost*? When *The State of Innocence* was registered with the Stationers Company in the spring of 1674, sales of Milton's poem had been steady, but *Paradise Lost* had not yet created much of a critical stir. By comparison, *The State of Innocence* flew off the bookstands; it reached eleven editions by 1703, although we do not know whether Dryden ever meant to have it performed." One answer to Welch's initial question is "that Dryden's opera aimed to make Milton's neglected poem more accessible to the Restoration public." Conversely, Welch argues that "[f]ar from encouraging readers to embrace *Paradise Lost* on its own terms, Dryden's goal was to *prevent* the poem from being read in the way that Milton intended. *The State of Innocence* was an early intervention in the reception history of *Paradise Lost*, a preemptive act of interpretation aimed both at correcting the poem's politics and rethinking its relationship with the epic tradition." Ultimately, Welch claims, "Dryden absorbs Milton's theological vision into the idiom of Continental romance partly to cultivate his readers' taste for the epic model most congenial to himself, but also to deactivate Milton's 'imaginary treason' by folding it up in fiction."

According to Elisabeth Liebert in "Through Eve's Looking Glass," Eve's account of her creation in book 4 of *Paradise Lost* "demonstrates a subjectivity that renders her a fit partner for the Adam who in book 8 will admit to loneliness. It demonstrates an essential likeness, an equivalent need." However, Liebert reads Eve's narrative as "illustrative of a volition that remains autonomous." She "is exercising her will to say. The dual contexts of romance and the marital ideal developed by Milton in the divorce tracts elucidate the nature of her choices in structuring this speech," and in so doing, Eve "[encourages Adam] toward the celebration of their union through its reenactment." In support of her assertion that Eve's first speech in Milton's poem "reflects . . . upon the mutuality necessary in relationships," Liebert turns to Imre Madách's dramatic poem *Az ember tragédiája*, written in Hungary in 1860, which, "in the absence of incontrovertible evidence" of Miltonic influence, nonetheless "rework[s] the story of the Fall in a way that provides an interesting counterpoint to Milton's epic." Liebert believes that, in her creation narrative, "[m]irroring God's words, mirroring Adam's," Eve "frames a looking glass that shows her husband to himself in the context of their relationship and serves to cherish and reincite with pleasing conversation" their marital bliss.

Turning to one of Milton's later works, Tim Moylan, in "Dramatic Silences: Interpretive Pauses in *Paradise Regained*," identifies what is not said in Milton's poem as significant to our understanding of the work: "Milton laces *Paradise Regained* with silences: moments of significant hesitation, some overtly identified, others easily overlooked and seemingly inexplicable. Interpretation of these silences depends heavily on textual cues, contextual familiarity, and ultimately on assumptions about the purpose of the poem as a whole. Milton employs two treatments of silence. The first he identifies and narrates; the second he implies. Both may be grouped according to the mental operation taking place during the silence." Moylan suggests "four kinds: silences of realization, diminution, recovery, and acceptance. Although these categories are not absolute, in each specific moment one mental and emotional action dominates. Attention to the presence of these silences and to what transpires within them offers greater insight into the thematic underpinnings of the work." Moylan's analysis of these silences leads him to conclude:

> To regain Paradise, Milton's Jesus must reestablish the proper order of priorities. This task underlies all the major and minor conflicts in the poem. In each case, the principal characters stand and wait rather than assert their will independent of divine direction. Silences of realization, diminution, and acceptance help to counter the natural rhythm of the

silently read text and provide for a dramatic interpretation that emphasizes the human struggle these choices involve. Criticism of the poem's
static characters and their lack of energy may be offset somewhat by a
sensitive reading that makes effective use of intentional hesitations and
of meaningful silences. An interpretive understanding of the doctrinal
issues that Milton addresses in the poem, and the application of those
understandings to the literal oral "reading" of the work, can use the device of silence, of hesitation, of significant pause, to tease out the implications, the meaning of the work.

Christopher Norton Warren, in "*Samson* and the Chorus of Dissent," examines the etymology of the title words "Samson" and "Agonistes" as a prelude to his discussion of the Chorus in Milton's poem.
"If," Warren asserts, "Samson, in English, means 'sun,' joined with 'agonistes,' the resulting noun 'sunagonistes'—one who shares with another in a contest, a fellow-combatant, coadjutor—is a word with potentially deep applications for the ensuing drama." Further, "[b]y
thinking with Milton about what it might mean for the Chorus to
'strive with' Samson," Warren "claims that the model of charitable,
doctrinal debate Milton dramatizes between Samson and the Chorus is
meant to contrast sharply with the model of 'force' exercised by the
Philistines." Warren believes "that the Chorus persists in doing just
what it needs to do, 'strive with' Samson," and hence serves as "an invaluable sounding board for Samson's thoughts, throes, and theories
and acts as a critical agent in the process that many critics have called
Samson's regeneration. . . . [F]allible though it may be, Samson's Chorus inherits what Samson's violent act bequeaths it: a world free of civil
laws in ecclesiastical matters, which is also free, incidentally, of an ascertainable divine will that had once adjudicated among the various
claims to truth." The conclusion of *Samson Agonistes*, Warren observes,
is the "tolerationist agon in which an individual can and should be less
an agonist, striving *against* others, than a sunagonist, striving *with*,
struggling *with*, contesting *with*, in advancement toward God. . . . In
the end the members of Milton's Chorus are co-adjutors, fighting together, striving, arguing, preaching in *faith*."

In " 'Intimate Impulses,' 'Rousing Motions,' and the Written Law:
Internal and External Scripture in *Samson Agonistes*," David V. Urban
considers "[a]n intriguing issue in *Samson Agonistes*," that is, "the problem of immediate spiritual revelation from God and whether Samson
discerns accurately God's 'promptings.' " As Urban says, "Milton raises
this question by portraying Samson's direct spiritual revelation as po-

tentially delusional, but also as a legitimate means of divine communication that, when correctly understood, can lead to redemption. In this sense, *Samson Agonistes* depicts a Hebrew God whose leadings may finally be known by the genuine servant of God who has first demonstrated obedience to the divine commands codified in the written Scripture." He continues:

> Throughout the drama, the matter of immediate revelation is addressed in conjunction with the question of whether a specific revelation can be trusted if it goes against the explicit teachings of the written Scripture. Milton's Samson considers himself to be the recipient of divine inspiration, for he believes God has led him to marry his two Philistine wives, the woman of Timna and Dalila, even though marrying a Canaanite woman goes against Mosaic Law. Indeed, Samson's violation of a clear scriptural command accomplishes God's broader commandment in written Scripture, for he obeys the larger sense of the Law. But in his discernment of God's "leadings" in his two marriages, Samson proves himself to be both a successful and an unsuccessful interpreter of special revelation: he properly recognizes God's true will in his first marriage, but because he has been deluded by his own lusts and presumption, he mistakes his unlawful desire for Dalila as God again leading him to marry a Philistine woman. By the end of the drama, however, we see Samson restored to his position as a useful servant of God. He has come to demonstrate an unswerving fidelity to the written Law, and Samson is once again able to discern divine promptings that lead him to obey God in a way that transcends the letter of the Law even as it fulfills the Law's greater purpose.

Using as his gloss Milton's distinction in *De Doctrina Christiana* between internal scripture and external, written Scripture, the former being superior, Urban's analysis brings him to the conclusion that

> Samson's decisions to follow the Officer, to perform at the festival, and to pull down the temple pillars, are all motivated by the same overarching leading of God's Spirit—the "internal scripture" of which *De Doctrina* speaks. In his "obedience unto death," Samson allows the new revelation of the internal scripture to guide him to a more perfect adherence to the external Law of God. Samson's obedience also demonstrates his resignation to the sovereign will of God, a resignation so unlike his earlier self-indulgence. This obedient resignation enables Samson to be used, once again, as God's instrument of judgment upon the Philistines; it also permits the Chorus to call—rightly so—the once-faithless Samson God's "faithful Champion." (1751)

As Bill Goldstein points out in "Samson Regained: A Play in Per-petual World Premiere," "[t]he extensive performance history of *Samson Agonistes* in the twentieth century has remained largely unexamined until only recently. This essay documents aspects of this largely un-known performance history and also explores the eighteenth- and nineteenth-century commentary on *Samson Agonistes* that in first imag-ining it as a stage-worthy dramatic poem established the critical foun-dation that made the long-delayed performances of Milton's supposed closet drama inevitable." Nonetheless, Goldstein counters,

> *Samson Agonistes* has a significant past as a play—but this is virtually hidden even from those Milton scholars most intimately familiar with it as a poem. It is also a past virtually unknown to those who today, and over the last century, have performed *Samson Agonistes* on the stage. Milton's tragedy, which seems to have been first performed in public in 1900, is a play with a performance history, but without the perfor-mance tradition, or development of stage conventions, that would be crucial for its continuing life in the theater. . . . The record of perfor-mances is largely buried in school or museum archives, traceable mainly through newspaper reviews of some performances and stray references to other planned or remembered performances.

Finally, Goldstein observes, "[b]y documenting the performance his-tory of *Samson Agonistes*, we can, I think, restore something of the play's heritage as a stage work, and perhaps point the way to its contin-uing future as drama, as a theatrical rather than academic affair."

These essays were originally among those presented at the 2003 Conference on John Milton, sponsored by Middle Tennessee State University, and, because of their merit as scholarly examinations of Milton, the authors were invited to expand their work for this collec-tion. Eclectic as they are in subject matter, approaches, and emphases, all demonstrate the rewards of "reading Milton deeply."

NOTES

1. John Milton, "Prolusion 3" and "At a Vacation Exercise in the College," in *John Milton: Complete Poems and Major Prose*, ed. Merritt Y. Hughes (New York: Odyssey, 1957). All references to Milton's poetry and prose in the introduction are to this edition and are cited parenthetically by page or line number(s) in the text. We would like to thank Glenn Sucich, whose essay in this collection brought together the two Miltonic quotations that serve as the basis for our title.

Milton and the Problems of Evil:
A Preemptive Modernism?

Annabel Patterson

To tackle this topic, at this stage of the game, may seem like re-inventing the wheel. But perhaps a better vehicle *can* be constructed, one with a twenty-first century design that does not do violence to Milton's late seventeenth-century mental technology. Let's begin with philology. The word "evil" in English derives from Old English, and there, as in all the other Teutonic languages except Scandinavian, it was once, according to the *Oxford English Dictionary*, "the most comprehensive adjectival expression of disapproval." Ubiquitous in the Middle Ages and the sixteenth century in England, it was deployed in all sorts of contexts, serious and banal, religious, moral, medical, used to describe bad times or harsh weather, a tasteless meal or a blunt tool. By the time the *OED* was last revised, shortly before the Second World War, it was reported as being "little used, such currency as it has being due to literary influence." That last phrase is of particular interest to us, for of whom could the compilers have been thinking if not of Milton? The primary cause of the retreat of *evil* from common parlance to the highly specialized terrain of literature is, of course, that English, unlike all the Romance languages, has another word for things we don't like, trivial or grand, namely *bad*. But the secondary cause, undoubtedly, is that *evil* became just too tendentious a term for casual use, thanks to the long philosophical struggle to define what it is and where it comes from. Sadly, the *Oxford English Dictionary* almost immediately became out of date in this instance, since Evil as a term to reckon with in everyday life made a strong reappearance in the rhetoric of the Second World War. We partly know how this turnabout in historical linguistics was effected. It began when, in 1945, during the last stages of the Second World War, Winston Churchill referred to

25

Japan, the only enemy left, as an evil nation. This was reinforced by Ronald Reagan, in his notorious "Evil Empire" speech, interestingly addressed to the British House of Commons on June 8, 1982, a speech recalling Churchill as a model but now applying the dark word, *Evil*, to the Soviet Union. In his State of the Union Address in January 2002, George W. Bush joined his two famous predecessors by coining the phrase "an axis of Evil" to refer to three states his administration regarded as particularly intransigent: Iraq, Iran, and North Korea. All three instances were moves in a very old game: to identify our adversaries as ontologically, metaphysically, theologically, the opposite of ourselves. We are the forces of Good, and they are the forces of Evil. A subtext of this essay, therefore, is to demonstrate that the recent revival of Evil in the political vocabulary is regressive, archaic, and bad for thought. Those responsible for it are either ignorant, or pretend to be ignorant, of the conceptual problems that serious thinkers about *evil* have wrestled with since serious thought began to be recorded.

What is called by philosophers the problem of evil is really at least four problems, which are often confused. The first I shall call "the problem of responsibility." Who (if anyone) is responsible for all the bad things that happen to us? The second, deriving from the first, is whether it is possible, for the purposes of answering the responsibility question, to distinguish between "natural" evils like floods, plagues, and earthquakes, and moral evils, like genocide. The third problem, equally deriving from the first, is whether we need to posit an Adversary figure in the cosmos to account for either natural or moral evils. And the fourth, perhaps the most subtle but seldom addressed, is the question of whether we can trace evil back to its origins, and what is the consequence of writing a *narrative* of its genesis. In all of these four areas of inquiry, areas, as it has turned out, of hopeless undecidability, Milton's great poem, *Paradise Lost*, made a thoughtful contribution, especially, of course, in developing the concept of the Adversary with an unprecedented imaginative brilliance. In my late rereading of the poem (my reinvention of the wheel) although Milton claimed he intended to write a theodicy, to "justify the ways of God to men" (1.26),[1] undecidability got the upper hand.

The problem of who is responsible for evil has always deserved first place. It is still unresolved. Comic proof of this is the 1987 film, *The Witches of Eastwick*, which, given its date, may well have been a response to the Reagan creation of an Evil Empire, the political version of the Adversary figure. Jack Nicholson, playing the devil, under the name of

Daryl Van Horne, is both a literalization and a critique of conventional ideas of Satan. He is the Seducer extraordinaire, rich, charming, intelligent, knows what every woman wants and gives it to her, so long as she plays his game. He has three beautiful sisters in his mansion, or coven, or harem. Eventually the sisters realize he is dangerous (someone has died a violent death as a result of his machinations), and plan to escape from his clutches by using his own demonic powers against him.

Blown into a New England church in the middle of a family service by his rebellious apprentices, filthy and covered in feathers, Nicholson fulminates: "When we make a mistake, they call it Evil. When God makes a mistake, they call it *Nature!*" He proceeds to ask a series of questions about the creation of Woman (the biggest mistake) which delineate, in however parodic a form, the central problem of evil as philosophers have wrestled with it. Who is responsible for all the bad things, horrible, painful, destructive, that happen in the world? Are they mistakes (which implies an intention by some superhuman agent to do otherwise), or part of a mysterious plan, or completely random? Should natural disasters, "like floods, plagues, and earthquakes," be included in our theory of evil, or are they just the effects of scientific preconditions, ultimately predictable, and hence, perhaps, ultimately preventable, or at least avoidable? Is there any ontological difference between natural disasters and human malice? And if so, where does human malice come from? Are there two competing forces in the world, one called God and another called Daryl Van Horne? If so, why does Nicholson, who seems so human most of the time, use the word "us" rather than the first-person singular in looking for the authorship of evil? And, most pertinently, is the word *evil* just a question of terminology, what we *call* it when things go wrong? This elegant and far from superficial inquiry can plausibly take its late place in the long, long history of philosophical and theological inquiry into the problem or problems of evil, which begins, in our culture, with the book of Genesis, and its derivate, the Judaeo-Christian myth of *human* responsibility.

According to the book of Genesis, *Evil* came into the world as a result of human disobedience, a willful act of badness on the part of Eve and her husband Adam. For eating the fruit of the Tree of Knowledge of Good and Evil these two and their descendants were condemned by God to live subsequently in a world no longer paradisal, but just like the one we know. Included in the costs of disobedience were bad weather, the back-breaking toil necessary to survive in a no longer

fruitful environment, the pain of childbirth, diseases, and the inevitability of death. Up to a point, this made sense. Something bad had
been done by humankind, and humankind was to suffer for it indefinitely. To a pessimistic mind that could swallow this logic, the question
might no longer be, why do natural disasters happen, but why are there
so few of them? Why do we still have spring and summer? Why are
there not *more* earthquakes, especially in California, where they have
more than their share of spring and summer?

It was evident, however, that some minds could *not* swallow this
logic, without asking a different set of questions, which pretty well
undid the causal solution offered by Genesis. What sort of God was
this, who would exact such a huge punishment for so small a fault?
What kind of Creator would let his once perfect world be messed up in
this way? A set of paradoxes once worked out by Epicurus in the third
century BC and transmitted by Lactantius in the fourth century AD
were restated at the very end of the seventeenth century by the French
philosopher Pierre Bayle, in his *Dictionnaire Historique et Critique*
(1697): "God is either willing to remove evil and cannot; or he can and
is unwilling; or he is neither willing nor able to do so; or else he is both
willing and able. If he is willing and not able, he must then be weak,
which cannot be affirmed of God. If he is able and not willing, he must
be envious, which is also contrary to the nature of God. If he is neither
willing nor able, he must be both envious and weak, and consequently
not be God. If he is both willing and able—the only possibility that
agrees with the nature of God—then where does evil come from?"[2]
Bayle ingeniously presented this Catch-22 merely as a quotation from
Lactantius's *De Ira Dei*,[3] but it formed the center of his provocative
essay on the Paulicians, a dualistic heretical sect of Christians whose
thought derived from Manichaeism. It was this essay that motivated
Leibnitz to write his 1710 rebuttal, *Essais de théodicée, oder betrachtung
der Gütigkeit Gottes, der Freyheit des Menschen und des Ursprungs des
Bosen* (that is, his Essays on theodicy, or a defense of God's goodness,
Man's Freedom, and the origins of Evil), a rigorously logical tract that
brought the word *theodicy* into the world, and tempts us, retrospectively, to apply that term to *Paradise Lost*. The appearance in 1697 of
Bayle's *Dictionary*, which should really be called an encyclopedia of
philosophy, marked the arrival of the Enlightenment and the beginning of the end of European theism.

But in the meantime, for many hundreds of years, Christianity and
then Islam attempted to rescue the idea of God from the charge of

weakness, stupidity, or malice by inventing an Adversary figure, a power who along with us humans could be held responsible for bringing evil into the world. I speak, of course, of the Devil, or Satan. The Hebrew name, Satan, or in Arabic Shaitan, simply means the Adversary. Scholars have argued that Satan was invented for the same reason that other mythologies invented adversary figures who challenged the gods, but, unlike the processes of Greek mythologization, the creation of an adversary for the Christian God was a relatively late development. There was no single, originary, myth retailing the career of Satan, in the sense that Genesis was an originary myth of *human* responsibility for evil. Instead, the Satan idea was pieced together from biblical fragments by those who *needed* a supernatural adversary figure, whether to take some of the heat off God, or to explain to themselves the disastrous experiences of their time.

The myth of Satan was in fact a pastiche, pasted together from biblical texts from quite different historical eras. Neil Forsyth has identified the most important of these. First, the "famous taunt" in Isaiah 14:12–13 against the king of Babylon. When we say Isaiah here, Forsyth warns, we are probably not referring to the genuine Isaiah, the Hebrew prophet of the eighth century BC, but to a text from some sixth-century writer who would have had an immediate interest in the downfall of Babylon.[4] In this passage is imagined, not without pathos, the defeat of a powerful political opponent. "How are you fallen from heaven, O Lucifer, son of the morning! How art thou cut down to the ground, which didst weaken the nations! For thou hast said in thine heart, I will ascend into heaven. . . . I will sit upon the mount of the congregation."[5] The second passage is from Ezekiel, announcing the downfall of the king of Tyre, Nebuchadnezzar, in equally poetic terms. It too has a political resonance, for the book of Ezekiel presents itself as contemporary with the Babylonian captivity of the Jews:

> Thou [art] . . . full of wisdom, and perfect in beauty;
> Thou hast been in Eden, the garden of God;
>
> . . . .
> Thou wast perfect in the ways from the day that thou wast created,
>   Till iniquity was found in thee.
> By the multitude of thy merchandise they have filled the midst
>   of thee with violence, and thou hast sinned:
>   therefore I will cast thee as profane out of the
>   mountains of God: and I will destroy thee,
> O covering cherub, from the midst of the stones of fire.

Thine heart was lifted up because of thy beauty,
    Thou hast corrupted thy wisdom by reason of thy brightness:
I will cast thee to the ground.

(Ezekiel 28:12–13, 15–17)

Needless to say, both passages are a form of wishful thinking, since the Judaean kingdom came to an end in 587/6 BC, with the capture of Jerusalem by Nebuchadnezzar and the second great Jewish exile.

From these two seminal, because imaginative, texts, speaking initially to the historical sufferings of the Jews and the hoped-for collapse of their enemies, speaking *metaphorically* about political events, it was possible for later theologues, especially St. Augustine, to construe the story of a great fallen angel. So now we have an Adversary figure, but one, importantly, necessarily, less powerful than God. This idea of a fallen angel, a once perfect creature, needed, however, to be assimilated to the very few Old Testament references to a satan figure. The satan in the book of Job is no once glorious rebel, but instead a bit of a busybody, going about the earth looking for trouble to make, and essentially a tempter. There may be more than one satan around. The only time that we find a figure who is apparently named "Satan" (since the word appears in Hebrew without the definite article) is in the book of Chronicles. He, too, is a tempter. He tempts David to number the people, that is to say, organize a census, which is opposed by his chief of staff, Joab, who is forced to comply nevertheless. For this mistake all of Israel is punished by a plague.[6] There are no details of the temptation, and indeed the Geneva Bible, seeing a problem, explains in the margin that census taking was in itself indifferent and usual, but that David's error was in glorying in the size of his kingdom and the number of his supporters. Both of these Old Testament tempters were subsumed in the New Testament accounts of the temptation by Jesus in the wilderness.

Finally (though in terms of composition probably contemporary with the Gospel of Mark), there was conceived the book of Revelation, in which rather human though diverse characterizations of the adversary give place to apocalyptic excess and Star Wars special effects. In Revelation, a great dragon, Satan, "that old serpent" (Rev. 12:9), attacks the stars and the child born of a woman clothed like the sun, resulting in a War in Heaven, in which the archangel Michael defeats Satan, who is cast out of heaven, but allowed to continue his bad ways on earth. Two beasts are his allies, one of which represents the Roman

Empire.[7] Forsyth argues that apocalyptic thinking of this kind originated among Christian sects such as the Essenes or the Jesus cults who felt isolated and intimidated and who chose to represent their own struggles as a battle between cosmic forces in which their side would finally be victorious. It is worth noticing that behind almost all of these constructions there lurks some form of political motivation, which disappeared from sight as theological motives became dominant.

However convenient might be the construction of an Adversary myth for those committed to theism, or reluctant to think through the alternatives so brutally outlined by Epicurus, Lactantius, and Bayle, this narrative solution to the problems of evil—what is it and where does it come from—only created another problem, that of dualism. Another term for dualism, when it refers to the good vs. evil dichotomy, is Manichaeism, designated heretical by those who kept guard over Christian theology. Manichaeism was thought up as an alternative religion by Mani in Mesopotamia in the third century AD. Influenced by earlier forms of Gnosticism, Mani imagined not one confused and impotent God, but two almost equal powers, Good and Evil, which Mani called Light and Darkness, locked in a conflict that seems eternal, which was initiated by Darkness and which results in the creation of Adam not by God but by the copulation between devils. This struggle will ultimately be resolved in the favor of Light, with the help of a Jesus figure. The clearest and probably most influential account of Manichaeism is to be found in the essay on "Paulicians" in Bayle's *Historical and Critical Dictionary*, the essay that Leibnitz found particularly upsetting.

While it solved the dilemmas posed by Epicurus and company by making the power of Light merely equal to, not stronger than that of Darkness, and while it also relieved mankind of responsibility for evil behavior—the voluntary fall of Adam disappears from the new version of the myth, which substitutes for human fallibility the struggle of cosmic forces—Manichaeism as originally formulated was clearly too loopy to last. St. Augustine fell prey to this idea in his youth, followed it for nine years, and spent the rest of his life arguing it out of existence. John Milton, it might be argued, while appearing on the surface to be utterly orthodox, gave dualism an imaginative run for its money in *Paradise Lost*.

We have now retraversed two of the four problems of evil, considered philosophically: the first, who is responsible, and the third, whether we need an Adversary figure. The second, whether we can draw

a distinction between natural and moral evils, as raised parodically by
Jack Nicholson in *Witches of Eastwick*, was supposedly settled shortly
after Leibnitz's largely unsuccessful argument that, despite all evidence
to the contrary, we live in the best of all possible worlds. According to
Susan Neiman, whose *Evil in Modern Thought* is concerned primarily
with this issue, Leibnitz was the last of those who attempted to write a
theodicy that covered both kinds of evil. For modern philosophy, the
Lisbon earthquake in 1755 was the turning point which made it essential to distinguish natural disasters like Lisbon from moral disasters
like Auschwitz. For Neiman, the capacity to make the distinction was a
form of growing up: "Radically separating what earlier ages called natural from moral evils was thus part of the meaning of modernity. . . .
Modern conceptions of evil were developed in the attempt to stop
blaming God for the state of the world and to take responsibility for it
on ourselves."[8]

There remains my fourth category of the problematics of evil, the
question of whether it is possible or necessary to write a *narrative* of the
origins of evil, a question obviously related to, but not identical with,
that of who is or was responsible. Thus if the third problem of evil is
whether we need an Adversary figure, the fourth is whether or not
there must be a narrative of how evil began. This too was addressed by
Kant in the later Enlightenment. In his 1793 treatise *Religion innerhalb
der Grenzen de blossen Vernunst (Religion, Within the Limits of Reason
Alone)*, Kant is characteristically determined to trace the origin of every
evil act to an act of the will, to voluntarism. Hence, he declares:

> However the origin of moral evil in man is constituted, surely of all the
> explanations . . . the most inept is that which describes it as descending
> to us as an *inheritance* from our first parents . . . in the manner of pre-
> sentation which the Scriptures use . . . the origin of evil in the human
> race [is] presented in a narrative, wherein what in its essence must be
> considered primary (without regard to the element of time) appears as
> coming first in time. . . . We must not, however, look for an origin of
> time of a moral character for which we are to be held responsible;
> though to do so is inevitable if we wish to *explain* the contingent exis-
> tence [of a propensity to evil in ourselves] . . . and perhaps it is for this
> reason that Scripture, in conformity with this weakness of ours, has
> thus pictured the temporal origin of evil. . . . Evil could have sprung
> only from the morally-evil . . . and yet the original predisposition
> (which no one other than man himself could have corrupted, if he is to
> be held responsible for this corruption) is a predisposition to good;
> there is then for us no conceivable ground from which the moral evil in

us could originally have come. This inconceivability . . . the Bible expresses in the historical narrative as follows. It finds a place for evil at the creation of the world, yet not in man, but in a *spirit* of an originally loftier destiny. Thus is the *first* beginning of all evil represented as inconceivable by us (for whence came evil to that spirit?); but man is represented as having fallen into evil only *through seduction*, and hence as being *not basically* corrupt.[9]

In other words, Kant explains the regression of Judaeo-Christian narrative to a previous Fall by Satan (a stage in the story that he does not apparently realize was a later construct) as a *representation* designed to satisfy our need for explanation, to drive away, by the seductions of narrative, the fear of inconceivability, the painful experience of running into a logical impasse.

Now the conventional way to situate Milton in this history of the problems of evil would be to place him firmly in the premodern, pre-Enlightenment era, within the constraints of the age of belief. Clearly Milton accepted the narrative of Genesis as literal truth, rather than as a construct designed to evade an impasse. Clearly Milton believed in God and stated his intentions to write a theodicy, though one extremely unlike the painful intellectual athletics of Leibnitz. Not only did Milton believe in the existence of an Adversary figure (presumably based on Scripture), but he took the concept and rendered it far more formidable, not least by inventing a complex psychological profile for his Satan. He dealt with the seam between the Adversary and the Tempter narratives by marking the seam *as* narrative, as a matter of chronology, with the first part of the poem dedicated to Satan as Adversary, the second half to Satan as Tempter. And yet, I shall shortly proceed to argue, everything he did to his inherited materials rather served to display the problems inherent in them than to resolve them. Everything he did seemed rather to anticipate the Enlightenment and even the modern concessions of philosophical defeat, if not quite the ironies and parodies of *The Witches of Eastwick*, then certainly the sense of ineptitude that Kant so brilliantly discerned in the Western myths of the origins of evil.

But before I advance this seemingly implausible, ahistorical argument, I want to suggest that it is, perhaps, not quite as ahistorical as it might first appear. For Milton had a colleague, not at all distant from himself either in religious upbringing or political experience, who produced a most interesting, preemptive version of modern thought on the subject of evil, of the skepticism of a Bayle or a Kant, if not of a

Nietzsche. That colleague was also a severe critic of Milton's handling of the problem, which might seem rather to differentiate than align them. But to put them side by side has the advantage of showing what was *thinkable* in the early modern period, as distinct from the truly modern period.

My early modernist is, or was, Daniel Defoe, known today primarily for *Robinson Crusoe*, his novel of self-help and survival when stranded on an island. In 1726 Defoe published a two-volume tract entitled *The Political History of the Devil*. Defoe was a Dissenter, a left-wing Protestant in a country dominated and partly run by the Established Anglican church, who had spent most of his life writing pamphlets intended to counter religious intolerance in England. He had been imprisoned several times, both for debt and for the so-called crime of "seditious libel," publishing something deemed disruptive of public order. By 1726 he was sixty-five and had recently endured surgery for bladder stones that, as was inevitable in the early eighteenth century, was performed without anesthesia, with the patient strapped to a table with his wrists tied to his ankles. This was an experience, we may surmise, likely to focus one's thoughts on the nature of evil. The next year he published *The Political History of the Devil*, nowhere near as famous now as *Robinson Crusoe*, but something of a blockbuster in his own day, being reissued in 1727 and quickly translated into French and German. It was republished in Philadelphia in 1837 and in January 2003 was republished by AMS Press, just a year after the Bush renovation of *evil* in the political vocabulary. This was probably just a coincidence.

Like Jack Nicholson in *The Witches of Eastwick*, Defoe makes wicked fun of the fact that man made Evil incarnate so as not to have to face the consequences of his own actions. *Evil* and *Devil* are, after all, nearly identical phonologically, so the slippage is demonically easy. Defoe's strategy is to make the devil or his subordinates responsible for everything atrocious or merely venal that happens in the world, to the point that it all comes to seem a huge hyperbole, a joke. At the beginning of both volumes of the work appears the same little verse, easy to pass over but crucial in explaining Defoe's intentions:

> Bad as he is, the Devil may be abus'd,
> Be falsly charged, and causelesly accus'd,
> When Men, unwilling to be blam'd alone,
> Shift off those Crimes on him which are their Own.[10]

To this end Defoe canvasses the Bible to see what authority it lends to the idea of an Arch-Enemy, and concludes, as modern scholars did subsequently, that a few chance mentions of a satan or devils have been blown up into a master concept. Defoe believes that a principle of evil exists, but he even more strongly believes that its incarnation has had dreadful results for the human capacity to take responsibility for evils caused by ourselves: "According to this usage of speech we go on to this day; and all the infernal things we converse with in the world are fathered upon the Devil, as one undivided simple essence, by how many agents soever working; Every thing evil, frightful in appearance, wicked in its actings, horrible in its manner, monstrous in its effects, is called the Devil . . . yet t'is remarkable, *the Devil* is no Old Testament word; and we never find it used in all that part of the Bible but four times, and then not once in the singular number; and not once, to signify Satan as it is now understood" (34).

Defoe proceeds to burst the bubble of the myth of Satan by blowing it up too far. He shows that by his time the idea of absolute evil is a patchwork not only of scriptural commentary but also of popular superstitions, including the belief that the Devil has a cloven hoof, that he makes pacts with humans for their souls, that he makes candles burn blue, and that he can be summoned up by any old woman with a bag of incantations, all rather beneath the dignity of a great fallen archangel. But at the same time Defoe has an enormously serious point to make: that there is some coherence between the vast variety of evils we experience and that some of them are much more evil than others. Right at the beginning he tackles the question of the role of religion in making not for less but for more evil in the world. The Devil himself, Defoe claims, is a believer and fears God. He offers to tell us later "who has the best claim to his brotherhood, the Papists or the Protestants, and among the latter the Lutherans or the Calvinists, and so descending to all the several denominations of the churches, see who has less of *the Devil* in them, and who more; and whether *less* or *more*, [see whether the Devil has] not a seat in every synagogue, a pew in every church, a place in every pulpit, and a vote in every synod" (8).

This catholicity or latitudinarianism, that is, an equal distribution of his cynicism to all religious groups and denominations, was not quite proof against Defoe's lifelong suspicion of Roman Catholicism. But it makes for a very radical idea of Christianity. "I think I do no injury at all to the Devil, to say that he had a great hand in the old holy war, as it was ignorantly and enthusiastically call'd," writes Defoe, "stirring up the christian princes and powers of Europe to run a madding after the Turks and Saracens, and make war with those innocent people, about a thousand miles off, only because they entered into God's heritage when he had forsaken it . . . spending the nations treasure, and embarking their kings and people, I say, in a war above a thousand miles off, filling their heads with that religious madness, call'd, in those days, *holy zeal*, to recover the *terra ancta* . . . and as they called it falsely, the *holy city*, though true religion says it was the accursed city, and not worth spending one drop of blood for" (8–9). This paragraph could easily have been written about America in the light of its Middle East policies today.

Everywhere we look, in national and international affairs, in politics, in high finance, in the law courts, we see, according to Defoe, the influence of the devil; but, so the implicit argument goes, if he is absolutely everywhere, and working on both sides of most issues, logic tells us that there can be no such person or entity.

In short, Defoe's agenda is mixed. Its primary focus is political, social, and religious satire. But part of it is serious history of ideas. He attempts to return to their proper status, not by rigorous argument but by joking and exaggeration, ideas of evil that were originally intended to be understood metaphorically or allegorically, such as that of hell as a place of fire and torment. Thus "Some tell us every single Man, every individual, has a Devil attending him, to execute the Orders of the (Grand Signior) Devil of the whole clan":

> that this attending evil Angel (for so he is call'd) sees every Step you take, is with you in every Action, prompts you to every Mischief, and leaves you to do every thing that is pernicious to your self. They also alledge that there is a good Spirit which attends him too: which latter is always accessory to every thing we do that is good and reluctant to evil; If this is true, how comes it to pass, that those two opposite Spirits do not quarrel about it, when they are pressing us to contrary Actions? And why does the evil tempting Spirit so often prevail? Instead of answering this difficult Question, I shall only tell you, it is a good Allegory indeed to represent the Struggle in the Mind of Man between good and evil Inclinations; but as to the rest, the best Thing I can say of it, is *that* I think *t'is a Fib*. (168–69)

That comical evasion, "Instead of answering this difficult Question," brings us back to *the* question—where does evil *really* come from. And here Defoe does something quite peculiar, which is of great advantage to us. He tackles the unanswerable question of the origin of evil in a perfect being—the greatest of the archangels—by complaining that Milton, in *Paradise Lost*, had fudged the issue. First, he homes in on the logical flaw in the myth of Satan by asking Kant's question: "How came seeds of crime to rise in the Angelic Nature, created in a state of perfect, unspotted holiness? How was it first found in a place where no unclean thing can enter . . . could untainted purity breed corruption?" (50). Then, in several saucy pages, Defoe enumerates the mistakes that Milton has made, dwelling particularly on his invention of a political reason for Satan's rebellion; namely, God's public promotion of the Son to Sonship. As Neil Forsyth explains, this was the most unbiblical, unauthorized part of the poem and of Milton's argument, even if it may be an adaptation of a heretical myth that had Satan rebel *after* the creation of man, of whom he was jealous and to whom he refused subjection.[11] As Defoe sardonically retells Milton's proposal, "The cause [of the origin of evil] must be thus: Satan . . . hearing this sovereign Declaration, that the Son of God was declar'd to be Head or Generalissimo of all the heavenly Host, took it ill to see another put into the high station, *over his head*, as the Soldiers call it; he, perhaps, being the senior Officer, and disdaining to submit to any but his former immediate Sovereign. In short, he threw up his Commission, and, in order not to be compell'd to obey, revolted, and broke out in open Rebellion" (57). To which Defoe objects, astutely, given our later grasp of Milton's half-hidden Socinianism, "that Mr. Milton is not orthodox in this part, but lays an avow'd foundation for the corrupt Doctrine of Arius, which says, there was a time when Christ *was not* the Son of God" (57). Finally Defoe declares that "the great Milton, after all his fine images, and lofty excursions upon the subject, has left it [the problem of the origin of evil] not one jot clearer than he found it" (59). "Here we must bid Mr. Milton good night; for in plain terms, he is in the dark about it, and so are we all" (56).

This critique of *Paradise Lost*, one part admiration for the poem, one part irritation at the boost that Milton had given to the myth of Satan, and one part acute detection of the argumentative flaws in the poem, computes with the feeling of many modern readers that Milton did not, after all, produce a successful theodicy. Perhaps they are not reading the poem against its historical grain. There are certain strains in the poem that almost seem to grant Defoe's point, or are, rather, Milton's admission that the task he had set himself was impossible.

The first thing to notice is that Milton seems to be obsessed with the *temporality* of evil (Kant's bugbear). In the first thirty-five lines of the poem Milton uses the word *first* five times, all of them in weight-bearing places, argumentatively speaking. "Of man's *first* disobedience . . . Sing, Heav'nly Muse" (1.1, 6). His was, he claims, the same muse that inspired Moses, "who *first* taught the chosen seed, / In the beginning how the heav'ns and earth / Rose out of Chaos" (8–10). "Say *first*" (27), he begs this Muse—the one who was responsible, apparently, for the writing of the book of Genesis, and then repeats himself "say *first* what cause / Moved our grand parents . . . to fall off / From their Creator. . . . Who *first* seduced them to that foul revolt?" (28–31, 33). What follows is the nonbiblical account of the fallen angels discovering themselves, after their fall, floating on the burning lake of Hell, their military regrouping, the building of Pandemonium, the demonic parliament, and the plan to take revenge on God by destroying his new creation, Man. Later, the archangel Raphael will fill in, as a flashback for the instruction of Adam, what had preceded the angelic debacle; the nonbiblical promotion of the Son, Satan's anger at his demotion, his fomenting a rebellion, and its conclusion in the three days battle in Heaven. All this to explain what happened "first," before the story of Genesis begins. But when it came to the crucial question asked by Defoe, "How came seeds of crime to rise in the angelic nature, created in a state of perfect, unspotted holiness?" Milton abandoned narrative and took refuge in allegory. At the gates of Hell, on his way to start his destructive mission against mankind, Satan encounters two figures of a different ontological nature—that is to say, more abstract than himself: Sin and Death. A female Sin and a male Death, both of which he is responsible for, without having the slightest knowledge of how he produced them. Sin tells Satan that she is his daughter, sprung mysteriously out of his head when he was in a dizzy trance. We recognize that Milton is here imitating classical myth, as Athena was said to spring fully formed from the head of Zeus. But we may have been too busy identifying the classical echo, and not focused enough on the trance, the state of unconsciousness that Milton invented. The trance came upon Satan just when he was articulating the case for rebellion. And then Sin tells him something else of which he is unconscious, that having produced her, he was immediately enamored of her and engaged in incestuous sex, a union that produced the ghastly mysterious shape of Death, "If shape it might be called that shape had none" (2.667). This is not narrative, though it imitates narrative's reliance on sequence. This is pure allegory, a way of describing that which simply cannot be described in the humanist terms that narrative requires. Satan himself never tells us how he came to conceive of rebellion. And Raphael's narrative of why it happened—the promotion of the Son—the part of the story that Defoe finds so ridiculous, is importantly never acknowledged by Satan himself.

So Milton asks the Muse to tell him what happened first, and when it comes to *the* originary moment, fudges. Surely, this fudging was intentional. He *wanted* his readers to notice the flaw in the argument from origins. He refused to try to solve the logical dilemmas posed by Epicurus, Lactantius, and Bayle. He actually undermined the initial project of the Satan mythologizers by inventing a reason for Satan's defection, a reason that ultimately puts the responsibility back in the hand of God, the then commander in chief.

Similar things take place at the philological level. For one way of thinking about *Paradise Lost* today is as an essay on the self-negating semantics of the term, *Evil*. There are few people who, having read *Paradise Lost* at some stage in their lives, are not able to quote the most striking instance, "Evil be thou my Good" (4.110), whereby Milton's Satan defies the theological tradition made central by Augustine. That is to say, Satan explicitly rejects Augustine's notion that evil is a nonentity, merely the absence of good, a space, as it were, where good ought to be. Instead, in Satan's mouth, the two terms have become interchangeable, and, at least at the level of language, equally powerful. It is just a question of where one stands—on the side of the winners or the losers. Here is a space—a semantic space—for dualism to creep back in. Later in the poem, though earlier in the poem's fictional chronology, Satan will reply to the archangel Michael's challenge to fight with a semantic twist which may sound familiar, and ever so slightly like Jack Nicholson: "so shall end / The strife which thou call'st evil, but we style / The strife of glory" (6.288–90). Michael's challenge had begun by calling Satan "Author of evil, unknown till thy revolt" (262), and he uses the word twice more in his brief speech; but Satan throws the triple usage back at him with the often unanswerable charge of relativism.

In this long, long poem, the term *Evil* is used with discretion, with frugality. It is almost as though Milton knew already, or was proposing, that it was not a word for general usage, not to be used promiscuously. The main appearances of the term are part of an ongoing argument that gets less certain of itself as it proceeds. Some are related to the in-

herently implausible notion that God permitted Satan his freedom to
induce the Fall of Man so that he could, out of his immense goodness,
as Adam enthusiastically declares in book 12, "All this good of evil . . .
produce, / And evil turn to good" (470–71). But this late statement of
orthodoxy, the notion that the Fall is, after all, not unfortunate but the
instrument of the Redemption, is shockingly anticipated by Satan's
second speech on the burning lake in book 1:

> If then his Providence
> Out of our evil seek to bring forth good,
> Our labour must be to pervert that end,
> And out of good still to find means of evil.
>   (162–65)

It is difficult not to exit from passages like this with the feeling that evil
and good are in some deep sense interchangeable, interdependent.

Sixteen of the occurrences of the word *Evil*, not surprisingly, occur
in book 9, the book in which the Fall of Man occurs. And perhaps the
most difficult of these appears during Satan's temptation of Eve, where
he argues precisely that she ought to want to know what evil is, that the
acquisition of such knowledge is heroic, Promethean:

> will God incense his ire
> For such a petty trespass, and not praise
> Rather your dauntless virtue, whom the pain
> Of death denounced, whatever thing death be,
> Deterred not from achieving what might lead
> To happier life, knowledge of good and evil;
> Of good, how just? of evil, if what is evil
> Be real, why not known, since easier shunned?
>   (692–99)

Note the connection between Satan's two evasions here: *whatever thing
death be*, and *if what is evil / Be real*. Each is more profound than its
disingenuous use in the temptation at first suggests. Satan himself only
knows Death as an allegorical shape, "If shape it might be called, that
shape had none." And the conditional clause, "if what is evil / Be real"
raises in stark form the central epistemological issue as to whether evil
really should be conceived in the aggregate, as an abstraction, as distinct from discrete events and actions.

Something else very interesting happens earlier in book 9, before
Satan, as the serpent, approaches Eve with this philosophical conun-

drum. Watching Eve, and observing "her graceful innocence" (459) among her flowers, Satan is, for a moment, no longer absolute evil:

> That space the Evil One abstracted stood
> From his own evil, and for the time remained
> Stupidly good, of enmity disarmed.
>
> (463–65)

The story does not need this moment. It is Milton's addition and invention. And it is hard not to believe that Milton is playing philosophical word-games here. If the phrase, "the Evil One," has been an abstraction of all our most miserable experiences, then to state that "the Evil One *abstracted* stood / From his own evil" seems to suggest, by way of another pun, that abstraction is a faulty reasoning process, that there is no such entity as absolute evil personified, but only conflicting impulses.

Furthermore, Milton wants us to recognize that evils, as experienced, are plural, multiple, and that they can be graded. During the War in Heaven, the rebels first experience pain, which they recognize as "the worst / Of evils" (6.462–63). After Adam has berated Eve for her "evil hour" (9.1067), he points out that they are now experiencing "shame, the last of evils" (1079), a subtle thought indeed. After his fall, Adam loosely applies the term *evil* to all the fearful visions of warfare, death, sickness, flood (that is, both moral and natural disasters), that Michael displays for his education before he leaves the Garden; that is, he refuses the modern philosophical distinction between natural and moral evils. And, perhaps most interesting of all, Milton admits that he himself is, if only in the writerly sense the Author of Evil, certainly its victim. At the beginning of book 7, having called on his muse to return him to his native element, lest, and the word is important, he "fall / Erroneous" (19–20), he tells us bizarrely that he has in fact fallen:

> More safe I sing with mortal voice, unchanged
> To hoarse or mute, though fall'n on evil days,
> On evil days though fall'n, and evil tongues.
>
> (24–26)

This marvelous chiasmus, "though fall'n on evil days, / On evil days though fall'n" brings his readers back with a start to the actual situation of this poet, once himself a firm supporter of a rebellion against Charles I. The evil days are those of the Restoration of the Stuart monarchy, but they are only evil for those who, like Milton, tried to prevent the Restoration from occurring. Thus the political roots of the epistemology of evil show themselves yet once more.

Following the semantic track of the term *evil* through Milton's complex, marvelous poem, we seem to have arrived at Kant's understanding *avant la lettre*; that theodicy is not well served by either the Genesis myth or the Satan myth. The more one expands and tries to rationalize those myths, the more one comes to the following conclusions: first, one will not conquer evil conceptually by tracking it to its origin, because the origin always recedes; two, that abstraction of the evils we experience into an idea of absolute Evil (thereby creating an Adversary) is no solution, since it only encourages either the return of dualism (or, in our day, the revival of bigotry). And three, that the only possible form of theodicy today, therefore, is to come up with a less complacent version of the Best Possible World theory proposed by Leibnitz; not that the world we inhabit is the Best Possible World, and that other versions of it would be worse, but that we can make it somewhat better than we find it. The tools of our remediation, a human remediation, as the last two books of *Paradise Lost* carefully explain, are humility, resignation, companionship, entrepreneurialism, hard work, control of our diet to avoid the worse diseases, and the capacity to look forward with hope rather than backward with regret. A great deal can be done, therefore, without the need for a supernatural redemption—and without the need for a mythical Adversary, who is all too easily confused with a political one, and even when Milton has done him imaginative justice, is a bit too much like us. These were, surely, strong, difficult, and daring thoughts for a seventeenth-century poet.

NOTES

1. John Milton, *Paradise Lost*, in *John Milton: The Complete Poems*, ed. John Leonard (New York: Penguin, 1998). All references to Milton's poetry are to this edition and are cited parenthetically in the text.

2. Pierre Bayle, *Historical and Critical Dictionary: Selections*, ed. and trans. Richard Popkin with the assistance of Craig Brush (Indianapolis, IN: Hackett, 1991), 169.

3. Ibid., 13.

4. Neil Forsyth, *The Old Enemy: Satan and the Combat Myth* (Princeton, NJ: Princeton University Press, 1987), 137.

5. All biblical references are to the King James Version and are cited parenthetically in the text.

6. Neil Forsyth, *The Satanic Epic* (Princeton, NJ: Princeton University Press, 2003), 17.

7. Ibid., 39–40.

8. Susan Neiman, *Evil in Modern Thought: An Alternative History of Philosophy* (Princeton, NJ: Princeton University Press, 2002), 4–5.

9. Immanuel Kant, *Religion, Within the Limits of Reason Alone*, trans. Theodore H. Greene and Hoyt H. Hudson (New York: Harper, 1960), qtd. in *The Many Faces of Evil: Historical Perspective*, ed. Amélie Oksenberg Rorty (New York: Routledge, 2001), 184–85.

10. Daniel Defoe, *The Political History of the Devil*, ed. Irving N. Rothman and R. Michael Bowerman (New York: AMS, 2003), frontispiece. All references to Defoe's work are to this edition and are cited parenthetically in the text.

11. Forsyth, *The Satanic Epic*, 180–81.

"Not Without Dust and Heat": Alchemy and *Areopagitica*

Glenn Sucich

THE INFLUENCE OF ALCHEMY ON MILTON'S PROSE AND POETRY HAS BEEN grossly underestimated. More than thirty years ago, Michal Lieb, in his appendix to *The Dialectics of Creation*, invited a more thorough investigation of alchemy's influence on Milton's poetics; unfortunately, his invitation has gone unheeded. As recently as 1996, Stanton J. Linden was left wondering why "there are relatively few modern scholarly investigations of Milton's alchemy, the topic often having been subsumed under the larger subjects of his science or philosophy." In fact, even those commentators concerned with Milton's science and philosophy have miscalculated the extent to which alchemy informs the poet's thought. Kester Svendsen, for instance, acknowledges Milton's debt to the occult tradition but concludes that, in Milton's mind, the alchemist's attempt to "short-cut the natural processes through which God works" align him with Satan, both guilty of "a sin of pride." Stephen Fallon, although alive to the implicit relationship between alchemical theories of matter and Milton's philosophical monism, limits his discussion of the connection, noting simply that "Milton was skeptical of occult phenomena and alchemical experiments." More recently, Sandy Feinstein has demonstrated the ways in which the alchemical meaning of the word "sublime" "informs [*Paradise Lost*] and its multiple levels of meaning." Like Svendsen, however, she suggests that "Milton may well be joining Chaucer and Dante before him and criticizing, if not damning, the practice of alchemy by associating it with Hell."[1]

In what follows, I argue for a more affirmative and constructive relation between the discourse of alchemy and Milton's thought. In particular, I demonstrate ways in which Milton employs alchemical im-

agery and ideas in *Areopagitica* to build his argument against prepublication licensing. My claim for the alchemical influence of the tract
rests on three related concepts: reduction to first principles, digestion,
and sublimation. These processes, which were all integral to the theory
and practice of early modern alchemy, shape Milton's overarching attempt to transform Parliament's decision regarding the Licensing Act
of 1643. They also inform Milton's efforts to promote the spiritual
health and moral integrity in individuals that he deems crucial to the
welfare of the English commonwealth.

To appreciate Milton's use of alchemical imagery, it is important
first to understand a key distinction in the alchemical tradition that
Milton and his milieu inherited. As early as the thirteenth century, the
Franciscan monk Roger Bacon distinguished between two branches of
alchemy, the operative and the speculative. The first was concerned
primarily with the transmutation of metals and inspired much of the
charlatanism that various authors, from Chaucer to Samuel Butler,
treated with derision. The second branch, speculative alchemy, was
more purely theoretical and attracted the attention of several prominent early modern thinkers, including Martin Luther, Francis Bacon,
and Isaac Newton.[2] Speculative alchemy was concerned with "knowledge of the secrets of nature, not for the purpose of achieving dominion over nature, as with the philosopher's stone or a magical elixir, but
rather a disinterested, unpragmatic knowledge of the origin, composition, and secret operations of all aspects of creation."[3] The Genesis account of creation, insofar as it was thought to resemble certain alchemical processes, corroborated the widespread belief that alchemy
could reveal Nature's most sacred secrets, including the correspon-
dences between the microcosm and macrocosm, cures for disease, and
the prolongation of life. More important, speculative alchemy was
characterized by a "concentration on spiritual and philosophical values
and ideals, especially as they impinge on the inner life of the individual
adept."[4] Sir Thomas Browne summed up the appeal speculative
alchemy held for many seventeenth-century thinkers when he admitted, "The smattering I have of the Philosophers stone, (which is something more then the perfect exaltation of gold) hath taught me a great
deale of Divinity."[5]

The line separating operative from speculative alchemy was often
blurred, and one finds in alchemical literature operative alchemists describing mundane operations with mystical rhetoric, and vice versa. In
Areopagitica, Milton is similarly ambivalent. In general, he communi-

cates the way to spiritual refinement through the language of operative
alchemy; in the process, he avails himself of "a devotional system
where the mundane transmutation of metals became merely symbolic
of the transformation of sinful man into a perfect being through . . .
submission to the will of god."[6] What unites both traditions of
alchemy, and what Milton exploits in his tract, are the related ideas of
transformation and purification. The quest for the philosopher's stone,
as we shall see, provided Milton a powerful metaphor for the pursuit of
moral and spiritual excellence that, in *Areopagitica*, is engendered by
reading.

First Principles

Milton begins his argument against prepublication licensing with an
explicit statement of his primary goal: to change Parliament's decision
regarding the Licensing Act of 1643. After praising the members of his
audience, Milton invokes as the model he plans to emulate the trans-
formational rhetoric of Isocrates, "who from his private house wrote
that discourse to the Parlament of Athens, that perswades them to
change the forme of Democraty which was then establisht" (2:489).[7]
Milton's acknowledgement of Isocrates' political success sets the stage
for the individual, moral transformations he hopes to effect with his
own discourse. His first step toward achieving this goal involves a return, or reduction, to first principles. He hearkens readers back to the
freedom enjoyed in ancient Athens and republican Rome, where even
Aristophanes, "the loosest of them all," and Lucretius were allowed to
circulate their works "without impeachment" (2:495, 498). Not until
the censorial policies of Augustus's successors, Milton claims, does the
world "meet with little else but tyranny in the Roman Empire" (499–
500).

Encouraging a return to the exemplary standards of the ancients
was, of course, a conventional strategy in humanist rhetoric. A further
implication, however, resides in Milton's invocation of Lucretius in
this context, for it intimates the relationship Milton conceives between
the first principles of moral reform, on the one hand, and the first
principles of natural science, on the other. As Richard DuRocher
points out, "Milton . . . regarded questions of natural philosophy as in-
separable from questions of metaphysics and theology"; for Milton science was "the vital, intimate link between knowledge of the world itself
and knowledge of God."[8] Ostensibly, Lucretius seems an odd figure for

Milton to use to suggest this link. The Roman writer was one of "two egregious poets" whom Milton's nephew, Edward Phillips, recalls being taught by his uncle, and Milton's contempt for Epicurean philosophy is well known. His disdain for Epicureanism, however, did not diminish Milton's regard for Lucretian natural science. In *Of Education*, he recommends Lucretius's *De Rerum Natura* in his ideal syllabus, and as Ernest Sirluck explains, "the natural science of the poem, not its Epicurean philosophy, is the basis of recommendation."[9] In the context of *Areopagitica*'s concern with first principles, Lucretian atomism provides a useful parallel: just as atoms are the basic elements from which matter assumes its final form, freedom is the basis for the moral growth with which Milton is primarily concerned. The Licensing Act, by depriving individuals of the freedom "to discover onward things more remote from our knowledge," stifles the individual's ability to develop, both spiritually and physically—an idea Milton expresses with organic metaphors such as "ripeness" and "growth" (550). Such deprivation, Milton maintains, violates the will of God: "For God sure esteems the growth and compleating of one vertuous person, more then the restraint of ten vitious" (2:528).

The connection between Lucretian atomism and Miltonic freedom might still seem tenuous. The works of Epicurus and Lucretius did, after all, inspire the movement most antithetical to Milton's own Arminian tendencies: the mechanistic philosophies of Hobbes, Descartes, and others. There was, however, another, equally viable interpretation of atomism available during the seventeenth century, one that emphasized atomism's relation to freedom and thus challenged purely mechanistic theories of matter-in-motion. John Rogers has demonstrated the currency of this "alternative materialism," which, he suggests, was the foundation of early modern individualism: "The infinitesimal unit of the mechanist's physical universe, the 'atom,' provided . . . one of the figural bases for the central element of the social universe, the 'individual,' a category of increasing interest to intellectual disciplines as diverse as Arminian theology and the nascent philosophy of political consensus."[10] The driving force behind this alternative materialism was vitalism, a philosophy of nature integral to both Milton's material monism and early modern alchemy.[11] Milton's invocation of Lucretius thus introduces the analogy between atoms, the first principles of matter, and freedom, the first principle of moral development.[12] It also points to the tradition that gives this analogy its particular force and meaning, the discourse of alchemy.

As Christoph Meinel has shown, the impetus for the seventeenth-century's interest in atomism came largely from "alchemists and practical men," who "did much to determine the questions of early modern theory of matter." Following the recovery of *De Rerum Natura* in 1417, Lucretius's exposition of atoms as the first principles of the material world "supplied the scheme according to which material change was assumed to occur in nature."[13] Because alchemical transmutation depended on such a scheme, Lucretius's poem became an important text for aspiring adepts (that is, those skilled in the theory and practice of alchemy). Before the alchemist could change base metals into gold, he had to reduce the metal to its purist, most elemental form, the *prima materia*. This idea, like the freedom it is meant to parallel in *Areopagitica*, had roots in the ancient world, particularly in the works of Aristotle. Although ancient atomism and Aristotle's theory of prime matter differed in certain respects, they shared a concern for the primeval stuff of the world, as well as for the nature of material change. Consequently, the two philosophies were often collapsed in seventeenth-century alchemical speculations.

Both atomism and Aristotelian natural philosophy offered insights into one of alchemy's overarching concerns, namely, "the connection between matter-theory and the theme of redemption by regeneration."[14] Against the prevailing dualism of Descartes and others, alchemists held to a dynamic, monistic conception of the material world. The perfection of metals, they believed, came about when the metal's inherent life principle, often conceived as its spirit, fully matured. Milton communicates a similar belief in the indivisible relationship between material and spiritual development in two passages that pun on the word "matter." In the first, he insists that it was "the favour and love of heav'n" that compelled England, above all nations, to lead the charge of religious reformation in Europe (552). Had it not been for "the obstinat perversnes" of English "Prelats," Wycliffe, rather than foreigners such as Luther and Calvin, would have won for England the "glory of reforming all our neighbours" (2:552–53). Instead, because the prelates suppressed Wycliffe "as a schismatic and innovator," "our obdurat Clergy have with violence demean'd the matter" (2:553).

The key word here is "demeaned." The *Oxford English Dictionary* cites this passage as an example of a neutral definition of the term, namely, "to manage" or "to deal with." The context of *Areopagitica*, however, argues for another, more charged meaning, also current during the seventeenth century: "to lower in condition, status, reputation or character."[15] Milton, in fact, exploits this latter sense of "demean" earlier in the tract, when he concedes the responsibility people have to keep "a vigilant eye how Bookes demeane themselves, as well as men" (492). In the case of the "obdurat Clergy," the violence that demeans, or lowers the condition of, matter—both the matter of reform and the matter of individuals—is the deprivation of freedom. This violence, Milton argues, has effectively reversed the natural process of material and spiritual growth that reading promotes; it has caused Englishmen to become "the latest and the backwardest Schollers, of whom God offer'd to have made us the teachers" (553). The denial of freedom and its detrimental effects on material and spiritual development stand in contrast to what can happen when people are granted their liberty: "that then the people . . . wholly tak'n up with the study of highest and most important *matters to be reform'd*, should be disputing, reasoning, reading, inventing, discoursing, ev'n to a rarity, and admiration, things not before discourst or writt'n of" (557; emphasis mine).

One of the matters to be reformed by *Areopagitica* is the individual her- or himself, and Milton's use of "rarity" here highlights the contrast between demeaned matter and reformed matter that underwrites his argument. The difference between material lightness and heaviness was a common and important distinction in alchemical parlance. Whereas alchemically re-formed matter was thought to be light, animated and fluid, demeaned matter remained heavy, immature, and stagnant. According to Milton, the licensing of books, by guaranteeing a limited and fixed body of knowledge, renders people equally heavy and static:

> Another sort there be who when they hear that all things shall be order'd, all things *regulated and setl'd*; nothing writt'n but what passes through the custom-house of certain Publicans that have the *tunaging and the poundaging* of all free spok'n truth, will strait give themselvs up into your hands, mak'em, & cut'em out what religion ye please; there be delights, there be recreations and jolly pastimes that will fetch the day about from sun to sun, and *rock* the tedious year as in a delightfull dream. What need they torture their heads with that which others have tak'n *so strictly, and so unalterably* into their own pourveying? These are the fruits which a *dull ease* and *cessation of our knowledge* will bring forth among the people. How goodly, and how to be wisht were such an obedient unanimity as this, what a fine *conformity* would it *starch* us all into? doubtles a *stanch and solid* peece of frame-work, as any January could *freeze* together. (545; emphasis mine)

This litany of sedentary and inert images reinforces Milton's conviction that licensing "starches" people in a state of relative ignorance, depriving the English their chance to become "a knowing people, a Nation of Prophets, of Sages, and of Worthies" (554). By contrast, liberty "is the nurse of all great wits. This is that which hath *rarify'd* and *enlighten'd* our spirits like the influence of heav'n" (559; emphasis mine). If censorship causes the English to "grow ignorant again, brutish, formall, and slavish" (559), the repeal of the licensing order will benefit "a Nation not slow and dull, but of a quick, ingenious, and piercing spirit, acute to invent, suttle and sinewy to discours, not beneath the reach of any point the highest that human capacity can soar to" (551).

Milton's claim that liberty has the capacity to rarify and enlighten human spirits "like the influence of heav'n" evokes another important idea in alchemical lore. Like most seventeenth-century Europeans, alchemists believed that celestial bodies exerted a direct influence on the terrestrial realm. These heavenly influences were thought to be responsible for the generation of metals, plants, and other living creatures. John Rumrich has argued that this "reproductive geology" was not alien to Milton, who "consistently worked it into his fictional premises and in so doing exploited the alchemical science of his day to elaborate the metaphorical motherhood of Earth."[16] A key component of this reproductive geology was the role that mercury played in the constitution of material bodies. Along with sulfur, mercury was considered one of the principles of metal. The French alchemist Joseph Duchesne, for instance, described mercury as "a sharpe liquor, passable and penetrable, and a most pure & Aetheriall substantiall body: a sybstance ayrie, most subtill, quickning, and ful of Spirit, the foode of life, and the Essence, or terme, the next instrument."[17] Like Duchesne's subtle and quickening mercury, Milton's idealized Englishmen are "of a quick, ingenious, and piercing spirit . . . suttle and sinewy" in their capacity for knowledge. That Milton describes the moral qualities of English citizens in language culled from contemporary natural philosophy lends credence to Lana Cable's claim that one of the chief resources for the "new ethics" Milton advocates in *Areopagitica* is the "intellectual milieu" of "scientific reformers."[18]

Milton renders clear the connection between alchemy and his goals in *Areopagitica* when he makes his most explicit reference to the science: "I am of those who believe, it will be harder alchymy than Lullius ever knew, to sublimat any good use out of such an invention [the Licensing Order]" (507). I will return to the connection between alchemy and sublimation below. Here, I want to suggest how this line functions in the structure of Milton's argument. More than just a convenient metaphor, the image acts as a hinge that moves Milton from the harmful effects of censorship to the salutary effects of free reading. Milton's choice of Ramon Lull, the medieval theologian and mystic whom Sirluck calls "a kind of patron saint of alchemists," is purposeful. Among his many influential works, Lull's exploration of chemical compounds and their behaviors had a profound effect on seventeenth-century alchemical and medical theory. A central tenet of Lull's alchemical philosophy was the power of the fifth essence, which he argued could be achieved through fermentation or digestion. In the sixteenth century, Lull's theory of digestion found its greatest advocate in Paracelsus, whom John Rogers calls "Milton's ultimate source for . . . digestive lore."[19] Milton's debt to these thinkers is important insofar as it illuminates the sources and pattern of alchemical thought he develops in *Areopagitica*. His use of Lull at this pivotal juncture allows Milton to condemn censorship while simultaneously condoning the potential of reading. If the Licensing Act cannot be transformed by the art of Lullius, readers (at least metaphorically) can be. In keeping with the connection Milton maintains throughout the tract between the health of the spirit and the health of the body, spiritual ascension is figured as a form of bodily digestion.

DIGESTION

Nigel Smith has argued that "eating" is "the central animating metaphor" of *Areopagitica*.[20] This fact assumes added significance when we remember that Milton "viewed digestion as a kind of natural alchemy."[21] The correlation between alchemical transmutation and digestion had, in fact, become a commonplace in seventeenth-century thought, providing alchemists as well as artists a powerful trope with which to express processes of purification, both material and spiritual. Duchesne, for instance, asserted that metals were made perfect in the womb of the earth not by the influence of the stars, a theory popularized by Ficino and, later, Agrippa, but by another source, "that is heate, by force whereof mettales congealed in the bowels of the earth are disposed, digested, and made perfect." Dryden expresses a similar idea in *Annus Mirabilis*:

> As those who unripe veins in mines explore,
> On the rich bed again the warm turf lay,
> Till time digests the yet imperfect ore,
> And know it will be gold another day.

And in Ben Jonson's *The Alchemist*, Face, when asked by Subtle if he had dissolved certain elements in his alembic, responds, "Yes, sir, and then married 'em , / And put 'em in a bolt's head, nipped to digestion, / According as you bade me."[22] Milton himself exploits the connection in *Paradise Lost*, when Raphael compares angelic digestion to the ability of the "Empiric Alchemist" who "Can turn . . . / Metals of drossiest Ore to perfet Gold" (5.440–42).[23] Indeed, Raphael's entire account of how our spirits may eventually be "by gradual scale sublim'd" (483) proves more a description of bodily digestion than a Neoplatonic allegory of the soul.[24]

In each of these examples, digestion is figured as a purifying or refining process. The source for this theory of digestion was Galen, who posited that food, when subjected to a gentle heat within the stomach, was "concocted," or broken down, into its constituent parts. The blood would absorb the useful nutrients, leaving any residual impurities to form the dead matter that Paracelsus would later call tartar. Alchemists believed they could replicate this natural process in the laboratory, using alembics and fire to purify metals the same way the stomach purified food. During the seventeenth century, Galen's theory of digestion came under fire, mainly because it assumed a passive ontology of matter: that certain nutrients were left unabsorbed by the blood meant that certain parts of matter were not animated by spirit. As vitalism increasingly took hold in Europe, Galen's theory was supplanted by iatrochemists (medical alchemists) such as Robert Fludd and Jean Baptiste van Helmont, who constructed theories of digestion on animist conceptions of matter. For these and other seventeenth-century alchemical thinkers, digestion provided an example of nature's tendency toward material perfection. The human body, in converting food to spirit, performed at the level of the microcosm what God performs at the level of the macrocosm.

Milton was certainly familiar with these theories of digestion. Around the time of *Areopagitica*, he was, according to Edward Phillips, "perpetually tampering with Physick," perhaps because he attributed his own failing vision to digestive problems.[25] During these years, the medical literature available to Milton had become increasingly alchemical and Hermetic in orientation. Paracelsus remained the leading figure of the "new medicine" well into the seventeenth century, and many of his followers, including Oswald Crollius, Andreas Libavius, and Thomas Tymme, published works that emphasized the superiority of Paracelsian remedies to traditional Galenic medicine. It makes sense, given this background, that digestion became integral to Milton's cosmogony and theology, leading him, in the words of Susannah B. Mintz, to put forth "bodily ingestion" as "the very pattern of spiritual ascension."[26]

In *Areopagitica*, Milton employs this alchemically oriented logic to describe how benefits may be digested, or "concocted," out of books. Following his allusion to the alchemy of Ramon Lull, Milton begins the ensuing section with another reduction to first principles. This time, in a move that recapitulates the tract's progress toward refinement, he invokes "the examples of Moses, Daniel, & Paul," who, like St. Jerome and Basil after them, put pagan authors to good use (2:507). These examples corroborate Dionysius of Alexandria's vision, in which God appeared to the bishop and "confirm'd him in these words: 'Read any books what ever come to thy hands, for thou art sufficient both to judge aright, and to examine each matter' " (511). Milton then elaborates this truth in a passage that trades on the relationship between knowledge and digestion. Under Paul's dictum, "To the pure all things are pure," Milton includes "not only meats and drinks, but all kinde of knowledge whether of good or evill. . . . For books are as meats and viands are; some of good, some of evill substance; and yet God in that unapocryphall vision, said without exception, Rise Peter, kill and eat, leaving the choice to each mans discretion." "Bad meats," Milton concludes, "will scarce breed good nourishment in the healthiest concoction" (512).

The comparison between books and food demonstrates the God-given gift of reason and its relation to choosing. When "God did enlarge the universall diet of mans body," writes Milton, "he then also . . . left arbitrary the dyeting and repasting of our minds" (513). When the Jews in the desert chose to eat only as much manna as they needed, it proved that "God uses not to captivat under a perpetuall childhood of prescription, but trusts him with the gift of reason to be his own chooser" (513–14). These passages initially seem consistent with Raphael's assertion, in *Paradise Lost*, that "Knowledge is as food" (7.127). In the epic, however, the analogy between knowledge and food clearly emphasizes the importance of "Temperance over Appetite"

(7.126); it serves as an explicit warning "not to know at large of things remote / From use, obscure and subtle" (8.191–92). In *Areopagitica*, Milton places no such restrictions on what humans can or should know. In fact, to be merely "worldy wise" is sarcastically dismissed: "Henceforth let no man care to learn, or care to be more than worldly wise; for certainly in higher matters to be ignorant and slothfull, to be a common, stedfast dunce will be the only pleasant life, and only in request" (2:535). On the contrary, unbridled reading is indispensable "to the search and expectation of greatest and exactest things" (559); it fosters "men of rare abilities, and more then common industry . . . to gain furder and goe on, some new enlighten'd steps in the discovery of truth" (566). In his emphasis on the limitlessness of human knowledge, Milton is closer to the young poet of the third prolusion, who insists that the "mind should not consent to be limited and circumscribed by the earth's boundaries, but should range beyond the confines of the world" ("Prolusion 3," 607).[27] In *Areopagitica*, what Milton wants to inspire in his readers is the desire to enter "the innermost shrines of the gods" and to search for "secret" things ("Elegy 5," 25, 24). The "prime Wisdom" (8.194) of *Paradise Lost*, with its clearly defined limits and their moral implications, is absent from the earlier tract, which depends on the conviction that true knowledge comes from "trying all things" (2:554).

Despite the occasional nod Milton gives to moderation, knowledge in *Areopagitica* is clearly the result of excess. Such excess "justifies the high providence of God, who though he command us temperance, justice, continence, yet powrs out before us, ev'n to a profusenes, all desirable things, and gives us minds that can wander beyond all limit and satiety" (527–28). This praise of the powers of individual thought recalls classical encomia on the mind, which Milton would have known from Lactantius, Plato, Ovid, and others. But it also has a source in seventeenth-century Hermetic literature. In the ancient dialogues attributed to Hermes Trismigestus, for instance, which Milton owned in Ficino's translation, the interlocutor known simply as Mind implores Hermes, "Make yourself grow to immeasurable immensity, outleap all body, outstrip all time, become eternity and you will understand god. Having conceived that nothing is impossible to you, consider yourself immortal and able to understand everything, all art, all learning, the temper of every living thing."[28] When Milton claims that God "gives us minds that can wander beyond all limit and *satiety*" (emphasis mine), he figures the production of knowledge through reading as a continual feeding of the mind that leads to ever more progressive degrees of understanding. Discrimination and choice remain important, but unlike in *Paradise Lost*, temperance is not the imperative. Rather, the individual must encounter as many different ideas as possible. Only the person who feeds on this wealth of ideas and has "tasted learning" will be able to "manage, and set forth new positions to the world" (567).

I emphasize the importance of Milton's metaphorics of eating because the idea of continually feeding an object to promote its growth and purity has a parallel in operative alchemy. For alchemists, feeding the metal—known in alchemical idiom as cibation or imbibation—was considered a crucial step toward achieving the elixir. The medieval adept George Ripley, whom one historian describes as "one of the most important early English alchemists for the seventeenth century," explained the process of refining metal in terms of eating.[29] In the section of *The Compound of Alchymie* entitled "Of Conjunction," Ripley explains how once the metal has stood in the alembic for five months, more heat should be applied, "Tyll bryght and shyneing in Whytenesse be thy Stone; / Then may thou opyn thy Glasse anone, / And fede thy Chyld whych ys then ybore, / Wyth mylke and mete ay more and more."[30] Feeding the stone was thought to increase not only its volume but its efficacy as well. Jabir Ibn Hayyan, the medieval alchemist known as Geber, describes the process succinctly when he instructs his readers to "Imbibe [feed] Calx or Body often-times, that thence it may be sublimed, and yet more purified then before."[31] While it remains uncertain how well Milton knew the work of these adepts, the connections among feeding, digestion, and spiritual growth were certainly in the air in Milton's England and were motivated, in large part, by the alchemists.

The perceived health benefits of feeding base metals point to another important attribute of early modern alchemy: its medical orientation. Alchemy, as several scholars have noted, "often drew on the theories and discourses of early western medicine."[32] One person for whom biological processes and morality were intimately related was Paracelsus, who regarded bodily disease as a sign of moral degradation. The relationship among food, disease, and morality also plays a central role in *Areopagitica*. Throughout the tract, Milton figures the dangers associated with "bad meats" (that is, immoral books) as a form of physical and spiritual contagion. Indeed, Milton was not alone among his contemporaries in connecting medicine and metaphysics. Nor were operative alchemy and iatrochemistry (medicinal alchemy) distinct en-terprises. In fact, "one must be careful not to err . . . by thinking of chyrsopoeians [gold seekers] and Paracelsian iatrochemists as wholly disjoined groups; in the seventeenth century there are quite a few notable overlaps."[33] Because of these overlaps, alchemists ascribed a great deal of importance to physicians, whose divine importance was affirmed in Ecclesiasticus: "Honor physicians for their services, for the Lord created them; / for their gift of healing comes from the Most High, and they are rewarded by the king."[34]

Milton displays his own reverence for physicians in *Areopagitica* when he asks his readers, "[H]ow can a man teach with autority, how can he be a Doctor in his book as he ought to be . . . whenas all he teaches, all he delivers, is but under the tuition, under the correction of his patriarchal licencer" (2:532–33)? By itself, Milton's suggestion that one "ought to be" a doctor in one's book is unexceptional; but together with the tract's other medical imagery, the doctor metaphor suggests that Milton may indeed have had Paracelsian iatrochemistry (medical alchemy) in mind. Consider, for instance, the extended passage in which he compares censorship with contagion. Milton refutes the arguments of those who warn of "the infection that may spread" if immoral books are allowed to circulate (517). He extends the contagion metaphor in the ensuing section, rebutting allegations against foreign books—the works of "heathen Writers of greatest infection"—on the grounds that these works are also available to "the worst of men, who are both most able, and most diligent to instill the poison they suck" (518). Licensing will ultimately prove ineffective, Milton insists, for "all the contagion that foreine books can infuse, will finde a passage to the people farre easier and shorter then an Indian voyage" (518). These images of diseases entering the body from the outside argue for Milton's familiarity with Paracelsian medicine. Paracelsus was one of the chief opponents of Galen's theory that disease was caused by an internally generated imbalance of the humors. Instead, Paracelsus maintained that disease was caused by external agents introduced to the body either through the air or food. Unlike Galen and his followers, who resorted to bloodletting, emetics, and other traditional remedies, Paracelsus insisted that medicines comprised of the disease itself should be administered to the sick.[35]

When Milton endorses the curative power of books, he does so in terms reminiscent of this new, Paracelsian medicine. To those supporters of licensing who allege "we must not expose our selves to temptations without necessity" nor "imploy our time in vain things," Milton responds, "to all men such books are not temptations, nor vanities; but usefull drugs and materialls wherewith to temper and compose effective and strong med'cins which mans life cannot want" (521). For Milton, a book becomes an effective medicine only if the reader exercises prudence. What is remarkable is how Milton describes this prudence and the fruits of choosing wisely in the language of alchemy. The reader who discriminates judiciously is "like a good refiner" who "can gather gold out of the drossiest volume" (521). Books, then, operate on our virtue as medicine operates on our body as refiners operate on base metals. In each case, purification occurs through a process that Milton imagines and describes in the language of alchemical digestion. The Licensing Order is "fruitlesse and defective" precisely because it impedes this digestive process (529); it "will operate," as Stanley Fish aptly puts it, "to eliminate the conditions of virtue's growth by removing the materials on which growth can *feed*."[36]

SUBLIMATION

Alchemical theories of digestion share important affinities with the third and perhaps most important alchemical process informing Milton's tract, sublimation. Like digestion, sublimation "was often viewed as a chemical reaction that brought about the 'reduction' of the elements to their essential form . . . by turning them into refined and spirituous essences."[37] In the case of sublimation, matter was reduced in this manner not by an internal bodily heat, but by being subjected to an external fire—a process alchemists often described as a trial or test. Indeed, as J. Andrew Mendelsohn observes, during the seventeenth century, "The English word 'test' itself, as contemporaries would have been aware, was emerging from alchemy and metallurgy (from *testum*, pot or earthen vessel) to wider meanings."[38] This etymological fact bears heavily on our reading of *Areopagitica*, for "if the *Areopagitica* is to be faithful to the lesson it teaches . . . it must offer *itself* as the occasion for *the trial* and exercise that are necessary to the constituting of human virtue."[39] By offering his own treatise as the occasion for such a trial, Milton invites his readers to undergo a transformation evocative of those being performed by alchemists in their labs. In lieu of the alchemist's fire, Milton's main instrument in this subliming process is his rhetorical tact. If readers are to be transformed, they must "try the matter," both of themselves and of Milton's tract, not by fire, but "by dint of argument" (2:562).

In operative alchemy, the coveted object of alchemical trials by fire
was the elusive *quinta essentia*, which Paracelsus described as a certain
matter "extracted from a substance—from all plants and from everything which has life—then freed from all impurities and all perishable
parts, refined into highest purity and separated from all elements."[40] As
Lyndy Abraham explains, the quest for the fifth essence grew out of ancient theories of prime matter: "The alchemical concept of the prima
material derives from the Hellenistic alchemists, who based their theory of nature on Aristotle's idea of the prima materia and on his idea of
the four elements from which the fifth element or quintessence was
synthesized."[41] Because all matter was thought to be alive, animated by
the same vital spirit with which God infused his entire creation, alchemists believed that, with enough diligence and piety, they could
achieve the elusive fifth essence and thus transform the material world.

That Milton had this alchemical concept of matter in mind while
composing *Areopagitica* is evinced by his use of "fifth essence," which
concludes a passage rife with vitalist and alchemical imagery. After describing the "potencie of life" and "active" nature of books, Milton
writes, "they do preserve as in a violl the purest efficacie and extraction
of that living intellect that bred them" (492). Because "a good Booke is
the pretious life-blood of a master spirit, imbalm'd and treasur'd up on
purpose to a life beyond life," censorship is akin to murder, "whereof
the execution ends not in the slaying of an elementall life, but strikes at
the ethereall and fift essence, the breath of reason it selfe" (493). Later,
Milton returns to the image of books as living organisms, this time to
condemn the Council of Trent and the Inquisition for the unprecedented restrictions they imposed on learning. Before the actions of
"the most Antichristian Councel and the most tyrannous Inquisition,"
"Books were ever as freely admitted into the World as any other birth;
the issue of the brain was no more stifl'd then the issue of the womb:
no envious Juno sat cros-leg'd over the nativity of any mans intellectu-
all off spring" (2:505).

Together these images—books instinct with life and a soul, a vial
that holds the purest extraction, and the ethereal fifth essence—create
a constellation of explicitly alchemical images. Merritt Hughes further
suggests the alchemical resonance of these passages. In a note glossing
Milton's use of "fifth essence," Hughes directs readers to Henry
Vaughan's "To My Books." Vaughan, along with his brother Thomas,
was perhaps the seventeenth-century's most renowned promoter of alchemical lore in his poetry.[42] In addition to the influence of Henry's

"To My Books," Milton's use of the vial metaphor anticipates Thomas Vaughan's use of a similar image in his alchemical poem "Hyanthe." There, Hyanthe, a personification of the alchemical elixir, tells her poet/alchemist lover just before she dies: "Let not this Vial part from Thee. / It holds my Heart, though now 'tis Spill'd, / And into Waters all distill'd."[43]

The vial image also figures prominently in Robert Fludd's *A Philosophicall Key*, published in 1617. There, Pan, the embodiment of Universal Nature, explains to man how he was created by Demogorgon, "who hath composed me of symmetry so diuine, and made me to represent the uniuersall mass of Watrÿ spirit, Wch he hath sublimed and refined bÿ the rectifying fire of his heauenlÿ Alchemÿ." After instructing Pan about how to create the race of men, Demogorgon offers up his essence, along with instructions to distribute the essence to humankind. This divine gift is presented to Pan in a vial: "With that he did commit unto mÿ custody a Christal glass or spirituall fioll [viol] of his diuine nature." Significantly, Fludd describes Demogorgon's divine nature as "supernaturall essence," "sparks of reason," and a "beame and quintessence of superstantiall light," images that all have close parallels in *Areopagitica*.[44]

By calling attention to these sources, I am not arguing for their direct influence on *Areopagitica*. I can only be suggestive. But Milton's use of images found in these alchemical sources lends a decidedly alchemical bent to the trial by fire motif that pervades *Areopagitica*. Milton introduces the issue of fire in a long section devoted to the importance of choice. After reminding readers how "the Books of Protagoras" were "commanded to be burnt," Milton insists that "the burning of those Ephesian books by St. Paul's converts" was a "privat" and "voluntary" act, one that we can either emulate or choose to avoid (494, 514). Milton follows this burning episode with his famous account of how good and evil "grow up together almost inseparably," his ultimate goal being to prove that "the knowledge of good is so involv'd and interwoven with the knowledge of evill" (514). He then arrives at arguably the most famous line in the tract: "I cannot praise a fugitive and cloister'd vertue, unexercis'd & unbreath'd, that never sallies out and sees her adversary, but slinks out of the race, where that immortall garland is to be run for, not without dust and heat" (515).

Most commentators have focused on the passage's allusion to the gospels of Paul and James, suggesting that Milton's concern is with winning Paul's prize through resisting temptation. This reading, useful as it may be, ignores the end of the passage, which suggests that the prize will be won "not without dust and heat." The literal meaning is clear: the race will be difficult and will involve the discomforts of dust and heat. Given the tract's alchemical undercurrents, however, and considering the fire imagery that introduces the passage, I suggest another allusion at work. In the alchemical quest for gold, the application of fire was the crucial step toward sublimating and refining matter. This process of material purification had for centuries been interpreted in spiritual terms. St. John of Damascus, for instance, described the Eucharist as a "purging from all uncleanness: should one receive base gold . . . [the alchemists] purify it by the critical burning lest in the future we be condemned with this world." One of Milton's favorite sources, du Bartas, also makes the association between alchemical trial and spiritual regeneration plain in the *Divine Weeks*: "Fire, that in Lymbec of pure thoughts divine / Doost purge our thoughts, and our dull earth refine." Finally, one of Milton's contemporaries, Gabriel Harvey, exploits a similar idea in a passage redolent of Milton's depiction of Adam's fatal experience of "knowing good by evill." In his animadversions against Thomas Nash, Harvey writes, "True alchemy can alledge much for her Extractions and quintessences; & true Phisique more for her corrections and purgations. In the best I cannot commende the badd, and the baddest I reject not the good, but precisely play the Alchimist in seeking pure and sweet balmes in the rankest poisons."[45]

During alchemical transmutation, the application of fire compelled the metal's finer qualities to ascend, leaving at the bottom of the alembic the dust or dregs. The sublimated material would then be reapplied to the metal and the process repeated several times. Many seventeenth-century thinkers used this process of separation to promote a brand of dualism that Milton likely would have suspected. There was, however, a longstanding tradition of alchemical thought that would have been more agreeable to Milton, who was considering his own monism at the time of *Areopagitica*.[46] Aristotle, for instance, likened the purified body or white dust of sublimated matter with the Hermes Bird: "Whiten the Earth, and Sublime it quickly with Fire, untill the Spirit which thou shalt finde in it goe forth of it, and it is called Hermes Bird; for that which ascends higher is efficacious purity but that which fals to the bottome, is drosse and corruption. This therefore is Dust drawn from Dust . . . the white foliated Earth, in which Gold is to be sown." George Ripley also refused an absolute distinction between body and soul. In the section of *The Compound of Alchymie* entitled "Of Sublimation," Ripley writes, "Folys do Sublyme, but Sublyme thou not so / For we Sublyme not lyke as they do I wys; / To Sublyme trewly therfore thou shall not mys: / If thou can make thy Bodys first spirituall, / And then thy Spyryts as I have tought the corporall." As C. G. J. Jung succinctly puts it, "matter in alchemy is material and spiritual, and spirit spiritual and material. Only, in the first case matter is *cruda, confusa, grossa, crassa, densa*, and in the second it is *subtilis*."[47]

As these passages suggest, during sublimation the separation of finer from grosser qualities was considered only temporary. Sublimated material, both that which ascends and that which remains below, remains material: dust is drawn from dust. The finer dust, after being cleansed by mercurial water, was then reapplied to its corrupted counterpart, in what alchemists called the chemical wedding. This reunion of separated forms of dust led to the regeneration of the metal. The important point is that both the purified and the corrupted dust remain on a continuum matter. In *Areopagitica*, Milton betrays his debt to this tradition of alchemical monism. After explaining that our bodies are healthiest when "the blood is fresh, the spirits pure and vigorous," he compares the human body to the body politic: "so when the cherfulnesse of the people is so sprightly up, as that it has, not only wherewith to guard well its own freedom and safety, but to spare, and to bestow upon the solidest and sublimest points of controversie, and new invention, it betok'ns us not degenerated, nor drooping to a fatall decay, but casting off the old and wrincl'd skin of corruption to outlive these pangs and wax young again, entring the glorious waies of Truth and prosperous virtue" (557). Nigel Smith has commented on the political implications of Milton's use of "sublime" in this context. According to Smith, Milton's use of the term here and elsewhere provides an example "of the generation of republican vocabulary in the 1640's."[48] His political analysis, however, overlooks the technical precision with which Milton uses alchemical matter-theory to expound his metaphysics. Milton's syntactical juxtaposition of "solidest and sublimest," for example, effectively conflates that which is solid (matter) with that which is sublime (spirit). This conflation of matter and spirit, body and soul, recalls Milton's earlier claim "that our faith and knowledge thrives by exercise, as well as our limbs and complexion" (543). It also reminds one of the Lady's assertion that Comus "hast nor Ear nor Soul to apprehend / The sublime notion and high mystery" (784–85) of "the sage / And serious doctrine of Virginity" (786–87). In *Areopagitica*, Milton puts this monist conception of matter into the service of his program for spiritual growth. Just as the alchemist's sublimated metal remains corrupt and degenerate *until* reunited with its better qualities, Milton's fellow citizens must cast off the old and wrinkled skin of corruption so that they can be reborn, purer and more alive to the ways of truth and virtue.

Was Milton, then, a closet alchemist? Hardly. The critical tradition that continues to emphasize Milton's doubts about alchemy and the occult finds support in passages from *Paradise Lost* and other works. Milton's sustained use of alchemical imagery in *Areopagitica*, however, suggests that he, like Sir Thomas Browne, may have identified "something more" than the transmutation of metals at the heart of alchemy. If, as Christopher Hill suggests, "The goodness of matter and the freedom of man's will are linked concepts for Milton," the discourse of alchemy might aid us in our continuing attempts to understand how and from what pool of ideas Milton forged that link.[49] At the very least, Milton utilized alchemical lore as a powerful aesthetic device, both in his verse and in his prose. And for a poet who was deeply invested in the relationship between the Word and Truth, language and virtue, this fact alone makes Michael Lieb's call for a deeper engagement with Milton's alchemy as urgent today as it was thirty years ago.

NOTES

1. Michael Lieb, *The Dialectics of Creation: Patterns of Birth and Regeneration in "Paradise Lost"* (Amherst: University of Massachusetts Press, 1970), 229–44; Stanton Linden, *Darke Hieroglyphicks: Alchemy in English Literature from Chaucer to the Restoration* (Lexington: University Press of Kentucky, 1996), 246; Kester Svendsen, *Milton and Science* (Cambridge, MA: Harvard University Press, 1956), 126–27; Stephen Fallon, *Milton Among the Philosophers: Poetry and Materialism in Seventeenth-Century England* (Ithaca, NY: Cornell University Press, 1991), 115; Sandy Feinstein, "Milton's Devilish Sublime," *Ben Jonson Journal* 5 (1998): 150, 161. See also Juliet Cummins, "Matter and Apocalyptic Transformation in *Paradise Lost*," in *Milton and the Ends of Time*, ed. Juliet Cummins (Cambridge: Cambridge University Press, 2003), 169–83. Cummins acknowledges that "The renewal of the heavens and earth at the apocalypse in *Paradise Lost* betrays the influence of contemporary alchemical theory," but her discussion of this influence centers on a few terms with "alchemical currency" and is thus limited in scope.

2. For a discussion of the difference between operative and speculative alchemy, see Allen G. Debus, *The Chemical Philosophy: Paracelsian Science and Medicine in the Sixteenth and Seventeenth Centuries* (New York: Dover, 2002), 18. For a discussion of the satirical tradition, see Linden, *Darke Hieroglyphicks*, esp. 26–36. As Linden explains, "The alchemists who are singled out for treatment by medieval and Renaissance satirists are generally adherents of the practical or exoteric type" (26). For

Luther's interest in alchemy, see Robert M. Schuler, "Some Spiritual Alchemies of the Seventeenth Century," *Journal of the History of Ideas* 41 (1980): 293–318; for Bacon, see Paolo Rossi, *Francis Bacon: From Magic to Science*, trans. Sacha Rabinovitch (Chicago: University of Chicago Press, 1968); for Newton, see B. J. T. Dobbs, *The Janus Face of Genius: The Role of Alchemy in Newton's Thought* (Cambridge: Cambridge University Press, 1991).

3. Linden, *Darke Hierogliphicks*, 8.

4. Ibid. Thomas Tymme, for instance, insisted that "Halcymie tradeth not alone with transmutation of metals (as ignorant vulgars think: which error hath made them distaste that noble Science) but she hath also a chirurgical hand in the anatomizing of every mesenteriall veine of whole nature: Gods created handmaid, to conceive and bring forth his Creatures" (qtd. in Linden, 6).

5. Sir Thomas Browne, *Sir Thomas Browne: Selected Writings*, 4 vols., ed. Sir Geoffrey Keynes (Chicago: University of Chicago Press, 1968), 1:50.

6. E. J. Holmyard, *Alchemy* (Harmondsworth, Middlesex: Penguin, 1957), 16.

7. John Milton, *Areopagitica*, in *Complete Prose Works of John Milton*, 8 vols., ed. Don M. Wolfe et al. (New Haven, CT: Yale University Press, 1953–82). All references to *Areopagitica* and other prose tracts are to this edition and are cited parenthetically in the text.

8. Richard Du Rocher, *Milton Among the Romans* (Pittsburgh, PA: Duquesne University Press, 2001), 36, 30.

9. Ernest Sirluck, *Complete Prose Works of John Milton*, 2:495 n. 35. On Milton and Epicureanism, see Fallon, *Milton Among the Philosophers*. As Fallon argues, "Not only did Epicurus's doctrine of the origin of the universe in chance collision of atoms threaten theism, but his materialism precluded the immortality of the soul and thus called into question the eschatological supports of morality" (20). See also John Leonard, "Milton, Lucretius, and 'the Void Profound of Unessential Night,' " in *Living Texts: Interpreting Milton*, ed. Kristin A. Pruitt and Charles W. Durham (Selinsgrove, PA: Susquehanna University Press, 2000), 198–217. Leonard discusses "the doctrinal gulf that separates the two poets" (199).

10. John Rogers, *The Matter of Revolution: Science, Poetry, and Politics in the Age of Milton* (Ithaca, NY: Cornell University Press, 1996), 36.

11. For a discussion of vitalism and alchemy, see B. J. T. Dobbs, "Alchemical Death and Resurrection: The Significance of Alchemy in the Age of Newton," in *Science, Pseudo-Science, and Utopianism in Early Modern Thought*, ed. Stephen A. McKnight (Columbia: University of Missouri Press, 1992), 55–87.

12. For a discussion of ways in which Lucretius's didactic style provided Milton a useful model in *Paradise Lost*, see Philip Hardie, "The Presence of Lucretius in *Paradise Lost*," *Milton Quarterly* 29 (1995): 13–24. "In both the *De Rerum Natura* and *Paradise Lost*," Hardie suggests, Lucretius and Milton "educate not simply through exposition but through a dramatization of the process of learning. The passage from error to truth, the function of the didactic, is written into these texts as figurations of the epic plots of struggle or journey" (13).

13. Christoph Meinel, "Early Seventeenth-Century Atomism: Theory, Epistemology, and the Insufficiency of Experience," *Isis* 79 (1988): 72, 85. See also Debus, *The Chemical Philosophy*. As Debus explains, "it is with Hermetic and chemical philosophers of the late sixteenth and the early seventeenth centuries that we first see a new growth of interest in the subject of atomism" (69).

14. Stephen Toulmin and June Goodfield, *The Architecture of Matter* (Chicago: University of Chicago Press, 1982), 117.

15. *Oxford English Dictionary Online*. 2nd ed. 1989. s.v. "demeaned." (http://dictionary.oed.com.turing.library.northwestern.edu/entrance.dtl)

16. John Rumrich, *Milton Unbound* (Cambridge: Cambridge University Press, 1996), 74.

17. See Allen G. Debus, *The English Paracelsians* (New York: Franklin Watts, 1966), 93.

18. Lana Cable, *Carnal Rhetoric: Milton's Iconoclasm and the Poetics of Desire* (Durham, NC: Duke University Press, 1995), 128.

19. Sirluck, *Complete Prose Works*, ed. Wolfe et al., 2:507, n. 74; Rogers, *Matter of Revolution*, 135. Rogers goes on to argue that Jean Baptiste van Helmont, who modified many of Paracelsus's theories, was "surely one of Milton's chief sources for his theodicial philosophy of fermentive vitalism" (135). For Lull's influence on early modern alchemy, see Michela Pereira, "*Medicina* in the Alchemical Writings Attributed to Raimond Lull (14th–17th Centuries)," in *Alchemy and Chemistry in the 16th and 17th Centuries*, ed. Piyo Rattansi and Antonio Cericuzio (London: Kluwer, 1994), 1–16.

20. Nigel Smith, "*Areopagitica*: Voicing Contexts, 1643–45," in *Politics, Poetics, and Hermeneutics in Milton's Prose*, ed. David Loewenstein and James Grantham Turner (Cambridge: Cambridge University Press, 1990), 109. Because "a contradiction appears between books as food and books as men, both of which can be eaten by other men," Smith sees this as "a crisis of production and consumption which remains unresolved in the imagistic subtext of the tract." See also Susannah B. Mintz, " 'On an empty stomach': Milton's Food Imagery and Disordered Eating," in *Reassembling Truth: Twenty-first-Century Milton*, ed. Charles W. Durham and Kristin A. Pruitt (Selinsgrove, PA: Susquehanna University Press, 2003), 145–72.

21. Fallon, *Milton Among the Philosophers*, 115.

22. Debus, *Chemical Philosophy*, 150; John Dryden, *Annus Mirabilis*, 553–56, in *Dryden: A Selection*, ed. John Conaghan (London: Methuen, 1978); Ben Jonson, *The Alchemist*, ed. Elizabeth Cook (New York: W. W. Norton, 1995), 2.3.73–75.

23. John Milton, *Paradise Lost*, in *John Milton: Complete Poems and Major Prose*, ed. Merritt Y. Hughes (New York: Odyssey, 1957). All references to Milton's poetry are to this edition and are cited parenthetically in the text.

24. See Lyndy Abraham, "Milton's *Paradise Lost* and 'the sounding alchymie,' " *Renaissance Studies* 12 (1998): 261–76. Abraham writes, "Milton clearly wished to underline the alchemical nature of angel digestion, by not only playing with the alchemical meanings of 'concoctive,' 'transubstantiate,' and 'transpires,' but also by comparing Raphael's transformation of the grosser fruits of paradise into ethereal substance with the empiric alchemist's task of turning the drossiest ore into pure gold" (269).

25. Edward Phillips, *The Life of Mr. John Milton*, in *The Early Lives of Milton*, ed. Helen Darbishire (London: Constable, 1932), 72. See Barbara K. Lewalski, *The Life of Milton: A Critical Biography* (Oxford: Blackwell, 2000), 181. See also William Kerrigan, *The Sacred Complex: On the Psychogenesis of "Paradise Lost"* (Cambridge, MA: Harvard University Press, 1983), esp. 192–262.

26. Mintz, "Disordered Eating," 145. Harinder Singh Marjara, in *Contemplation of Created Things: Science in "Paradise Lost"* (Toronto: University of Toronto Press,

1992), makes a similar point: "Milton's spirits, whatever their manifestation, are apparently the end-products of the vertical movement that begins with the ingestion and 'concoction' of food by the body" (233). It is worth noting that the official *Pharmacoepia* (1618), issued by the College of Physician's, included Paracelsian remedies alongside more traditional Galenic treatments. This new Paracelsian medicine emphasized a spiritualized, monistic model of the material world.

27. The passages also recall the ambitious idealist of "At a Vacation Exercise," who desires to go "where the deep transported mind may soar / Above the wheeling poles, and at Heav'n's door / Look in, and see each blissful Deity" (33–35).

28. Hermes Trismegistus, *Hermetica: The Greek "Corpus Hermeticum" and the Latin "Asclepius" in a New English Translation*, ed. and trans. Brian P. Copenhaver (Cambridge: Cambridge University Press, 1992), 41.

29. Schuler, "Some Spiritual Alchemies," 294.

30. George Ripley, *The Compound of Alchymie*, in *Theatrum Chemicum Britannicum*, ed. Elias Ashmole (New York: Johnson Reprint Corporation, 1967), 147.

31. Arthur Dee, *Fasciculus Chemicus, Translated by Elias Ashmole*, ed. Lyndy Abraham (New York: Garland, 1997), 42.

32. Gareth Roberts, *The Mirror of Alchemy: Alchemical Ideas and Images in Manuscripts and Books, from Antiquity to the Seventeenth Century* (Toronto: University of Toronto Press, 1994), 37.

33. Lawrence Principe, *The Aspiring Adept: Robert Boyle and His Alchemical Quest* (Princeton, NJ: Princeton University Press, 1998), 42. With respect to Milton, Kerrigan suggests that, because of the poet's "spiritual materialism," "Medicine and moral theology would seem to be, on his own account, aspects of the same subject" (*Sacred Complex*, 201).

34. Ecclesiasticus, in *The New Oxford Annotated Bible*, ed. Michael D. Coogan (Oxford: Oxford University Press, 2001), 38:1–2.

35. In his *Chemical Philosophy*, Allen Debus writes, "[Paracelsus] had rejected the traditional view that disease was a disturbance of the humoral balance and had emphasized instead the importance of outside agents which entered the body and like parasites took possession of an organ and gradually consumed it" (133).

36. Stanley Fish, *How Milton Works* (Cambridge, MA: Harvard University Press, 2001), 202; emphasis mine.

37. Marjara, *Contemplation of Created Things*, 233. Marjara here is describing the "digestive process," but his description applies equally well to sublimation, which in alchemical lore was closely aligned with digestion.

38. J. Andrew Mendelsohn, "Alchemy and Politics in England 1649–1655," *Past and Present* 135 (1992): 70.

39. Fish, *How Milton Works*, 203; emphasis mine. Denise Gigante has argued that "Milton himself was aware of the epistemological implications of taste, whereby the Latin *sapere* can mean both 'to taste' and 'to know' " ("Milton's Aesthetics of Eating," *Diacritics* 30 [2000]: 88). I would argue that Milton exhibits the same etymological acumen in his treatment of trial and its cognate "test."

40. Paracelsus, *Selected Writings*, ed. Jolande Jacobi, trans. Norbert Guterman (Princeton, NJ: Princeton University Press, 1988), 145–46.

41. Lyndy Abraham, *A Dictionary of Alchemical Imagery* (Cambridge: Cambridge University Press, 2000), 153.

42. Merritt Hughes, ed., *Complete Poetry*, 720 n. 23. See Thomas O. Calhoun, *Henry Vaughan: The Achievement of "Silex Scintillans"* (Newark: University of Delaware Press, 1981), 101–30.

43. Thomas Vaughan, *Magia Adamica*, "Hyanthe," in *The Works of Thomas Vaughan*, ed. Alan Rudrum (Oxford: Clarendon, 1984), 206, lines 42–44.

44. Robert Fludd, "A Philosophicall Key," in *Robert Fludd and His Philosophicall Key, being a Transcription of the manuscript at Trinity College, Cambridge*, ed. Allen G. Debus (New York: Science History Publications, 1979), 79, 82, 81.

45. St. John of Damascus, qtd. in Claude N. Stulting Jr., " 'New Heav'ns, new Earth': Apocalypse and the Loss of Sacramentality in the Postlapsarian Books of *Paradise Lost*," in *Milton and the Ends of Time*, ed. Cummins, 186; Guillaume du Bartas, *The Divine Weeks and Works of Guillaume de Salustre Sieur du Bartas*, ed. Susan Snyder, trans. Josuah Sylvester, 2 vols. (Oxford: Clarendon, 1979), 1:328, 427–28; Harvey, qtd. in Lynn Veach Sadler, "Relations Between Alchemy and Poetics in the Renaissance and Seventeenth Century, with Special Glances at Donne and Milton," *Ambix* 24 (1977): 72.

46. See John Rogers, *The Matter of Revolution*. Rogers rightly argues that "an early engagement of the monistic union of body and spirit can be detected" in *Areopagitica* (104).

47. In Dee, *Fasciculus Chemicus*, 61–62; Ripley, *The Compound of Alchymie*, 171; C. G. J. Jung, *Alchemical Studies*, trans. R. F. C. Hull (Princeton, NJ: Princeton University Press, 1983), 140.

48. Smith, "Voicing Contexts," 110.

49. Christopher Hill, *Milton and the English Revolution* (New York: Viking, 1977), 326.

Circe's Best Boy

William Shullenberger

"LIMINALITY" BETOKENS A THRESHOLD OR LIMIT, A BOUNDARY SPACE FOR transition and transformation. In the liminal stage of traditional rites of passage, initiates undergo a period of testing and instruction, frequently in a forest or waste space marked off by the society as beyond the reach of its law and order. They endure a series of ordeals and instructions, which may include concealment or seclusion, ritual humiliation marked by binding, blinding, taunting, aggressive mock courtship, ritual drinking, and purifying baths. Masked elder figures who embody the central myths and traditions of the culture orchestrate these experiences, thus exposing initiates to the formative stories and operative metaphors that organize their symbolic universe. The rite of passage is completed by a celebratory return of the initiates from the liminal zone to the gathered company of family and community, to reenter the social structure as newly empowered and acknowledged adults. The central actions of Milton's *A Mask Presented at Ludlow Castle*, which stages the fifteen-year old Alice Egerton's passage from girlhood to womanhood, occur in such a liminal zone.

The three mythic figures the Lady encounters are the *Mask*'s equivalent to the supernatural apparitions to whom the initiate is exposed in traditional rites of passage: "Masked figures, representing gods, ancestors, or chthonic powers may appear to the novices or neophytes in grotesque, monstrous, or beautiful forms. Often, but not always, myths are recited explaining the origin, attributes, and behavior of these strange and sacred habitants of liminality."[1] Each of these symbolic figures has a role to play in the Lady's initiation. The Attendant Spirit presents himself first and last as a trustworthily omniscient master of ceremonies, who establishes the mythic framework, sets the cosmic and terrestrial stage, provides plot outlines in his expository prologue

(1–92) and visionary epilogue (976–1023), and serves as the male elder guiding the brothers in their efforts to rescue the Lady (490–658, s.d., 813).[2] Sabrina's epiphany signals Milton's tacit recognition that the Lady's initiation into female mysteries requires a female rather than a male sponsor and guide. Sabrina appears as a fairy godmother. A riverine goddess of flow and fertility, Sabrina completes the Lady's initiation with a ritual anointing (910–21) that lubricates, purifies, and mobilizes her signature virtue, chastity, transforming it from a necessarily rigid and self-defensive posture of resistance into an ardent, energetic, generous, and questing disposition of the loving soul.[3]

The Lady's ritual antagonist Comus, what he represents and what he calls forth from the Lady, will be the primary subject of the rest of this essay. The master of the nocturnal revels that parody and pervert the framing entertainment of Milton's *Mask*, Comus serves as the Attendant Spirit's dark double and the Lady's parodic initiator. The *Mask* assigns to Comus a ritual position like that of a "mock bridegroom" figure to threaten and tempt the Lady. In rites of passage like the *chisungu* practiced by the Bemba people of Zambia, the mock bridegroom's role involves sexual teasing and threats to the initiate—a ritual analogue to the contemporary American judicial term "sexual harassment." These actions provide adversarial instruction to the girl in the dangers of aggressive male sexual potency and in the management of her proper response to it.[4] Milton makes this ritual archetype culturally specific. Since this initiation performs itself in the specific social setting of Caroline England, by means of the masque, a genre of social drama favored by its ruling class, we can see in Comus's ritual aggression against the Lady a self-dramatization of the aristocratic excesses that Milton intends to critique and reform. The namesake of the belly-god of Puteanus's *Comus* and of Jonson's masque *Pleasure Reconciled to Virtue*, Comus is a suppler and subtler avatar than they for moral anarchy and spiritual gluttony.[5] Although Milton follows Jonson in consigning his Lord of Misrule to the antimasque, he expands Comus's role beyond the conventional containing structure of the antimasque, assigns a significant set of culturally recognizable arguments to him, and endows him with a mesmerizing eloquence to elaborate them. Sleek and sexy as a rock star, he is no slothful Silenus or fat clown. So it is impossible to dispel Comus's charms through laughter. In his extravagance, libertine cynicism, shallow rhetorical ease, and moral triviality, he implicitly represents the decadent spirit lurking beneath the apparent idealism of the Stuart masque itself: "As a satir-

ical embodiment of contemporary masquing practices, Comus justifies the Puritan critique of the form. The revelry he supervises shows
masquing at its worst, reflects its encouragement of immorality, its
false elitism, its self-congratulation, and, perhaps most dangerously, its
superficial elegance, which obscures the moral bankruptcy of its practices."[6]

In the cultural coding of Jacobean and Caroline poetics, Comus expresses most explicitly the predatory allure of libertine sexuality. In his
initial, almost formulaic pass at the Lady, he greets her in terms of conventional masque flatteries and vanities:

> Hail foreign wonder
> Whom certain these rough shades did never breed,
> Unless the Goddess that in rural shrine
> Dwell'st here with Pan or Silvan, by blest Song
> Forbidding every bleak unkindly Fog
> To touch the prosperous growth of this tall Wood.
> (265–70)

This flattery positions itself suggestively in the canon of Milton's work.
It recalls, indeed virtually reiterates, the praises of the Countess Dowager of Derby, stepmother of Lady Alice's father John Egerton, for
whom Milton had collaborated with Lawes to compose *Arcades* two
years prior to *Comus:* "Such a rural Queen / All Arcadia hath not seen"
(94–95). Within the *Mask*, it forecasts, by an irony unknowable to
Comus himself, the countervailing, healing powers of Sabrina (842–
47), the authentic genius loci invoked by the Attendant Spirit to "listen
and save" (866, 889) at the epiphanic climax of the plot. And it anticipates the hyperbolic Petrarchan flatteries with which Satan will initiate
his courtship of Eve in *Paradise Lost* (9.532–48). By rewriting his former praises of the Countess of Derby as the easy, glozing pickup lines
of Comus that menacingly anticipate Satan's erotic bravado, Milton in
effect distances himself from the conventions of masque rhetoric in
which he had formerly participated and exposes them as seductive
idolatries.

Although Comus intimates an aristocratic palate of refinement,
his libidinal appetite discloses itself as crudely binary: either the Lady
is to be part of his "well stock't . . . fair . . . herd" (152)—one more
good breeder or good piece of flesh for the harem—or "she shall be
my Queen" (265)—set apart from cruder pleasures of the flesh for
delights reserved for the most cultivated tastes.[7] These two images of

women exist in complementary rather than oppositional relation to one another, endlessly succeeding one another as libertine desire circulates forever between aspiration and possession, idolatry and degradation, absolute singularity and monotonous anonymity. To imagine that the Lady would be his Queen is, ironically, for Comus to imagine for her a more or less conventional place in the masque of cupidity which he proceeds to orchestrate around her. The Queen, like James I's Anne and Charles I's Henrietta Maria, can be both patron and star of the masque. The masque is a privileged form for the staging of queenship. Yet even in the apparently feminized court extravaganzas of the Jacobean and high Caroline periods, masques stage the power of court women as self-containing fantasies that ritually disguise, libidinize, and renew their dependence on and subjection to the King.[8]

A perverse logic links Comus's fantasy about the Lady as his Queen to his captivity of her in the enchanted chair. Schooled in the libertine idea that women desire and need subjection, Comus creates in his palace of worldly delights a mise-en-scène for what he expects to be the Lady's ready submission of the will:

> The Scene changes to a stately Palace set out with all manner of deliciousness; soft Music, Tables spread with all dainties. Comus appears with his rabble, and the Lady set in an enchanted Chair, to whom he offers his Glass, which she puts by, and goes about to rise.

> *Comus.* Nay Lady, sit; if I but wave this wand,
> Your nerves are all chain'd up in Alabaster,
> And you a statue; or as Daphne was,
> Root-bound, that fled Apollo.
> (s.d., 659–62)

This mise-en-scène recurs in literary bondage fantasies from Amoret's masochistic suffering in Spenser's House of Busyrane (3.11–12), to 0's adventures at Roissy, and Stanley Kubrick's stylized adaptation of them in the ponderous orgy scene of *Eyes Wide Shut*.[9] The Lady finds herself perversely enthroned by Comus's fantasy of her, simultaneously idolized and held captive. The seat of her prestige is the site of her bondage. It might be read as a mirroring parody of the seat of power occupied by her father as a witness to Milton's *Mask*.[10] Milton's structuring of the seduction episode implies that the Lady's plight is a cultural position inevitably assigned to women by the erotic imagination of the conventional masque and of the culture that sustains and is sustained by it.

In Milton's mythic analysis of libertinism, Comus is the bastard son of the transformative sex goddess Circe and the Greco-Roman god of ecstatic release, Bacchus, or Dionysus. This means double trouble for those who encounter him. Angus Fletcher neatly characterizes this double threat: "Comus, child of Circe, is a false virtuoso whose 'gay rhetoric' is the maddened freedom of ecstasy without form. He is one of the Dionysian archetypes of the ancient myth, the Loosener."[11] Each of these mythic parents of Comus is in turn double in character and potential. Dionysus, whose presence in the *Mask* deserves more thorough consideration than this essay can here give, offered release from the burden of selfhood, which Euripides and Ovid ironically dramatize in myths of ruthless physical transformation, savage misperception, and dismemberment. His greatest expositor, Nietzsche, would extoll the annihilating gift of Dionysus as explosive freedom from the illusion of individuality.[12] He is the god who presides over tragedy, and his devotees, the Bacchae, so lost to self and abandoned to the god as to become his hunting dogs, are, as Michael Lieb recounts, a constant specter haunting Milton's aspirations toward the Orphic mastery of poetry.[13] As Comus himself is double natured, Comus's "rout of Monsters" (s.d., 92) are both the Circean feral sports and the bacchic troupe of Milton's *Mask*. If the "orient liquor" (65) distilled from his mother's charms by Comus promises self-forgetful degeneration of human form into sensual folly and spiritual lassitude, the restless circling of his horde suggests the possibility of physical dismemberment suffered by those who deny Dionysus's compelling power. Circe, whom the Attendant Spirit indicates is the dominant parental influence on Comus— "Much like his Father, but his Mother more" (57)—is a witch goddess whose metamorphic power was read in the English Renaissance primarily in terms of the enervating and dehumanizing lure of "sensual Folly and Intemperance" (975).[14] In his notes on Aurelian Townshend's allegory of *Tempe Restored*, a recent masque precedent for Milton, Inigo Jones explains Circe's double nature thus: "Circe here signifies desire in general, the which hath power on all living creatures, and being mixed of the divine and sensible, hath diverse effects, leading some to virtue and others to vice. She is described as a queen, having in her service and subjection the nymphs, which participate of divinity, figuring the virtues, and the brute beasts, denoting the vices."[15] In the plot of *Tempe Restored*, Townshend's Circe, potentially disposed toward spiritual beauty, virtue and reason, and capable of motivating men to seek and achieve them, signifies her willing submission to these higher orders of value by yielding her rod of enchantment to Minerva. Milton eschews mythic bipolarity of this sort; he will allow no such disposition toward the good nor change of heart to his tempter figure. He is less sanguine about the easy idealization of desire, or its ready submission to the claims of virtue, and so he revises the happy ending of *Tempe Restored*.[16] Like other Miltonic tempters, Comus appears to be unreformable, thus unredeemable: the one who tempts and runs away lives to tempt another day. Comus manages to escape with his rod in hand (s.d., 813, 814–20), a sign of Milton's ethical realism regarding the recalcitrance of self-willed desire to domestication by virtuous intentions in a still fallen world.

As the Attendant Spirit explains to the brothers, Comus has inherited the dark sanctuary of liminal testing, "the navel of this hideous Wood" (520), as well as his metamorphic powers, from Circe. Mircea Eliade describes the liminal forest space in which traditional rites of passage occur as a maternal space of spiritual disintegration and gestation, analogous to Comus's "thick shelter of black shades" (62): "The bush symbolizes both hell and cosmic night, hence death and virtualities; the cabin [where initiates are secluded and tested, as the Lady is in Comus's "stately Palace"] is the maw of the devouring monster, in which the neophyte is eaten and digested, but it is also a nourishing womb, in which [s]he is engendered anew."[17] Comus's power center, the imbowered and labyrinthine shades of the uroboric forest, "the perplex't paths of this drear Wood" (37), materializes the self-entangling and regressive cycle of the pleasures he proffers. He only comes out at night, and he chants and speaks, as he dances, in circles:

> We that are of purer fire
> Imitate the Starry Choir,
> Who in their nightly watchful Spheres,
> Lead in swift round the Months and Years.
> The Sounds and Seas with all their finny drove
> Now to the Moon in wavering Morris move,
> And on the Tawny Sands and Shelves
> Trip the pert Fairies and the dapper Elves;
> By dimpled Brook and Fountain brim,
> The Wood-Nymphs deckt with Daisies trim,
> Their merry wakes and pastimes keep:
> What hath night to do with sleep?

Night hath better sweets to prove,
Venus now wakes, and wak'ns Love.
Come let us our rites begin,
'Tis only daylight that makes Sin,
Which these dun shades will ne'er report.

(111–27)

Pert, dapper, dimpled, trim, and merry: Comus casts himself as carnival barker for the festal games and morris dances of Merrie Olde England at their most wholesome, natural, and innocent. At first glance, who could fault him for this, or resist his invitation, with its promise of tireless pleasure and life renewal? To sublunary spirits it certainly sounds like more fun than the frosty solemnities and sober patriarchal hierarchies of those "Regions mild of calm and serene Air" (4) from which the Attendant Spirit has just reluctantly descended. Still, the dramatic evidence of the antimasque contradicts his self-promotion: he is not surrounded by delicate and weightless folk sprites like Peaseblossom, Cobweb, Moth, and Mustardseed, but by monsters. Comus's merry-go-round of pleasure traces the cycle of club-drug addiction: this endless spinning in circles driven by the wheels of stars and seasons would become frantic, then monotonous, after awhile. Rosamond Tuve observes that in Comus's vision, the universal process of existence is purposeless: "the vast skiey system is nothing but one grand and idiotic whirligig."[18]

If we set the opening of Yeats's "Sailing to Byzantium" next to Comus's opening cadences, we can recognize the melancholy undertow of Comus's sprightly carousel of natural pleasure:

That is no country for old men. The young
In one another's arms, birds in the trees—
Those dying generations—at their song,
The salmon-falls, the mackerel-crowded seas,
Fish, flesh, or fowl, commend all summer long
Whatever is begotten, born, and dies.
Caught in that sensual music all neglect
Monuments of unaging intellect.[19]

Comus would no doubt respond, if he could, that Yeats's speaker against "that sensual music" is one of those aging spoilsports, spokesmen of "sour Severity" (109), against whom he rails. And he would be in part right. But that would be a way of distracting from the question of what it is that Comus offers when he conjures up his promises of terrestrial delight. Cyclical repetition, confined to the reiteration of natural process, is one component of his lifestyle. Another is the either/or habit of compartmentalizing experience that belies the fluidity and energy he claims to speak for. He associates the night world with revelry, youth, abandonment, joy, and pleasure. He associates the daylight with effort, age, law, duty, and repression. This polarization is as insufficient in its comprehension of the complexities of experience as the severe, repressive, and voyeuristic society of elders he imagines peeping in on him from the other end of the diurnal pole. Comus cannot imagine the possibilities of *daylit* joys and pleasures, as his innocent prototype, the speaker of "L'Allegro," can.

This is no doubt because Comus seems to have no direct experience of daylight activity. The containment of his experience to the night world links Comus subliminally to folk spirits of the night and the forest more ambiguous and less innocent than the Fairies, Elves, and Nymphs of his imagined train. He joins the "flocking shadows pale" and "fetter'd Ghosts" who flee the daylight in Milton's Nativity Ode (232, 234), as they are also said to do in *A Midsummer Night's Dream* (3.2.378–87) and *Hamlet* (1.1.148–56).[20] It is not so surprising that when he invokes supernatural sponsorship of his revels, Comus turns to the dark goddesses Cotytto and Hecate, as his own cadences momentarily lengthen and gather weight, turning from light tetrameters into somber pentameters, loaded with harsh glottals and plosives, and melancholic nasals:

> Hail Goddess of Nocturnal sport,
> Dark veil'd Cotytto, t' whom the secret flame
> Of midnight Torches burns; mysterious Dame,
> That ne'er art call'd but when the Dragon womb
> Of Stygian darkness spits her thickest gloom,
> And makes one blot of all the air,
> Stay thy cloudy Ebon chair
> Wherein thou rid'st with Hecat' and befriend
> Us thy vow'd Priests, till utmost end
> Of all thy dues be done, and none left out.
>
> (128–37)

The tone darkens, and the dancing measure falters here. Midsummer or Michaelmas festivities, encouraged by the Crown and by the Church of Archbishop Laud, yield to darker pagan solemnities that

Milton leaves largely to the imagination.[21] But an audience imagination informed by Ovid's treatment of Medea's witchcraft (*Metamorphoses* 7.192–301) would not likely shrug off the reference to Hecate as preparation for some good clean fun.[22] Comus's invocation, with its specification of dues owed to the Goddess in her form as the Teeth Mother, implies ritual sacrifice, and sacrifice requires a victim, preferably a pure one.[23] The Lady's arrival is timely for the rite that Comus wishes to stage as antithesis to the framing rite which Milton has composed. Comus's invocation here provides an additional ritual framework in which to read his capture of the Lady, and the malevolent catechism he will subject her to. His enchanted chair serves as a potential altar of blood sacrifice to the dark mother goddesses to whom he devotes himself. Comus's *carpe diem* appeal is rather a *carpe noctem* appeal, warping desire toward the darkness and stagnancy of an eternal round of "barbarous dissonance" (*Paradise Lost*, 7.32) over which these goddesses preside, far from the light of day.

As an energy god driven by the rhythms of seasons and tides, Comus stakes out a position for himself as Nature's advocate. Yet for all his enthusiasm about Nature's bounty in his appeal to the Lady, he expresses a curiously utilitarian notion of the uses of Nature. He understands divinely ordained plenitude primarily in terms of supply and demand. Although he condemns the temperate use of natural gifts as living "like Nature's bastards, not her sons" (727), he is in fact Nature's bastard, and glamorizes the bastardization of nature, the self-gratifying libertine exploitation of its secret resources. The specious magnificence of his paean to natural fertility conceals a raging hunger:

> Wherefore did Nature pour her bounties forth
> With such a full and unwithdrawing hand,
> Covering the earth with odors, fruits, and flocks,
> Thronging the Seas with spawn innumerable,
> But all to please and sate the curious taste?
>
> (710–14)

In *Paradise Lost*, Milton will lift the glamorous mask of Comus and disclose that it is Death who wears it:

> To mee, who with eternal Famine pine,
> Alike is Hell, or Paradise, or Heaven,
> There best, where most with ravin I may meet;

> Which here, though plenteous, all too little seems
> To stuff this Maw, this vast unhide-bound Corpse.
>   (10.597–601)

Comus's palate appears to be more sophisticated, and his manners a bit neater, than Death's, yet he is driven by the same immense hunger. What fills him ultimately doesn't seem to matter, for the overbundance he assigns to Nature leads to a breakdown of qualitative distinctions between "odors, fruits, and flocks," the natural goods of the earth as objects of insatiable desire for incorporation.

What makes Comus so voracious? Angus Fletcher notes that "in *Comus* the most important instance of subsurface implication is the use of the myth of Circe. . . . Milton is withholding much of the direct narrative content of the myth of Circe, and it is this withheld context that fills the interior spaces of the myth of Comus, Thyrsis, the Lady, her brothers, and Sabrina."[24] Circe's latent influence, in other words, permeates the *Mask*. Fletcher implies that Circe is what Freud might call the repressed unconscious material of both Comus the character and *Comus* the ritual drama of initiation. We can begin to explicate this "withheld context" if we raise the question, provoked by the text of the *Mask*, of Comus's relation to his mother: what would maturation be like for a Dionysian manchild who has had Circe, sensual desire personified, as his single mother? The Attendant Spirit observes that Comus is "Much like his Father, but his Mother more" (57). A strange elision creates a telling ambiguity in this observation. The primary meaning of the line seems to be "Much like his Father, but [like] his Mother more." The absence of the second "like," which would establish a likeness between Comus and his Mother analogous to that between him and his Father, suspends and oddly intensifies the nature of the maternal bond. Syntactic compression for the sake of scansion creates the effect of linguistic deterioration into a more archaic, imprecise, less clearly differentiated mode of articulation. With its lulling, suckling alliterations and its suspension of contextual anchors, "his Mother more" is orally evocative of the primal romance of nursing, where subject and object and act dissolve in one another. More like his Mother, Comus likes his Mother more. His ambition at maturity is both to "[Excel] his Mother at her mighty Art" (63), and to recreate, in the "thick shelter of black shades imbow'r'd" (62), "the navel of this hideous Wood" (520), the womblike maternal surround of his upbringing.

Virgil's Aeneas has a comparable problem, as the offspring of the elusive, tantalizing, and irresistible Venus Generatrix, against whom he complains as she darts away from him:

> Why do you mock your son—so often and
> so cruelly—with these lying apparitions?
> Why can't I ever join you, hand to hand,
> to hear, to answer you with honest words?[25]

Ironically, his goddess mother's very elusiveness creates the saving possibility of Aeneas's heroism. Her distanced, protective, yet evocative relation to him sets him on the road of self-disciplined sublimation of desire to the higher and long-deferred calling which will be Rome. But Comus as tempter has the temper of a spoiled child. His mother seems never to have taught him to know what No means. Consequently, the course of self-indulgence rather than self-restraint seems natural and inevitable to him. Comus never had it so good as when he was Circe's baby boy. Bereft of her, he tries to recapitulate the luscious sensual fullness of his infancy. He can never get enough of what he imagines Nature, in Circe's place, has to offer. Comus populates his imaginative world with maternal figures who appear irresistible, virtually omnipotent and potentially all-consuming, yet who invite aggression and possession. This suggests that his desire is ultimately regressive and infantile, and that it involves reproducing such desire in the objects of his desire. His impossible longing to excel his mother is also a longing to restage the scenario of his mother's ego-dissolving tendernesses. So he parodies the perverse and promiscuous fertility of Circe by using her cup of pleasure to give birth to monsters.

As we have noticed, Comus serves the spectral mother figure Cotytto and her crony Hecate, dark surrogates and analogues for Circe, in the hallucinatory night world of his "conceal'd Solemnity" (142). Wicked female grotesques, as we can see in Jonson's *The Masque of Queens,* or the masque scene in Beaumont and Fletcher's *The Maid's Tragedy,* are no strangers to the anarchic uproar of antimasques, but Comus's goddesses derive added sinister force by the very invisibility of their sponsorship of his revels. The infernal orgiast Cotytto, consorting with Hecate, usurps the patriarchal domain of the stars (1–5) and blurs its celestial mapping with a stratospheric menstrual discharge:

> mysterious Dame,
> That ne'er art call'd but when the Dragon womb
> Of Stygian darkness spits her thickest gloom,
> And makes one blot of all the air.
>
> (130–33)

Comus also reminisces more bucolically about

> My mother Circe with the Sirens three,
> Amidst the flow'ry-kirl'd Naiades,
> Culling their Potent herbs and baleful drugs,
> Who as they sung, would take the prison'd soul,
> And lap it in Elysium; Scylla wept,
> And chid her barking waves into attention,
> And fell Charybdis murmur'd soft applause.
>
> (253–59)

This narcotic lullaby, Comus testifies, "in pleasing slumber lull'd the sense, / And in sweet madness robb'd it of itself" (260–61). In this concentrated allusion to the sites of greatest danger to the resourceful and steadfast will of Odysseus—Circe, Sirens, Scylla and Charybdis—Comus discloses his nostalgia for a menacing yet cradling sensuality where he found himself most cosily at home.

Surprisingly, then, Comus's ostensible function in the *Mask* as a male sexual aggressor entails a complementary and more subtle threat, the lure of regressive absorption in the mythic Mother Goddess. William Kerrigan notices this linkage between phallic assertiveness and longing for the maternal surround, although he diagnoses it as Milton's problem rather than Comus's: "Perhaps this fusion of oedipal with preoedipal wholeness shows us why the phallic magic of Comus should reside in the navel of the woods, filling the scar that marks our original dismemberment."[26] Circe, Nature, Cotytto, Hecate: by whatever name he evokes her, Comus's mythic Mother keeps her children mesmerized with the lure of "th'all worshipt ore" (719) hutched "in her own loins" (718). Comus conjures up a Mother Nature who longs to be violated. If her riches were to go unplundered by her ungrateful children, she

> would be quite surcharg'd with her own weight,
> And strangl'd with her waste fertility;
> Th'earth cumber'd, and the wing'd air dark't with plumes,

The herds would over-multitude their Lords,
The Sea o'erfraught would swell, and th'unsought diamonds
Would so emblaze the forehead of the Deep,
And so bestud with Stars, that they below
Would grow inur'd to light, and come at last
To gaze upon the Sun with shameless brows.

(728–36)

When we have analogous cataclysms in Shakespeare, they are produced by violations of, or dissensions within, natural order: the murder of a King *(Macbeth,* 2.4.1–20),[27] the "dissension" over a foundling child *(A Midsummer Night's Dream,* 2.1.81–117). Comus ironically conjures the prospect of an apocalypse produced by the *refusal* to violate Nature. This bizarre suggestion of an apocalypse of undevoured excess has psychological, ecological, and political ramifications. It is a dark and extravagant parody of the ecological reciprocities that will obtain in Milton's Eden, where Nature, requiring a gentler kind of human culling and cultivation, "Wanton'd as in her prime, and play'd at will / Her Virgin Fancies, pouring forth more sweet, / Wild above Rule or Art, enormous bliss" *(Paradise Lost,* 5.294–97). The Nature over which Adam and Eve are called to exercise their creative stewardship is innocent.[28] Her fancies are virginal, and her abundance invites and responds to the delicate touch of human husbandry. By contrast, Comus imagines that his Mother Nature is neither virginal nor fanciful, but a kind of Queen Bee or Termite. Her indiscriminate and ultimately self-smothering fecundity erases difference of species in the world order, disturbs class boundaries in the social order, and dissolves ego structure in the order of the psyche, until the very logic of generational distinction and progression collapses. Exploiting her riches will keep things in balance, Comus argues. More accurately, it will preserve the social order that supports and supplies aristocratic tastes and privileges. The ecological catastrophe resulting from Nature's unchecked fecundity would produce the political catastrophe of a world turned upside down, where "herds would over-multitude their Lords" and "they below / Would grow inur'd to light, and come at last / To gaze upon the Sun with shameless brows." The economic and ecological implications of Comus's position, with its legitimization of the rarefied tastes and extravagances of an aristocratic leisure class, are particular to the cavalier fancies of the Stuart era, yet the supply side logic of unrestricted wish fulfillment makes his pitch anticipate the thematics of the political economy of postmodern consumer capitalism.

Comus's personal investment in and reproduction of his mother's arts account for the power of his appeal. He participates in and presides over a mythological projection of the cultural and psychological domain that the psychoanalyst Jacques Lacan calls the Imaginary order.[29] In Lacan's account, the Imaginary order distills itself from the child's mirroring primary relation to the mother. Lost in one another's gaze, suffused by the mutual warmth of nursing, mother and child seem a world apart, sufficient unto themselves. The child gains a sense of a surrounding world overabundantly poised and disposed to his wishes, and flirts with the sense of omnipotence. At the same time, the child's own wishes form themselves responsively to the nurturing mother's wish for him, and of this interplay of desire is woven a rudimentary yet enduring subjectivity, a preliminary sense of self.[30]

Lacan observes, "man's desire finds its meaning in the desire of the other, not so much because the other holds the key to the object desired, as because the first object of desire is to be recognized by the other.[31] The primary other in Lacan's developmental scenario, as in Comus's experience, is the mother. This means both that the child desires the mother as his primary object choice, and that the child's desire mimics the mother's desire for the child. The Imaginary, where the child's desire continually reflects and is reflected in the desire of the mother, is typified by the fullness of a field of erotically charged, intense yet briefly lived images: the Imaginary is "a 'dual relationship,' an ambiguous redoubling, a 'mirror' reflection, an immediate relationship between the subject and its other in which each term passes immediately into the other and is lost in a never-ending play of reflections."[32] Any single image in the Imaginary register tends to usurp the consciousness as an absolute and absorbing object, even as it quickly recedes into the inexhaustible visual plenum of other images generated in the confusion of the mirroring relationship.

In the psychoanalytic paradigm of Lacan, the father eventually intervenes in this charmed circle. His role in the family, and in the culture which the family represents, is to alienate the child's desire from the all-absorbing desire of the mother, and to redesignate it according to the order of culture, which is, for Lacan, structured by language and structured like language. This order of culture, where we are fated to mature our identities and destinies, linguistically instructed and organized by the patriarchal mystique which Lacan associates with "the

Name of the Father," is called the Symbolic order.[33] Nothing in the human psyche is ever destroyed, although it may be powerfully repressed or displaced. The Symbolic is a culturally patterned template for the social formation of a desire that is already, and always will be, charged with phantasmal objects and intentions that resist the threats, entitlements, and enticements of culture. Outbursts from the circuitry of the Imaginary register continually flare up to startle, disrupt, and redirect the Symbolic orchestrations of conscious intention. In effect, Comus represents such an outburst in the Symbolic psychodrama of Milton's *Mask*. A mediator of the Symbolic, speaking in the Name of the Father, the Attendant Spirit intends to orchestrate the initiation of Alice Egerton and her brothers into the securities and opportunities of a patriarchally stabilized culture. His parodic counterpart, at once master and captive of the Imaginary, Comus plays out the archaic and presocial claims of the Mother of desire, whose regressive call and mesmerizing image float through the liminal spaces of psyche and culture, resistant to and uncolonized by more complex, stressful, and morally charged forms of cultural knowledge.

"Ripe and frolic of his full grown age" (59), Comus plies his illusions and champions moral dissolution to restore the maternal enclosure and to replicate the dream world of oneness with the mother. Bacchus, not surprisingly a footloose father, doesn't seem to stick around for long after Comus's birth to play the conventional paternal role in his son's development, to introduce the demands for self-discipline required for maturation and social engagement (55–58); nor would it be in Bacchus's nature as energy-god to do so. The eventual rupture of the charmed circle of his own infantile enchantment with Circe leads Comus in the furious circling dance of endlessly generated, endlessly displaced, endlessly unsatisfied desire. The "light fantastic round" (144) of his dance is a figure for his longing and his lostness, his slippage through the labyrinthine self-entangled womb-world of unstable spectacle. The "light fantastic round" is a figure too for the Imaginary desire that drives his rhetoric. That he is a fast talker, a rhetorical whirligig whose images have the momentary and affective brilliance of an extraordinarily brief half-life, is a sign of his attempt to subject language—the signifying materialization of the Symbolic register, in Lacan's account—to the destabilizing momentum of the Imaginary. He himself can't slow down, in effect, because his rapid-fire free-associative bravado is a way of veiling the anxious suspicion that he is tap dancing across metaphysical quicksand. Strangely but inevitably,

Comus himself discloses, in his initial gambits of seduction, the spiritual exhaustion of the Imaginary roller coaster he is riding. Trying to soften the Lady up, he offers her the sprightly cordial in his magic glass:

> Not that Nepenthes which the wife of Thone
> In Egypt gave to Jove-born Helena
> Is of such power to stir up joy as this,
> To life so friendly, or so cool to thirst.
>
> (675–78)

"You must be tired; have a refreshing drink." This sounds like an inviting gesture of conventional hospitality until we consider the context of Comus's Homeric allusion. In the palace of Menelaos, Helen offers the drug to her husband and to their melancholic young guest Telemachos, as an anodyne and sedative to quiet the youth's grieving for the lost father he seeks, and to ease the sorrow it stirs in Menelaos as guilty survivor of the war over his marriage. Nepenthes: No Pain. The drug's effect is not to stir up joy, but to douse pain and memory in oblivion:

> Into the wine of which they were drinking she cast a medicine
> of heartsease, free of gall, to make one forget all sorrows,
> and whoever had drunk it down once it had been mixed in the wine
>   bowl,
> for the day that he drank it would have no tear roll down his face,
> not if his mother died and his father died, not if men
> murdered a brother or a beloved son in his presence
> with the bronze, and he with his own eyes saw it.
>
> (4.220–26)[34]

In the *Odyssey*, Helen is quick to offer this anodyne. In the haunted splendor of their golden palace, unblessed by male children of their own and surrounded by the memories of all who have died and all that has been destroyed for their sake, Helen and Menelaos might be presumed to depend on Nepenthes as the drug of choice to make their lives bearable.[35] Comus offers his potion to another wandering child on the threshold of maturity. Bereft of family and searching for home, the Lady is both Telemachos the searcher and Odysseus the lost wanderer. In Comus's hands, Helen's narcotic cup is also Circe's potion of sensual self-abandonment. It is not surprising that Comus resorts to a pharmacopia of narcotics, distilled by skilled enchantresses, if his project is the dissolution of selfhood in the interests of primordial motherhood. But it is surprising that he would hint this so explicitly, so early in his seduction effort, to a well educated and self-aware Lady who is already on her guard, and hardly subject to the spiritual enervation to which he appeals.[36]

Comus continues to ply his offer of solace and refreshment by teasing the Lady for

> Scorning the unexempt condition
> By which all mortal frailty must subsist,
> Refreshment after toil, ease after pain,
> That have been tir'd all day without repast,
> And timely rest have wanted; but, fair Virgin,
> This will restore all soon.
>
> (685–89)

Comus slows his pacing to intensify his appeal here, through the hypnotic tempo of slow-breathed lines, and phrases spaced by languorous pauses, and the alternation of consonant rhymes that quietly seal off each line. This is a hypnotic incantation that seeks to produce the spiritual condition of exhaustion and relaxation by the act of description. Comus models this appeal on the virtuouso performance of one of Spenser's great rhetorical enchanters. Despayre offers death to the Redcrosse Knight as the final solution, as solace and refreshment for a wayfaring, warfaring, conscience-stricken life:

> Is not short paine well borne, that brings long ease,
> And layes the soule to sleepe in quiet graue?
> Sleepe after toyle, port after stormie seas,
> Ease after warre, death after life does greatly please.
>
> (Faerie Queene, 1.9.40, 6–9)

Comus more or less successfully effaces his master source here, and gives a more upbeat twist to the outcome of his offering. But the voice, the very word, of Despayre surfaces in "Refreshment after toil, ease after pain," and in the promise of "timely rest."[37] This tells us more about Comus, at this stage of the ritual, than it does about the Lady. He attempts to project on her his own spiritual condition, as Despayre seeks to make men feel what he always and already is. It is strange to discover from this slight but emphatic Spenserian echo that Comus's libertine vitalism is a disguised version of the voice of despair, and despair is what he hopes to provoke in his test of the Lady's chastity. Still young in the career of chastity, the Lady has hardly reached the stage of afflicted conscience and battle fatigue that renders the Redcrosse Knight so vulnerable to Despayre's seduction. But Comus's cup of refreshment is no less deadly in its consequences than the dagger that Despayre offers to Spenser's hero. His rhetoric is a suicide bomb with a slow fuse.

As the Lady's opening soliloquy has intimated (170–229), Comus answers to, embodies, and appeals to the pressure of Imaginary desire. He makes explicit the shadowy calling of desire by giving voice and substance to the "calling shapes and beck'ning shadows dire, / And airy tongues that syllable men's names" (207–8) that well up out of her liminal isolation and lostness. Making the potential self-gratificatory indulgence of her newly awakened desire explicit, Comus's desire is to prevent the ritual of the *Mask* from "growing a girl" into a woman.[38] There is double trouble, with both a masculine and a feminine allure, in his temptation and his threat to her. As the "mock bridegroom" of the rite of passage, he provokes and tests her curiosity and fear about male desire, seeking her subjection to libertine versions of sexuality and social order. As Circe's best boy, advance man for the claims of an ego-dissolving maternity, he spins out regressive notions of womanhood as models for self-fashioning. Comus tries to cultivate the Lady's emerging desire into a selfhood whose primary obligation is to saturate and dissolve itself in pleasures. Even as Milton's *Mask* stages the ritual formation of the Lady as self-conscious and autonomous moral agent and experiential center of the world, it also represents in the figure of Comus a canny dream manufacturer who reifies a parody of that self: a perpetual consumer who would be in turn consumed by the artificial construction of appetite.[39] Yet in the moral dialectic characteristic of Milton, Comus ironically performs a cultural service he seeks to subvert. A demonic catechist, he prefigures the Satan of *Paradise Regained*, and, more obliquely, the antagonists of *Samson Agonistes*. Every one of his claims becomes a test of what the Lady thinks about God, nature, desire, economy, labor, beauty, philosophy, and language. His attempted seduction provides the opportunity for her to make clear to herself what she believes about what she has been taught, and, in the public ritual, to iterate her newly and personally claimed beliefs in the presence of her family and community. The first true Miltonist, for whom poetry is the highest form of prophetic social action, the Lady changes the primary subject of the conversation from sex to economic justice and its relation to authentic piety. She translates erotic self-abandonment, the subtext of Comus's appeal, into conscientious and other-directed husbandry of resources: personal, social, natural, and rhetorical resources (762–78). In response to the smothering overfecundity of his vision of Nature, the Lady articulates natural law in terms of the principles of equity, self-discipline, and thrift that govern the early modern Puritan household, and the wider social order in which the household is situated and upon which it is founded. She thereby projects an ecology and an economy that reconfigure desire into social and political goods beyond the reach of immediate self-gratification. In response to Comus laying a world of equivocal and fleeting pleasure at her feet, the Lady thus masters and integrates the primary lessons of natural and social wisdom that will order her mature life in the world. Having dramatically confronted, identified, and repudiated Comus's regressive trajectory of desire, which conceals beneath the pretense of self-gratification a dynamic of despairing self-consumption, the Lady returns to her home as Milton's triumphant exemplar of the autonomous ethical self of progressive Reformation culture. Comus, the "mock bridegroom" of the Lady's initiation, proves to be the great pretender and demonic type of the divine love for whom her initiation prepares her and toward whom it directs her.

NOTES

1. Victor Turner, *Dramas, Fields, and Metaphors* (Ithaca, NY: Cornell University Press, 1974), 239.

2. John Milton, *A Mask Presented at Ludlow Castle*, in *John Milton: Complete Poems and Major Prose*, ed. Merritt Y. Hughes (New York: Odyssey, 1957). All references to Milton's poetry are to this edition and are cited parenthetically in the text.

3. For a more detailed account of Sabrina's role in the Lady's initiation, see William Shullenberger, "Girl, Interrupted: Spenserian Bondage and Release in Milton's Ludlow *Mask*," *Milton Quarterly* 37 (2003): 184–204.

4. Audrey Richards, *Chisungu: A Girl's Initiation Ceremony among the Bemba of Zambia* (London: Routledge, 1988), 122.

5. R. H. Singleton studies the influence of Puteanus's *Comus* on Milton's *Mask* in "Milton's *Comus* and the *Comus* of Erycius Puteanus," *PMLA* 68 (1943): 949–57. Although the direct influence of Jonson's Comus in *Pleasure Reconciled to Virtue* upon Milton's conception is debatable, since Jonson's masque was not published and publicly available until 1640, John G. Demaray suggestively notes character parallels in *Milton and the Masque Tradition: The Early Poems, "Arcades," and "Comus"* (Cambridge, MA: Harvard University Press, 1968): both characters "share the same dedication to libertine wantonness" (87). More recently, Ross Leasure studies

the relation of the *Mask* to Puteanus, with particular attention to the motif of homoerotic threat, in "Milton's Queer Choice: Comus as Castlehaven," *Milton Quarterly* 36 (2002): 63–86.

6. Maryann Cale McGuire, *Milton's Puritan Masque* (Athens: University of Georgia Press, 1983), 42. See also Cedric C. Brown, *John Milton's Aristocratic Entertainments* (Cambridge, MA: Cambridge University Press, 1985), 64–73; David Norbrook, *Poetry and Politics in the English Renaissance* (London: Routledge, 1984), 257; and Andrew Hubbell, "*Comus*: Milton's Re-Formation of the Masque," in *Spokesperson Milton: Voices in Contemporary Criticism*, ed. Charles W. Durham and Kristin Pruitt McColgan (Selinsgrove, PA: Susquehanna University Press, 1994), among others, on Milton's critique of customary masque extravagances.

7. Leonora Leet Brodwin makes the interesting argument that, in light of Comus's testimony of "such a sacred and home-felt delight, / Such sober certainty of waking bliss" (262–63) stirred by the Lady's song to Echo, Comus's intention is to "reclaim his own better nature from its profligate indulgence through marriage to her. . . . He tempts her to renounce not premarital chastity for promiscuity but the ideal of virginity for that of marriage." This strikes me as a charming but far-fetched premise in light of Comus's sinister behavior both before and after this testimony, but it is ironically consonant with what I consider Comus's ritual role as a "mock bridegroom." See Brodwin, "Milton and the Renaissance Circe," *Milton Studies* 6 (1974): 48–50.

8. On the role of the queens in Stuart masques, see Barbara Kiefer Lewalski, *Writing Women in Jacobean England* (Cambridge, MA: Harvard University Press, 1993), 15–43; McGuire, *Milton's Puritan Masque*, 132–35; Suzanne Gossett, " 'Manmaid, begone!': Women in Masques," *English Literary Renaissance* 18 (1988): 96–113.

9. Edmund Spenser, *The Faerie Queene*, ed. Thomas P. Roche Jr. (New York: Penguin, 1987). All references to *The Faerie Queene* are to this edition and are cited parenthetically in the text. See also Pauline Reage, *The Story of 0*, trans. Sabine d'Estree (New York: Ballantine, 1973); Stanley Kubrick, dir., *Eyes Wide Shut* (1999).

10. William Kerrigan reads the Lady's "root-bound" condition as a sign of Milton's ambivalence toward the virgin chastity his heroine professes. On the one hand, the Lady's intact virtue "is a suppressed indictment of the community of parents who, guilty themselves, impose on their children obedience to the law they defile." On the other hand, "Hers is a root-bound virtue, caught in reaction formation to oedipal temptation. It is not free. It is in bondage to the desire denied." See *The Sacred Complex: On the Psychogenesis of "Paradise Lost"* (Cambridge, MA: Harvard University Press, 1983), 53, 55. Christopher Kendrick suggestively interprets the Lady's fixed silence in her chair as a sign of Milton's displacement of her father's, and thus the king's, presiding authority; see "Milton and Sexuality: A Symptomatic Reading of *Comus*," in *Re-Membering Milton: Essays on the Texts and Traditions*, ed. Mary Nyquist and Margaret W. Ferguson (New York: Methuen, 1988), 58–61.

11. Angus Fletcher, *The Transcendental Masque: An Essay on Milton's "Comus"* (Ithaca, NY: Cornell University Press, 1971), 245.

12. Friedrich Nietzsche, *The Birth of Tragedy and The Case of Wagner*, trans. Walter Kaufman (New York: Random House, 1967); Marcel Detienne, *Dionysos at Large*, trans. Arthur Goldhammer (Cambridge, MA: Harvard University Press, 1989). A companion piece to this essay, comparing Milton's treatment of the Dionysus myth to Nietzsche's strong interpretation of it, appears in William Shullenberger, "Nietz-

sche for Girls," in *Milton's Legacy*, ed. Kristin A. Pruitt and Charles W. Durham (Selinsgrove, PA: Susquehanna University Press, 2005), 116–35.

13. Other crucial poetic sites instantiating Milton's anxieties, about bacchic threats of dismemberment include *Lycidas*, 58–63, and *Paradise Lost*, 7.32–39. See Michael Lieb, *Milton and the Culture of Violence* (Ithaca, NY: Cornell University Press, 1994), 46–51.

14. For an overview of the significance of the Circe myth in Milton's *Mask*, see especially Brodwin, "Milton and the Renaissance Circe," 21–83; and Rosamond Tuve, *Images and Themes in Five Poems by Milton* (Oxford: Oxford University Press, 1957), 130. Consistent with the Renaissance allegorizations of her, Erich Neumann analyzes Circe as the "young witch" formation of the Goddess archetype, who lures to the transformation and disintegration of the psyche: she is one of the negative manifestations of primordial goddesses in whom "the character of enchantment leading to doom is dominant." See Neumann, *The Great Mother: An Analysis of the Archetype*, trans. Ralph Mannheim (Princeton, NJ: Princeton University Press, 1973), 81, 288.

15. Inigo Jones, notes for Aurelian Townshend, *Tempe Restored*, in *Court Masques: Jacobean and Caroline Entertainments, 1605–1640*, ed. David Lindley (Oxford: Oxford University Press, 1995), 163.

16. On the relation of *Comus* to *Tempe Restored*, see especially Demaray, *Milton and the Masque Tradition*, 79–83.

17. Mircea Eliade, *Rites and Symbols of Initiation: The Mysteries of Birth and Rebirth*, trans. Willard R. Trask (New York: Harper and Row, 1958), 36–37.

18. Tuve, *Images and Themes*, 144.

19. W. B. Yeats, "Sailing to Byzantium," in *The Collected Poems of W. B. Yeats*, Definitive Edition, with the author's final revisions (New York: Macmillan, 1956), 1–8.

20. William Shakespeare, *A Midsummer Night's Dream*, ed. Wolfgang Clemen (New York: Signet, 1963). All references are to this edition and are cited parenthetically in the text. William Shakespeare, *Hamlet*, ed. Edward Hubler (New York: Signet, 1963). Each text treats the status of its supernatural spirits ambiguously. Although Oberon insists that "we are spirits of a different sort" than the nightbound spirits of evil (3.2.388), both the Faeries of *A Midsummer Night's Dream* and Hamlet's Father's Ghost confine themselves to nocturnal activity.

21. Comus represents as well some of the nonsanctioned and potentially dangerous excesses that spilled over from Michaelmas harvest celebrations, when, as the Lady worries, "the loose unletter'd Hinds, / . . . for their teeming Flocks and granges full / In wanton dance . . . praise the bounteous Pan / And thank the gods amiss" (174–77). On ex officio outbursts of rural lawlessness during Michaelmas festivities, see James Taaffe, "Michaelmas, the 'Lawless Hour,' and the Occasion of Milton's *Comus*," *English Language Notes* 6 (1968–69): 257–62. On Milton's critical opposition to the official toleration and encouragement of "holiday sports" by the regime of Charles I, see Leah Sinanoglou Marcus, *The Politics of Mirth: Jonson, Herrick, Milton, Marvell, and the Defense of Old Holiday Pastimes* (Chicago: University of Chicago Press, 1986).

22. See Allen Mandelbaum, *The Metamorphoses of Ovid* (New York: Harcourt, 1993), 215–21. Medea's invocation of Hecate is preparatory and essential to the grisly blood rites of her black magic.

23. The "Teeth Mother" is Robert Bly's designation of the Terrible Mother of Neumann's archetypal analysis. See Neumann, *The Great Mother*, 147–73; also see

Robert Bly, "The Teeth Mother Naked at Last," in *Sleepers Joining Hands* (New York: Harper and Row, 1973).

24. Fletcher, *The Transcendental Masque*, 245–46.

25. Virgil, *The Aeneid of Virgil*, trans. Allen Mandelbaum (Berkeley: University of California Press, 1982), 1.581–84.

26. Kerrigan, *The Sacred Complex*, 53.

27. William Shakespeare, *Macbeth*, ed. Sylvan Barnet (New York: Signet, 1963).

28. Good starting points for an overview of the nature of Nature in Milton's poetry are William G. Madsen, "The Idea of Nature in Milton's Poetry," in *Three Studies in the Renaissance: Sidney, Jonson, Milton*, ed. Richard B. Young et al., Yale Studies in English, no. 138 (New Haven, CT: Yale University Press), 181–283; and more recently, Diane Kelsey McColley, "Beneficent Hierarchies: Reading Milton Greenly," in *"All in All": Unity, Diversity, and the Miltonic Perspective*, ed. Charles W. Durham and Kristin P. McColgan (Selinsgrove, PA: Susquehanna University Press, 1994), 231–48. For the conceptualization of Nature in Milton's *Mask*, see A. S. P. Woodhouse's foundational argument, "The Argument of Milton's *Comus*," *University of Toronto Quarterly* 11 (1941–42): 46–71; also, Joan Bennett, "Virgin Nature in *Comus*," *Milton Studies* 23 (1987): 21–32; James Andrew Clark, "Milton *Naturans*, Milton *Naturata*: The Debate Over Nature in *A Maske Presented at Ludlow*," *Milton Studies* 20 (1984): 3–25.

29. The primary development of Lacan's schematization of the Imaginary and the Symbolic orders appears in *The Language of the Self: The Function of Language in Psychoanalysis*, trans. Anthony Wilden (New York: Dell, 1968). Anthony Wilden's commentary, "Lacan and the Discourse of the Other," is particularly useful in clarifying the differences between the Symbolic and the Imaginary orders, in Lacan's thought; see this essay in *The Language of the Self*, especially 161–66, 185–88. See also Fredric Jameson, "The Imaginary and the Symbolic in Lacan: Marxism, Psychoanalytic Criticism, and the Problem of the Self," *Yale French Studies* 55–56 (1977): 338–95; and Joseph H. Smith, *Arguing with Lacan: Ego Psychology and Language* (New Haven, CT: Yale University Press, 1991), 95–106, 119–22.

30. Although it may be argued that I reproduce the gender biases of standard grammatical practice and of psychoanalysis, I use the masculine pronoun here deliberately for several reasons. Although the differentiation into male and female human subjects, the gender-marking of desire, occurs decisively in the drama of the oedipal crisis, and thus later than the relationship I am trying to describe, "it" as a gender-neutral term is not appropriate to designate an emerging human subject. The masculine pronoun follows the protocols of psychoanalytic discourse at this point. Although it could be argued that this is a sexist privileging of the masculine—a point that I would not dispute in many instances of standard pronominal usage—it might also be argued that in the preoedipal emergence of the human subject, all children are "masculine" in relation to the "feminine" presence of the mother.

31. Lacan, *The Language of the Self*, 31.

32. Jameson, "The Imaginary and the Symbolic," 378.

33. Lacan, *The Language of the Self*, 35–42. See also Lacan's discussion of "the Name of the Father" in "On a question preliminary to any possible treatment of psychosis," in *Ecrits: A Selection*, trans. Alan Sheridan (New York: W. W. Norton, 1977), 198–99.

34. Homer, *The Odyssey of Homer*, trans. Richmond Lattimore (New York: Harper & Row, 1967).

35. For an analysis of the melancholy that haunts Menelaos's magnificent palace, and its relation to the temptation of immortal ease, see William Anderson, "Calypso and Elysium," in *Essays on the Odyssey*, ed. Charles Taylor (Bloomington: Indiana University Press, 1963), 73–86.

36. George William Smith Jr. makes the case that Comus is not a very competent seducer because Milton's revisions of the *Mask* de-emphasize the temptation element in Comus's exchange with the Lady in order to sharpen the differences between them into a debate. See "Milton's Revisions and the Design of *Comus*," *English Literary History* 46 (1979): 56–80.

37. James Andrew Clark notes Comus's adaptation to his own purposes of Despayre's seduction of the Redcrosse Knight, in "Milton *Naturans*, Milton *Naturata*," 26.

38. John Leonard offers a sharp critique of William Kerrigan's psychoanalytic discussion of *Comus* in "Saying 'No' to Freud: Milton's *A Maske* and Sexual Assault," *Milton Quarterly* 25 (1991): 129–40. Leonard would probably be suspicious of my suggestions about the fascinated ambivalence expressed by the Lady in lines 205–9. In rescuing the Lady's honor—and Milton's—from Kerrigan's account of the Lady's chastity as a troubled and unsuccessful reaction formation against a desire in which she is implicated, Leonard perhaps overreacts. He forecloses the possibility that Comus may indeed be addressing—admittedly perversely and dishonestly—the anxieties, uncertainties, and fantasies typical of puberty, which the *Mask* as an initiation is designed to articulate and integrate into her virtue. Deborah Shuger studies the intersection of the physiological and theological concerns of the *Mask* in " 'The Bliss of Dreams': Theology in Milton's *Maske*," *Hellas* 7 (1996): 39–53. Although Shuger traces possible patristic sources for the "gums of glutinous heat" (917) that glue the Lady to Comus's enchanted chair, her discussion of the theological reflection on involuntary and voluntary sexual arousal becomes something of a tease, because of the suggestive indeterminacy of her management of the drama. She does not make clear who she believes is aroused in the *Mask*'s plot: Comus, the Lady, Milton, the reader/audience, or all of the above.

39. In her study of Milton's construction of marriage in the divorce tracts and *Paradise Lost*, Maria Magro interestingly describes the emergence of "what we might anachronistically call an ethical Protestant subject of the Weberian type" ("Milton's Sexualized Woman and the Creation of a Gendered Public Sphere," *Milton Quarterly* 35 [2001]: 101). Magro argues that the emergence of this implicitly male-gendered early modern subject depends upon the construction of the private domestic sphere with which the female is associated and to which she is confined. Although Magro's account of the emergence of the modern ethical and political subject and property owner is persuasive, I think the gender segregation she describes is problematized by figures like the Lady, who exemplifies the citizen-subject that Magro describes and whose rebuttal of Comus transforms his private party room into a veritable public sphere where politics, economics, ecology, and ethics can be debated—by women as well as men. The same could be observed of Eve in *Paradise Lost* 9, when she raises the question of division of labor and holds her ground. Of this crucial exchange, Magro only remarks, "After the serpent has whispered in her ear . . . Eve attempts to control and dictate her own and Adam's work schedule, forgetting that 'nothing

lovelier can be found / In woman, then to studie household good, / And good works in her Husband to promote' (9.232–34), as Adam gently reproves" (108). This dismissive assessment serves to put Eve in the (domestic) place where Magro argues that Milton's construction requires her to belong, but it seems to neglect both the learning curve charted for her in books 5–8 and the rational integrity and force of the argument by which she persuades Adam to acknowledge her freedom. John Rumrich argues that the paradigm of the Protestant ethic offered by Max Weber is inappropriate to a description of early to mid-seventeenth-century social and psychological formation; see Rumrich, *Milton Unbound: Controversy and Reinterpretation* (Cambridge, MA: Cambridge University Press, 1996), 35–36. Magro nicely finesses this potential critique of her thesis by acknowledging the potential "anachronism" of her description.

Infernal Preaching:
Participation, God's Name, and the Great Prophesying Movement in the Demonic Council Scene of *Paradise Lost*

Bryan Adams Hampton

THE DEMONIC COUNCIL SCENE HAS BEEN APPROACHED FROM A NUMBER of provocative perspectives, but as yet no one has approached it within the context of preaching.[1] Jameela Lares comments that the "seventeenth-century mind . . . accepted angels as types of preachers," and she examines the angelic speeches of Raphael and Michael delivered to Adam as sermons.[2] The influential Puritan divine William Perkins explicitly links ministers with angels: "are they *Gods Angels*? therefore they must preach Gods word," and, "Art thou therefore an *Angell* of God, then magnifie the Spirit of God, and not thy self in thy preaching of his word."[3] To be sure, ministers and angels alike had the supreme duty of delivering the "good news": the eruption of the Divine into the world through the mystery of the Incarnation. What is more, many radical preachers, such as the Independent John Everard, the Army chaplain John Saltmarsh, or the Quaker James Nayler, figured themselves and other genuine believers as "incarnations" or embodiments of Christ acting in and speaking to the world.

But we ought perhaps to be more suspicious on Milton's behalf if we are to regard angels as preachers and preachers as incarnations. As Milton the "Church-outed" poet-preacher well knew, these angelic preachers have their demonic counterparts not only in hell, but also on earth. The task before us, Milton repeatedly charges in his anticlerical prose tracts, is to discern true preachers from false and dissembling ones. We find a picture of the latter in book 2 of *Paradise Lost*. The dynamics of the demonic council scene are reminiscent of the "Great

91

Prophesying Movement" of the late sixteenth and seventeenth centuries, wherein a panel of Puritan ministers gathered to deliver a series of sermons on the same text of Scripture. In this essay I argue that these infernal preachers deliver sermons on the same "text": the Name of God. As separatists who dissent from participating in divine rest, and as champions of the liberty of individual conscience and exegesis, the restless demons play language games that attempt to "unsay" the Name of God. Their linguistic attack on the Name is also a metaphysical assault on God's essence, and the performative manifestation or "Bright effluence" of that "bright essence" in the Anointed Son, as they loosen the Name from its mooring as defining Presence (3.6).[4] Rather than fulfilling what promises to be a proliferation of meaning through the freedom of individual reading, however, I aim to show that their language games paradoxically inscribe them within a calculus of sameness, and a "form of life" whose performance is characterized by aggression and violence, manipulation and self-interest.

It is not too much of a stretch to say that popular preachers, who exuded charisma, could wittily turn a phrase, or stir the passions of their audience, were to the early modern world what rock stars are to contemporary culture. Broadsides announced the details of their forthcoming engagements, young men and women met in audience or accompanied each other on the way, verbal quarrels ensued over points of doctrine, and members of every social class departed abuzz with devotional zeal. William Haller aptly describes this age of the sermon as the "vital rage for utterance," and early modern audiences displayed their own vital rage for hearing them.[5] Many Puritans not only heard several sermons on Sundays, but also gave their ear to four or five sermons during the week, and they discussed them at length during their times of work and leisure.[6] Moreover, we need only to look to the popular phenomenon of "gadding" to sermons, wherein English parishioners traveled miles outside their own parish for the purposes of hearing a particularly striking preacher, to confirm the point.[7] As Bryan Crockett surmises, the sermons delivered at Paul's Cross by the most prominent divines attracted audiences as large as six thousand! Because these sermons were usually about two hours in duration, preachers had to rely on every rhetorical device and dramatic tactic in their performative arsenal to keep the crowds from becoming unruly.[8] Preachers at such large sermon gatherings were frequently met by laughter, jabbering, or other disruptive behavior from the audience, in just the same manner as acting companies in the playhouse. So much was riding on capturing the attention of the crowd—no less than their salvation as well as the preacher's own livelihood, if not bodily health. With such crafted attention paid to one's performance, it is no wonder that the pulpit and the playhouse contended for the same audience until the 1583 ban on Sabbath-day theatrical productions.[9]

Stephen Denison, whose preaching was akin to a theatrical performance, advocates that the preacher ought to be a "son of thunder" in the pulpit.[10] But many preachers were deeply conflicted over the extent to which "man-made" eloquence and dramatic performance ought to enter into the preaching of the Word, for fear of compromising the work of the Spirit or creating verbal idols.[11] While George Herbert claims that the preacher "procures all attention by all possible art," Bartimaeus Andrewes upbraids those preachers who "thinke Christ too base to bee preached simply in him selfe . . . and thinke that Christe commeth nakedly, unlesse clothed with vaine ostentation of wordes."[12] For many early modern divines, book 4 of Augustine's *On Christian Doctrine* helped define the parameters for the use of rhetoric in the construction of sermons. Central to Augustine's thoughts on eloquence in the pulpit, shared by Milton as we will see in a moment, is the theology of participation—the doctrine that all creation, including human language, participates and finds its proper telos in the Being of God.

Augustine begins with a disclaimer that he will not, as some of his readers apparently had hoped, "give the rules of rhetoric which I learned and taught in the secular schools." The reason for Augustine's demur appears to be that he does not want to be responsible for disseminating rules that could be used in the employ of evil and the propagation of falsity. Strangely, however, Augustine's refusal does not arm the "good man" with these rules either. Augustine assumes that his primary readership is already well versed in the rules and arts of rhetoric. As he sees it, his job is to clarify to what end rhetoric is to be used, and in the process he reflects on the telos of language itself. He acknowledges that rhetoric is a vital and necessary avenue of study for preachers. "Should [the pagans] speak briefly, clearly, and plausibly," he objects, "while the defenders of truth speak so that they tire their listeners, make themselves difficult to understand and what they have to say dubious?" By no means. Those who "oppose the truth with fallacious arguments and assert falsehoods" must be met with equal eloquence by the "defenders of truth" who are armed to "oppose the false."[13]

For Augustine, eloquence has a proper end: to move the hearts and minds of men and women toward the saving knowledge of God; subsequently, that knowledge spurs congregants to conversion and virtuous action in the world. In the *Enchiridion* Augustine writes, "speech was given to man, not that men might therewith deceive one another, but that one man might make known his thoughts to another. To use speech, then, for the purpose of deception, and not for its appointed end, is a sin."[14] Augustine's thoughts on the "appointed ends" of speech and rhetoric are modeled on the Incarnation. Just as "the Word of God was made flesh without change that He might dwell among us," our thought "remains entire in itself and assumes the form of words by means of which it may reach the ears without suffering any deterioration in itself." Like the Son, whose divine participation and performance points to the Father, eloquence and rhetoric do not draw attention to themselves for their own sake. Crucially, they point to the Beauty, Truth, and Goodness of the God who is their source. Augustine is thus able to affirm the use of rhetoric as long as it satisfies this condition of participation. Christ is the "cure" for humanity, and the implication is that human words have the potential to cure and restore others.[15] Thus, to use language improperly denies on a fundamental level the Incarnation and all that follows according to Christian theology: healing, hope, unity, and charity.

This doctrine of participation is of crucial importance to Milton as well. Over "what," we might imagine Milton asking, is language and the preacher's performance in the pulpit "suspended": over the One in whom, by whom, and through whom all things move and have their being (Acts 17:28); or over the "dark unbottom'd infinite Abyss" where "all life dies, death lives, and nature breeds, / Perverse, all monstrous, . . . / Abominable, inutterable, and worse" (*Paradise Lost*, 2.405, 624–26)?[16] True preachers who participate in the former can incite personal, national, and ecclesial revolution. The sermons of false preachers who participate in the latter, however, produce not the internal seeds of virtue or the fruits of salvation (Rom. 10:13–14); they "produce," rather, nothing, for the bellies of the "hungry Sheep" in their congregation are "swoln with wind" and "rank mist" (*Lycidas*, 125–26).

As David Loewenstein ably demonstrates,[17] part of Milton's multifaceted attack on the Presbyterian ministers in *The Tenure of Kings and Magistrates* (1649) is directed against these "prevaricating Divines" perverting the ends of language by saying one thing and doing another

(3:232).[18] Theirs is a sophistical language and politics of equivocation and flux; like Satan, they "say and straight unsay" (*Paradise Lost*, 4.947). Playing "fast and loos" with the truth, and full of "falshood and dissention," these "Ministers of sedition" and "Mercenary noisemakers" broker language with their forked tongues to serve their selfish purposes (*Tenure*, 3:232, 235–36). Seven years earlier in *The Reason of Church Government*, Milton had scorned the prelates for neglecting the supreme duty of "healing our inward man." Their failure to do so is the result of an impoverished language that does not participate in the divine because it issues from their own spiritually bankrupt and undisciplined souls. Effective "public preaching is . . . the gift of the Spirit"; for Milton, the true preacher seeks to create disciplined souls and infuses in the hearts of his congregants the godly desire for personal and public virtue, the "visible shape . . . given to divine things" (1:751). The personal failure of the prelates to cultivate these divine fruits results in massive public failure; as John Morgan observes, the preacher's personal failures endanger the eternal fate of their congregants.[19] Rather than establishing a church that reflects "all her glorious lineaments and proportions" in Christ, the words of this Wordless clergy bring only a plague of spiritual maladies, sloth, and disorder.

For Milton, as for Augustine, the beauty of rhetoric and the preacher's performance in the pulpit hinge on the doctrine of participation. Sever that connection, Milton would have us believe, and satanic and sophistical performances in the pulpit and in the world are all that remain: "Ambiguous words . . . to sound / Or taint integrity" and "calumnious Art / Of counterfeited truth" to hold, entertain, or delight our ears with their false eloquence (*Paradise Lost*, 5.703–4, 770–71). In their rhetorical performances in the pulpit, Milton asks, do God's anointed spokesmen bear true witness to the Speech of God, whom the Father calls the "Son of my bosom" and "effectual might," and who has "spok'n as my thoughts are, all / As my Eternal purpose has decreed" (*Paradise Lost*, 3.169–72)? Or, do the preachers dissemble and manipulate "with clov'n tongues of falshood and dissention," and rely on the thunderous "affected zele of thir pulpits" (3:235; 5:449)?

This is the question that Milton takes up in the demonic council scene, for the devilish false preachers have radically severed their own linguistic participation in the divine. The "infernal councilors are *not* attempting to investigate reality," John M. Steadman emphatically writes, "but to argue the merits or demerits of a proposed course of action. . . . Political orators rather than philosophers, they are concerned less with knowledge than with persuasion and dissuasion."[20] Steadman is only partially right: the demonic orators are certainly concerned with persuading their peers toward a course of action. Where Steadman errs is in his assertion that the devils are not concerned with "reality." To the contrary, the demons must come to grips with the novel, tortured reality that confronts them as a result of their separation from divine participation *before* they can decide what to do next. They are newly fallen, tossing upon the furious waves of Hell's lake, licked by the "livid flames" and "o'erwhelmed / With Floods and Whirlwinds of tempestuous fire" (*Paradise Lost*, 1.182, 76–77). The anguish of this new reality is what motivates Satan to gather his council together in the first place. In their own "process of speech," they attempt to redefine and recreate a world apart from God (7.178).

The key to their being able to accomplish this lies in their fallen understanding of that which had previously grounded their reality and language: the Name of Names that is eternity and existence itself, the expression of "God's self" and "his real person."[21] William Perkins states, "Our dutie is, to labour to bee setled and assured in our conscience that God is our God: for first in this assurance is the foundation of all true comfort."[22] Consolation for Perkins derives from God's Name as the secure anchor of hope as one navigates the troubling waters of spiritual existence. The demons, however, have lost that anchor; despite their desperate search for it, there can be no genuine comfort. Satanic language—the loss of the Sacred Grammar—allows them to go on, "therapeutically" we might say, as they play language games that empty God's Name of its metaphysical ultimacy and remove the Word from the word. In the infernal sermons that ensue, they "say and straight unsay" the Name (4.947); their sermons are intended to both console their chthonian congregation through the "cure" of language, and move them to "virtuous" action and application. Consequently, we will find that of all the sermon types, the infernal preachers are most given to the consolatory mode wherein language is the only consolation.[23]

Gathered together in a "Synod of Gods" (2.391), the infernal ministers deliver a series of redargutive and consolatory sermons in quick succession. We might say that Beëlzebub, Satan's second in command, acts as a kind of moderator for the ministerial panel; his penultimate sermon, "first devis'd / By Satan, and in part propos'd" (2.379–80), sets up Hell's senior minister to deliver the keynote address. Intriguingly, the gathering of this synod and the delivery of sermons by a panel of

ministers bear a striking resemblance to the highly controversial assemblies of Puritan ministers during the "Great Prophesying Movement" of the late sixteenth and early seventeenth centuries. These assemblies caused a political and ecclesial uproar of which Milton would
no doubt have been mindful. They threatened to tear apart the fragile
fabric of the Elizabethan church, challenged the "reasons" of church
government, became a vital part of the Puritan underground in the
reigns of James and Charles, and modeled what would become the ideological core of the Presbyterian contingent in the 1640s, against whom
Milton leveled some of his polemical attacks.

In the late summer and early fall of 1576, the Puritan Thomas
Wood exchanged a series of letters with the Earls of Warwick and Leicester, both important and influential allies to the Puritans. The purpose of these letters was to dissuade the Earls from following through
with the Queen's wishes to censure the "godly exercises" of ministers
throughout England. To Wood, these exercises provided ministers
with a "benefitt . . . the like whereof were never erected in England before." When Leicester responds (August 19, 1576), the Earl defends
his many past actions in support of the Puritans, but he expresses reserve that "there be and have bene some places of exercises used that I
doe mislike, and some over curious ministers also that give cause of the
breach of the unity of our Church." Leicester having expressed this
reservation, and fearing that the Earls would not give their full support
of the continuance of the exercises, Wood responds (September 7,
1576) that when the exercises are stamped out, "perseqution is like to
followe" from "byshops . . . whom the Prince of this world hath be-
witched with such welth and pufte up with such pride. . . ."[24]

Even before the fall of 1576 when Wood writes his letters, the exercises had stirred up controversy. In 1574 Archbishop Parker ordered
Bishop Parkhurst "to suppress those vain prophesyings," an alternate
name for the exercises, in Norwich.[25] Translated to Canterbury in early
1576 and summoned before the royal presence at the end of that year,
Archbishop Edmund Grindal was ordered by Elizabeth to convey to
his bishops the "utter suppression" of all "learned exercises and conferences" and for the "abridging" of the number of preachers.[26] In early
December of 1576 Grindal wrote a lengthy letter to Elizabeth refusing
to follow her order: "I am forced, with all humility, and yet plainly, to
profess, that I cannot with safe conscience, and without the offense of
the majesty of God, give assent to the suppressing of the said exercises."[27] Grindal, not surprisingly, was immediately suspended and fell

from royal favor. By 1577 the Queen herself stepped in and suppressed the exercises in the southern provinces. In a final letter to Warwick and Leicester (undated 1577), Wood reacts with profound sadness and prophetic judgment. To him and many others the censures represent "not only a great rejoysing to all God's enemies but such a service to Sathan as unles the whole religion shold be overthrowen a greater could not be done." He writes with indignation, "this is but the beginning of greater plagues, whereof the stopping of the course of Christ's Gosple is a most fearfull signe."[28]

What were these "godly exercises" that caused so much trouble, that led to the silencing of thousands of preachers, the altercation between the Queen and her Archbishop, and that threatened to split the Elizabethan church apart? What, finally, would Milton's interest be in them many decades removed from the controversy? Patrick Collinson, the foremost authority on the exercises, admits that the ecclesiastical record on the proceedings of these exercises or "prophesyings" is scant. The prophesyings were modeled on a method of biblical study that many English preachers, having returned from Marian exile, adopted from churches on the Continent. Their purpose was to bring out the "true" sense of the text by inviting several clergy to comment on the same passage of Scripture. In England they served the crucial functions of educating the laity in the Reformed religion and educating the clergy on doctrinal issues. Ministers derived scriptural authority for them from 1 Corinthians 14:29–30: "Let the prophets speak two or three, and let the other judge. . . . For ye may all prophesy one by one, that all may learn and all may be comforted." This is a strange prooftext, given that this section of Paul's epistle deals with the restriction of the speaking of tongues in the church. Nevertheless, like the gift of tongues, the prophesyings were intended to edify all those present.

The proceedings, many times taking place in the market towns and open to large crowds of the laity, had assumed by Grindal's time a common pattern. A senior minister, sometimes with the consent of the bishop and often without it, would call together a session. He acted as moderator for a panel of three to four preachers who took turns preaching a sermon on the same text of Scripture. If an audience were present, the moderator would ask if any learned man wished to agree or disagree with the exposition of the text. The senior minister would then deliver a sermon of his own, after which the ministers would disperse to eat a meal and to discuss privately issues of doctrine, leaving lay audiences to debate what they had heard. According to Collinson, the practice helped to promote "a unity of belief based on instruction and assent rather than on ecclesiastical authority."[29]

Herein lies the threat to the Elizabethan church, and why Milton would have found these proceedings so provocative. The prophesyings were often the sites of controversy and scandal as much as they were places of edification. Moreover, in Scotland the exercises were seen as presbyteries; thus, when the prophesyings began to flourish in England in the 1570s, there was already a common assumption that these exercises were presbyteries "in embryo."[30] From these Scottish exercises had matured the full-blown classes and synods which constituted a genuine threat to episcopacy. Collinson reminds us, however, that the English exercises still maintained a sense of hierarchy. They were frequently convened by the bishops, who in turn required parishioners to attend; furthermore, the exercises were often moderated by the same distinguished clergymen. The potential threat loomed too large, however, for the Queen to tolerate. Enemies of the more extreme Puritans colored the exercises with insinuations of enthusiasm, even though for the most part the prophesyings were strictly moderated.[31] Thousands of preaching licenses were revoked, preachers were silenced, and Elizabeth commanded that any who continued in the proceedings were to be imprisoned.[32] These actions did not, however, have the intended effect. By the 1580s these prophesyings had gone underground, meeting in clandestine classes and synods, and remained so into the next century. There is evidence to suggest that some form of the prophesyings continued in the county of Suffolk as late as 1636.[33] By the early 1640s the exercises would have been associated with the various radical separatist groups working outside sanctioned ecclesiastical authority.

In *Eikonoklastes* (1649) Milton writes, "I never knew that time in England, when men of truest Religion were not counted Sectaries" (3:348). The demons are sectaries and separatists of the most radical sort. Significantly, Milton describes Lucifer's refusal to sleep, wherein "All but the unsleeping eyes of God" close at twilight in order to participate in divine rest, as "dissent" (*Paradise Lost*, 5.647, 679). This refusal to participate in rest and "communion sweet" marks the beginning of the rebels' violent breach and initiates their fall (637). The exaltation of the Son, the anointing and granting of the name and title Messiah by the Father, awakens the "envy" and "Deep malice" that prevent Lucifer from sleeping (662, 666). While this restless angel indicates to the unnamed Beëlzebub that he takes offense to the "new

Laws thou see'st impos'd" (679), the true source of his dissent from sleep is his inability to accept that another has been granted a name and proclamatory and performative role that he desires: Anointed One, the One who represents and speaks for God. For Milton, the ideal preacher acts as God's anointed spokesman on earth because he embodies "true eloquence" and charitably "infuses" the "good things" of God's Good Speech into his hearers (*An Apology against a Pamphlet*, 1:949). The War in Heaven begins with a dissent from the doctrine of participation, as this radical preacher "infus'd / Bad influence into th' unwary breast[s]" of "the Congregation call'd" together in assembly (*Paradise Lost*, 5.694–95, 766).

Like many dissenters in Milton's turbulent age, these sectaries declare their freedom to read and interpret God's Word without political interference and against the ecclesial monopoly. But their declaration of freedom is a hermeneutical assault *on* God's Word, as they question the meaning of the Anointed One and his semiotic relation to the divine Text of which he is a part and expression. In his massive compendium *Gangraena*, the heresiographer Thomas Edwards upbraids the "antiscripturist" sects who cast doubt on the infallibility of God's Word: "right Reason is the rule of Faith," they assert, "and we are to believe the Scriptures, and the Doctrine of the Trinity, Incarnation, and Resurrection, so far as we see them agreeable to reason, and no further."[34] This first dissenting angel, an antiscripturist of the highest caliber, appeals directly to reason as he questions God's decree and the Son's status. The "Orders and Degrees" of God, he reasons, "Jar not with liberty." This Antiscripturist wonders, "Who can in reason then or right assume / Monarchy" over those who are his equals in freedom (5.792–97)?

Lucifer's subjecting the exaltation of the Anointed One to interpretation occurs in spite of the Father's eternal "Decree, which unrevok'd shall stand" (5.602). This decree, the scripture or text that Satan reads and "reasonably" questions, is the Father's proclamation that the Son, who is the "Effulgence of my Glory" and "in whose face invisible is beheld / Visibly, what by Deity I am," shall reign as "Vice-gerent" (6.680–83, 5.609). The Protestant preacher William Ames writes that any decree of God "is his determinate purpose of effecting all things by his almighty Power, and according to his counsel. . . . In the decree of God there appeareth his constancy, truth, and faithfulnesse. . . . Every Decree of God is eternall."[35] God's decree—His "speech"—is also an expression of his character and essence. In his dissent from participation in divine rest, Satan claims the hermeneutical authority to read the "texts" of God's essence: His Name, and the in/visible expression of it in the Son who is, as Paul Ricoeur aptly puts it, the "exegesis of God."[36] Consequently, Lucifer's questioning and rejection of God's unflagging decree and apodictic government through his Son limit God's own freedom to choose, and open up a critical metaphysical, theological, and linguistic fissure. A satanic hermeneutics of flux enters, one based on the liberty of a dissenting conscience. The infernal sermons declare the freedom to "create" a new politics of reading and preaching, a new metaphysics and theology of language that is severed from the "constant," "true," and "faithful" essence of God that Ames describes.

For Moloch, the first infernal preacher of this prophesying assembly of divines, the Name has been interpreted both as the "Torturer" and the "fierce Foe" (2.64, 78). The first name suggests that Moloch is actually exegeting two "texts": not only the Name of God, but also the pain of his own body. We must remember how novel and overwhelming the sensation of pain is for these fallen angels; it defines the reality they face and the culture they inhabit. "[W]hat can be worse," he asks, "[t]han to dwell here, driv'n out from bliss, condemn'd / In this abhorred deep to utter woe[?]" Here there is "pain of unextinguishable fire / . . . without hope of end" (85–89). Hell's crucible of suffering drives Moloch to disregard the niceties of the rhetorical rules altogether; as a sermonist, he skips the introduction (*exordium*) to move directly to the announcement of his subject (*propositio*), and the removal of objections (*confutatio*). To many Reformation sermon theorists the *confirmatio*, or treatment of the subject, is the most vital part of the sermon, but without properly preparing an audience in the *exordium*, the preacher runs the risk of losing his audience before he even begins.

As a malevolent preacher and "son of thunder," however, Moloch prefers verbal combat and relies more on the ferocity of his own figure and thunderous delivery. Consolation for their pain, Moloch asserts, is to be found in aggression and intimidation, and his language reflects his participation in a culture of violence; consequently, his exegesis of the Name is also his own performance. The narrator describes him as the "Scepter'd King" who "Stood up, the strongest and fiercest Spirit / That fought in Heav'n; now fiercer by despair," and he wastes no time in stating his thesis and admitting his lack of eloquence (43–45). His "sentence is for open War," for "Of Wiles, / More unexpert, I boast not . . . " (51–52). The treatment (*confirmatio*) of Moloch's text is one of "negative consolation" whose purpose "shew[s] that either there is no evill at all, or that it is not so great, or so unavoidable," as William Chappell describes.[37] Moloch, whose "trust was with th'Eternal to be deem'd / Equal in strength," minimizes the threat (46–47). Striving for eloquence is a waste of time for Moloch; it is a delay tactic and an exercise characterized by weakness; his *confutatio* thus begins immediately and continues throughout his sermon. What if the way is difficult? Ascent to their "native seat" is their "proper motion" (75–76). What if we provoke more wrath? Nothing can be worse than our current pain (85–92). What if we are destroyed? Rejoice to be "happier far / Than miserable to have eternal being" (97–98). The Torturer is the Foe, and Moloch advises that they can gain consolation only through attempting "Revenge" (105). Consolation is to be found in the application (war) of his exegesis of a name that lacks any sense of eternity or omnipotence. His sermon is delivered, and the *peroratio* (conclusion) is found in Moloch's frowning face (106), an image that probably is mirrored in the faces of his assembly as well.

Moloch's lack of eloquence is juxtaposed against Belial's calm demeanor, and Belial delivers the lengthiest sermon. He is the sophistical preacher whose "Tongue / Dropt Manna" and who could "make the worse appear / The better reason" (112–14). Belial at least makes attempts to address his audience in his *exordium* "O Peers" (119), a strategy that singly displaces Moloch's impressive figure and bellicose delivery, but we get the feeling that Belial's whole strategy is an extended *exordium*. Belial makes it clear that unlike Moloch he will not use intimidation. Instead, he will appeal to fellowship and his fellow sufferers' reason. His *confirmatio* reveals that his speech begins as a redargutive sermon, employed to correct the "doctrine" that Moloch's sermon expounded. Moloch's exegesis of the Name promised revenge; Belial's exegesis is full of questions without answers.

Interestingly, Belial is the most agnostic and therefore the most "reverential" of the infernal preachers in his sermon on the Name. God is the "Enemy," the "Almighty Victor," "angry Foe," "Conqueror," and "Supreme Foe" (137, 144, 152, 208, 210). The seeming deference he pays in "Almighty Victor" grows not out of respect or awe, but out of his dubious knowledge of the extent of God's power to inflict even more pain. God's Name is thus the seat of nothing more than potential pain, and the uncertainty of the degree of that pain is reflected throughout the sermon by questions: What revenge can we possibly extol on an "Impregnable" fortress (129–42)? Will God even grant our destruction if we fail (146–59)? Is this place the worst punishment God can deliver to us (162–74)? What if God has only partially bestowed his wrath (174–85)? Open war? Not for Belial. The weight of these questions is his strategy; his sermon is intended, paradoxically, to move his audience to inaction—a suffocating paralysis. He switches his redargutive tact to one of consolation. But where Moloch offers negative consolation, attempting to minimize the power of the Name, Belial offers positive consolation. As William Chappell comments, the "Positive good tends to that, that if it cannot remove the evill of punishment (as sometimes it cannot) yet it may . . . make it tolerable."[38] Belial ends his sermon with "positive" consolation; if they can "sustain and bear" their "doom," perhaps their "Supreme Foe in time may remit / His anger . . . " and this present "horror will grow mild, this darkness light" (208–9, 220). What is Belial's *peroratio* and application? A deflated gesture toward "ignoble ease, and peaceful sloth" (227). This sloth is the outcome of their liberty; far from the divine rest that Satan and his cronies deemed a servility born of sloth (6.165–67), this existence is characterized, ironically, by restlessness: "Not peace," as the narrator clarifies (2.228).

The third infernal preacher is Mammon and his sermon is the shortest—odd, given his penchant for luxurious excess. His exegesis of the Name emphasizes God as king: "Heav'n's Lord," "envied Sovran," and "Heav'n's all-ruling Sire" (236, 244, 264). But God is a king not worthy of serving; he is a tyrant who commands subjection and imposes "Strict Laws" (241). Any service offered to a tyrant amounts to extortion and "servile Pomp" (257); if they return to Heaven they are doomed to utter "warbl'd Hymns" and "Forc't Halleluiahs" (242-43). For Mammon there is no place in Heaven for them "unless Heav'n's Lord supreme / We overpower" (236–37). Rather than risk war and incur wrath, the application that Mammon suggests in his exegesis is that they appropriate the kingly names for themselves: fashion the kingdom of Hell to rival Heaven.

While God's throne in Heaven is obscured with the darkness of thick clouds, Hell's throne will be brilliant with the reflected light of precious gems and the shimmer of gilded gold. Mammon, the "least erected Spirit that fell," is in fact the one responsible for erecting their grandiose underworld whose temple-like description extends for over twenty lines (1.710–30). But Milton undermines its lustrous exterior with a single phrase when he describes it as an "ascending pile" (722). This indicates not only that their temple is a confused heap, but that it is a scatological nightmare (the *Oxford English Dictionary* cites hemorrhoids as one possible early modern connotation for "pile"). The demons "Rifl'd the bowels of thir mother Earth" and "Op'n'd into the Hill a spacious wound" in order for the work to be accomplished (687, 689). Like Satan's "calumnious Art" that in the end is all breath and no substance, through their "wondrous Art" Mammon and his crew manage to raise "like an Exhalation" what can only be likened to a dung pile poised to fall (5.770, 1.703, 711). "What we see here," Stanley Fish asserts, "is the piling up of signs—lighting effects, tall structures made of diamond and gold—that strive to pass themselves off as signifieds, that present themselves not as the theater of glory but as the real thing."[39] Mammon builds on this precarious foundation in a sermon that makes attempts at consolation as well. He uses positive consolation to encourage his listeners to "raise / Magificence" from the "hidden lustre" of Hell (2.271–73). He uses negative consolation to minimize the pain; thinking that their fiery torments "may in length of time / Become our Elements," he hopes that "our temper [may be] chang'd / Into their temper" (274–77). Mammon's double consolation wins the favor of all those present as his sermon is met with riotous applause.

Beëlzebub, who in rising "[d]rew audience and attention still as Night," steps in as moderator of the infernal prophesying (308). His *exordium* is formal as he reminds his audience of their due right: "Thrones and Imperial Powers, off-spring of Heav'n / Ethereal Virtues" (310–11). In his *confirmatio* he corrects (redargutive mode) the misguided "doctrine" of Moloch and approves the doctrine espoused by the exegesis of both Belial and Mammon: God is the "Conqueror" who will not be defeated, war is pointless, and the devils can build their own empire. But this senior minister appeals to another Name of God, even though he does not say it. Beëlzebub's strategy is to refocus, through a *digressio*, the attention from God as King, Foe, and Conqueror to God as Creator. He remembers a decree in Heaven regarding the creation of "another World, the happy seat / Of some new Race call'd Man" (347–48). So sure is he that his plan either to "waste his whole Creation" or "[s]educe them to our Party" will prove profitable, that he bypasses the *confutatio*—there are no objections to answer (365, 368). His sermon, too, tends toward consolation and his *peroratio* moves his audience, as "joy / Sparkl'd in all thir eyes" (387–88). It also serves as a platform of praise for the one who will accept the hazardous quest; here Beëlzebub, in cahoots with Satan

(378–80), sets up the senior preacher to deliver the final sermon and accept the challenge.

Satan's exegesis of God's Name never takes place; after four sermons on the Name, the Arch preacher sidesteps it completely. God has been successfully exegeted into virtual nonexistence. The senior minister's sermon is one long *digressio* as he describes the various dangers of the journey ahead of him, only to refocus the attention on his glory and translation to Hell's "anointed one" (445–50). His *exordium*, like his predecessor's, is formal. But despite his appeal to parity in the "us" of line 432 and the appeal to "O Peers" in line 445, the narrator twice refers to him as a monarch (428, 467). This prophesying meeting is not as presbyterian in nature as we might first construe, and Satan reveals himself to be not a minister among the many in this synod, but a kind of bullying bishop, a "New Presbyter" who is "but Old Priest writ Large" ("On the New Forcers of Conscience," 20). The dreaded speaker rises after his sermon "and prevented all reply" (*Paradise Lost*, 2.467). His terrifying presence, his massive body, and his heroic exploits as he ascends from Hell are to be their new scriptures.

Relying on his prodigious figure and terrifying tongue to silence his fellows, he assumes an authority that actually prevents participation and manages to "unsay" not only God's Name, but also the sermons that have preceded. He is the *only* anointed prelate of Hell; his thunderous voice is the only that will be heard; and, his bullying church government is the only that shall rule: end of discussion. Unlike the exercises of the 1570s, Satan does not conclude this exercise by asking if there are any "learned" devils in the audience who would like the opportunity to confute his message. Intimidated by his aggressive bearing, the assembly "Dreaded not more th'adventure than his voice / Forbidding; and at once with him they rose" (474–75). The prophesying over, the fellowship disperses to occupy themselves in entertainments, games, exploring, singing, writing poetry, and philosophizing: all of these activities are gestures to find ease for their pain until their anointed son of thunder returns.

The demons' fall from Heaven, an act of religious and political separation and dissent, is also a fall into culture—a radically different culture with a radically different conception of language as the infernal sermons reveal. In the culture of Hell, language barely rises above the level of being a tool for aggression, manipulation, or temporary consolation. The well-turned phrase, the most "eloquent" of arrangements, and the thundering dramatic performances can be little more than smoke and mirrors that either promote self-interest or attempt to "charm / Pain for a while or anguish, and excite / Fallacious hope" (566–68).

Intriguingly, we might construe this council scene as Milton's brilliant anticipation of Ludwig Wittgenstein's notion of language games: the simple but powerful thesis that the meaning and purpose of language is in its *use*, and "to imagine language is to imagine a form of life." For Wittgenstein, language is not a system of signs but a structure of practice. A word "hasn't got a meaning given to it, as it were, by a power independent of us, so that there could be a kind of scientific investigation into what the word *really* means," but "a word has the meaning someone has given to it." Instead, we should think of words "as instruments characterized by their use, and then think of the use of a hammer, the use of a chisel, the use of a square, of a glue pot, and of the glue."[40] This is the nature of the language game: words have meaning according to the "rules" or "grammars" of the game in which they are used.

Milton's devils play language games with the Name of God, a Name that is drained of metaphysical reality and eternal essence; those language games generate and are generated by the culture of Hell, a "form of life" as Wittgenstein puts it.[41] The "use" to which the demons put the Name is to cast God in a limited role as the Foe. In his envy of the Son, unfallen Lucifer desires a Name which secures meaning as God's Anointed One, the Word in the word. When he cannot possess it, his fall secures another name that will constantly call the meaning of the Name into question: the Enemy. Lucifer does not recognize the freedom he already has in the surplus and saturation of meaning generated by the Name of Names because he sees the Name as a tyrannical totality instead of as infinity.[42] As Satan the Enemy of God, he actually casts himself and his demons within the narrowest scope of meaning, and inscribes them within a constricted narrative role they cannot escape. His satanic language promises individual freedom to interpret the Signified according to one's own conscience; rather than resulting in a promising proliferation of meaning through this "new found" liberty, however, what emerges is vapid sameness. This sameness is the culture and language game of Hell, where language is cast against the Abyss with a desperate faith that beauty alone, divorced from the Good and the True, will ease or divert the sameness of their painful existence. The language of Milton's Hell is the language of exile, "wand'ring [in] mazes lost" (2.561).

The Milton of *Paradise Lost* stands on the cusp of modernity: Bacon's *Novum Organum* (1620) battles against metaphysics in science; Descartes' *Meditations* (1641) begins the epistemological turn inward; and the Rationalist project is only decades away and probably already existed in embryo. As Milton looks forward he prophetically envisions new language games of science, of mathematics, of economics, and of philosophy which will create and be created by new communities. As he looks back (nostalgically?), he sees that the Name that once dominated and defined the singular language game of science, mathematics, and philosophy will no longer hold sway. If this is the case, then we might also construe Milton's investigating language games in Heaven and unfallen Paradise as well. Language there has *use* as well within a (now separate) community: praise, hymns, celebration, liturgy—all to the end of participating in and bringing glory to the infinite Name. In Milton's Heaven the angels are engaged in reverently praising the Name that cannot be exhausted:

> Thee Father first they sung Omnipotent,
> Immutable, Immortal, Infinite,
> Eternal King; thee Author of all being,
> Fountain of Light, thyself invisible
> Amidst the glorious brightness where thou sit'st
> Thron'd inaccessible.
>
> (3.372–77)

God's "inaccessibility" paradoxically permits hermeneutical abundance. Moreover, the glorious works generated in abundance by the decree of that holy Name are praised and celebrated by "Millions of spiritual Creatures" who "walk the Earth / Unseen, both when we wake, and when we sleep" and "[sing] thir great Creator" (4.677–78, 684). What emerges in *Paradise Lost*, then, are two competing language games, two competing "cultures." Although he does not pose it in quite the same way, I think this is what Stanley Fish has in mind when he points to the competing "storytellers" of the narratives of Heaven and Hell.[43]

Milton himself is convinced of the superiority of the one language game and narrative over the other, and he demonstrates it in the heavenly council scene. Having foreseen that humanity will be seduced by Satan's language game—Satan transfers the qualities of the Name to Eve as "sovran Mistress," "Celestial Beauty," "Queen of this Universe," until she and Adam become "Gods"—the Father recognizes that fallen man will no longer be a participant in the language game of Heaven (9.532, 540, 684, 712). "So will fall / Hee and his faithless Progeny. . . ." The "fault" lies only with them, and in a moment of sadness the Father laments, "ingrate, he had of mee / All he could have" (3.95–98). The Father's use of "ingrate" reveals that fallen language will be characterized by ingratitude: self-praise, self-interest, and self-imprisonment as "free they must remain, / Till they enthrall themselves" (124–25). This satanic freedom is the "false freedom of irresponsibility," one that is "initially exhilarating" but that gradually becomes a prison, for "the more fictions you proliferate, the greater distance between you and what is real and true."[44] Human beings will fall from participating in the culture and language game of Heaven, in order to dwell in their own fictions. As Milton depicts, this is an unbridgeable gap—unbridgeable, that is, until the Son reestablishes the possibility for participation in it again.

When the Son declares, "Behold mee then, mee for him, life for life / I offer, on mee let thine anger fall; / Account mee man" (236–39), we might add "language for language" as well. Now the Word will inhabit the word at the Incarnation (282–85); crucially, the Son reestablishes the heavenly language game by *out-narrating* the language game of Hell through his exercise of virtue and obedience to the Father:

> So Heav'nly love shall outdo Hellish hate,
> Giving to death, and dying to redeem,
> So dearly to redeem what Hellish hate
> So easily destroy'd, and still destroys
> In those who, when they may, accept not grace.
>   (3.298–302)

Satanic language and the form of life that it generates will continue, observes Milton, but it does not have to dominate fallen language games. Grace provides entrance once again into participation with the Divine. Here we see that Milton embraces a kind of narrative theology in which witness, the narrative of one's own life, demonstrates the vitality of the vocabulary of one language game over another.

Stanley Hauerwas observes that the story embodied in any tradition "directs us to observe the lives of those who live it as a crucial indication of the truth of their convictions. . . . At least part of what it means to call a significant narrative true is how that narrative claims and shapes our lives."[45] The Name, said and unsaid by Satan and his demons in a single breath, is said, and said, and said, and said ad infinitum—proclaimed—through the obedience of the Word. It is also proclaimed through the exercise of virtue and obedience on the part of a poet who was devoted to out-narrating and out-preaching his contemporaries in so many ways, armed with a powerful language and vocabulary that participated in a gaze that bestows "[b]eatitude past utterance" (*Paradise Lost*, 3.62). He sees the narrative of his own life as a performance that, like the Jesus of *Paradise Regained*, causes his antagonists to stand in awe, "mute [and] confounded what to say, / What to reply, confuted and convinc't / Of [their] weak arguing and fallacious drift" (3.2–4). While their lives are characterized by the duplicity, false eloquence, and restless "drifting" of the Adversary, Milton sees his life as that of the anchored Christic reader and preacher who is "suspended" over the One in whom, by whom, and through whom all things move and have their being. For Milton, doxology, and the doxological life of virtue, is the saying that can never be unsaid.

NOTES

Debts of gratitude belong to Regina Schwartz, Michael Lieb, Ethan Shagan, and Steve Long, all of whom read and commented upon an early draft of this essay.

1. See, for instance, the following contributions: Catherine Canino, "The Discourse of Hell: *Paradise Lost* and the Irish Rebellion," *Milton Quarterly* 32 (1998): 15–23, supplies us with a fascinating glimpse into Milton's relations with the Irish after the Irish Rebellion of 1641; Todd H. Sammons, "Ciceronian *Inventio* and *Dispositio* in Belial's Speech During the Debate in Hell," *Milton Quarterly* 25 (1991): 14–22, explores Belial as Ciceronian orator in conjunction with Thomas Wilson's 1560 *The Arte of Rhetorique*; Robert Thomas Fallon, *Captain or Colonel: The Soldier in Milton's Life and Art* (Columbia: University of Missouri Press, 1984), 156–64, finds parallels with Cromwell's exchange with the Earl of Manchester; and E. H. Visiak, *The Portent of Milton: Some Aspects of His Genius* (London: W. Laurie, 1958), 116, argues that the debates in Hell reflect speeches in Parliament.

2. Jameela Lares, *Milton and the Preaching Arts* (Pittsburgh, PA: Duquesne University Press, 2001), 153; for the angelic sermons, see chap. 4.

3. William Perkins, *Of the Calling of the Ministerie* (London, 1605), 7.

4. John Milton, *Paradise Lost*, in *John Milton: Complete Poems and Major Prose*, ed. Merritt Y. Hughes (New York: Odyssey, 1957). All references to Milton's poetry are to this edition and are cited parenthetically in the text.

5. William Haller, *The Rise of Puritanism, Or, The Way to the New Jerusalem as Set Forth in Pulpit and Press from Thomas Cartwright to John Lilburn and John Milton, 1570–1643* (New York: Columbia University Press, 1938), 258.

6. Christopher Durston and Jacqueline Eales, eds., *The Culture of English Puritanism, 1560–1700* (New York: St. Martin's, 1996), 20.

7. For more on "gadding," see Patrick Collinson, *The Religion of Protestants: The Church in English Society 1559–1625* (Oxford: Clarendon, 1982), chap. 6. For a revisionist account of gadding, see Christopher Haigh, "The Taming of Reformation: Preachers, Pastors and Parishioners in Elizabethan and Early Stuart England," *History* 85 (2000): 572–88.

8. Bryan Crockett, *The Play of Paradox: Stage and Sermon in Renaissance England* (Philadelphia: University of Pennsylvania Press, 1995), 38.

9. For more on the shared audience of the pulpit and playhouse, see Martha Tuck Rozett, *The Doctrine of Election and the Emergence of Elizabethan Tragedy* (Princeton, NJ: Princeton University Press, 1984), 15–25.

10. See Peter Lake, *The Boxmaker's Revenge: "Orthodoxy," "Heterodoxy" and the Politics of the Parish in Early Stuart London* (Stanford, CA: Stanford University Press, 2001), 56. Denison's flair could, at times, backfire. When Denison was occupied in the vestry following one of his sermons, one Mistress Rose Law assumed the pulpit to parody the preacher for her friends, causing such laughter that Denison rushed back into the sanctuary to witness her make "an immodest and unseemly gesture, not fit to be used in the church." Not surprisingly, the incident spurred a church court case in March 1617.

11. The best study on the relation between preaching and rhetoric is Deborah K. Shuger, *Sacred Rhetoric: The Christian Grand Style in the English Renaissance* (Princeton, NJ: Princeton University Press, 1987).

12. George Herbert, *The Priest to the Temple, or The Countrey Parson* (London, 1652), 22; Bartimaeus Andrewes, *Certaine Verie worthie, godly and profitable . . . Sermons* (London, 1583), 26.

13. Augustine, *On Christian Doctrine*, trans. D. W. Robertson Jr. (Upper Saddle River, NJ: Prentice Hall, 1958), 4.1.2, 4.2.3.

14. Augustine, *The Enchiridion on Faith, Hope, and Love*, trans. J. F. Shaw (Chicago: Regnery Gateway, 1961), 22.

15. Augustine, *On Christian Doctrine*, 1.13.12, 1.14.13.

16. See John Milbank, "Suspending the Material: The Turn of Radical Orthodoxy," in *Radical Orthodoxy: A New Theology*, ed. John Milbank, Catherine Pickstock, and Graham Ward (London: Routledge, 1999), 1–20. Milbank and the other contributors to the volume reassess the doctrine of participation within postmodern categories.

17. See David Loewenstein, *Representing Revolution in Milton and His Contemporaries: Religion, Politics, and Polemics in Radical Puritanism* (Cambridge: Cambridge University Press, 2001), 180–201.

18. John Milton, *The Tenure of Kings and Magistrates*, in *Complete Prose Works of John Milton*, 8 vols., ed. Don M. Wolfe et al. (New Haven, CT: Yale University Press, 1953–82). All references to Milton's prose are to this edition and are cited parenthetically in the text.

19. See John Morgan, *Godly Learning: Puritan Attitudes Towards Reason, Learning, and Education, 1560–1640* (Cambridge: Cambridge University Press, 1986), 99.

20. John M. Steadman, *Milton's Epic Characters: Image and Idol* (Chapel Hill: University of North Carolina Press, 1968), 242.

21. *The Interpreter's Dictionary of the Bible*, 4 vols. (New York: Abingdon Press, 1962), 2:408. For more on Milton and the Name of God, see Michael Lieb, *Poetics of*

the Holy: A Reading of "Paradise Lost" (Chapel Hill: University of North Carolina Press, 1981), chap. 8.

22. William Perkins, "A Godly and Learned Exposition Upon the whole Epistle of Jude," in *The Workes of That Famous and Worthy Minister of Christ in the Universitie of Cambridge, Mr William Perkins*, 3 vols. (Cambridge, 1608–13), 3:520.

23. For more on the sermon types, see Lares, *Milton and the Preaching Arts*, 56–80. By the middle of the sixteenth century, sermon types were more or less fixed: doctrinal (to teach correct doctrine), redargutive (to reprove incorrect doctrine), correction and instruction (to urge virtuous habits or action), and consolation.

24. The exchange is partially reprinted in Patrick Collinson, *Godly People: Essays on English Protestantism and Puritanism* (London: Hambledon Press, 1983), 92, 96, 99–100.

25. Qtd. in Patrick Collinson, *The Elizabethan Puritan Movement* (Berkeley: University of California Press, 1967), 192.

26. Patrick Collinson, *Archbishop Grindal 1519–1583: The Struggle for a Reformed Church* (London: Jonathan Cape, 1979), 16.

27. Collinson, *The Elizabethan Puritan Movement*, 195.

28. Collinson, *Archbishop Grindal*, 104–5.

29. Collinson, *The Elizabethan Puritan Movement*, 175.

30. Ibid., 179.

31. Ibid., 173–74, 179. For more on the various ways in which invectives between Catholics and Protestants, and between factions of Protestants, shaped religious discourse, impacted public policy, and intensified paranoia especially during the Jacobean and Carolingian reigns, see Anthony Milton, *Catholic and Reformed: The Roman and Protestant Churches in English Protestant Thought, 1600–1640* (Cambridge: Cambridge University Press, 1995).

32. See Richard Baxter, *An Apology for the Non-Conformists Ministry* (London, 1668, 1681). Nonconformist preachers were also silenced after the Restoration, and Baxter's treatise is an ordered and reasonable defense of preaching.

33. Collinson, *Godly People*, 474–77.

34. Thomas Edwards, *Gangraena: or a Catalogue and Discovery of many of the Errours, Heresies, Blasphemies and pernicious Practices of the Sectaries of this time* (London, 1646), 1.19; for more on the "anti-scripturists," see Christopher Hill, *The English Bible and the Seventeenth-Century Revolution* (London: Penguin, 1993), 223–38.

35. William Ames, *The Marrow of Sacred Divinity* (London, 1642), 23.

36. Paul Ricoeur, "The Hermeneutics of Testimony," in *Essays on Biblical Interpretation*, ed. Lewis S. Mudge (Philadelphia: Fortress Press, 1980), 119–54. Originally published as "The Hermeneutics of Testimony," *Anglican Theological Review*, 61 (1979).

37. William Chappell, *The Preacher, or the Art and Method of Preaching* (London, 1656), 184.

38. Ibid., 182.

39. Stanley Fish, *How Milton Works* (Cambridge, MA: Harvard University Press, 2001), 90.

40. Ludwig Wittgenstein, *The Blue and Brown Books* (Oxford: Blackwell, 1972), 28, 67–68.

41. There is a great deal of disagreement among philosophers about what Wittgenstein means by this phrase. See Ludwig Wittgenstein, *Philosophical Investigations*,

trans. G. E. M. Anscombe, 2nd ed. (Oxford: Blackwell, 1958), 19: "to imagine a language means to imagine a form of life." In *The Blue and Brown Books*, Wittgenstein indicates that a language is also a culture (134).

42. Cf. Emmanuel Levinas, *Totality and Infinity: An Essay in Exteriority*, trans. Alphonso Lingis (Pittsburgh, PA: Duquesne University Press, 1969).

43. Fish, *How Milton Works*, 92.

44. Ibid., 91.

45. Stanley Hauerwas, *A Community of Character: Toward a Constructive Christian Social Ethic* (Notre Dame, IN: Notre Dame University Press, 1975), 97.

"Strange point and new!": Satan's Challenge to Nascent Christianity

Pitt Harding

Milton's Satan acquires so many pejorative epithets over the course of *Paradise Lost*—he is introduced as "th' infernal Serpent" even before being named—that it is tempting for readers to assume his seduction of Eve is what casts him irrevocably "into utter darkness" (1.34, 5.614).[1] Yet Satan first earns that grim distinction by committing what Milton frames as the primal sin: he refuses to worship the Son of God. This essay examines Milton's innovation in giving ultimate temporal priority to the begetting of the Son. By disputing the Son's priority, I will argue, Satan embodies an ancient skepticism regarding what became a central tenet of Christian faith, one so firmly established in orthodoxy as to be practically invisible: the doctrine of the Son's preexistence. At the chronologically earliest point in a narrative that thrives on disclosing ever-earlier points of origin, Satan ignites a conflict over the very idea of origins. In effect, he contests the validity of the epic's first "first."

I

Adam's "Divine / Historian" Raphael (8.6–7) discloses the story's point of origin only in the middle books of the poem. Having seen the Son enthroned beside the Father in book 3, readers have been tutored to regard the Son's eminence as being part of the heavenly order. Hence his anointment in book 5 seems less surprising than it otherwise might. The revelation of his begetting appears simply to confirm what we, and the angels, already know or believe. By a narrative reversal of priority, that is, something new is made to seem old. As though to confirm the impression that nothing new is happening, Milton alludes to familiar biblical passages when his God announces what amounts to the birth of Christianity:

> This day I have begot whom I declare
> My only Son, and on this holy Hill
> Him have anointed, whom ye now behold
> At my right hand; your Head I him appoint;
> And by my Self have sworn to him shall bow
> All knees in Heav'n, and shall confess him Lord.
>
> (5.603–8)

The novelty lies partly in Milton's use of Scripture. A primary source of the passage, Psalm 2, has a puzzling intermediate source in Milton's 1653 translation. As many readers have noticed, his translation includes a parenthetical clause that is absent from the Hebrew original:

> I, saith hee,
> Anointed have my King (*though ye rebel*)
> On Sion my holi' hill. A firm decree
> I will declare; the Lord to me hath said,
> Thou art my Son, I have begotten thee
> This day.
>
> (11–16; emphasis mine)

The psalm's historical context apparently justifies Milton's interpolation of the words "(though ye rebel)." Neil Forsyth explains that the psalm is thought to be a coronation hymn whose opening verses represent "an announcement by the king that he is adopting a new and powerful 'son' in order to put down a serious challenge to his power."[2] The parenthetical insertion seems almost calculated to enhance this scriptural authority for *Paradise Lost* to portray the Son's begetting as the cause of Satan's revolt. Since the juxtaposition of these two events lacks a precedent in Christian tradition, it is as though Milton had modified the psalm to justify his own innovation. At the same time, casting the ancient Hebrew psalm as a prophetic reference to Jesus (as Milton does by alluding to it in God's decree) exemplifies a familiar practice of Christian exegesis. The validity of this practice—which assumes that Jesus's coming was anticipated in veiled words whose meaning was revealed only later—depends upon faith in the power of a later vision to illuminate earlier texts. As I hope to show, it is partly because Satan lacks this faith (or something analogous to it) that he will indeed rebel.

Milton's other primary source for God's decree illustrates the interpretive method by which Psalm 2 was read as a Christian text. The New Testament's Epistle to the Hebrews quotes the psalm and refers it to Jesus (as does the apostle Paul, for example, in Acts 13:33). Hebrews describes the Son's exaltation through a series of rhetorical questions that place strong emphasis on his superiority to the angels. The Son, according to Hebrews, "sat down on the right hand of the Majesty on high; Being made so much better than the angels, as he hath by inheritance obtained a more excellent name than they. For unto which of the angels said he at any time, Thou art my Son, this day have I begotten thee? And again, I will be to him a Father, and he shall be to me a Son? And again, when he bringeth in the firstbegotten into the world, he saith, And let all the angels of God worship him" (Heb. 1:4–6).[3] Insisting that God put the Son "above thy fellows," the author of Hebrews asks: "to which of the angels said he at any time, Sit on my right hand?" (9, 13). Readers of Milton who are led by editors' notes to this scriptural source may be startled to find these questions harping so insistently on the Son's superiority: they read like a provocation for the envy and injured pride of Milton's Satan. Forsyth puts the point starkly. Noting that "the inferiority of the angels is rather cruelly stressed," he adds: "On a strong reading one may hear sneering, and thus angelic resentment just below the surface of the Hebrews text."[4] Along with its Christian reading of Psalm 2, then, the epistle's emphasis on the Son's superiority furnishes Milton with another pre-text for Satan to rebel. The innovation lies in consolidating the Son's begetting (foretold in Psalm 2, according to traditional Christian readings) with his posthumous exaltation (as described in Hebrews) and moving this new configuration back in time to prompt the angelic revolt.[5]

This innovative handling of Scripture contradicts the views set forth in Milton's own *De Doctrina Christiana*. Hebrews asserts that the Son was exalted after "he had by himself purged our sins" (1:3)—that is, after the death and resurrection of Jesus. Consequently, for Milton and others of his day, writes William B. Hunter, "the passage in Psalm 2 was metaphorically referred to the resurrection of Jesus from the dead and to his concomitant exaltation."[6] In Milton's treatise, accordingly, Psalm 2 is said to refer to the Son's "metaphorical generation, that is resurrection from the dead or appointment to the functions of mediator," just as the psalm is interpreted in Hebrews (6:206).[7] Milton goes on to argue that the psalm's term "begotten" refers to the Son in just this metaphorical sense (6:210).[8] While insisting that the Son was indeed created, distinct from the Father, Milton's treatise never specifies when this creation occurred; nor does it relate his creation to the angels' rebellion. To consolidate his begetting with his exaltation, and portray this event as the motive for Satan's revolt, requires moving it back not only before the Resurrection but before the creation of the world. Maurice Kelley, in his illuminating study of the treatise, observes that Milton does so "without sanction or authority of his own systematic theology," thereby creating a "theological fiction."[9]

Kelley's implication that epic fiction can be readily distinguished from doctrinal fact perhaps understates the hermeneutical crosscurrents that run through *Paradise Lost*. Milton's negotiations with his heavenly muse, the accommodated speech of Adam's "Divine Interpreter" Raphael (*Paradise Lost*, 7.72), and the poem's pervasive allusions to Scripture all suggest that mediation is inescapable. Divine truth reaches human ears only through intermediaries. Even Satan's challenge to the Son is mediated through his confrontation with the faithful Abdiel, conveyed in turn through the "text" of Raphael's narrative. This process of mediation, including the delayed and secondhand revelation of the Son's priority, seems to reflect in epic terms the process of gradual disclosure that early Christians took to be God's way of manifesting himself in history. Compared to the ancestral deities of the Greeks and Romans, the Christian Son of God appeared relatively late, in the midst of a civilization possessing a vivid cultural memory. Precisely because the new faith emerged in historical time, it was an abiding concern of early Christian apologists to establish that the Son preexisted his incarnation as Jesus. Their approach was to offer readings of the Jewish Scriptures based in allegory and typology. By such methods, in the words of C. A. Patrides, early Christians "endeavored to prove that their faith was not a novel religion but the culmination of God's gradual revelation to mankind."[10] Partly in response to objections raised by dissenters such as Marcion, who found the God of the Old Testament incompatible with the Father of Jesus (and who was consequently deemed heretical), the early apologists insisted on a continuity between the Old Testament and the New. Confidence in the validity of divining a hidden sense in earlier texts became a fundamental condition of faith. The second-century apologist Justin Martyr, for example, asked: "How could we believe that a crucified man is the first-born of the ingenerate God . . . were it not that we have found testimony borne prior to His coming as man, and that we have seen that testimony exactly fulfilled?"[11] The priority of Jesus as the "first-born" of God involved interpreting an ancient non-Christian tradition as containing *testimonia* of the new dispensation. This method of exegesis was employed by patristic writers following a precedent set in the gospels, allowing them to read the Old Testament as being "Christian through and through."[12]

Faith in the power of revelation to illuminate Scripture helped to sustain the contention that the Son of God not only fulfilled Scripture but also preexisted it. His preexistence was taken for granted by most of the early apologists; so, too, was his role in the creation.[13] Justin Martyr argued that God addressed the words "Let us make man in our own image" to the Son,[14] thereby unveiling his hidden presence in Genesis just as Satan was found, by later exegetes, to have been lurking in the Genesis serpent. Ignatius argued that the Son "existed with the Father before the ages" and Origen insisted it cannot be said that "there was when He was not."[15] Despite such patristic affirmations of the Son's preexistence, Milton did not hold the Son to be coeternal with the Father. In his treatise he points to the temporal marker "today" in scriptural passages which Christians referred to Christ, concluding that the Son was begotten at some definite (if unknowable) point in time (6:210).[16] And time, according to *Paradise Lost* as well as *De Doctrina Christiana*, is an inviolable medium of motion and change predating the Creation (6:313–14).[17] Milton's God beholds "past, present, future" (*Paradise Lost*, 3.78) and identifies his omnipotent will with fate (7.173), but he never exerts his omnipotent will to alter the past. Finding that Eve has fallen, Adam credits time with an inexorability which no character in the poem disputes: "But past who can recall, or done undo? / Not God omnipotent, nor Fate" (9.926–27). This respect for temporal sequence presents a difficulty for the epic narrator similar to one that early Christians faced in trying to convince pagan opponents that their new religion had roots reaching back before the creation. Milton apparently wished to give his epic an absolute beginning,[18] and to make his cosmos fully Christocentric by honoring the Son with that originative event. Perhaps, too, the Son's absolute priority represents a kind of epic refutation of heresies like Socinianism, active in Milton's day, which held that Jesus was initially not the divine Son of God.[19] Yet to treat his begetting as the primal cataclysm—as the

first event with a bearing on human destiny—reverses the temporal sequence established by tradition and accepted in Milton's own treatise,
exalting the Son in advance of his incarnation. It takes traditional exegesis to a hyperbolical extreme. (It comes, moreover, at the cost of a
circular causality. For if the "Merit more than Birthright" [3.309] that
elevates the Son subsists in his volunteering to redeem humankind,
then his meritorious deed sets in motion the very events that make it
needful: angelic rebellion, leading to the Fall.)[20] I am suggesting, then,
that Milton applies traditional exegesis so creatively here as to call attention to that interpretive activity. Adapting Scripture to accord priority to the Son frames in extreme terms the point of Christian doctrine that incredulous skeptics might consider most astonishing. It
bestows priority on the Son's begetting after the fact, in a belated revelation that appears unremarkable even as it illuminates and transforms
that which has come earlier.[21] What Satan finds himself opposing, in
effect, is an innovation that supplies the epic's origin and its most original narrative stroke.

II

Satan's resistance to innovation is well attested in the poem. His sensitivity to issues of established rank and seniority are suggested even at
the level of wordplay. When Raphael describes him as "of the first, / If
not the first Arch-Angel" (5.659–60), the term "first" evokes both
precedence and temporal priority. He is among the "Sons of morn,"
and of course the name Lucifer associates him with "the Morning
Star" (5.716, 708). The rebel angels are linked to him in a comparison
that mutates into images of earliness: they are "Innumerable as the
Stars of Night, / Or Stars of Morning, Dew-drops" which, however (in
a pun that seems to divest them of self-origination), owe their existence to "the Sun" (5.745–46). The morning star Satan feels "eclipst"
by the newly exalted Son (5.776). In response, he claims hereditary
privilege. In Hell he calls Heaven "our ancient seat" and the rebellion
an effort "To claim our just inheritance of old" (2.394, 38). He appeals
to settled law and tradition when he assures the rebels that he leads
them through "just right and the fixt Laws of Heav'n" (2.18). On first
inciting rebellion, he calls them "Natives and Sons of Heav'n possest
before / By none" (5.790–91). This appeal to nativist sentiment—"we
were here *first*"—will lead to his calling Abdiel's "new" point of doc-

trine "strange" (that is, foreign). The unwarranted innovation of the Son's elevation, in Satan's mind, justifies the further novelty of opposing God: "New Laws from him who reigns, new minds may raise / In us who serve" (5.680–81).[22]

This new mind is surprised to hear, from Abdiel, that the angels derive from a still earlier source. To Satan's insistence that the angels are natives of Heaven, Abdiel retorts that they came into being through the agency of the Word. They all derive from the "begotten Son, by whom / As by his Word the mighty Father made / All things, ev'n thee" (5.835–37). According to Abdiel, the Son holds not only the preeminence newly proclaimed by God, but also a temporal and creative priority that the archangel and morning star Satan is loath to concede.

Readers have already heard Abdiel's words affirmed in the (chronologically later) praise of the Son in book 3. There, the good angels proleptically ratified Abdiel's interpretation by characterizing the Son as being "of all Creation first, / Begotten Son" (3.383–84) and by singing that God created the angels through his agency. For readers, this affirmation tends to undermine Satan's protest in advance.[23] In book 5, however, only Abdiel asserts that the Son served to create the angels. After the Son's exaltation, that is, the faithful angel becomes his first apostle by interpreting his preeminence to mean that the angels are derivative, secondary, and contingent on the Word. Like an early Christian finding prefigurations of Jesus in the Jewish Scriptures, Abdiel reveals in God's announcement a significance undisclosed at the time it was made. His words, in turn, come to us through the mediation of Adam's "Divine Interpreter" Raphael (7.72). As in the history of Christian doctrine, a hermeneutic sequence driven by controversy asserts the Son's priority after the fact.

When Satan disputes the Son's priority, then, he rejects a revelation that interprets the Word of God in a way that radically transforms the present. He questions whether the past can be "read" so as to legitimate a present innovation:

> That we were form'd then say'st thou? and the work
> Of secondary hands, by task transferr'd
> From Father to his Son? strange point and new!
> Doctrine which we would know whence learnt.
>
> (5.853–56)

Abdiel never says whence he has "learnt" the new doctrine. Presumably, it must be taken on faith.[24] In his incredulity, Satan repudiates an origin that only now has been retrospectively ordained for him, one that radically alters his place in the celestial scheme. He refuses to acknowledge one "before" him in precedence or priority, and he disdains to have been "the work / Of secondary hands."[25]

Satan's claim to self-origination has been undermined in advance through a reversal of temporal priority in the narrative structure itself. Not only have the loyal angels already praised the Son as God's creative agency but also Satan's claim has been undercut further when he first alights on Earth and acknowledges, in his soliloquy on Mount Niphates, that God made him an exalted heavenly being: "he created what I was / In that bright eminence" (4.43–44). Although a reader encounters these passages earlier in the poem, their placement represents the transposition of chronologically later events into earlier narrative time. When Satan hears that the Son created the angels, then, his surprise must be considered genuine.[26] As Empson points out, it is only when facing visible evidence of the Creation, in book 4, that Satan admits God's limitless creative potential. This realization motivates his anguished soliloquy. Before he speaks, "horror and doubt distract / His troubl'd thoughts" when he first views the created world: "Sometimes towards Eden which now in his view / Lay pleasant, his griev'd look he fixes sad, / Sometimes towards Heav'n and the full-blazing Sun" (4.18–19, 27–29). This observation deepens his despair and prompts his spiteful apostrophe to the sun.[27] It may reveal Satan's lack of faith that he requires visible evidence before he admits God's creative power; but then his rejoinder to Abdiel may reveal not willful fraudulence but this same lack of faith. In his rejoinder, moreover, Satan makes the extraordinary claim to have been "self-begot" (5.860) only after he registers "haughty" disdain for Abdiel's assertion that the Son preceded the angels and served as the instrument of their creation. Both Satan's and Abdiel's claims, like early Christian doctrines, are forged in the heat of controversy.[28] Yet Milton manages, by undercutting Satan's claims earlier in the narrative, to make Abdiel's news seem old.

While raising the rebel host, Satan further contests the unwelcome news. He lays emphasis on the innovative aspect of the Son's exaltation by repeating the words "now" and "new": he objects that "Another *now* hath to himself ingross't / All Power" because he is the image of God "*now* proclaim'd" (5.775–76, 784; emphasis mine). He refers to

the "new commands" the Son may issue, and he hurls a veiled threat
with sarcastic emphasis on the word "new" when he says that the
rebels will receive the Son with "honors new" (5.691, 780). In refusing
to worship the Son, then, Satan not only rejects what he perceives as
the tyranny of the omnipotent; he eloquently rejects the gospel of the
new.

Satan's rejection of creaturely status, his refusal to believe there was
a time before him and without him, contests the doctrine of the Son's
preexistence even as it mirrors and mimics it. By consolidating the
Son's begetting with his exaltation, and moving this event back in time
to motivate Satan's revolt, Milton puts Satan in opposition to his own
creative innovation. This opposition seems to pose an imaginative
parallel to early skeptics' resistance to emergent Christianity. As the
first to hear the Word and disbelieve, Satan anticipates the ancient objection that Christianity could not be eternally true because it was so
manifestly new. In matters of religion, Graeco-Roman society prized
ancestral custom and distrusted innovation. Early Christianity, therefore, stood exposed to "the censure of noveltie," as Milton observes
in *Eikonoklastes* (3:534). The "proof from antiquity," discussed above,
defended the new faith from that censure by claiming a venerable an-
cestry in ancient Jewish poetry and prophecy. For skeptics trained in
classical literature, however, the Hebrew Scriptures adduced by Christians to establish their faith's antiquity appeared "barbaric" and "alien."[29]
Satan levels a similar charge in terming Abdiel's doctrine "strange"
and "new." The confrontation between Abdiel and Satan thus recapitulates a dynamic that is visible in the work of early apologists writing
to defend the new faith against pagan detractors. Even as Milton effects a striking innovation, he appropriates the rhetorical energy of
an apologetic intent on proving that the new covenant was no mere
novelty.

III

Milton's boldness in permitting Satan to challenge the Son on grounds
of priority becomes clear by comparison with his foremost classical
model. In the *Aeneid*, vindictive Juno obstructs Aeneas and strives to
hinder Fate, but her schemes unwittingly serve to fulfill Roman destiny. They leave intact the revisionist strategy that allows Virgil to construct mythical antecedents for Roman preeminence. Virgil highlights

the perverseness of her wrath in his proem by asking *tantaene animis caelestibus irae*? (1.11),[30] a question that Milton adapts for Raphael to pose in regard to Satan: "In heav'nly Spirits could such perverseness dwell?" (6.788). In Milton's epic, however, the strategy that produces authoritative origins is strongly contested. In the heavenly rebellion and war, as we have seen, positive assertions of the Son's priority stand in tension with the objection that an innovation has been wrought which lacks legitimacy and should therefore fail to command assent. It is the unfolding revelation of the Son's preeminence that the rebels seek to hinder, and their disbelief involves rejecting an interpretative maneuver that revises the past—their own creation—by granting priority to the Son.

The validity of this mode of interpretation will ultimately be affirmed, when the angel Michael leads Adam through an exercise in hermeneutics. Step by step the angel discloses that the judgment passed on the serpent—that the "Woman's Seed, obscurely then foretold" (12.543) will bruise the serpent's head—actually contains, in veiled and mysterious terms, the protevangelium promise of a Savior to redeem humankind.[31] By rejecting a reading of God's word that gives priority to the Son, then, Satan rejects a mode of interpretation that will also show Adam the way to redemption. It does so by transferring the Christian redemptive promise back to the Hebrew text of Genesis, in effect giving the new covenant priority over the old.

The priority of Christian revelation over pagan historiography is similarly suggested in juxtaposed allusions to the gospels and the *Aeneid*. To take one example, Raphael echoes Virgil's proem while describing how the Son, revealed in his power and glory in the climactic phase of the War in Heaven, encountered the obduracy of the satanic host:

> In heav'nly Spirits could such perverseness dwell?
> But to convince the proud what Signs avail,
> Or Wonders move th' obdurate to relent?
> They hard'n'd more by what might most reclaim,
> Grieving to see his Glory, at the sight
> Took envy.
>
> (6.788–93)

An allusion to a key question posed in Virgil's epic on the foundation of Rome—do heavenly powers behave as though driven by wrath and envy?—is followed by an allusion to a key document in the establishment of the new faith that would supersede Roman institutions and values.[32] Although the terms "Signs" and "Wonders" are annotated in most editions of Milton as an allusion to Exodus, they refer perhaps more aptly to the Gospel of John (4:48).[33] There, having performed his first miracle, Jesus tells a man who beseeches him to heal his dying son: "Except ye see signs and wonders, ye will not believe." In their obduracy and "envy" the rebel angels persist in disbelief, prefiguring pagans and Jews who doubted that Jesus was the prophesied "Messiah" (6.796). Driving the devils to the brink of Heaven (6.856–62), the Son becomes the precursor of Jesus driving the devil-infested Gadarene swine to destruction (Mark 5:11–13). Acclaimed in song by the faithful angels, he rides "Triumphant through mid Heav'n, into the Courts / And Temple" (*Paradise Lost*, 6.889–90), in a prefiguration of Jesus's triumphant entry into Jerusalem (Mark 11.7–10). Even as these prefigurations make the Son ancestral to the Jesus of the gospels, Satan's host becomes ancestral to disbelieving pagans and Jesus's skeptical coreligionists.

Objections to the new faith's claim to priority are clearly audible in the responses they elicit in the Gospel of John. The synoptic gospels are silent on the Son's preexistence, but the Johannine gospel sets his origin "in arche" as the divine logos: "In the beginning was the Word, and the Word was with God . . . All things were made by him" (John 1:1, 3). Repeatedly in the gospel as a whole, such affirmations come in response to expressions of incredulity and anger (including threats of stoning). Doubters question Jesus's claim to supernatural authority on the basis of his origin: "Is not this Jesus, the son of Joseph, whose father and mother we know? how is it then that he saith, I came down from heaven?" (6:42). Perhaps in answer, the gospel elaborates a paradox of temporal reversal in which the new does not merely supersede but *precedes* the old. "How can a man be born when he is old?" asks Nicodemus, as though speaking on behalf of more ancient religions: "can he enter the second time into his mother's womb, and be born?" (3:4). The gospel insists that the new teaching can indeed reveal a new origin, and that receiving this revelation is tantamount to a second birth. Jesus instructs his disciples that the meaning of present events will be revealed only by the light of a later revelation: "What I do thou knowest not now; but thou shalt know hereafter" (13:7). The disciples will learn only in retrospect that their actions have fulfilled early prophecies (12:16). Meanings concealed in the Scripture will come to light only when revealed as anticipations of Jesus: indeed, events in his life have occurred as they have so that "the scripture might be fulfilled" (19:24). Faith in the ancient patriarchs is contingent, paradoxically, on faith in the living Jesus: "had ye believed Moses, ye would have believed me: for he wrote of me," Jesus tells his fellow Jews. "But if ye believe not his writings, how shall ye believe my words?" (5:46–47). Perhaps because such reversals of priority require a transcendent atemporality, the Gospel repeatedly asserts the Son's preexistence and temporal ubiquity, most dramatically when it quotes Jesus as saying: "Before Abraham was, I am" (8:58).

When Milton's Abdiel asserts the Son's priority in the face of skeptical challenge, then, he may be said to reenact (or, by Milton's fictive chronology, to foreshadow) a drama recorded in some of the earliest Christian documents. Satan's rebellion includes resistance to the interpretive strategies visible in those texts. Among the first to encounter such resistance, of course, was the apostle Paul. Parallels between Paul and Abdiel include repeated allusions to the Pauline Epistles in the faithful angel's rebuke to Satan, as Hunter has observed.[34] It seems to be equally the case that Satan embodies the hostile disbelief which Paul encountered. In Acts, the apostle propounds a reading of Scripture that provokes a reaction not unlike that of Satan: the leaders of the Jewish community, hearing his novel interpretation of Psalm 2, are "filled with envy" at the sight of the multitudes gathered to hear him preach (13:45). Arriving at Athens, the apostle is questioned by Epicurean and Stoic philosophers, in terms to which Milton may be alluding in Satan's response to Abdiel: "they took him, and brought him unto Areopagus, saying, May we know what this *new doctrine*, whereof thou speakest, is? For thou bringest certain *strange* things to our ears: we would know therefore what these things mean" (17:19–20; emphasis mine). The question posed of Pauline Christianity by the cultural descendants of Moses and Plato resonates in the verbal challenge that Satan hurls at Abdiel's "doctrine" by exclaiming: "Strange point and new!"

From Paul's confrontations with skeptics to the apologists' defense of the new faith against pagan attack, early Christian doctrines were forged amid controversy. Satan's challenge to the Son's priority appears to reflect those ancient disputes. Among many other things, Satan appears to be the ancestor of skeptics within the Roman world who challenged the "new doctrine" taught by Christianity, implicitly questioning an exegetical practice that furnished ancient foundations for the new faith. By disputing Abdiel's attribution of priority to the Son, Satan confirms his role as the primal adversary: he rejects a hermeneutics that makes the Christian epic possible.

NOTES

I would like to thank Stephen B. Dobranski for much helpful advice on an earlier version of this essay.

1. *John Milton: Complete Poems and Major Prose*, ed. Merritt Y. Hughes (New York: Odyssey, 1957). All references to Milton's poetry are to this edition and are cited parenthetically in the text.

2. Neil Forsyth, *The Satanic Epic* (Princeton, NJ: Princeton University Press, 2003), 55.

3. All references to the Bible are to the Authorized Version and are cited parenthetically in the text.

4. Forsyth, *Satanic Epic*, 183, 184–85. Forsyth notes that the epistle was probably intended to end a controversy in the early Jewish Christian community over whether Christ was, or was not, an angel. Its unknown author adduces scriptural *testimonia*, including Psalm 2:7, "that had previously been collected in the early Church to show the Son as eternal and divine" (183). "Elsewhere in the primitive Church," Forsyth continues, "this *testimonium* was applied to the Resurrection, not the generation of the Son. . . . Here in Hebrews, though, it is used to distinguish the Son from the angels, since they also existed before the creation of the world, and are called 'Sons of God' " (184). Ironically, Forsyth notes, the decree announced by Milton's God provokes the type of dissent that Milton's primary sources seem to be aimed at suppressing.

5. Milton's innovation has been widely remarked. In his study of traditional treatments of the Fall, J. Martin Evans found that "nothing quite like this had ever appeared before" (*"Paradise Lost" and the Genesis Tradition* [Oxford: Clarendon, 1968], 224). Christopher Hill terms it "one of Milton's inventions" (*Milton and the English Revolution* [New York: Viking, 1977], 367), while William B. Hunter argues that Milton innovates here for reasons other than "the purpose of fictional motivation" ("The War in Heaven: The Exaltation of the Son," in *Bright Essence: Studies in Milton's Theology* [Salt Lake City: University of Utah Press, 1971], 115–30), and Dennis Danielson defends his "narrative ingenuity" (*Milton's Good God: A Study in Literary Theodicy* [Cambridge: Cambridge University Press, 1982], 220). Forsyth finds it "the most original narrative choice in the poem" and notes its self-referential character: in the middle of an epic that seeks to disclose ultimate origins comes "this ironic commentary on its own project" (*Satanic Epic*, 187).

6. Hunter, "War in Heaven," 117.

7. John Milton, *De Doctrina Christiana*, in *Complete Prose Works of John Milton*, 8 vols., ed. Don M. Wolfe et al. (New Haven, CT: Yale University Press, 1953–82). All references to Milton's prose are to this edition and are cited parenthetically in the text.

8. Milton argues that the generation of the Son "took place within the bounds of time . . . (the insertion of the word *today* makes this quite clear)" (6:209–10). The temporal marker "today" occurs in Psalm 2 and in Hebrews 1:5 and 5:5–6, as well as in Acts 13:32–33. The Yale editor, Maurice Kelley, notes that three paragraphs earlier Milton had held that all these scriptural passages refer not to the literal but to the metaphorical generation of the Son, and asks whether Milton has contradicted himself (6:210 n. 24).

9. Maurice Kelley, *This Great Argument: A Study of Milton's "De Doctrina Christiana" as a Gloss upon "Paradise Lost"* (Princeton, NJ: Princeton University Press, 1941), 100.

10. C. A. Patrides, *Premises and Motifs in Renaissance Thought and Literature* (Princeton, NJ: Princeton University Press, 1982), 111.

11. Justin Martyr, *First Apology*, 53, qtd. in J. N. D. Kelly, *Early Christian Doctrines*, 2nd ed. (New York: Harper, 1960), 66.

12. Kelly, *Early Christian Doctrines*, 65.

13. Ibid., 95.

14. Ibid., 92.

15. Ibid., 93, 128.

16. Milton appears to have taken the scriptural "today" as authority for rendering the premundane begetting of the Son as a singular event giving rise to Satan's revolt.

17. In *De Doctrina Christiana*, Milton disputes the notion that time did not exist before the creation.

18. Milton's absolute point of origin may be an illusion, even within the epic itself. Forsyth points out that the memorial emblems held aloft by the angels (*Paradise Lost*, 5.593–94) on the day of the Son's begetting seem to indicate a heavenly history prior to that event (*Satanic Epic*, 173–74). Stella Revard notes that the prelapsarian Satan never appears in the poem (*The War in Heaven: "Paradise Lost" and the Tradition of Satan's Rebellion* [Ithaca, NY: Cornell University Press, 1980], 49). Milton's elision of Heaven before Satan's fall—incomplete though it may be—avoids the possibility that obedience to God might ever have excluded worship of the Son.

19. For Milton's participation in the Socinian controversy, see Stephen B. Dobranski, "Licensing Milton's Heresy," in *Milton and Heresy*, ed. Stephen B. Dobranski and John P. Rumrich (Cambridge: Cambridge University Press, 1998), 139–58; Hill, *English Revolution*, 285–96; H. John McLachlan, *Socianism in Seventeenth-Century England* (Oxford: Oxford University Press, 1951), 160–62, 189–90.

20. William Poole notes that Milton "engineers a circularity at the heart of his poem," in that "the remedy of the Fall is also its possible cause" (*Milton and the Idea of the Fall* [Cambridge: Cambridge University Press, 2005], 162).

21. Retrospective clarification occurs repeatedly in Milton's narrative. Satan in Hell, for instance, attributes his defeat to a "Potent Victor" whom "force hath made supreme / Above his equals" (1.95, 248–49). Only in book 6 does Raphael's account of the war reveal that these periphrases refer to the Son. Thus, readers first encounter the Son in a veiled form whose interpretive key the poem provides only later. This retrospective disclosure seems analogous to early Christian attempts to disclose testimonies of Christ in the Hebrew Scriptures.

22. Forsyth observes that in using Psalm 2 as the basis of God's speech announcing the Son's begetting, "Milton almost has his God, like Hesiod's Zeus, be the rebel, the one who disturbs the settled order of Heaven" (*Satanic Epic*, 186). To the extent

that Milton's God instigates revolutionary change, I think it must be the case that Satan defends what he believes to be the *status quo ante*.

23. According to Forsyth's sympathetic reading of Satan, Milton's disruption of linear chronology "adds to the validity of Satan's complaint" (*Satanic Epic*, 177). But its initial effect on readers is surely to undermine his complaint. Further, I think it mimics historical reality by confronting readers with the revelation of the Son's priority after the fact.

24. William Empson surmised that Abdiel received word that God created the angels through the agency of the Son at some point between the time of God's pronouncement and Satan's midnight rally (*Milton's God*, rev. ed. [London: Chatto and Windus, 1965], 83). Similarly, Alastair Fowler conjectures that Abdiel has learned the doctrine by some means not disclosed in the poem: "Either an obedient angel can intuit it, or else God's speech at v 600–15 was fuller than Raphael gives it" (*Paradise Lost*, 2nd ed. [London: Longman, 1998], v 855 n). Perhaps Milton deliberately gives no answer: the doctrine of the Son's creative agency must either be rejected, as Satan rejects it, or taken on faith.

25. Milton might have borrowed Satan's indignation over loss of priority from the rabbinical text *Vita Adae et Evae*, where Satan defies a command to worship Adam with the words: "I will not worship an inferior and younger being (than I). I am his senior in the Creation, before he was made was I already made" (qtd. in Evans, *Genesis Tradition*, 56. See also Forsyth, *Satanic Epic*, 180–81). Among the church fathers, Lactantius was the first to speculate that a heavenly adversary rebelled through envy of the Son's priority: God first begot the Son, then made "another being" who "passed from good to evil" and "cursed his predecessor" (qtd. in Evans, *Genesis Tradition*, 226). Forsyth provides a lucid account of how the figure of Satan was forged amid controversies within the early church in *The Old Enemy: Satan and the Combat Myth* (Princeton, NJ: Princeton University Press, 1987), 309–440.

26. "The point *must* be new, or [Satan] could not in full assembly say it was," as A. J. A. Waldock notes (*"Paradise Lost" and Its Critics* [Cambridge: Cambridge University Press, 1947], 71), in response to C. S. Lewis's disparagement of Satan (in *A Preface to "Paradise Lost"* [London: Oxford University Press, 1942], 94–103).

27. Empson, *Milton's God*, 47–48, 61–65.

28. Forsyth concludes that Milton's familiarity with patristic sources and his engagement with the theological disputes of his day made him aware "that Christianity had formed itself as a religion of controversy, indeed that many of its fundamental doctrines arose from the quarrel with what came to be called heresy. That quarrel he dramatized in the figure of Satan and his wholly credible opposition to God" (*Satanic Epic*, 74).

29. Pagan views of the Hebrew Scriptures are characterized thus by Frances Young, "Greek Apologists of the Second Century," in *Apologetics in the Roman Empire: Pagans, Jews, and Christians*, ed. Mark Edwards, Martin Goodman, and Simon Price (Oxford: Oxford University Press, 1999), 93.

30. Virgil, *P. Vergili Maronis Opera*, ed. R. A. B. Mynors (Oxford: Clarendon Press, 1969).

31. Michael's protracted tutoring of Adam in the protevangelium is elucidated as a model of Protestant exegesis in Patrides, *Premises and Motifs*, 90–104.

32. Another significant preemption of Virgil occurs when Michael's prophecy that the Son will "bound his Reign / With earth's wide bounds, his glory with the

Heav'ns" (12.370–71) revises the prophecy of Virgil's Jove that Caesar Augustus will gain boundless fame (*Aeneid* 1.287). That the temptation scene assigns Satan responsibility for classical values condemned by early Christians is argued in Pitt Harding, "Milton's Serpent and the Birth of Pagan Error," *SEL* 47 (2007): 161–77.

33. Exodus 14:4–8 describes the hardening of Pharaoh's heart but with no explicit reference to signs or wonders.

34. Hunter, *Bright Essence*, 127.

Satan's Supper:
Language and Sacrament
in *Paradise Lost*

Jamie H. Ferguson

I‍T HAS OFTEN BEEN CLAIMED THAT MILTON'S *PARADISE LOST* PORTRAYS, concomitant with the Fall of Eve and Adam, a fall of language. I shall argue here, to the contrary, not that Eve's taking the fruit leads to fallen language, but rather that the disobedient act derives in part from a fall *into* language, which the poem presents as an inherently unstable medium. This view of language is illuminated by Milton's comments, in *De Doctrina Christiana*, on another kind of token, the Eucharist; the same view is illustrated poetically in the Temptation sequence, the conversation between Satan and Eve prior to the Fall. Moreover, given the presence of language before and after the Fall, this view of language as inherently unstable perhaps informs the tragic sense pervading the poem's portrayal of mankind's Fall: namely, the visiting of catastrophic consequences on behavior that appears somehow inevitable.

In book 1, chapter 28 of *De Doctrina Christiana*, Milton observes that, when Jesus spoke the Words of Institution ("those words of *Take, eat, this is my body,*")[1] he intended these words as a "trope, or a figurative usage of speech" (*tropus sive usus loquendi figuratus*); the Roman tradition, however, misled by the "utmost connection between sign and thing signified" (*inter signum et rem signatam ratio summa*), conflates them (*WJM* 16:198; *CPW* 6:555).[2] The Roman reading of the copulative *is* in the Institution, not as meaning "figures" or "represents" but taken literally, underlies the doctrine of transubstantiation, according to which the eucharistic wafer is Christ's body *revera* ("actually"—etymologically: the *res vera*; *WJM*, 16:210, 198; *CPW*, 6:559, 555).[3] For

Milton, word and wafer alike are cut off from their figurative content and assigned a dangerous autonomy.

Milton's discussion of the Eucharist in *De Doctrina* constitutes a comprehensive attack on the doctrine of Real Presence; Milton argues instead for a dualistic opposition between the Eucharist and the body of Christ—between matter and spirit, corporeal and incorporeal.[4] Recent studies of the place of Milton's eucharistic theory in the poetics of *Paradise Lost* have focused, for obvious reasons, on a passage that seems to imply a very different conception: namely, Raphael's meal with Adam and Eve in book 5. Here is the one occurrence in the poem of the word *transubstantiate*, used moreover in reference to a meal shared by man and spirit.

> So down they sat,
> And to their viands fell, nor seemingly
> The angel, nor in mist, the common gloss
> Of theologians, but with keen despatch
> Of real hunger, and concoctive heat
> To transubstantiate.
>
> (5.433–38)[5]

In light of Milton's fervent opposition to the Roman Mass, Raphael's "real hunger," his transubstantiation of earthly "viands," is surprising. Both John King and Regina Schwartz have highlighted the liturgical allusions in the *table* and *naked ministering* attending this meal (5.443–44), as opposed to the railed altars and priestly vestments of the Laudian church.[6] This revision of the Roman concept of transubstantiation is sandwiched between a pair of disquisitions made by Raphael, evoking the "consubtantiality" of matter and spirit on a cosmic level:[7]

> and food alike those pure
> Intelligential substances require
> As doth your rational; and both contain
> Within them every lower faculty
> Of sense, whereby they hear, see, smell, touch, taste,
> Tasting concoct, digest, assimilate,
> And corporeal to incorporeal turn.
>
> (407–13)

Further, Raphael instructs,

> one almighty is, from whom
> All things proceed, and up to him return,
> If not depraved from good, created all
> Such to perfection, one first matter all,
> Indued with various forms, various degrees
> Of substance, and in things that live, of life;
> But more refined, more spirituous, and pure,
> As nearer to him placed or nearer tending
> Each in their several active spheres assigned,
> Till body up to spirit work.
>
> (469–78)

This vision of the ultimate reconciliation of matter and spirit—illustrating a doctrine Stephen Fallon has termed "animist materialism"[8]—would seem to offer an alternative to Roman doctrine, "transforming" the notion of transubstantiation "from the popish cannibalistic rite . . . into a different conceptual possibility: the entire universe is ceaselessly engaged in transforming substances, in turning into God."[9]

John Ulreich has argued that the monism so richly evoked in Raphael's speech is incompatible with the "absolute separation of matter and spirit" implicit in Milton's discussion of the Eucharist in *De Doctrina*.[10] But does philosophical assent to monism imply that (in Regina Schwartz's cannily disingenuous statement) "the body of God would surely be in the wafer and the wine too"?[11] Milton contends that the Roman conceptions of "consubstantiation, transubstantiation, and the Papist $\alpha\nu\theta\rho\omega\pi\omega\phi\alpha\gamma\iota\alpha$" are "utterly alien to sacred teaching [that is, scriptural revelation] . . . [and] to the ordinary custom of speech" (*a doctrina sacra . . . a communi more loquendi . . . alienissimae*; *WJM*, 16:198; *CPW*, 6:555).[12] Evidently Milton understands the sacrament according to the classical linguistic opposition between sign and referent; the doctrine of transubstantiation he dismisses as an accretion, a human tradition. The dualism in Milton's discussion of the Eucharist in *De Doctrina* thus belongs to the realm of sign-theory; the monism evoked in the poem to that of cosmogony. Mankind creates signs, God the cosmos: Milton would have recognized the confusion of the two categories as an old error: "Your turning of *devises* shal it not be estemed as the potters clay? for shal the worke say of him that made it, He made me not?" (Isa. 29:16).[13] The Roman Mass assigns the eucharistic sign the self-sufficiency of the idol, the human "device" that asserts an impious autonomy.

Milton pursues this idolatrous elevation of the sign, polemically in *De Doctrina* and dramatically in *Paradise Lost*. Satan's temptation of Eve in book 9 alludes suggestively to what Milton called the "Missa Papistica"; the parallel suggests that theological polemic and poetic drama might be read as facets of a single, comprehensive project. In *De Doctrina*, Milton defines his notion of the Eucharist, in conformity with Huldrych Zwingli's Reformist denial of Real Presence: "since every sacrament is a seal [*obsignatio*] of the covenant of grace, it is evident that the Papists err, attributing to the external sign [*externo signo*] the power—by the effect of its operation [*ex opere operato*], as they say—to work salvation or grace; for the sacraments by their own action confer neither salvation nor grace, but only seal or represent [*vel obsignant vel repraesentant*] both for believers" (*WJM*, 16:200; *CPW*, 6:556). This opposition between secondary signification (Latin *signum* and its derivatives) and intrinsic operation reappears in *Paradise Lost*. The "interdicted" fruit is consistently described as strictly a "sign" (4.428) or "pledge" (3.95) of obedience; the "effect of its operation" is something very different, as becomes clear following the transgression (9.1011ff.). When Satan, in the form of the proverbially rapacious cormorant, perches on the Tree of Life, the narrator makes a point regarding the misuse of that tree that again suggests a sacramental reference:

> nor on the virtue thought
> Of that life-giving plant, but only used
> For prospect, what well used had been the pledge
> Of immortality.
>
> (4.198–201)

There is firm distinction here between the intrinsic potency of a sacred thing and the various uses and misuses to which it may be put; clearly the potency is not essential to the thing itself, the "external sign," but depends on an interaction between the "pledge" and the right intention of the participant. The narrator goes on to allegorize the image of Satan's misuse of this "pledge," in such a way as to suggest a contemporary relevance for the distinction between "best things" and their use or abuse:

> So little knows
> Any, but God alone, to value right
> The good before him, but perverts best things
> To worst abuse, or to their meanest use.
>
> (201–4)

The narrator turns Satan himself into a sign here, a figure of general theological error. The words "worst abuse" and "meanest use" in reference to this "pledge of immortality" recall Milton's description of the implications of Roman belief in the Real Presence: for the communion bread to become the flesh of Christ would mean that the ceremony—following Christ's vile crucifixion and exaltation to the right hand of the Father—has "dragged back" (*retrahit*) Christ's flesh to "a state of humiliation more disgraceful and wretched [*miseriorem atque indigniorem*] than before" (*WJM*, 16:212–13; *CPW*, 6:560). Investing the sacramental sign with recapitulation of Christ's bodily experience of disgrace and wretchedness would indeed demean His presence. Satan's abuse of this "pledge" thus parallels neatly Milton's diagnosis of Roman eucharistic error.

Satan ministers the fruit to Eve in terms that recall the specific form of communion Milton attributes to Roman doctrine in *De Doctrina:* Satan tempts Eve with ascension to the rank of goddess through ingestion of an object whose intrinsic character he consistently emphasizes. In the "Papist Mass," the "very flesh" (*caro vera*) of Christ, the *res* itself, is ingested (*WJM*, 16:194; *CPW*, 6:553). Similarly, Satan emphasizes the material aspect of the forbidden fruit: he claims that as the serpent he previously perceived nothing "but food . . . / Or sex," so that his initial perception of the fruit was but of "a savoury odour blown, / Grateful to appetite"—answering, by wicked coincidence, to Eve's noon-time "eager appetite" (9.573–74, 579–80, 739–40); likewise, the formerly "abject" serpent "apprehended nothing high," so that his taking of the fruit represented nothing more than a physical climb to branches "high from ground"—a height belonging properly, as he notes, to Eve's "utmost reach or Adam's" (572, 574, 590–91). Another ascension, to divinity through "participating god-like food" (717), furnishes the capstone of Satan's indoctrination of Eve and recalls the eucharistic context even more explicitly. Satan's emphasis of the intrinsic character of the fruit obscures the contradiction in Eve's imagining of what "participation" with God might mean: taking the fruit, she flatly opposes the deity that she imagines will be "communicated" by it (755). This is much the kind of contradiction asserted in the Reformers' criticism of the Roman Mass: the doctrine of transubstantiation inculcates complete indifference as to the inner state of the communicant—"real presence" functions *ex opere operato* regardless of who ingests (whence Reformers' repeated and indignant references to nibbling church mice.)[14] Eve takes and eats a sign that she no longer perceives as a sign but as a vividly material thing, possessing an intrinsic, mystical *operatum* disassociated from its ostensible frame of reference. Pulled free, in other words, from reference to God's law, the palpably, "really" present fruit, it seems to Eve, operates autonomously.

This eucharistic travesty has a linguistic dimension: that is, this negative image of eucharistic *usus* is translated into a *usus loquendi*. In his role as pontifical surrogate,[15] Satan has to detach the fruit from its meaning, obedience, by emphasizing its intrinsic properties, both physical and mystical. This recalls Milton's contention that Roman eucharistic doctrine collapses the *res signata* into the *signum* (Christ's flesh into its token) and so strips the Eucharist of its properly tropic reference. In the Temptation, Satan exposes language's lack of determinate meaning—which is to say, in the prelapsarian context, he exposes the lack of naturalness in putatively natural language.[16] Satan effects this primarily by means of the figure antanaclasis, the repetition of the same word in differing senses.[17] By definition, exact homonyms worry the notion of natural language, and the figure antanaclasis points up this tension by juxtaposing homonyms in close proximity to one another, urging polyvalence on the presumptively stable connection between word and meaning. Absent a fixed frame of reference, meaning becomes contingent, dependent on context.[18]

This verbal affectation is emblematized by the body of Satan's chosen vehicle, the serpent. Satan's selection of this creature is so fitting as to strain credulity in God's (or the Son's) statement that the serpent, along with the rest of Creation, is "entirely good" (7.549).[19] Nevertheless, if a head "well stored with subtle wiles" might not seem uncomplicatedly good, at least it is "not nocent" (9.184, 186; cf. 7.498). In the event, the serpent's body, a "labyrinth of many a round self-rolled" (183)—the "fold above fold" of a body that "floated redundant" (499, 503)—provides a figure of Satan's way of speaking to Eve. As in the figure of antanaclasis, Satan consistently repeats words, in differing senses, eventually bringing Eve, on the brink of her Fall, to do the same. Repetition of the same, reiteration, redundancy are the master figures of this style of speech, as they are the physical characteristics of the snake's body, and this verbal redundancy has a corrosive effect on the semantic confidence associated with natural language. Satan evokes this kind of pernicious verbal redundancy with reference to a series of key words, in an effort to lodge a conceptual wedge between prohibition and choice.

The first word Satan speaks to Eve, "wonder," illustrates this process. "Wonder not" is itself a kind of prohibition, which, however, is immediately undermined, and not only by the conditional "if perhaps / Thou canst," but also, and more strikingly, by the repetition of the word in the middle of the following line: "who art sole wonder" (532–33).[20] "Wonder" in the first instance is synonymous with "be struck with surprise" and bears the negative connotation of "arm / Thy looks," its coordinate in the following clause (533–34); both the wondering and the arming are things not to be done. Yet in the second instance the word's sense is entirely positive or appreciative. "Wonder" is a verb, then it is a noun; it is something not to be done then it is something singularly to be admired; it is something Eve might do, it is something Eve is. Taken as a group, these equivocations suggest that the word's meaning is indeterminate, a question of context. Given that it is his intention all along to bring Eve to ignore his "Wonder not," Satan has here his first success overturning a prohibition.[21] In this instance the prohibition is of his own invention and seems rather innocuous; he will go on to widen the scope of his rhetoric until it encompasses another prohibition, that of God Himself.

John Leonard has framed the verbal dimension of the Temptation as a "contest between Satan and Eve for mastery and interpretation of the natural language."[22] Throughout their dialogue, the two do indeed pass key words back and forth—words such as "God," "death," and "evil"—each asserting his or her own constructions. In Eve's response to Satan's opening sally, it is "wonder" that explains her desire to hear more: "such wonder claims attention due" (566). Significantly, Eve's "wonder" has a double aspect: it is an objective description of the "miracle" of the serpent's becoming "speakable of mute" (562, 563); at the same time it coyly acknowledges the admiration with which the serpent has so copiously plied her: "thou . . . / To me so friendly grown" (563–64). Not only does Eve take up one of the key words in Satan's initial speech, and not only does she make it a key word in her response, but she uses that word with the kind of equivocation that Satan has tried to inculcate. The equivocation casts a shadow on Eve's integrity, as she quietly folds the effect the serpent's praise has had on her into surprise at his speaking at all; this anticipates her response to his next barrage of hyperbolic laudatives:

> Serpent, thy overpraising leaves in doubt
> The virtue of that fruit, in thee first proved:

But say, where grows the tree [?]

(615–17)

Despite the supercilious check, "yet more amazed unwary" Eve is ready to follow (9.614).[23] Satan might well laugh at her attempt to maintain appearances. On seeing the tree at issue, however, Eve arrests the process, taking up the word "wonder" yet again and this time defining it unequivocally as a thing requiring restraint: "Wondrous indeed, if cause of such effects. / But of this tree we may not taste nor touch" (650–51). This firm assertion follows Eve's initial response to the Tree, a demurring double-entendre, which, Fowler has suggested, shows Eve "[s]lipping into the serpent's wordplaying style":[24] "our coming hither, / Fruitless to me, though fruit be here to excess" (647–48). Certainly neither she nor Adam has said anything like this before. Nevertheless, the play is innocent: there is self-conscious levity in it, but no speciousness. Eve does not try to collapse one meaning into another or otherwise sophisticate. If there is something of the mere serpent's redundant subtlety here, Eve, as we have seen, at once puts the restraints on "wonder" that Satan has been trying to loosen.[25]

Satan immediately takes up the word with which Eve toys, turning her playful equivocation to pernicious obfuscation: "Hath God then said that of the fruit / Of all these garden trees ye shall not eat?" (656–57). The fruit of this tree, of all the trees—which fruit? Countering this effort to confuse the meaning of the word, Eve proceeds to carefully distinguish one fruit from another:

> Of the *fruit*
> Of each tree in the garden we may eat,
> But of the *fruit* of this fair tree amidst
> The garden, God hath said, Ye shall not eat
> Thereof, nor shall ye touch it, lest ye die.
> (659–63; emphasis mine)

This use of antanaclasis corresponds to Quintilian's definition of how the figure may be employed with "better propriety" (*elegantius*): "in distinguishing among aspects of the referent" (*proprietate rei*).[26] In fixing the meanings of one word, however, Eve only provides her opponent with more crucial verbal targets for his duplicitous rhetoric. In anticipation of this speech, the serpent rises to full height "in himself collected" (673); Fowler paraphrases "in control of himself,"[27] but this ignores the particulars of the bodily form that Satan has adopted and, more specifically, the echo of the serpent's "many a round self-rolled" (183). Visually speaking, Satan is "self-raised" (5.860)—on a pillar of redoubled self. The comparison to an orator who has risen to speak recalls Belial's puns conflating physical matter with the matter of rhetorical discourse (6.621–22, 624) and suggests the verbal dimension of the temptation that Satan is now to bring to a head. The purpose of this onslaught is to worry the words undergirding the Prohibition, beginning with "death."

> do not believe
> Those rigid threats of *death*; ye shall not *die*:
> How should ye?
> . . . .
> whom the pain
> Of *death* denounced, whatever thing *death* be,
> Deterred not from achieving what might lead
> To happier life
> . . . .
> So ye shall *die* perhaps, by putting off
> Human, to put on gods, *death* to be wished.
> (684–86, 694–97, 713-14; emphasis mine)

Death is variously a thing threatened and denounced, a thing to be welcomed, a thing that will not happen, a thing that may well happen, and a thing with no clear meaning. [28] The third passage above is part of another series of equivocations—around the word "God."

> will *God* incense his ire
> For such a petty trespass
> . . . .
> *God* therefore cannot hurt ye, and be just;
> Not just, not *God*;
> . . . .
> and ye shall be as *gods*,
> Knowing both good and evil as they know.
> That ye should be as *gods*, since I as man,
> Internal man, is but proportion meet,
> I of brute human, ye of human *gods*.
> So ye shall die perhaps, by putting off
> Human, to put on *gods*,
> . . . .
> And what are *gods* that man may not become

> As they, participating *godlike* food?
> The *gods* are first.
>   (692–93, 700–701, 708–14, 716–18;
>   emphasis mine)

Most prominently, Satan draws the latter word from monotheistic to polytheistic reference, from *God* to *gods*—a singularly momentous equivocation (though one fraught with ambiguity, considering Milton's anti-Trinitarianism).[29] The word is also subject to constant, more local shifts of reference: God is prepared to pardon lesser offences, then he is only God insofar as he represents perfect justice; deity is approachable only by analogy, then it represents an entirely new stage distinct from humanity; deity inheres in certain foods, or perhaps it is simply a matter of primogeniture. In each of these speeches, Satan provides several discrete, incompatible definitions of the given word, yet no definition is given priority over any other.[30] This is not, in other words, the sort of Miltonic lexis that provokes the "active process of recognizing and resolving complexity, of distinguishing and determining between alternatives."[31] Nor does it seem ultimately true that "words are being fought for in the Temptation, some reaching out for their fallen meanings, while the finer senses of others are not voiced."[32] Rather Satan provides a conglomeration of alternatives that go unreconciled. Satan does not so much assign new meaning to words as assign so many meanings to the same words, in such quick succession, as to suggest that the words may not have any determinate meaning at all. I would modify Leonard's characterization ("a contest between Satan and Eve for mastery and interpretation of the natural language"): it is not mastery of the natural language that is at stake, but the very possibility that language may be "natural" at all.[33]

The strategy is successful: in her final speech prior to taking the fruit, Eve both uses words in the way Satan has taught, and acts on the semantic uncertainty introduced by this *usus loquendi*. This speech, miming the verbal wedge Satan has interposed between obedience and autonomous choice, is full of antanaclasis: Eve applies the figure to a series of words—associated with the Temptation ("praise," "beast,") and the original Interdiction ("forbid," "good," "unknown," "had," "fear") respectively. Though she seems unable or unwilling to abuse the word "God" in this way, she does take up the other central word that Satan has worried, that is, "death":

> But if *death*
> Bind us with after-bands, what profits then
> Our inward freedom? In the day we eat
> Of this fair fruit, our doom is, we shall *die*.
> How *dies* the serpent?
> . . . .
>   For us alone
> Was *death* invented?
>   (760–64, 766–67; emphasis mine)

In the wake of Satan's play on the word, Eve proposes a series of answers to the question: what does the word "death" mean?[34] Is it an inevitability that contradicts her impression of freedom? Is it the immediate effect of eating the fruit? But then in what sense can it be applied to the serpent? Is it a punishment reserved for humankind? Eve does not arrive here at a new sense of the word, nor has Satan tried to teach her a new sense; rather she follows Satan's verbal technique and so arrives at the point Satan wants: namely, "this ignorance of good and evil, / Of God or death, of law or penalty" (774–75).[35] Like the victim of a shell game, Eve chooses without recognizing what is in front of her: none of these words retain determinate meaning for her. Satan has taught Eve that the meaning of words derives from verbal context, from other words.[36] Meaning, as a modern poststructuralist might say, is revealed to be "relational" rather than "referential," and language autonomous.[37] Verbal autonomy is immediately translated into psychological or spiritual autonomy, as Eve takes and eats.[38]

The figure antanaclasis provides Satan with an effective tool for demonstrating that words—the words associated with obedience to God and words in general—bear no necessary relation to any particular referents, that language is inherently unstable. Allusions to the Roman Mass in and around the Temptation sequence suggest a parallel between this conception of language and Milton's discussion, in *De Doctrina*, of the sheer indeterminacy of the eucharistic sign independent of its recipient. The structural analogy between eucharistic doctrine and literary semantics reinforces the impression, of increasing interest to recent scholars of the Renaissance and Reformation, that the period's intense doctrinal polemics concerning the status of the Eucharist provide an important source of comparative insight into the period's abiding preoccupation with defining the nature of language. The analogy between sacrament and language also casts light on perennial critical cruxes in the poem. The possibility of natural language or linguistic truth is normally considered in connection with judgment of Eve: as blame for the Fall is withdrawn from Eve, so it is assigned to ambiguous language, and thence to Milton for imposing the Fall's consequences undeservedly. The dichotomy is misleading. If the invention of the human in *Paradise Lost* belongs to the locus of tragedy, the vehicle of that tragedy is language, from which neither poet nor protagonists could escape.

NOTES

I am grateful to Judith H. Anderson, Herbert Marks, and the editors of this volume for comments on earlier drafts of this essay.

1. English version of the Words of Institution cited in *The Doctrine and Discipline of Divorce*, in *Complete Prose Works of John Milton*, 8 vols., ed. Don M. Wolfe et al. (New Haven, CT: Yale University Press, 1953–82), 2:325.

2. John Milton, *De Doctrina Christiana (DDC)/Christian Doctrine (CD)*. In citations, I have consistently modified the available English translations. The Latin text is taken from *De Doctrina Christiana*, trans. C. S. Sumner, in *The Works of John Milton* (New York: Columbia University Press, 1934), vol. 16 (*WJM*). The other English translation I have consulted is *Christian Doctrine*, trans. John Carey, in *Complete Prose Works of John Milton*, vol. 6 (*CPW*). Unless otherwise noted, all references to *De Doctrina Christiana* are to both editions and are cited parenthetically in the text, *DDC* from *The Works of John Milton* and *CD* from *Complete Prose Works of John Milton*.

3. On the "is" in the English version of the Words of Institution—that is, on the problems involved in the "translation of nominal to verbal sentence structure" (23)—with reference particularly to early sixteenth-century polemics around the Eucharist, and on the implications of these polemics for Renaissance (and modern) conceptions of metaphor, see Judith H. Anderson, "Language and History in the Reformation: Translating Matter to Metaphor," *Renaissance Quarterly* 54 (2001): 20–51.

4. Regina Schwartz has written compellingly on the relevance of eucharistic theory for the study of early modern culture generally. "During the Reformation, discussions about how to understand and ritually perform the ingestion of the body of God or the ingestion of a wafer that brought to mind the presence of the body of God, materially, spiritually, or symbolically, reflected assumptions about the entire world. What was at stake in these debates was not only the obvious issue of redemption, but also the relation of matter to spirit, the universal to the particular, the self to the other, language to its referents. . . . That is, along with religion, one's ontology, epistemology, poetics and politics were bound up with his understanding of the Holy Communion" ("Real Hunger: Milton's Version of the Eucharist," *Religion and Literature* 31 [1999]: 1). For general comments on Milton's role in Reformation polemics over the sacraments, see C. A. Patrides, *Milton and the Christian Tradition* (1966; reprint, Hamden, CT: Archon Books, 1979), 217–19. Compare also Robert Whalen's recent argument, with reference especially to Donne and Herbert, that "[s]acrament's cultural centrality in the later sixteenth and early seventeenth cen-

turies . . . was perhaps an effect of its conceptual applicability to analogous contemporary sphere of inquiry" (*The Poetry of Immanence: Sacrament in Donne and Herbert* [Toronto: University of Toronto Press, 2002], 176).

5. John Milton, *Paradise Lost*, in *Milton: "Paradise Lost,"* ed. Alastair Fowler, 2nd ed. (New York: Longman, 1998). All references to *Paradise Lost* are to this edition and are cited parenthetically in the text.

6. John N. King, *Milton and Religious Controversy: Satire and Polemic in "Paradise Lost"* (Cambridge: Cambridge University Press, 2000), 135–41; Schwartz, "Real Hunger," 2–8. King reads these allusions as "parodic" (152), while Schwartz sees Milton as "creating his own theology of the eucharist and his own eucharistic poetics" (10). See also Thomas N. Corns, *Milton's Language* (Oxford: Basil Blackwell, 1990), 106.

7. John C. Ulreich Jr., "Milton on the Eucharist: Some Second Thoughts about Sacramentalism," in *Milton and the Middle Ages*, ed. John Mulryan (Lewisburg, PA: Bucknell University Press, 1982), 39.

8. Stephen Fallon, *Milton Among the Philosophers: Poetry and Materialism in Seventeenth-Century England* (Ithaca, NY: Cornell University Press, 1991), 79–110.

9. Schwartz, "Real Hunger," 13.

10. Ulreich, "Milton on the Eucharist," 36–37.

11. Schwartz, "Real Hunger," 11. Schwartz goes on to argue that the image of cosmic consubstantiality belongs to the prelapsarian world, that for Milton and reformers like him, "excommunionicated" as it were, "the vision holds out the ideal of union with all matter and spirit, each other, God, the universe; but it is a repast offered to Tantalus" (15).

12. Compare Schwartz, "Real Hunger," 6.

13. English translation taken from the Geneva Bible (*The Geneva Bible: A Facsimile of the 1560 Edition*, with introduction by Lloyd E. Berry [Madison: University of Wisconsin Press, 1969]). "Devises" is a particularly felicitous choice of words in the context of idolatry, suggesting an *invention* that effects *division* (*OED*, s.v. *Device*, 7.a; s.v. *Devise*, *sb*.).

14. "The Papists hold that it is Christ's actual flesh which is eaten by all in the Mass. But if this were so, even the most wicked of the communicants, not to mention the mice and worms which often eat the eucharist, would attain eternal life by virtue of that heavenly bread" (*CPW*, 6:553).

15. I do not mean that the significance of the temptation can be reduced to historical allegory. If anything, for Milton, the reference would likely run in the other direction.

16. Satan's words themselves are imbued with a sense of intrinsic, physical presence; they are twice described as making their way "Into the heart of Eve" (9.550, 734), using a figure of physical penetration to describe psychological affect; his words are imagined as physical conveyors of their content ("replete with guile" [733], "impregned / With reason" [737–38]) and leave in their wake a physical residue ("in her ears the sound / Yet rung" [736–37])—recalling Satan's resounding voice in Hell (1.314–15).

17. "Eiusdem verbi contraria significatio" is Quintilian's paraphrase of the Greek αντανάκλασις: "a single word with varied meaning" (Quintilian, *Institutio Oratoria*, trans. Donald A. Russell [Cambridge, MA: Harvard University Press, 2001], 140 [9.3.68]—translation modified). George Puttenham, with his penchant

for interlingual nicknaming, englishes antanaclasis "the Rebounde": the word bounced, homonyms used within earshot of one another (George Puttenham, *The Arte of English Poesie*, in *Elizabethan Critical Essays*, ed. Gregory Smith [London: Oxford University Press, 1904], 2:170).

18. Compare Stanley Fish's discussion of the "moral and linguistic anarchy," "the awful freedom of complete relativity," of the fallen angels in Hell (*Surprised by Sin: The Reader in Paradise Lost* [London: Macmillan, 1967], 95, 104). However, in demonstrating that Satan and his followers are made to guide the reader through the sequence: "mistake—correction—instruction" (104), Fish seems to condemn them first for "fail[ing] to realize that physical posture has nothing to do with virtue" and then for "fail[ing] to see that physical configurations are to be interpreted morally" (98–100)—that is, first for treating signs as arbitrary and then for treating them as determinate. Evidently, the fallen angels' relation to signs is not ultimately the object of Fish's criticism.

19. Joseph Summers has set a firm line against what he calls "short cuts" in the interpretation of *Paradise Lost*: "No human quality or achievement is presented apart from its relationship to a state of mind and heart, to action, and to a total context of good and evil; it is only through such relationships, Milton believed, that events and qualities achieve moral status and human significance" (*The Muse's Method: An Introduction to "Paradise Lost"* [1962; reprint, Binghamton, NY: Medieval and Renaissance Texts and Studies, 1981], 28). But compare William Empson's remarks on the patently unfair punishment of the serpent following the Fall (*Milton's God*, rev. ed. [Cambridge, MA: Cambridge University Press, 1981], 197).

20. "Wonder not" are the first words of the Temptation, Satan's effort to bring Eve, as he says, to "participat[e] godlike food" (9.717). Compare Raphael's instruction that Adam "Wonder not" in an exactly, though inversely, symmetrical situation: namely, when the angel participates manlike food, eats with Adam and Eve; Raphael comments that "time may come when man / With angels may participate" (5.491–94). Empson notes a related parallel, pointing out that words Eve hears in her satanic dream ("Thyself . . . sometimes in the air, *as wee*, sometimes / Ascend to Heav'n") are repeated in Raphael's speech ("Your bodies . . . winged ascend / Ethereal, *as wee*"; 5.78–80, 497–99, Empson's repetition italicized and his citation of old spelling followed here): "the voice of the mysterious dream and the spokesman to God are not merely saying the same thing (that God expects them to manage to get to Heaven, and that what they eat has something to do with it) but even using the same tricks of speech." Empson concludes that God—responsible for this parallel ("all such accidents lie within his Providence")—"has thus made it baffling for her to gauge his intentions" (150). In a way that is characteristic of his approach, Empson scrutinizes the poem's unlit corners by bringing the poem's assumptions (in the above case: God's omnipotence, Eve's incomplete knowledge of what is going on around her) to bear on passages where the poem's concerns are elsewhere. If this procedure is "brilliantly perverse" (Fish, *Surprised by Sin*, 46), it is also cogent enough to suggest that a "perverse" reading will be any that does not "always expect to find that Milton's intention is perfectly matched by his performance" (A. J. A. Waldock, *"Paradise Lost" and Its Critics*, 3rd ed. [Cambridge, MA: Cambridge University Press, 1964], 25). Though these episodes in the Milton Controversy are grounded in evaluative criteria of moral and/or aesthetic coherence that probably seem dated today, they do raise with remarkable clarity—and a refreshing lack of dis-

cursive theorization—the effort to "read against the grain" that, if it has lost its need to defend its procedures explicitly, is nonetheless an aspect (retooled as "reading *across* the grain"?) of the contemporary critical apparatus.

21. Compare John Steadman's comment that "Wonder not" is "calculated to produce exactly the opposite effect" (*Epic and Tragic Structure in "Paradise Lost"* [Chicago: University of Chicago Press, 1976], 108, qtd. in John Leonard, *Naming in Paradise: Milton and the Language of Adam and Eve* [Oxford: Clarendon, 1990], 199).

22. Leonard, *Naming in Paradise*, 199.

23. Compare Fowler's annotation: "Eve, *unwary*, almost flirts—'Silly compliments like that don't say much for the tree's effect on you' " (*Paradise Lost*, 505 n. ix 616).

24. See Fowler, ed., *Paradise Lost*, 507 n. ix 647–50.

25. Compare Leonard's comment, that Eve "scores many local victories before yielding Satan the linguistic mastery" (*Naming in Paradise*, 199). See Christopher Ricks on the "fruitless"/"fruit" pun, as well as on the implications of "to excess" (*Milton's Grand Style* [Oxford: Clarendon Press, 1963], 73–74).

26. Quintilian, *Institutio Oratoria*, 142–43 (9.3.71). Again, I have modified Russell's translation.

27. Fowler, ed., *Paradise Lost*, 509 n. ix 670–6.

28. Compare Kristin A. Pruitt's similar comment on these lines, considering however their cumulative impact in light of Eve's ignorance of death prior to her conversation with the serpent (*Gender and the Power of Relationship: "United as one individual Soul" in "Paradise Lost"* [Pittsburgh, PA: Duquesne University Press, 2003], 142).

29. See Christopher Hill, *Milton and the English Revolution* (New York: Viking Press, 1978), 285–96.

30. Compare Leonard on 9.700–701: "the serpent darts into the gap between 'God' and 'just' and exploits this gap to deny that God is God. Satan speaks of 'God' so as to cancel the word. He never speaks it again" (*Naming in Paradise*, 201). As Leonard acknowledges, however, Satan does subsequently use the word "gods" (202). If the words "God" and "gods" necessarily have different referents (if, as Leonard says, "God is God"), then it is true that Satan does not use the word again after line 701; if, alternatively, the word "God" (in the singular or plural) has no determinate referent—the condition, I would argue, that Satan is trying to bring about—then the word "God" does reappear after line 701, only it is unaccompanied by its accustomed referent.

31. Corns, *Milton's Language*, 111.

32. Leonard, *Naming in Paradise*, 212.

33. Compare Herbert Marks's discussion of the poem's ambivalence with regard to the very possibility of "nominal truth" ("The Blotted Book," in *Re-membering Milton: Essays on the Texts and Traditions*, ed. Mary Nyquist and Margaret W. Ferguson [New York: Methuen, 1988], 211–33). John Leonard responds in effect that, unless "there are such things as 'true names' in *Paradise Lost*" (291), his book-length discussion—of Milton's poetic "striv[ing] . . . for the unfallen" in the face of "the darker notes of the fallen world" (292)—"follows from a false premise" (2). This seems drastic. Even if the poem's claims on the possibility of linguistic truth are ultimately ambivalent, that fact would not obviate the distinction between language that "strives" for such possibilities and language that deliberately opposes them, a distinction whose validity both Leonard and Marks endorse.

34. Compare J. B. Broadbent's comment, in passing, that Satan "circles round a few key-words" and that Eve "drifts round the circle of traductio after him" (*Some Graver Subject: An Essay on "Paradise Lost"* [New York: Barnes & Noble, 1960], 257).

35. Leonard suggests, "Where Satan had been a master of rhetoric, Eve has become its slave" (*Naming in Paradise*, 209).

36. Satan's focused and successful inducement of this relation to words answers the charge of J. M. Evans (and others) that "Milton was working very much on an *ad hoc* basis in this part of the poem, that he was more concerned with making Eve's conduct seem plausible than with exemplifying any particular doctrinal interpretation of her actions" (*Paradise Lost and the Genesis Tradition* [Oxford: Clarendon, 1968], 280). This aspect of my argument could be framed as an attempt to provide what Waldock despaired of finding: "a satisfactory formula for the fall of Eve" (25).

37. The implications of this verbal autonomy in book 9, as I interpret them, are anticipated eerily by Paul de Man's discussion of the "autonomous potential of language," a potential that "gives the language considerable freedom from referential restraint . . .its use can no longer be said to be determined by considerations of truth and falsehood, good and evil" ("The Resistance to Theory," in *Twentieth-Century Literary Theory: A Reader*, ed. K. M. Newton [New York: St. Martin's Press, 1988], 159–60). For an application of Saussurian language theory to Renaissance literature, see Richard Waswo, *Language and Meaning in the Renaissance* (Princeton, NJ: Princeton University Press, 1987), esp. 8–47.

38. The genesis of this link between verbal and spiritual autonomy is set out in Satan's initial monologue in book 1. Satan's tendency in this speech is to destabilize the meaning of words by means of antanaclasis. This affectation provides internal profile to the dramatic situation Satan finds himself in: namely, the nature of his and his fellows' identities now that their autonomy from God has seemingly become fact. His lack of certainty as to Beelzebub (is this *thou* that *he*?) leads to a remembrance of Beelzebub's "brightness" that outshone others "bright" (86–87), evoking an oddly circular comparison. There follows a series of verbal repetitions:

> he whom mutual league,
> United thoughts and counsels, equal hope
> And hazard in the glorious enterprise,
> *Joined* with me once, now misery hath *joined*
> In equal ruin.
> . . . .
>   Yet not for those,
> Nor what the potent victor in his rage
> Can else inflict, do I repent or *change*,
> Though *changed* in outward lustre.
> . . . .
> His utmost *power* with adverse *power* opposed.
> . . . .
>   What though the field be *lost*?
> All is not *lost*.
>   (87–91, 94–97, 103, 105–6; emphasis mine)

In each of these passages, the rapid shift of context wrenches the repeated word away from determinate meaning. The frequency of the gesture suggests that it mirrors the dramatic situation of the speaker. Aside from anything else, of course, this speech derives rhetorical power from the verbal coordination (as in "what pit . . . what ruin" [91]), but the internal coherence that comes with such repetition is reinforced "to excess" (9.648). In Satan's speech, this potential for verbal autonomy is implicated in a dangerous autonomy vis-à-vis God. Satan's words are made to be as irreconcilable to stable meaning as he is toward God. Satan's speech enacts semantically the dramatic situation in which he finds himself. See also the play on etymology in Satan's later speeches to his followers: "but still his strength concealed, / Which *tempted* our *attempt*" (1.641–42), and the stunning catachresis, "*Surer* to *prosper* than *prosperity* / Could have *assured* us" (2.39–40; emphasis mine).

Transforming the "Corporal Rinde": The Songs of Milton's *A Mask Presented at Ludlow Castle*

Eliza Fisher Laskowski

IN HIS CRITIQUE OF JOHN MILTON'S *A MASK PRESENTED AT LUDLOW CASTLE*, Dr. Johnson was characteristically quick with both praise and condemnation:

> The greatest of his juvenile performances is the masque of *Comus*, in which may very plainly be discovered the dawn or twilight of *Paradise Lost*. Milton appears to have formed very early that system of diction and mode of verse which his maturer judgment approved, and from which he never endeavored nor desired to deviate.
>
> As a series of lines, therefore, it may be considered as worthy of all the admiration with which the votaries have received it.
>
> As a drama it is deficient.[1]

An obvious unease with the perceived disconnect between aesthetics and form that Johnson here articulates permeates the remainder of his critique: "The following soliloquies of Comus and the Lady are elegant, but tedious. The song must owe much to the voice, if it ever can delight."[2] Johnson's discomfort with the work manifests almost exclusively in questions of genre,[3] and his discomfort has been rearticulated by countless critics who likewise struggle to pigeonhole *A Mask* in a precisely labeled generic box. For instance, in his 1968 *Milton and the Masque Tradition*, John G. Demaray asserts that "*Comus* is frequently adduced as the death blow of the masque,"[4] yet in the same year, in *A Maske at Ludlow: Essays on Milton's "Comus,"* C. L. Barber enthusiastically declares "Invited to consider Milton's masque as a comedy, I report back after six months that Milton's masque is a masque!"[5] The generic conundrum seems to become especially acute when the masque is examined in close parallel to the royal entertainments of the Jacobean and Caroline court;[6] Milton's work appears to violate the rigid form developed by Ben Jonson and embraced by Thomas Carew, James Shirley, William Davenant, and the later Caroline dramatists.[7] In her *Milton's Puritan Masque*, Maryann McGuire examines the poet's discomfort with and rejection of the cult of love so popular at the Stuart court during his youth: "Despite Milton's obvious disagreement with the Neoplatonic cult, he appeared to offer in his masque something that superficially resembles dramas that grew out of the tradition. . . . However, such similarities are only superficial."[8] The songs of Milton's masque and its tidy resolution appear to impose a Platonic, Jonsonian structure that would otherwise be absent from the entertainment. Yet, Milton was no Platonist. At its core, neither is his masque. Ultimately Milton's songs are another layer through which he interrogates the larger theological issues of body and soul. Every permutation of the continuum of body and soul—immortality, divinity, mortality, bodied, disembodied—is created, evaluated, and explored within these musical moments.[9] A close examination of the songs of *A Mask*, and the bodies presented within them, indicates that Milton was actually seeking to revise the genre he inherited from Jonson, transforming it in a way that anticipates a conception of bodies and souls consonant with the monism of his mature epic works.

I

Although considerably less lavish than the entertainments at the Stuart court, Milton's *A Mask Presented at Ludlow Castle* does resemble its grander cousins from an exclusively technical standpoint.[10] Where the masques presented at Whitehall had required approximately a dozen noble dancers, scores of professional actors/dancers, and the extensive services of the King's Music and the Children of the Chapel, Milton's masque needed only three nobles, three actors/singers, and enough actors/dancers to fill out Comus's band of beasts and Sabrina's bevy of nymphs. Only a limited number of musicians would have been required for the one antic dance, five songs, and brief revels associated with the performance.

A Mask retains the technical elements of dramatic plot, songs, and dances that characterize court masque in the most general terms; yet,

Milton extends or manipulates the formal qualities of masque as it is developed by Ben Jonson, the primary author of masque at court from around 1605 to 1631. Jonson's masques follow a very specific pattern: one or more antimasques, the overturning of the antimasque world and establishment of the masquers representing the forces of order, masque dances (single sex dances by the masquers) alternated with songs, and finally measures and revels dances initiated by the descent of the masquers from the stage into the audience.[11] Philosophically, Jonson intends that the forces of disorder be vanquished by divine Order, represented through the noble masquers. In most cases, the masquers are described as envoys or extensions of a supremely powerful figure—perhaps Jove, the Sun, or Virtue—allegorically representing the king.[12] Divine Order is then bestowed upon the entire court through the descent of the masquers for the revels. John G. Demaray describes a "heaven on earth" created through a rigid allegorical process centered on a Platonic concept of cosmic order and originating from "the power of a loving king."[13] Masquers and actors descend — are lowered physically by "cloud machines"—from a perfect heavenly realm and overturn or displace the imperfect, disordered world of the masque, thus creating a perfect world at the level of the stage. After descending from the stage, the masquers perform dances that represent the perfect harmony of not only the fictitious world of the masque, but also the actual performance hall itself, bringing that perfection directly to the level of the spectators. The revels dances, in which the masque dancers partner with spectators, and those spectators with other audience members for the duration of a ball, transmit perfection throughout the "realm" of Whitehall. Order and perfection are, therefore, symbolically established within the entire kingdom through a hierarchical progression of Platonically "perfect" characters who descend and interact with less perfect beings below them, bringing the forces of virtue and order along.

Milton complicates the precise working out of a Jonsonian-type masque very quickly. The rowdy antimasque characters of Comus's band open the masque appropriately enough, but there is no establishment of perfect order when the riotous dancers are disbursed.[14] At the entrance of the Lady, where the transformation scene should occur, there is instead an increase of danger. When the scene does change, to a palace—a common location for Jonson's virtuous masque characters to inhabit—it is not a domain of nobility and order, but one of danger and sensual folly. The debate that follows, between the

Lady and her would-be seducer, is pure drama, not the end-stopped encomium of courtly masque. Indeed, Milton's heavy use of blank verse, the single incident of song and single dance of the "masque" up to line 860,[15] the point when the lady is rescued by her young brothers and the attendant Spirit summons Sabrina, are much more like drama than the rhyming couplets of the Jonsonian pattern. After 860, however, *A Mask* is all quatrain couplets and song, with dancing announced but not stage directed; at this point it looks much more "masque-like."

Although Milton forces his ending into the established pattern and restores song and formal dancing at the end, he seems to have violated the philosophical conventions of his courtly predecessor. Order is not neatly imposed through a Platonic descent, and only after a series of complications is the "neat" finish of a Jonsonian masque allowed to occur. Yet, at the end of the mask, as Demaray observes, "the noble Peer in his seat of state is not elevated . . . to the position of an angel or a heavenly figure before an earthly or heavenly temple. . . . He remains an archetypal lord and father governing under Jove and a hierarchy of pagan gods at an ideal, earthly castle."[16] The abrogation of the perfect order inherent in the Jonsonian pattern aligns with the poet's postlapsarian conceptions of earth; humans, no matter how good and virtuous, can never become wholly divine. The ordered progression from immortal and divine to human, however, is not entirely absent from *A Mask*; Milton's use of masque song is an attempt to enunciate and activate those philosophic forces his dramatic structure has abridged.

II

Sabrina, entering at line 890, fulfills the divine savior/orderer role in Milton's text. Described as a minor deity, Sabrina is prayerfully invoked by the Spirit. He recounts the story of her "quick immortal change / Made Goddess of the River" (841–42), after she has been revived with "nectar'd lavers strew'd with Asphodil" and "Ambrosial Oils" (838, 840). She has the power to right many wrongs "with pretious viold liquors" (847). Though she is intimately linked with water, in both the Spirit's song and her own, Sabrina's divinity takes on another, more airy characteristic as well. After alighting from her "sliding Chariot" (892), she seems to walk on water:

> Whilst from off the waters fleet
> Thus I set my printles feet
> O're the Cowslips Velvet head,
> That bends not as I tread.
>   (896–99)

Sabrina leaves no trace of her weight while she walks across the land. The banks of the river are unmarred by her footprint, and the nearby vegetation is undisturbed by her passing. Though she is a river goddess, fully associating herself with both the blues and greens of water and also the "fleet," ductile quality of the liquid (892–96), her divinity takes on a floating or weightless quality when she tranverses the land. Milton is not taxing his audience's credulity by equating a river goddess with weightlessness. Folk tradition frequently calls for supernatural creatures such as angels and fairies to fly, and many things, both animate and inanimate, are able to float in water. Sabrina's weightlessness, however, seems to be of a different sort from that of either angels, fairies, or fish. She has no wings and no flippers; though description is lavished on her hair, neither wings nor fins nor flippers are alluded to. In line 897, she specifically mentions her feet, curtailing the possibility that she became mermaid-like upon transformation. Her song also indicates that she uses a chariot, a terrestrial vehicle, to move through the water; therefore, in the river, her primary mode of locomotion is neither swimming nor floating. Actually, the Spirit, in his invocative song, hints that, instead of swimming in the water, Sabrina lives under it:

> Sabrina fair
> Listen where thou art sitting
> Under the glassie, cool, translucent wave.
>   (859–61)

Because she is clearly residing beneath the water, she must either have physical weight to keep her down or she must have become part of the river itself, taking on the "glassie, cool, translucent" qualities of the liquid in which she exists. However, because she remains weightless upon land, she cannot have the physical weight to hold her under the water while she is in the river. Therefore, when she was rescued by Nereus and transformed into a deity, Sabrina must have become a physical part of the river; in becoming immortal, the goddess of the Severn has also become noncorporeal. Her form, her body, can be seen, but it has no mass or substance to it.

In the closing moments of the masque, Sabrina's noncorporeal weightlessness is overtly extended to the nobility and thematically extended to the Lady. In the Spirit's final song, which both announces the measures and revels and also "presents them to their father and mother" (Flannagan, 167), the frolicking dance of shepherds is contrasted with the noble measures dance that will shortly commence:

> Back Shepherds, back, anough your play,
> Till next Sun-shine holiday,
> Here be without duck or nod
> Other trippings to be trod
> Of lighter toes, and such Court guise
> As Mercury did first devise
> With the mincing Dryades
> On the Lawns and on the Leas.
>
> (958–65)

Banishing the shepherds, the Spirit links courtly dance with the classical god Mercury and the Dryades, female members of the minor pantheon. While these minor deities' dance is "mincing," defined by the *Oxford English Dictionary* as "[showing] affectation or affected delicacy in manner or gait," the courtiers will have "lighter toes" for their "trippings." Both the Dryades and courtiers dance primly and decorously, signaled by the words "mincing" and "lighter," but the noble dancers seem to have natural lightness, while the Dryades must, surprisingly, work for theirs. Milton, by juxtaposing the image of weightlessness with the nobility, not the deities, inverts the pattern he has previously established with Sabrina, but at the same time equates Sabrina's noncorporeal weightlessness with the aristocratic audience who has just been called to dance.

The Lady, transformed by Sabrina's touch, becomes the conduit for divine weightlessness from the goddess to the audience. As Comus's prisoner, she has already privileged spirituality over corporeality:

> Fool do not boast,
> Thou canst not touch the freedom of my minde
> With all thy charms, although this corporal rinde
> Thou haste immanacl'd, while Heav'n sees good.
>
> (662–65)

By unbinding the body from the mind, thus isolating the mind from any harmful actions taken upon the body, the Lady begins the process of divine transformation that will be completed by Sabrina. Though she has asserted that her soul or her mind is free, the Lady's body still remains to imprison her in Comus's palace. Either she is bound because "Your nervs are all chain'd up in Alablaster, / And you a statue" (660–61) or the "marble venom'd seat / Smear'd with gumms of glutenous heat" (916–17) has caught her as sure as birdlime; it is clear that the physical matter of her body has been used to entrap her.

At Sabrina's touch, however, "the Lady rises out of her seat" (Flannagan, 165). Several verbal constructions could have comprised an appropriate stage direction—"The Lady stands"; "the Lady is released"; "The Lady is helped to her feet";—yet Milton instead chooses the verb "rises," a verb connoting weightlessness and grace, the same verb he uses to direct Sabrina's entrance: "Sabrina rises, attended by water-Nymphs" (Flannagan, 163). Milton's stage direction at this point reflects the pattern of noncorporeal weightlessness he has already established through the Spirit's song to Sabrina and the goddess's response. Moreover the laying on of hands that Sabrina performs on the Lady resembles the same process Sabrina herself underwent to become divine. Nereus raised the girl's "lank head," caused her to be bathed in nectar and Asphodel, and finally anointed her with Ambrosial Oils (835–40). The now-immortal Sabrina uses a similarly miraculous liquid to revive and transform the chair-bound Lady:

> Thus I sprinkle on thy brest
> Drops that from my fountain pure,
> I have kept of pretious cure,
> Thrice upon thy fingers tip,
> Thrice upon thy rubied lip.
>
> (911–15)

Both virgins have forsaken physical nature, one by self-destruction and the other by renunciation, and both are consequently transformed by an immortal who touches and anoints them. As a result both Sabrina and the Lady represent noble virtuousness that transcends corporeal nature. Although the substance of her body remains and she continues to move across the stage, the Lady has become, like Sabrina, a noncorporeal female, transformed by the divine.

Through female weightlessness or bodilessness, established primarily in the songs of his masque, Milton is able to enact the philosophic conceptions of the Jonsonian form that would otherwise have been absent in his version. The Spirit's first song and Sabrina's song unite the qualities of divinity with noncorporeal weightlessness; that weightlessness is bestowed upon the Lady, who in turn conveys it to the aristocratic audience through the measures and revels dancing at the close of *A Mask*. The Spirit's second song signals the divine transformation that is about to occur in the revels; in taking a partner's hand to dance, Lady Alice will have completed the symbolic chain of hands from Nereus to the members of the audience. Although he circumvents the rigid formality of the Jonsonian pattern, Milton nevertheless succeeds in establishing the philosophic impetus informing Jonson's structure. Noble perfection, order, and divinity are thematically ascribed to the aristocratic audience through, not a series of Platonic descents, but instead a series of transformations, transformations that foreground the loss of the body or weightlessness as a symbol of divine status.

III

Through the Spirit's and Sabrina's songs, Milton seems to have activated the Jonsonian structure in which a perfect, divine being bestows divinity to the less perfect beings below. This neat connection, however, is complicated, even contradicted, by the initial song of the masque, the Lady's invocation of Echo. The opening of the Lady's song closely parallels the structure of the opening of the Spirit's song to Sabrina:

> Sweet Echo, sweetest Nymph that liv'st unseen
>   Within thy airy shell
> By slow Meander's margent green.
>
> (230–32)

Each song begins by calling upon a bodiless female to grant aid and then proceeds to describe the river with which each spirit is associated. The green banks of "slow Meander" are the Grecian equivalent of Sabrina's Severn. The greenness and motion of that river are directly connected to the "Turkis blew, and Emrauld green" (894) and the straying "channell" (895) that Sabrina will later use to describe her watery home. Unlike Sabrina, though, there is no doubt about the status of Echo's body.[17] Of all the weightless and bodiless virgins that Milton presents in *A Mask*, Echo is the most weightless, the most without body. Just as the Spirit calls to Sabrina, the Lady prays to Echo to bring relief. "Canst thou not tell me of a gentle Pair / That likest thy Narcissus are?" (236–37). Where the Spirit is unhesitating in his faith in Sabrina's ability to bring assistance, the Lady instead seems to bargain with Echo:

> Tell me but where
> Sweet Queen of Parly, Daughter of the Sphear,
> So maist thou be translated to the skies,
> And give resounding grace to all Heav'ns Harmonies.
> (240–43)

The Lady knows that Echo is not a deity, though she is immortal. In return for aid, the Lady offers the grace of a higher power to transform Echo again, "translat[ing]" her to heaven, completing the process of bodily dissolution and divine fulfillment that, for the forlorn Nymph, has only been partially accomplished. Although Echo is the most disembodied female in the masque, her bodilessness has not been supplanted with a spiritual perfection that enables her to intervene for prayerful supplicants. Consequently, she utterly fails to assist the troubled Lady who calls to her. It is Comus, instead, who responds to the Lady's plaintive voice.

Because the Lady's song precedes the Spirit's song, it complicates, even contradicts, the later action of the masque. The Lady beseeches Echo; a little more than six hundred lines later, the Spirit beseeches Sabrina in a song that offers close parallels to the song of the Lady. Echo's earlier failure to assist the Lady is further recalled by the Spirit's hesitating and uncertain attempt to summon Sabrina, "If she be right invok't in warbled Song, / . . . this will I try" (854, 857). As the Spirit begins to sing, the appearance of the Maid of the Severn is by no means assured. Perhaps more critical are the similarities between Echo and the Lady. Both maidens find themselves alone in the woods, seemingly rejected or abandoned by trusted and beloved young men; indeed Echo's status as a solitary woodland figure makes her the ideal protectress of the equally solitary Lady. Furthermore, in a crisis, both girls reject physical nature, the Lady through her words and Echo, like Sabrina, through her actions, by refusing physical comforts and sustenance until her body has literally vanished. The disembodied virtue upon which the Lady resolves is essentially no different from the disembodied virtue of Echo. Yet, Echo's virtue has done little to benefit her, leaving her forever a voice, alone and powerless in the woods. The Lady's virtue is, fortunately, never put to extremes, for her body has been made just as helpless as Echo's, bound fast to Comus's luxurious chair.

Of course, neither the Lady nor Echo has been deified, as Sabrina has been. Sabrina's power to render aid is a direct result of her divinity. That Echo has not been deified, however, further complicates the division between corporeality and spirituality that Milton here interrogates. He depicts powerless, disembodied immortals, weightless goddesses who really cannot have a body but who do have the power of divine intervention, transcendent and spiritual mortals who reject corporeality but remain somehow simultaneously corporeal and weightless. Bodilessness may or may not be linked with divinity; bodies may or may not be joined to spirits. The nobles may or may not be transformed by an unbroken succession of transcendent, weightless women who have themselves been transformed into creatures of pure spirit.

Ironically, the character described as "attendant Spirit" further confuses any attempt to distinguish body from spirit within the masque. At his first entrance the Spirit either "descends or enters" (Flannagan, 123), but for his second entrance "The attendant Spirit habited like a Shepherd" (Flannagan, 145) must walk on stage, as any other mortal would do, to meet the brothers. The stage directions for the Spirit's final entrance ask only for a speech,[18] though the first line hints at aerial capabilities: "To the Ocean now I fly" (976). Lawes's character is indeed a spirit, but one who may or may not be able to rise or float above the earth. Through the end of the masque, the Spirit continues to be ambiguous about his movement between the spiritual and the mortal worlds: "But now my task is smoothly don, / I can fly, or I can run" (1012–13).[19] In the closing couplets of the performance,[20] the Spirit even discusses the manner in which humans with bodies can achieve divine status, a process that has nothing to do with weightlessness or flying:

> Mortals that would follow me,
> Love vertue, she alone is free,
> She can teach ye how to clime
> Higher then the Spheary chime;
> Or if Vertue feeble were,
> Heav'n it self would stoop to her.
> (1018–23)

Despite the obvious pattern the songs of the attendant Spirit establish between noncorporeality and divinity, his physical motions and his words, undoubtedly sung during the original performance, contradict the connection. Sabrina, the Lady, and the noble dancers may have the ability to float weightless above the earth, but the Spirit seems very physical in his groundedness. His costume change to meet the brothers as Thyrsis further accentuates his corporeality, reminding the audience that the Spirit, like the antimasque villain Comus, has a physical form that can be covered or altered at will. Indeed his claim "I would not soil these pure Ambrosial weeds, / With the rank vapours of this Sin-worn mould" (16–17) establishes the intrinsic connection between his divine status and his tangible, physical form from the opening moments of the masque.

Lawes's Spirit further problematizes the already tricky relationship between bodies and spirits presented in *A Mask*. He is at once the most corporeal and most divine of all the characters Milton depicts in the entertainment. As such, the Spirit becomes not merely a foil to Sabrina, his fellow guardian spirit, but also a tangible—truly physical—contradiction to the noncorporeal, perhaps divine, process of transformation that the maid of the Severn represents. In addition, his final lines, the closing lines of the masque, reject a superficial, physical metamorphosis, the hallmark of the Jonsonian masque pattern, as the key to achieving divinity; instead mortals must "Love vertue" to reach heaven. While Echo merely undermines the pattern of noncorporeal weightlessness that activates a Jonsonian structure in *A Mask*, the Spirit, in body and soul her precise antithesis, transforms the genre itself.

In his long monologue defining the nature of his sister's chastity, the Elder brother foreshadows the transformation, grounded exclusively upon inner "vertue," with which the masque concludes. Indeed his description of permeable bodies and malleable spirits, ebbing and flowing in a never-ending cycle of mutual action and reaction, anticipates the complicated exploration of corporeality and spirituality presented in the remainder of the text. The Elder brother explains that angels protect and interact with a virtuous soul:

> Till oft convers with heav'nly habitants
> Begin to cast a beam on th' outward shape,
> The unpolluted temple of the mind,
> And turns it by degrees to the souls essence,
> Till all be made immortal.
>
> (459–63)

Alternatively, sin, both of the body and of the mind, allows "defilement to the inward parts" (467), until the soul "quite loose / The divine property of her first being" (468–69). In this account of spiritual transformation—and its converse, spiritual corruption—the body, the mind, and the soul remain discrete entities, yet act with and upon each other "by degrees," slowly bringing an individual closer to or further from the divine. During this gradual change, only the "essence" of the "outward shape" is transformed; its tangible, physical characteristics seem to remain unaltered. Moreover, this process of transformation requires that the quality of divinity be something entirely distinct from the seat of human spirituality, the soul. Throughout *A Mask*, Milton's metaphysics, precociously given voice here by an eleven-year-old boy, is exemplified through the complicated, contradictory corporeal and spiritual natures of the Spirit, Sabrina, Echo, and the Lady. Ultimately, the implications of the brother's speech and the masque's conclusion are one and the same: achieving divinity is a gradual, internal process, not an instantaneous, external metamorphosis.

IV

Defining the nature of bodies in *A Mask Presented at Ludlow Castle* becomes not only an interesting academic problem, but also a hint in determining Milton's ideas about the body/soul division from his youthful writings.[21] Several early critics of Milton attempted to explain the obvious connections between the physical and spiritual in *A Mask*.[22] However, it is not until Milton's mature works are read against the masque that the early text's elusive philosophical underpinnings are more comfortably explained. In "Of the Creation," book 1, chapter 7 of his posthumously published *De Doctrina Christiana*,[23] Milton writes: "But, you will say, body cannot emanate from spirit. My reply is, much less can it emanate from nothing. Moreover spirit, being the more excellent substance, virtually, as they say, and eminently contains within itself what is clearly the inferior substance; in the same way as the spiritual and rational faculty contains the corporeal, that is, the sentient and vegetative faculty" (6:309). Milton's complex rhetoric veils a very simple proposition: the spirit contains the body as part of itself. This simple idea was, however, considered a heresy—monism—in the seventeenth century, a heresy with which Milton's mature works are nonetheless replete. As he explains in "Of the Creation," the poet embraces monism because "this original matter" emanated from God at Creation, "in an incorruptible state, and even since the fall it is still incorruptible, so far as its essence is concerned" (309). Milton continues: "Really it is not the matter nor the form which sins. When matter or form has gone out from God and become the property of another, what is there to prevent its being infected or polluted, since it is now in a mutable state?" (309). Milton's monist philosophy, linking body and spirit through original, created "matter," unifies all of creation with and through God.[24] Because Milton interprets the scriptural account as *creatio ex Deo*, and not *ex nihilio*,[25] everything that exists, from the inanimate clay to the noncorporeal soul, before it was given "a mutable state," was once prime matter brought into existence by the divine. D. Bentley Hart summarizes Milton's ideas succinctly: "Spirit and flesh are not different realities, but different manifestations of one reality."[26]

Yet in " 'Matter' versus Body: The Character of Milton's Monism," Phillip J. Donnelly articulates a vital semantic distinction in Milton's Latin prose,[27] allowing a further refinement of the poet's monist principles. Donnelly finds a crucial rhetorical difference between "matter" and "body" in the *De Doctrina* passage: "Milton is, however, quite precise in his usage; only in reference to original creation does he use *materia*, while only in the latter discussion of substances does he use *corpus*."[28] Original "matter," emanating from God, should not be confused with corporeal nature or "bodies." This matter, from which both body and spirit derive, creates a "continuum" of creation. Although Donnelly carefully explores this continuum through the angelic digestion passage and other cruxes of *Paradise Lost*, a fledging exploration of monism could also account for the problematic bodies and spirits in *A Mask Presented at Ludlow Castle*.[29]

Though many critics notice the fluidity of bodies and spirits in the work, *A Mask Presented at Ludlow Castle* continues to be read primarily as a dualist text, with no more than a hint of the monism and mortalism that would inform Milton's later writings.[30] A close reading of the songs of the masque, however, reveals a much more complicated metaphysical world, a world where the bodied and bodiless, the mortal, immortal, and divine are repeatedly juxtaposed and evaluated. In this world, the relationship of body to spirit is unfixed, a continuum rather than a rigid distinction. Here noncorporeal virtue, sanctified by divine intervention and touch, thematically unites Sabrina and the Lady; yet, the powerless nature of the equally noncorporeal female body is exemplified by both the Lady and Echo. Because he frustrates the clean solution of the deus ex machina, Milton also frustrates the "proper" ending of his masque. Through Echo's problematic bodilessness, the poet calls into question Sabrina's true ability to offer divine assistance and ultimately taints the symbolic transformation of the court at the end of the performance. Spiritual transcendence cannot, finally, be accomplished through the laying on of hands or the dropping of oil, no matter how sacred some may claim the hands or the oil to be.

In *A Mask Presented at Ludlow Castle*, Milton has created courtly entertainment that both conforms to and rejects the Jonsonian-type pattern. Far from "the death blow of the masque," Milton's creation is instead the prototype for a transfigured genre, one that emphasizes, through all its artistic elements, the potential for inner transformation. Though Dr. Johnson essentially dismissed their poetic value, the songs of Milton's masque become a keystone for not only understanding Milton's generic expansion, but also for aligning the implications of the masque more closely with the poet's mature works, giving the masque more in common with the epics than merely a "system of diction and mode of verse." The complicated tangle of the bodied and the bodiless, the illusion of the spiritual represented as the temporal and the temporal as the spiritual, the questionable nature of transcendence from without, not from within, all of these problems are interwoven through five seemingly straightforward musical moments within the masque. Along the banks of the Severn, in the woods beyond Ludlow Castle, bodies and souls do not seem to exist in rigid distinction; the boundaries between them are as quick and liquid as the waters of the neighboring river.

NOTES

1. Samuel Johnson, "'John Milton,' *The Lives of the Poets*," in *Samuel Johnson: Selected Poetry and Prose*, ed. Frank Brady and W. K. Wimsatt (Berkley, CA: University of California Press, 1977), 429.

2. Johnson, "John Milton," 430.

3. For a further discussion of Johnson's reaction to the masque, see C. L. Barber, "*A Mask Presented at Ludlow Castle*: The Masque as a Masque," in *A Masque at Ludlow: Essays on Milton's "Comus,"* ed. John S. Diekhohff (Cleveland, OH: Case Western Reserve University Press, 1968), 188–89.

4. John G. Demaray, *Milton and the Masque Tradition: The Early Poems, "Arcades," and "Comus"* (Cambridge, MA: Harvard University Press, 1968), 74.

5. Barber, "The Masque as a Masque," 188.

6. For further comparison between Milton's masque and other examples of the genre, see Cedric C. Brown, *John Milton's Aristocratic Entertainment* (Cambridge, MA: Cambridge University Press, 1985); Maryann Cale McGuire, *Milton's Puritan Masque* (Athens: University of Georgia Press, 1983), 75–76, 167–70.

7. For a discussion of the typical structure of a Jonsonian masque, see Peter Walls, *Music in the English Courtly Masque 1604–1640* (Oxford: Clarendon, 1996), 2–3.

8. McGuire, *Milton's Puritan Masque*, 137.

9. Philip J. Donnelly, in " 'Matter' versus Body: The Character of Milton's Monism," *Milton Quarterly* 33 (1999): 79–85, makes similar use of the term "continuum" (81, 82).

10. Because there are multiple editions and manuscripts of Milton's masque, the choice of text for use in this paper must be addressed. Like Roy Flannagan, editor of *The Riverside Milton* (New York: Houghton Mifflin, 1998), many critics agree that the Trinity Manuscript "is only a working draft" (115); therefore, it will not be of much concern while examining the songs. Critically, the accepted performance text—the Bridgewater Manuscript—and the printed editions have some variation in the number of songs. There is the potential for eight songs in the Bridgewater Manuscript; these potential songs include: (1) the opening and (2) closing songs performed by Henry Lawes, (3) the Lady's "Echo" song, (4) the Spirit's invocation of Sabrina, (5) his call to the revels dances, (6) the "dialogue" following the call to Sabrina, (7) Sabrina's song at her entrance, (8) and the presentation of the children to their parents. To complicate a precise understanding of the number of songs in the masque, however, the Bridgewater stage directions indicate flexibility at performance in two places; these vague stage directions are: line 787 "*The verse to singe or not*" ("The Bridgewater *Comus*: Text of *A Maske*," in *A Maske at Ludlow: Essays on Milton's "Comus*," ed. Diekhoff, 235), introducing the dialogue after the call to Sabrina, number 6 above; and line 896 "*the / Dæmon singes or sayes*" (239) found before the closing lines, number 2 above. Moreover, the opening lines of the masque, text for which there is both music and a widely accepted belief in the performance of that text as song, are not stage directed as song at all; immediately under Milton's title, "A Maske," are the directions: "*The first sceane discovers a wild wood, then a guardian spiritt or demon descendes or enters*" ("The Bridgewater *Comus*," 210). For a discussion of the possible performance of the opening lines of the masque, see both Lady Alix Egerton, *Milton's "Comus" being the Bridgewater Manuscript with Notes and a Short Family Memoir* (London: J. M. Dent & Sons, 1910), 30, and John S. Diekhoff, "A Maske at Ludlow," in *A Maske at Ludlow: Essays on Milton's "Comus*," ed. Diekhoff, in which Henry Lawes's desire to "open the performance with a song and close it with a song, songs of his own composition, with himself as singer" (2) is described. Complete settings of the first five songs survive in an autograph manuscript by Henry Lawes, reproduced in "The Airs of the Songs by Henry Lawes with His Version of the Words," in *A Maske at Ludlow: Essays on Milton's "Comus*," ed. Diekhoff, 241–50. Published versions of the Bridgewater Manuscript can be found in "The Bridgewater *Comus*: Text of *A Maske*," in *A Maske at Ludlow: Essays on Milton's "Comus*," ed.

Diekhoff, 207–40, and Lady Alix Egerton, *Milton's "Comus" being the Bridgewater Manuscript*.

Conversely, the published versions of Milton's masque, according to the stage directions, contain only five songs altogether; with reference to the numbers above, these songs are: (3) the Lady's "Echo" song, (4) the Sprit's invocation of Sabrina, (7) Sabrina's song at her entrance, (5) the Spirit's call to revels dances, and (8) his song presenting the children to their parents. Of these five, only numbers 3, 4, and 5 exist in the Lawes's settings of the music. An important omission from the stage directed songs is the twenty lines opening the Bridgewater text, the Spirit's opening song "From the Heavn's now I fly," song 1 above, appearing as "To the Ocean now I fly" in the published versions. These lines, widely accepted as song during the performance, have been relocated to the end in the published versions, following the presentation of the children but before the closing twelve lines, "But now my task is smoothly done." Critically, the lines have been specifically translated to speech: "*The dances ended, the Spirit Epiloguizes.*"

The Bridgewater Manuscript was a collaborative project, and the 1637 edition, according to Roy Flannagan in *The Riverside Milton*, appeared through the efforts of Henry Lawes, seemingly without the author's contribution (116). But the 1645 edition was published under Milton's supervision and seems to be the clearest indication of "authorial intent" for the masque; it is, more importantly, the most explicit with stage directing musical moments. Therefore, the 1645 text found in *The Riverside Milton*, edited by Roy Flannagan, is the text from which this paper primarily proceeds. However, Bridgewater's opening and closing songs—"From the Heavn's now I fly" and "But now my task is smoothly done"—un–stage directed but with extant music, will also be considered.

11. Walls, *Music in the English Courtly Masque*, 2–3.

12. For a discussion of the centrality of the monarch to the allegory of the masque, see Stephen Orgel, *The Jonsonian Masque* (Cambridge, MA: Harvard University Press, 1967) and Stephen Orgel and Roy Strong, *Inigo Jones: The Theatre of the Stuart Court*, 2 vols. (Berkeley: University of California Press, 1973).

13. Demeray, *Milton and the Masque Tradition*, 28.

14. For further consideration of Milton's changes to masque conventions, see McGuire, *Milton's Puritan Masque*, 113–15.

15. John Milton, " '*Comus* (1634)' in *1645 Poems*," in *The Riverside Milton*, ed. Roy Flannagan (New York: Houghton Mifflin, 1998), 120–71. All references to *A Mask Presented at Ludlow Castle* are to this edition and are cited parenthetically in the text.

16. John G. Demaray, "The Temple of the Mind," *Milton Quarterly*, 21 (1987): 71.

17. Ovid's story "Echo and Narcissus" appears in book 3 of *Metamorphoses*, trans. Rolfe Humphries (Bloomington: Indiana University Press, 1983), 67–73. Echo, her capacity for spontaneous speech previously cursed by Juno for assisting Jove's infidelities, sees Narcissus in the woods. Burning in love, she follows him after he becomes separated from his hunting companions. The nymph attempts to communicate with him, but is cruelly spurned by the arrogant boy. Deeply hurt and ashamed, Echo retreats to live in caverns and deep forests, until love-sickness eventually destroys her:

> She frets and pines, becomes all gaunt and haggard,
> Her body dries and shrivels till voice only

> And bones remain, and then she is voice only
> For the bones are turned to stone. She hides in woods
> And no one sees her now along the mountains,
> But all may hear her, for her voice is living.
>
>   (69)

18. This is the text relocated, with some changes, from the opening of the masque in the Bridgewater Manuscript, text for which music does exist.

19. This is also text for which music exists.

20. For a discussion of the continuing importance of this couplet to Milton, see Brown, *John Milton's Aristocratic Entertainment*, 3.

21. Because they are easily defined, this essay focuses primarily on the five songs stage directed in the 1645 edition, but the texts of these songs remain unchanged from the Bridgewater Manuscript; therefore, these songs do indeed represent Milton's youthful writings.

22. Among these early critics are A. S. P. Woodhouse who, in "The Argument of Milton's *Comus*," in *A Maske at Ludlow: Essays on Milton's "Comus*," ed. Diekhoff, describes "the natural level" and the "order of grace" and the ways in which four principle "doctrines" of the masque create a spectrum between the two realms (20–21). Sears Jayne, alternatively, proposes a rigid allegorical interpretation in "The Subject of Milton's Ludlow *Mask*," in *A Maske at Ludlow: Essays on Milton's "Comus*," ed. Diekhoff: "Alice, the soul, lost and wandering away from home toward the body in the dark of the physical world," contrasts with "Sabrina . . . the Mens . . . that part of the soul which remembers its home with God and leads the soul there" (174–75). In "Metamorphosis and Symbolic Action in *Comus*," *ELH* 34 (1967): 49–64, Richard Neuse maintains the emphasis on dualism, but discards an exacting nomenclature: "Sabrina becomes a symbolic expression of man's lower nature seen truly in a new light, transformed, namely as no longer in conflict with spirit and reason, but as harmoniously responsive to them" (58).

23. John Milton, "*Christian Doctrine*," in *Complete Prose Works of John Milton*, 8 vols., ed. Don M. Wolfe et al. (New Haven, CT: Yale University Press, 1953–82). All references to Milton's prose are to this edition and are cited parenthetically in the text.

24. For discussion of monism and Milton's works see D. Bentley Hart, "Matter, Monism, and Narrative: An Essay on the Metaphysics of *Paradise Lost*," *Milton Quarterly* 30 (1996): 16–27; Maurice Kelley, *This Great Argument: A Study of Milton's "De Doctrina Christiana" as a Gloss upon "Paradise Lost"* (Princeton, NJ: Princeton University Press, 1941); C. A. Patrides, *Milton and the Christian Tradition* (Oxford: Clarendon, 1966); and Stephen M. Fallon, *Milton among the Philosophers: Poetry and Materialism in Seventeenth-Century England* (Ithaca, NY: Cornell University Press, 1991).

25. Hart, "Matter, Monism, and Narrative," 23.

26. Ibid.

27. Donnelly, "'Matter' versus Body," 79.

28. Ibid., 80.

29. For consideration of the angelic digestion passage from book 5 of *Paradise Lost*, see Donnelly, " 'Matter' versus Body," 82.

30. Though most critics, like Jason P. Rosenblatt in "The Angel and the Shepherd in *Lycidas*," *Philological Quarterly* 62 (1983): 252–58, recognize "the interdepen-

dence of body and spirit" (254) in Milton's early works, they are still reluctant to ascribe latent monism to Milton's masque. See also William Kerrigan who argues, "these works [his early poems] yield no traces of nascent mortalism" in "The Heretical Milton: From Assumption to Mortalism," *English Literary Renaissance* 5 (1975): 127, but instead claims that Milton embraces the non-heretical concept of assumption in his early work. Stephen Fallon maintains, in *Milton among the Philosophers*, that the masque is still firmly within a dualist tradition, containing "the seeds of change" only (81).

Milton's Other Worlds

Lara Dodds

"[I]n such abundance lies our choice"
(*Paradise Lost*, 9.620).

MY EPIGRAPH COMES FROM EVE'S CONVERSATION WITH THE SERPENT.[1] He reports the false virtues and powers of the fruit he has eaten; she responds with knowledge of the scope of God's providence in the natural world. We, who know the outcome of this choice, read her response as naïve. She does not yet know that the serpent's offer is not part of the abundance of choice, but the one choice she and Adam must not make. But her answer is also true, a gesture toward the wonder and variety of Milton's Paradise. Adam and Eve live in a world in which wonders remain undisclosed, as the rest of the passage suggests:

> For many are the trees of God that grow
> In Paradise, and various, yet unknown
> To us, in such abundance lies our choice,
> As leaves a greater store of fruit untouched,
> Still hanging incorruptible, till men
> Grow up to their provision.
>
> (9.618–23)

Eve's response evokes the freedom and variety, the choice, that distinguishes Milton's prelapsarian world. She describes a choice that is unconstrained but also "unknown." Defined only through its abundance, this choice is nevertheless already embedded within its future consequences. This passage captures beautifully what might be called the doubleness of *Paradise Lost*. Eve's speech preserves the image of the "fruit untouched," a perfect and eternal Paradise, while her invocation

164

of future generations is Milton's acknowledgment of his readers who have grown to their provision in a very different world.

The particular narrative challenges of *Paradise Lost* require such doubleness, as Milton must contrive a poetic structure that accommodates an as-yet-unmade choice with known consequences. In this essay I propose that the controversy surrounding the plurality of worlds provides Milton with a vocabulary for expressing the conditions and consequences of such choice. Alan Gilbert wrote long ago that "Milton never falls into the error of making *world* and *earth* synonyms."[2] For Milton "world" often has the now archaic sense of the cosmos, or the whole created universe.[3] When Satan first sees "this pendant world" (2.1052) or the Son uses the golden compasses to "circumscribe / This universe, and all created things" (7.226–27) with the pronouncement "thus far extend, thus far thy bounds / This be thy just circumference, O world!" (7.230–31), the "world" is the world, a single and unified system. And yet in *Paradise Lost*, the world is not always singular. "Space" may produce "new" (1.1650) and "his dark materials" "more" worlds (2.916), while the cosmic voyages of both Satan and Raphael are through an environment that seems to be populated with "other worlds" (3.566).[4] Likewise the poem depends on the reader's simultaneous perception of multiple worlds that must be understood as both separate and coexistent. These worlds include the separate spaces of Heaven, Hell, and Earth, and extend to worlds that are bounded in other ways: fallen and unfallen; male and female; mortal and angelic; past, present, and future. Milton wrote during a century in which the concept of "world" took on new senses, including those areas of the Earth recently defined as the "new world"[5] and those real or imagined planets and stars that might be inhabited "worlds."[6] Mary Campbell has suggested that what the plurality of worlds offered the seventeenth-century literary imagination was the potential for "the separate, the distant, the alternative, the other."[7] In *Paradise Lost* the potential of a plurality of worlds performs this function in a particularly complex way. For the poem's reader, the other world preserves the fragile possibility of the "fruit untouched," while for Adam and Eve, the lesson of the world and of potential multiple worlds becomes a necessary means of negotiating agency and authority.

Readers have long identified Milton's response to seventeenth-century astronomical debates and, in particular, Galileo's telescope as important elements of *Paradise Lost*.[8] Perhaps the narrative demands of Milton's fable required the representation of astronomical spaces, but the conspicuous dialogue on the merits of the geocentric and heliocen-

tric models as well as the repeated references to the most famous as-
tronomer of the age suggest that for Milton astronomy was much more
than necessary poetic background. For many scholars, the repeated citation of astronomical issues is one means by which Milton explores
questions of observation, vision, and the limitations of human knowledge. The poem's frequent return to Galileo's telescope as a means of
and figure for sight suggests both the necessity and difficulty of seeking
knowledge of the world.[9] As Maura Brady has recently argued, the instruments of Galileo are "signs for the labor by which knowledge is
constructed" and proof that "the hard work of intellectual inquiry, with
all its attendant confusions is unavoidable."[10] Thus for Milton the telescope is a marker of his century's reexamination of human ways of
knowing.[11] In this essay, however, I will be concerned with what rather
than how the telescope allows us to see. One of the most significant
claims of Galileo's landmark *Sidereus Nuncius* (1610) was the visual
demonstration that the moon was surprisingly like the earth.[12] In fact it
is this "discovery" that Milton alludes to in his first reference to Galileo, where Satan's shield is compared to the "spotty globe" (1.291) of
the telescopic moon. One consequence of such discoveries by Galileo
and others was renewed speculation about the possibility of a plurality
of worlds.[13] Though this possibility had caused speculation and controversy since ancient times, Copernicus's heliocentric hypothesis and the
telescope gave the controversy greater urgency. These innovations
demonstrated that bodies in the heavens could look like worlds, and
provided arguments that placed the earth and planets on a par, thus
prompting questions about the size of the universe and the status of
man's unique place in it. *Paradise Lost* frequently incorporates the possibility of a plurality of worlds, yet few critics have attended to this aspect
of Milton's interaction with contemporary astronomy.[14] For Milton and
his contemporaries, the plurality of worlds was a potent symbol of the
spatial and epistemological problems posed by the heliocentric hypothesis. Replacing a single world (or Word) with worlds, the plurality of
worlds substitutes horizontally differentiated centers of authority for a
single vertical hierarchy.[15] In *Paradise Lost*, such concerns become central to Adam and Eve's negotiation of their places and their choices.

PLURALITY OF WORLDS

Adam and Eve's story is haunted by glimpses of and speculations about
what goes on in other worlds. Of course the poem begins in Hell,

which is initially cordoned off from the "new world" (2.403) in which
Satan will seek the Earth. Later, Raphael narrates events in Heaven
that occurred when "yet this world was not" (5.577) and engages in
speculation about "other worlds" (8.175). At these moments, and elsewhere in the poem, Milton contrives for his readers and his characters
to understand a world as, to use Campbell's terms, separate, distant,
other. I'd like to focus first, however, on Satan's journey to the Earth.
Describing the environment encountered by Satan immediately following his breech of the world (that is, universe), Milton introduces
here concerns associated with the plurality of worlds throughout *Paradise Lost*. Satan travels

> Amongst innumerable stars, that shone
> Stars distant, but nigh hand seemed other worlds,
> Or other worlds they seemed, or happy isles,
> Like those Hesperian Gardens famed of old,
> Fortunate fields, and groves of flowery vales,
> Thrice happy isles, but who dwelt happy there
> He stayed not to inquire.
>
> (3.565–71)

Satan's movement amongst the celestial bodies demonstrates how the
discoveries of the telescope gave new life to the idea of a plurality of
worlds; from afar, the stars are stars, but draw near and they are worlds,
perhaps inhabited as the Earth is. Yet significantly, the image of the
other world is here associated with a moment of choice. In this case,
that choice is Satan's decision to pass by these "worlds" in order to seek
out and tempt the inhabitants of Earth. These other worlds are not
simply the environment through which Satan travels, but a potential
space for Satan's action. Here the plurality of worlds becomes an image
of another Paradise and another story. But Satan doesn't pursue this alternate narrative. He stays "not to enquire," but in this moment the
reader catches a brief glimpse of possibilities foreclosed by the narrative of the poem—of people who remain happy in their garden, unmo-
lested and untempted by Satan. Furthermore, Milton's allusion to a
classical paradise suggests the primary theological objection to the plurality of worlds as well. Like the ancient worthies (or the Native Amer-
icans), the inhabitants of other worlds challenge the singular narrative
of Christian salvation.[16]

Satan's brush with other worlds in book 3 provides an outline of the
major issues raised by Milton's frequent use of the trope of the plural-

ity of worlds. Other worlds teem with wonderful, untapped potential
for alternative narratives, even the possibility of a different outcome
for Milton's poem, but the path to these other worlds, and their meaning for those who seek them, is never clear. In this respect, *Paradise Lost*
incorporates the perspectives of both the enthusiastic advocate for the
"new science" and the skeptical traditionalist whose books were among
Milton's sources for astronomical knowledge. As Grant McColley has
shown, Milton was probably familiar with books by John Wilkins and
Alexander Ross, which, respectively, defended and attacked the idea of
a plurality of worlds.[17] Wilkins's *The Discovery of a World in the Moone*
(1638) and *A Discourse Concerning a New Planet, Tending to Prove that 'tis
Probable our Earth is one of the Planets* (published with *The Discovery* in
1640) and Ross's 1646 reply, *The New Planet No Planet*, popularized the
astronomical discoveries of the past century through the controversy
over the plurality of worlds. Consequently, these books suggested that
what was at stake in these astronomical controversies was a re-defini-
tion of such fundamental terms as *world, earth,* and *moon*. For example,
the title of one of Wilkins's chapters, "That as their world is our
Moone, so our world is their Moone," threatens to collapse the categories of earth and moon, while the very title of Ross's book resists this
reversal: *The New Planet No Planet*. This challenge to such basic categories is central to the philosophical and cultural questions raised by
the plurality of worlds.

For John Wilkins (1614–72), the possibility of a world in the moon
broadened the horizons of man and opened new aesthetic vistas for the
human imagination. Wilkins, perhaps best known as a founder of the
Royal Society and the author of the ambitious language reform project, *An Essay towards a Real Character and Philosophic Language* (1668),
wrote his books on astronomy to demonstrate that there was no essential contradiction between Scripture and post-Copernican develop-
ments in astronomy.[18] Wilkins argues in *The Discovery of a World in the
Moone* that the discoveries of the telescope prove the moon to be a
body very much like the earth. Wilkins even considers it likely that the
moon is inhabited. He celebrates this primary insight of the new astronomy as "a compendium of providence, that could make the same
body a world, and a Moone, a world for habitation, and a Moone for
the use of others, and the ornament for the whole frame of nature."[19]
The moon is both alien and home, both familiar nightly companion
and exotic other world. This act of speculation releases the moon from
her Aristotelian sphere and her traditional meanings in human philos-

ophy, poetry, and mythology to become a world in her own right. Wilkins is careful to identify each of these multiple meanings of the moon as elements of providence, God's care and beneficence in the disposition of nature. But naturally, these same arguments set the earth adrift as well. In fact, this speculation about the moon allows Wilkins to imagine the earth itself as seen from the moon: "suppose we were in the Moone, where wee might see the whole earth hanging in those vast spaces where there is nothing to terminate the sight . . . we may easily conceive, that our earth appears as bright to those other inhabitants in the Moone, as theirs doth to us."[20] By providing his readers with this radically alien view of earth (much as Milton does with his angels), Wilkins collapses the distance between the earth and the planets and establishes the other world as an alternative narrative space.[21] The discovery of a world in the moon prepares the imagination for the possibility, mined by later writers of science fiction, that if worlds are multiple, the earth and its ways may not be singular.

Wilkins and others popularized the contention that the planets may be worlds and its corollary that the earth may be a planet, but these claims always drew scientific and theological objections. Both Protestant and Catholic theologians perceived the idea of a plurality of worlds to be a challenge to revealed Scripture and a threat to the position of man, with his singular relationship with God, in the universe.[22] Alexander Ross, in his reply to Wilkins, *The New Planet No Planet*, makes these consequences explicit.[23] Ross objects to the disorder and confusion a plurality of worlds would bring to the hierarchy of the universe by wittily suggesting how such change must be promulgated, literally, to all parts of daily life. He asks whether the earth "may be an eighth Planet, that so wee may make up our week of eight days; for why should not mother Earth have one day of the week, as well as the other Planets, to carry her name? And so let there be *dies terrae*, aswell as *dies Solis*, & *Lune*, Earth day, as well as Sunday or Moonday."[24] Though this argument may seem specious because it does not engage with the actual claims of the Copernican hypothesis (which, of course, does not require that we add an extra day to correspond to an extra planet), Ross's objection acknowledges (and insists upon) the submerged metaphorical function of the traditional universe.

Ross warned that acknowledging other worlds would, by dispensing with a single hierarchically arranged cosmos, inevitably challenge traditional sources of authority. Translating astronomical controversies to the political realm, Ross invokes images of carnival and the world turned upside down: "You would make the common-wealth of heaven like many disordered common-wealths here on earth, where the inferiour and meaner sort of people will take upon them to rule and guide their superiors, Princes and Magistrates, and then all comes to confusion; the horses run away with the coach and coach-man."[25] Ross's projection of what he perceives as political disorder into the heavens suggests what is at stake in this controversy. The debate over plurality of worlds led the human imagination to inaccessible realms, but also raised questions closer to home. During a period in English history when the construction of a new political world was a reality, the claim that the earth and the moon (and perhaps innumerable other heavenly bodies) are now equivalent *worlds* threatened the traditional hierarchies that constituted both nature and society.

The possibility of other worlds prompted a wide range of responses in the seventeenth century. For all his enthusiasm about the philosophical, aesthetic, and even economic benefits of the other world, even Wilkins was careful to qualify his argument with a quibble on what he calls the "double sense" of *world*. He distinguishes between *world* used "more generally for the whole Universe, as it implies in it the elementary and aethereall bodies, the starres and the earth" (of which there is one) and "an inferiour World consisting of elements" (of which there are many).[26] Wilkins reconciles his arguments for a plurality of worlds with the one world of Creation by suggesting that many worlds in the second sense (what we might call planets) may exist within one world in the first sense (what we might call the solar system or universe). *Paradise Lost* has been described as enacting a similar equivocation by establishing "the concept of infinite space even within an apparently finite Ptolemaic universe."[27] Thus Satan's voyage through the multiple worlds of the Copernican universe (Wilkins's second sense) is framed within the one world of the Aristotelian (the first sense). Before traveling past "worlds" (3.566), he must first move "down right into the world's first region" (3.562).

But if theologians challenged the existence of other worlds, they could not deny that an omnipotent God had the ability and power to create such other worlds. Characteristically, *Paradise Lost* contains this argument as one of its many responses to the plurality of worlds. Flying through chaos, Satan is presented with the potential of other worlds: chaos is matter that remains ever "confused" "unless the almighty maker them ordain / His dark materials to create more worlds" (2.915–16). Milton writes into chaos a potential for other worlds that rests in the creative ability of God. What follows these lines, however, is an image of the very disruption that opponents of the plurality of worlds feared. Chaos is a "wild abyss" (2.917), characterized by unbearable noise that is no

> less than if this frame
> Of heaven were falling, and these elements
> In mutiny had from her axle torn
> The steadfast earth.
>
> (2.924–27)

In this simile, the Earth is torn from its position as the stationary center of the world. Such transformation and displacement recall perhaps the most famous seventeenth- century image of the new astronomy, in which "the Sun is lost, and the earth, and no mans wit / Can well direct him, where to look for it."[28] Again Milton's verse depends on the simultaneous perception of two models of the world. His "dark materials" contain both the potential for other worlds and, through that potential, a threat to the traditional world of Milton's readers.

The discovery of other worlds is a discovery that must necessarily be staged more than once in Milton's narrative, and the consequences of this discovery are varied. Critics have attempted to determine whether Milton believed in the existence of other worlds, but the poem's narrative would seem to require both Wilkins's excitement at the imaginative possibilities of other worlds and Ross's dismay at their disruptive effects. The recognition of other worlds in *Paradise Lost* is both cause for celebration and a symbol of absolute loss. So, when the angels sing their hymn to Creation, new worlds magnify and reflect God's glory:

> Witness this new-made world, another heaven
> From heaven gate not far, founded in view
> On the clear hyaline, the glassy sea;
> Of amplitude almost immense, with stars
> Numerous, and every star perhaps a world
> Of destined habitation.
>
> (7.617–22)

As with Wilkins's moon, the existence of bodies that may be both stars and worlds is a sign of marvelous providence. Yet when Adam and Eve (or the reader) seek to learn of other worlds, Eden is always shadowed by that other, fallen world that is to come. Even after Raphael instructs

Adam to "Dream not of other worlds" (8.175), the poem is haunted by
their possibility. Raphael must warn Adam about the future world his
disobedience could bring into being: "and this happy state / Shalt loose,
expelled from hence into a world / Of woe and sorrow" (8.331–33).

Milton's seemingly contradictory treatment of the plurality of worlds
can be explained through the separate yet coexistent worlds *Paradise
Lost* represents for its readers. The demands of the narrative are well
served by the trope of the other world. Adam and Eve, in their prelapsarian state, have before them the potential for one world. When, by
"long obedience tried" they are led "Up hither" (7.159), there will no
longer be a plurality of worlds: "And earth be changed to heaven, and
heaven to earth, / One kingdom, joy and union without end" (160–61).
For the readers of the poem, however, the boundaries have been re-
drawn already to exclude this potential world as well as the Paradise so
vividly represented in the poem from the world made by Adam and
Eve's choices. The success of Milton's theodicy depends upon the construction of other worlds that the reader may recognize as containing
not only the origin of his or her story, but also the potential for other
stories.

WORLDS AND SELVES IN
PARADISE LOST, BOOK 8

Historians and philosophers of science have traditionally found the
questions raised by the possibility of a plurality of worlds—what is the
shape of the universe and what is the human place in it?—at the center
of the transformations wrought by seventeenth-century astronomy. In
From the Closed World to an Infinite Universe, Alexandre Koyre describes
the development of a modern cosmology as the replacement of a "conception of the world as a finite, closed and hierarchically ordered
whole (a whole in which the hierarchy of value determined the hierarchy and structure of being)" by an "indefinite and even infinite universe which is bound together by the identity of its fundamental com-
ponents and laws."[29] In other words, modern cosmology replaced a
single, vertically integrated hierarchy with a universe in which difference had to be understood as horizontal as well as vertical. Book 8,
which brings together a dialogue about the spatial arrangement of the
physical world (or worlds) with a dialogue concerning the social arrangement of the human world suggests the further significance of the
plurality of worlds to the poem's central action. Adam's two conversa-

tions with Raphael, which may be seen as the culmination of his prelapsarian education, may be understood as working through this transformation from a vertical hierarchy to the recognition of horizontal differentiation.

Of course the dialogue on astronomy is not explicitly concerned with the question of whether the universe contains a plurality of worlds. Rather, the dialogue begins when Adam, prompted by Eve's earlier question about the function of the stars,[30] questions the economy that disposes the great light of the stars and planets in service of the Earth. Adam, who presumes a single world, is nevertheless concerned that his experience does not match his presumptions about the universe. He wonders how the Earth, "a spot, a grain, / An atom" (17–18) can be the center of a much greater world. Raphael's famous response—"whether heaven move or Earth, / Imports not" (70–71)—subordinates questions about the physical disposition of the world to the proper understanding and worship of God. Beyond this, however, Raphael explains Adam's questions about the spatial organization of the world with reference to questions of social organization. Raphael suspects that Adam's discomfort concerning the apparent disproportions in the world arises from his social identity as father and leader (86). Adam thus thinks that

> bodies bright and greater should not serve
> The less not bright, nor heaven such journeys run,
> Earth sitting still, when she alone receives
> The benefit.
>
> (87–90)

Raphael counters this kind of thinking, which is attributed to Adam's expectation of hierarchical deference, with a useful warning against mistaking "great / Or bright" for "excellence" (90–91) or appearance for reality. Raphael's answers to Adam's questions reaffirm the centrality of humanity and a proper awe for God's power, but they also provide advice against constructing hierarchies of worth based on irrelevant characteristics. Adam, it seems, is to be reminded of his place in the world, but not to become too comfortable in it.

But what are we to make of the fact that it is Raphael who introduces the possibility of a plurality of worlds only to exclude them from Adam's ken? Here other worlds establish the boundaries of human comprehension and of human action:

> Think only what concerns thee and thy being;
> Dream not of other worlds, what creatures there
> Live, in what state, condition or degree.
>
> (174–76)

These lines may be read as limitations on human knowledge, but in
practice they prepare for the expansion of such knowledge: the rest of
book 8 focuses on Adam's growing self- awareness. Thus the effect of
this boundary making is not only to separate Earth from Heaven, but
also to demarcate a world for Adam's own story. The overall effect of
his dialogue is to open rather than close new sources of narrative. Book
8 of *Paradise Lost* yokes together the dialogue on astronomy and
Adam's narrative of his own origins. The combination of these two
topics is not accidental. Rather, the central question of the astronomical dialogue—what is my place?—defines Adam's struggle for self-def-
inition in the rest of book 8, which is framed for the reader as both natural philosophy and an exchange that brings the distinctly human into
the poem.[31] Adam takes Raphael's hint that he should be "lowly wise"
(173), and shifts the conversation to, quite literally, his turf: "Therefore
from this high pitch let us descend / A lower flight, and speak of things
at hand / Useful" (198–200). Adam says, "now hear me relate / My
story" (204–5), and the rest of the book establishes the bounds of his
competence and mastery. Book 8 begins with worlds Adam cannot
reach, but this speculation and the boundaries it constructs are actually
what inserts the human world into the poem. For example, in books 6
and 7, Raphael tells of the creation of the plants and animals, but here
Adam recounts his ability to "name / What e'er I saw" (272–73) and
therefore domesticate these creatures for the pleasure and benefit of
man. The account of the naming of plants and animals confirms the
passage of created things into human culture. The reader has already
heard Eve's own account of her creation, but in his tale Adam recalls
the definitive act of naming—"woman is her name, of man" (496)—
that should preempt that narrative. The book that begins with the possibility of worlds whose "state, condition or degree" (176) can never be
known and great uncertainty about the disposition of the heavens ends
with an earth populated with all the familiar creatures and the begin-
nings of a family.

The story Adam tells, of his own birth and of Eve's, is the story of
the innovation of horizontal differentiation in Paradise. In book 5, Raphael carefully describes the hierarchically arranged universe of *Paradise*

Lost, and Eve's place in this hierarchy is clearly defined throughout the poem: "He for God only, She for God in him" (4.299). Yet what Adam asks for is something different. He desires not to fill a gap in the vertical hierarchy, but rather another creature like himself, for "Among unequals what society / Can sort, what harmony or true delight?" (8.383–84). Adam recognizes Eve as a horizontally differentiated creature: "so absolute she seems / And in her self complete, so well to know / Her own" (547–49). She is, perhaps, her own world. Raphael's reaction to Adam's expression of this desire is to reassert a vertical organization.[32] But Raphael's lecture has in some sense already been preempted by his insistence that Adam shift his frame of reference from Heaven to the Earth. It is finally Raphael who blushes, while Adam describes this new thing of sex as indeed building a new world that is authorized not by the observation of the external world, but by the experience of the self:

> I to thee disclose
> What inward thence I feel, not therefore foiled,
> Who meet with various objects, from the sense
> Variously representing; yet still free
> Approve the best and follow what I approve.
>   (607–11)

Here Adam insists that he has learned Raphael's lesson. He will not mistake appearance for reality or bright for excellent, but rather will "approve" and "follow" the best. Raphael is not convinced, and knowledge of this story's outcome perhaps leaves the reader unconvinced as well, but this conclusion reflects Adam's broad-minded response to the possibilities of Raphael's discourse. The plurality of worlds implies a shift in the poetics of the universe, from vertical to horizontal, and Adam's narrative encompasses a similar shift. Adam's conversation with Raphael puts him in his place but also leads him to question the notion that the universe is a closed system. Adam is made to acknowledge his inferiority and dependence upon Heaven, but in doing so to find Earth and recognize his desire and responsibility for his earthly companion.

One function of the presence of other worlds in book 8 of *Paradise Lost* is to authorize Adam's narrative of his own world and provide the grounds for the inclusion of human narrative in the poem. For Eve, however, the possibility of other worlds presents a different set of problems. It is Eve who first asks the question that prompts Adam's dialogue with Raphael, even though she doesn't stay to hear the angel's answer: "But wherefore all night long shine these, for whom / This glorious sight, when sleep hath shut all eyes?" (4.657–58). Eve also arrives at the question posed by the plurality of worlds: what lies outside one's perception and experience? Adam answers Eve by directing her thoughts to the future: to the peoples and stories to which they are parent and origin:

> Those have their course to finish, round the earth,
> By morrow evening, and from land to land
> In order, though to nations yet unborn,
> Ministering light prepared, they set and rise.
> (661–64)

Just as Satan's brush with possible other worlds during his flight occasions a brief alternative narrative, Eve's questions about astronomy force her outside her emerging understanding of the world.

But Eve's transit through the perils of the other world is not as smooth as Adam's. If for Adam the contemplation of the other world leads back to Earth, for Eve it draws her repeatedly into an improper relation to the heavens. Satan's dream-temptation of Eve begins with an echo of her question about the function of the stars but transforms this question so that Eve is the necessary receiver and observer of the stars' light. Satan makes explicit the implicit assumption of Eve's question, by suggesting that the moon shines

> in vain,
> If none regard; heaven wakes with all his eyes,
> Whom to behold but thee, nature's desire,
> In whose sight all things joy, with ravishment
> Attracted by thy beauty still to gaze.
> (5.43–47)

First, Satan confirms Eve's intuition about the stars and moon but places her in the position she assigned to Adam: Eve becomes the reason for the Heavens' light and the object of their gaze. As the dream continues, she is drawn to believe that she is flying. With a movement opposed to that of Adam's narrative in book 8, Eve gets an astronomical view of the Earth. In this scene, knowledge of the stars and the privileged view of the Earth provided by a distant perspective (associated in the poem with the view provided by the telescope) draw Eve (temporarily, this time) into a story in which her narrative diverges from that of the earthbound Adam. In the dream she is tempted with Heaven, with other worlds:

> Taste this, and be henceforth among the gods
> Thy self a goddess, not to earth confined,
> But sometimes in the air, as we, sometimes
> Ascend to heaven.
>
> (77–80)

Eve's astronomical vision offers her other worlds and other stories that disrupt her position in the hierarchy of Milton's Paradise. Later as the serpent, Satan echoes the language of Eve's dream. For Raphael, the lesson of astronomy is wonder. Adam and Eve are to learn from the contemplation of the stars to worship and "admire" (8.75); Satan's language transforms this response—wonder—into idolatry. He describes Eve as "sole wonder" (9.533) and later praises her "celestial beauty" (540) and "thy beauty's heavenly ray" (607). Eve recognizes the "overpraising" of the fruit (615), but not of herself. Her choice is framed by celestial language of the plurality of worlds, which for her are no more than the illusory, and finally false, worlds Raphael warned against.

But before concluding that Eve's attraction to the other world merely results from and confirms her inferior sex, consider the complications that the poem's multiple perspectives bring to the representation of the plurality of worlds in *Paradise Lost*. For Adam and Eve, who have an angel to introduce them to Heaven and Hell and even the origin of their own world, perhaps it is enough to heed Raphael's advice to "Dream not of other worlds." However, for Milton, writing in the world that he did not choose, and his "fit audience, though few" (7.31), the trope of the plurality of worlds preserves the possibility of the other, the alternative. Eve's fatal choice is a transgression, a failure to recognize the boundaries of her world and her obedience. It also confirms the danger Raphael predicted in the plurality of worlds, but the choice of the other world is not only that. By embedding the recognition of difference within the dialogue on astronomy, Milton constructs *Paradise Lost*, which is itself a representation of a plurality of worlds, so that it preserves the principles of freedom and choice. Adam is reluctant to let Eve go when she suggests they should work separately, and subsequent events (along with the traditional gendered readings of the Fall) encourage readers to interpret this decision as error: Eve is willful, or Adam unable, as Raphael suggests he must, to make Eve "to realities yield all her shows" (8.575). But Eve's arguments for their separation are no mere "shows"; they echo Milton's arguments for choice in *Areopagitica*.[33] Eve confirms Adam's human challenge to Raphael's rebuke by suggesting the role of choice and independent agency for maintaining even the unfallen world. "Frail is our happiness, if this be so," she warns, "And Eden were no Eden thus exposed" (9.340–41).

"Some say": Cosmology, Choice, and Consequence in *Paradise Lost*

Though the convergence of the trope of the plurality of worlds and the problems of agency and choice is suggestive, in the end, of course, Adam and Eve's choice is not between this world and another or between different cosmologies, but between obedience and disobedience. The distance between these choices is marked by the fact that *Paradise Lost* contains two speculative cosmologies and two actual cosmologies. The tension between the two speculative cosmologies, figured most frequently by the plurality of worlds, serves to leave open the possibility of choice and the recognition of difference within the vertical hierarchy of Milton's narrative. The two actual cosmologies, however, reflect directly the consequences of choices made and forsaken. One of the most widely cited outcomes of the Scientific Revolution was the establishment of a new relationship between the individual and the natural world.[34] The apologists for natural philosophy argued that new models of the universe would be reflected in a transformation of human communities.[35] *Paradise Lost*, however, shows the reverse to be true. When the human community is altered (through human action and human choice), the structure of the world itself is altered:

> Some say he bid his angels turn askance
> The poles of earth twice ten degrees and more
> From the sun's axle; they with labour pushed
> Oblique the centric globe: some say the sun
> Was bid turn reins from the equinoctial road.
>   (10.668–72)

Again, Milton does not choose between a heliocentric or geocentric universe. He can not tell us whether it was the Earth or sun that was

shaken by the Fall. Both alternatives are marked by the same, equivocal "some say." Here, it truly "imports not" whether the sun or Earth
lies at the center. If the cause is unknown, the effect is undeniable. The
effect of this choice is the invention of seasons and of the world we
know. The separate worlds of the poem are here collapsed, as Adam
and Eve come to experience what Milton's readers know all too well:
"cold and heat / Scarce tolerable" (653–54), "Decrepit winter" (655),
and winds that "bluster to confound / Sea, Air, and shore" (665–66).
This record of the two actual cosmologies in the poem marks the consequences of choices made and describes the fallen world familiar to
the reader. The two speculative cosmologies, however, are never resolved and, through the trope of the plurality of worlds, preserve the
freedom to choose worlds not yet made: "The world was all before
them, where to choose / Their place of rest, and providence their
guide" (12.646–47).

NOTES

1. John Milton, *Paradise Lost*, in *Milton: "Paradise Lost*," ed. Alastair Fowler, 2nd
ed. (New York: Longman, 1998). All references to *Paradise Lost* are to this edition
and are cited parenthetically in the text.

2. Allan Gilbert, "The Outside Shell of Milton's World," *Studies in Philology* 20
(1923): 444.

3. See *OED*, "world," s.v. 9.

4. Raphael's flight is "between worlds and worlds" (5.268).

5. See *OED*, "world," s.v. 11.

6. See *OED*, "world," s.v. 8b. The earliest citation for this sense is 1713, but it
seems clear that "world" was used thus during the seventeenth century. Wilkins is
very careful to distinguish this meaning from the older sense (see below p. 181) as
early as 1638. Milton implies this sense at several points in *Paradise Lost*, perhaps
most unambiguously at 3.566, 3.567, and 8.175.

7. Mary B. Campbell, *Wonder and Science: Imagining Worlds in Early Modern England* (Ithaca, NY: Cornell University Press, 1999), 122.

8. See especially Marjorie Hope Nicolson, *Science and Imagination* (Ithaca, NY:
Great Seal, 1956).

9. On Milton's constructive use of astronomy generally and the telescope particu-
larly as a figurative mediation of human knowledge and its limitations, see Amy
Boesky, "Milton, Galileo, and Sunspots: Optics and Certainty in *Paradise Lost*," *Mil-
ton Studies* 34 (1996): 23–43; Donald Friedman, "Galileo and the Art of Seeing," in
Milton in Italy: Contexts, Images, Contradictions, ed. Mario A. Di Cesare (Binghamton,
NY: Medieval and Renaissance Texts and Studies, 1991), 159–74; Judith Scherer
Herz, " 'For Whom This Glorious Sight?': Dante, Milton, and the Galileo Ques-
tion," in *Milton in Italy: Contexts, Images, Contradictions*, ed. Di Cesare, 147–57; Regina

Schwartz, "Through the Optic Glass: Voyeurism and *Paradise Lost*," in *Desire in the Renaissance: Psychoanalysis and Literature*, ed. Valeria Finucci and Regina Schwartz (Princeton, NJ: Princeton University Press, 1994), 146–68. Some critics have seen Milton's use of contemporary astronomical imagery as primarily a rejection of scientific thought. See especially Roy Flannagan, "Art, Artists, Galileo, and Concordances," *Milton Quarterly* 20 (1986): 103–5; Neil Harris, "Galileo as Symbol: The 'Tuscan Artist' in *Paradise Lost*," *Annali dell' Instituto e museo di storia della scienza di Firenze* 10 (1985): 3–29. Flannagan's claims have been persuasively countered, however, by Julia M. Walker, "Milton and Galileo: The Art of Intellectual Canonization," *Milton Studies* 25 (1989): 109–23.

10. Maura Brady, "Galileo in Action: The 'Telescope' in *Paradise Lost*," *Milton Studies* 44 (2005): 129. Brady is careful to distinguish between the modern telescope and the instruments of either *Paradise Lost* or Galileo.

11. Some scholars have viewed Milton as unknowledgeable about or even hostile to the fundamental transformation in scientific thought undertaken in many disciplines during the seventeenth century. See Kester Svendsen, *Milton and Science* (Cambridge: Harvard University Press, 1956), and Stanley Fish, *Surprised by Sin*, 2nd ed. (Cambridge, MA: Harvard University Press, 1997), 107–30. Recent work by Catherine Gimelli Martin corrects some misconceptions of earlier scholarship and describes Milton as a Baconian poet. See Martin, " 'What if the Sun be Centre to the World': Milton's Epistemology, Cosmology, and Paradise of Fools Reconsidered," *Modern Philology* 99 (2001): 231–65. Further studies that explore the connection between Milton's poetry and the epistemology of his scientific contemporaries include Karen Edwards, *Milton and the Natural World: Science in "Paradise Lost"* (New York: Cambridge University Press, 1999), and Joanna Picciotto, "Reforming the Garden: The Experimentalist Eden and *Paradise Lost*," *ELH* 72 (2005): 23–78.

12. Albert Van Helden, "Galileo, Telescopic Astronomy, and the Copernican System," in *Planetary Astronomy from The Renaissance to the Rise of Astrophysics*, ed. Reni Taton, Curtis Wilson, and Michael Haskin (Cambridge, MA: Cambridge University Press, 1989), 86–87.

13. For the intellectual history of the plurality of worlds controversy, see Steven J. Dick, *Plurality of Worlds: The Origins of the Extraterrestrial Life Debate from Democritus to Kant* (Cambridge, MA: Cambridge University Press, 1982); Karl S. Guthke, *The Last Frontier: Imagining Other Worlds, from the Copernican Revolution to Modern Science Fiction*, trans. Helen Atkins (Ithaca, NY: Cornell University Press, 1990).

14. Two exceptions are Grant McColley, "The Theory of a Plurality of Worlds as a Factor in Milton's Attitude Toward the Copernican Hypothesis," *Modern Language Notes* 47 (1932): 319–25, and John S. Tanner, " 'And Every Star Perhaps a World of Destined Habitation': Milton and Moonmen," *Extrapolation* 30 (1989): 267–79. McColley argues incorrectly that the theory of a plurality of worlds "taints" Milton's attitude toward the "simple" Copernican perspective (324). Tanner notes Milton's "keen awareness of the issue" and describes his attitude as "cautious skepticism" (269). Both studies are concerned with Milton's attitude to the theory, while in this essay I consider the plurality of worlds as a figurative and narrative resource in the poem.

15. Fernand Hallyn, *The Poetic Structure of the World: Copernicus and Kepler*, trans. Donald M. Leslie (New York: Zone, 1993); Alexandre Koyre, *From the Closed World to the Infinite Universe* (Baltimore: Johns Hopkins University Press, 1957).

16. Tanner, "Milton and Moonmen," 273. Tanner cites the eighteenth-century thinker Thomas Paine: "are we to suppose that every world in the boundless creation had an Eve, an apple, a serpent and a Redeemer?"

17. Grant McColley, "Milton's Dialogue on Astronomy: The Principle Immediate Sources," *PMLA* 52 (1937): 728–62. McColley argues persuasively for Milton's knowledge of these works through the identification of many specific verbal parallels between *Paradise Lost* and the Wilkins and Ross texts. These were, however, probably not Milton's only source for astronomical knowledge. For Milton's knowledge of or debt to Galileo's *Dialogue Concerning Two Chief World Systems* and other works, see Alan Gilbert, "Milton and Galileo," *Studies in Philology* 19 (1922): 152–85; Francis Johnson, *Astronomical Thought in Renaissance England* (New York: Octagon Books, 1968); Boesky, "Milton, Galileo, and Sunspots"; Friedman, "Galileo and the Art of Seeing"; Martin, "What if the Sun be Centre to the World." In this essay I focus on Wilkins and Ross because of their explicit concern with the plurality of worlds and its attendant controversies.

18. See especially *Discourse Concerning a New Planet* (1640), which considers and refutes each of the supposed contradictions between Scripture and the new astronomy, in John Wilkins, *The Mathematical and Philosophical Works of the Right Reverend John Wilkins, Late Bishop of Chester* (London, 1708). For a study of Wilkins's career, see Barbara Shapiro, *John Wilkins, 1614–1672* (Berkeley: University of California Press, 1969). Shapiro notes that Wilkins wrote in English out of a "desire to spread scientific information" (30).

19. John Wilkins, *The Discovery of a World in the Moone* (1638; rept., Delmar: Scholars' Facsimiles & Reprints, 1973), 43.

20. Ibid., 165–66.

21. Campbell traces the moon as narrative destination in *Wonder and Science*.

22. For further detail on arguments for and against plurality of worlds throughout the early modern period, see Dick, *Plurality of Worlds*.

23. Alexander Ross (1591–1654) was an Anglican minister, schoolmaster, and a prolific author. For a positive assessment of Ross's contribution to philosophy, see David Allan, " 'An Ancient Sage Philosopher': Alexander Ross and the Defence of Philosophy," *Seventeenth Century* 16 (2001): 68–94.

24. Alexander Ross, *The New Planet No Planet, or, the Earth No Wandring Star, except in the Wandring Heads of Galileans* (London, 1646), sig. A 3r.

25. Ibid., 88.

26. Wilkins, *Discovery*, 41.

27. Malabika Sarkar, " 'The Visible Diurnal Sphere': Astronomical Images of Space and Time in *Paradise Lost*," *Milton Quarterly* 18 (1984): 1.

28. John Donne, "The First Anniversary," *Complete English Poems*, ed. C. A. Patrides (London: J. M. Dent, 1994), 255.

29. Koyre, *From the Closed World to the Infinite Universe*, 2.

30. See *Paradise Lost*, 4.657–58.

31. For another reading of the coherence of book 8, see John Guillory, "From the Superfluous to the Supernumerary: Reading Gender into *Paradise Lost*," in *Soliciting Interpretation: Literary Theory and Seventeenth-Century English Poetry*, ed. Elizabeth D. Harvey and Katharine Eisaman Maus (Chicago: University of Chicago Press, 1990), 68–88.

32. See *Paradise Lost*, 8.589–94.

33. Ibid., 9.322–41.

34. See Steven Shapin's useful synthesis in *The Scientific Revolution* (Chicago: University of Chicago Press, 1998).

35. See especially Francis Bacon's *The New Atlantis* (1626) in which the exceptional order and prosperity of the community is a reflection of the scientific activities of Solomon's House. But see also Thomas Sprat, *History of the Royal Society of London* (1667), which projects numerous benefits for English society as a result of the improvement of scientific knowledge.

Reassessing Milton's Republicanism: History, Machiavelli, and *Paradise Lost*

William Walker

Over the last twenty years, several leading Miltonists have argued that, rather than signaling the poet's retreat from political engagement, *Paradise Lost* is in fact a further expression of "Milton's republicanism." By this they mean mainly that the poem describes and refers (if obliquely) to agents and events in mid-seventeenth-century England, draws from the principal sociopolitical vocabularies and debates of this period, and affirms some of the principles and beliefs of the revolutionaries and supporters of the English commonwealth.[1] But it is clear that in making this case for the poem's republicanism, several of these critics also mean that it conforms in important ways with the *tradition* of political thought running from Aristotle to Machiavelli that has been documented so impressively by scholars such as J. G. A. Pocock and Quentin Skinner. Reflecting what David Norbrook refers to as its "republican milieu,"[2] that is to say, *Paradise Lost* is also now widely seen to reflect the republican tradition of political thought that so strongly informed it.

Some Miltonists and historians of political thought, have, however, questioned the going argument for the classical and Machiavellian credentials of Milton's republicanism in particular and English republicanism at large. In some cases, this questioning has been driven by the feeling that, as Jonathan Scott has recently put it, "the greatest shortcoming of the existing literature on English republicanism [is] the relative neglect of its religious dimension."[3] A much more complicated and problematical picture of mid-seventeenth-century English political thought is emerging from this scholarship, and it is to such a picture that I propose to add some details, not so much by observing the religious dimension of Milton's republicanism as by observing how the

religious dimension of his thinking *conflicts* with many of the tenets of
the classical and Machiavellian republicanism with which he has been
aligned. The comprehensive case for how the heterodox Protestantism
expressed in *Paradise Lost* and other texts differs from and indeed
openly repudiates aspects of the tradition of republican political
thought would need to take into account how Milton deals with all of
those issues, treatments of which various scholars have located at the
heart of this tradition. That is to say it would need to observe how the
poet differs from the republicans on civil liberty, forms of government,
virtue, eloquence, empire, and history. Here I propose to deal only
with the last of these, though as we will see, an understanding of how
Milton responds to the republican vision of history provides considerable insight into how he differs from the republicans on these other issues as well.

That a way of thinking about human experience over time is one of
the defining elements of republican tradition is suggested by the fact
that most of the texts which are commonly taken to be the major texts
in this tradition are not works of philosophy or political theory, but
works of history and historical commentary. Thus, when Blair Worden ventures to identify the main sources of the "English republicanism" of which he sees Milton (at least up until *Paradise Lost*) as a major
spokesman, he lists Aristotle's *Politics*, Polybius's *Histories*, Plutarch's
Lives, Cicero's writings on justice and government (which contain substantial histories of Rome), Livy's history of Rome, Tacitus's history of
Rome, "the histories of Sallust and Quintilian," Machiavelli's commentary on Livy's history of Rome, and *The Prince*.[4] If we take this to
be the canon of classical and Renaissance republicanism, it is clear that
the affirmation of what are thought of as "republican principles" and
"republican values," and the implementation of "republican language"
or "republican discourse" occur within descriptions and analyses of the
experience of particular nations and peoples over long periods of time.
As Pocock observes in connection with Machiavelli and the early modern Florentines, "a vital component of republican theory consisted of
ideas about time, about the occurrence of contingent events of which
time was the dimension, and about the intelligibility of the sequences
. . . of particular happenings that made up what we should call history.
It is this which makes it possible to call republican theory an early
form of historicism." Building on Hans Baron's postulation of a Florentine "revolution in historiographical concepts," Pocock goes on to
claim that a particular vision of history is that from which early mod-

ern republican political discourse (which Pocock also calls "civic humanism") derives, and that a particular historical problem (which Pocock sometimes calls "the Machiavellian moment") is that which this discourse was meant to articulate and solve. "The language," he writes, "for which the term 'civic humanism' may appropriately be used can be traced, deriving from the assertion of a republican vision of history, and employed for a variety of purposes among which by far the most important was that of asking whether the vivere civile and its values could indeed be held stable in time."[5]

In *Paradise Lost*, Milton presents a vision of history which not only differs from but openly repudiates major aspects of the understanding of history which Pocock and many others rightly place at the heart of republican political thought. This becomes clear if we compare the ways in which Milton and Machiavelli (who, as we will see, in many ways follows but in some ways departs from the classical republicans) treat the history of Rome and Israel, the causes of human experience, the overall shape of this experience, and its meaning and value. Given the importance of ideas about history to republican tradition, this understanding of how Milton stands apart from them will help us move toward a more refined understanding of "Milton's republicanism."

I

In the Preface to the *Discourses*, Machiavelli laments that men now shun "what history has to say about the highly virtuous actions performed by ancient kingdoms and republics, by their kings, their generals, their citizens, their legislators, and by others who have gone to the trouble of serving their country."[6] It is in part to get men out of this wrong way of thinking about history and to allow them "more easily [to] draw those practical lessons which one should seek to obtain from the study of history" that Machiavelli claims to present a commentary on Livy which contains "what I have arrived at by comparing ancient with modern events" (99). Over the course of the work, Machiavelli does indeed comment on the history of several ancient kingdoms and republics, such as Israel, Sparta, and Athens, and he compares the important events in these nations with what for him was the recent history of Florence, Venice, and other western European nations. But in some cases, such as ancient Israel, Machiavelli's comments amount to no more than citations of further instances or examples of things evident elsewhere (102, 133, 166, 176, 296, 486). In all cases, his treatment of events in these ancient and modern states is cursory compared to his treatment of the history of one ancient kingdom and republic in particular—Rome. This is in part because, like Polybius and many classical Roman poets and historians, he feels that because Rome was so successful in defeating and ruling other nations of the Mediterranean, he sees the history of Rome as the history of the world (267).[7]

Though human history is described throughout *Paradise Lost*, by far the most comprehensive account is that in the final books when, following God's command, Michael reveals to Adam "what shall come in future days / To thee and to thy Offspring" (11.357–58).[8] That this revelation, deriving in many ways from descriptions of and allusions to history earlier in the poem, will be fundamentally at odds with the republican vision of history is clear from the start when Michael leads Adam to the summit of the highest hill in Paradise from which "His Eye might . . . command wherever stood / City of old or modern Fame, the Seat / Of mightiest Empire" (385–87). From here, Adam certainly sees "where Rome was to sway / The World" (405–6), but Michael is about to follow neither Virgil nor Augustine, upon whose Christian historical consciousness Rome impinged so deeply. Rome is just one seat of empire among a host of others listed by the narrator, all of which are dismissed out of a concern for "nobler sights" (12.411). For the classical republicans and Machiavelli, there *were* no sights nobler than the sight of republican Rome and its empire, and the notion that scenes of fratricide, disease, misery, and death deriving from man's natural pravity (with which Michael begins), and scenes of persecution and crucifixion would qualify as such sights would have struck them as being ludicrous. Moreover, whereas *patriotism* was a major driving force of the historiographical practice of both the classical Roman and Florentine republicans, Milton conveys a vision of history by way of an angel who has no nation and who pays no attention whatsoever to the poet's own nation, the subject of his "republican historiography" in *The History of Britain*.[9] And whereas Israel is treated by the classical republicans as simply one of Rome's troublesome territories and by Machiavelli as simply one nation among others that furnishes evidence for his claims about men and politics, it is of course central to Michael's vision of the history of the world.

Ignoring Rome and Britain and foregrounding Israel in this way, Michael conforms with his explicit account of what is and is not worthy of record. Referring to the days of the giants described in Genesis 6:4, but also taking shots at the Romans and their triumphs, Michael claims that "in those days Might only shall be admir'd," and that "what most merits fame" shall be "in silence hid" (11.689, 699). This critique of military prowess, which runs through the entire poem and which Michael repeats before his account of Noah, is commonly taken to be directed against the pagan epic poets who supposedly glorified it. But it is important to see that such a critique applies just as much to the ancients and Machiavelli, since they, too, were preoccupied with military deeds, taught that such deeds were heroic and therefore worthy of record and imitation, established to an important extent the fame, renown, and glory enjoyed by those who performed them, and tended to remain silent about that which most merits fame. What most merits fame, as we know from the invocation to book 9, is "the better fortitude / Of Patience and Heroic Martyrdom" (9.31–32). Working against both the pagan epic poets and historians, Michael celebrates this fortitude by observing the acts of the heroes of faith and the "God-like act" performed by the Son (12.427). Michael thus clearly does not just happen to treat things that are different from those treated by the republicans. He does so out of an explicitly stated commitment to entirely different criteria for identifying what is heroic and virtuous and so worthy of renown and fame.[10]

II

Machiavelli's analysis of the causes of most of the events he takes to be history is comprehensively naturalistic. First of all, in both *The Prince* and the *Discourses*, he commonly explains human experience in terms of how the base "matter" or "material" of humanity has, as a result of forms of education, law, custom, and ways of life, become a structure of passion, desire, and humor which he calls a "disposition," "character," or "nature." That is to say that he commonly sees what men do and experience as being a direct result of their natures and dispositions (*P*, 65, 80–81; *D*, 430–32, 465–71, 503–5). In addition, Machiavelli often points to specific actions, strategies, policies, and procedures when he is explaining the causes of other specific events. Thus, in the *Discourses*, taking issue with Livy and Plutarch who claim that "the Roman people was indebted for the empire it acquired rather to fortune than to virtue," he follows Polybius and claims that "it was the virtue of her armies that caused Rome to acquire an empire, and it was her constitutional procedure and the peculiar customs which she owed to her first legislator that enabled her to maintain what she had acquired" (270). When in this work he discusses the downfall of Rome, he continues to provide a thoroughly naturalistic causal explanation, though he departs from his emphasis on the reliance on mercenaries which features in *The Prince*: he claims that the two main causes of the dissolution of the republic were "the disputes which arose concerning the Agrarian law" and "the prolongation of military commands" (473). It is, moreover, this kind of naturalistic analysis that prevails in Machiavelli's account of the causes of a wide range of other kinds of incidents that recur in human experience, such as the rise of tyranny, the difference between the ancients and the moderns, success and failure in war, the loss of kingdoms, and the failure and success of conspiracies.

This is not to say that Machiavelli does not also grant some power to the supernatural agency to which he occasionally refers as "fortune" and "Fortune." In a famous passage in *The Prince* he goes so far as to grant that "fortune is the arbiter of half the things we do leaving the other half or so to be controlled by ourselves" (79), and there are several occasions in the *Discourses* where he identifies fortune as an active force in human affairs. But in both works, Machiavelli deeply qualifies the power of this apparently supernatural agency by observing that individuals and institutions that have virtue are not subject to it (*P*, 46; *D*, 375–76, 488, 492). In addition, not only in the *Discourses* but also in *The Prince*, Machiavelli so commonly chastises those who identify fortune as the cause of their losses and failures that one could reasonably say that human freedom *from* the power of fortune (and therefore human responsibility *for* what happens to them) is an important theme of both works. Moreover, in some of the causal chains Machiavelli likes to construct, he makes "fortune" itself the effect of other naturalistic causes, and so implicitly denies it the status of some kind of independent supernatural agent that directs the course of human affairs (113, 141, 272–74). Indeed, in many cases, "fortune" ends up being nothing more than those events that constitute history itself and that may be either "good" or "bad." Given this treatment of fortune, and his relentless account of how tumults, the virtue of founders, the virtue of commanders, the free choices of individuals, education, the simple virtue of one man alone, customs, human passions and desires, and civil laws cause specific historical events, it must be said that Machiavelli's conception of the causes of human experience is predominantly naturalistic. He may thus reasonably be seen to follow Polybius, Cicero, and Sallust, for while all of these figures acknowledge a supernatural power of fortune in various ways, their causal analyses of the major aspects of the Roman experience that interest them are predominantly naturalistic, with Roman virtue and the republican constitution occupying major causal roles.[11] Besides aligning him with the classical historians, this naturalistic outlook also aligns Machiavelli with the Renaissance humanists.[12]

Like Machiavelli, Milton in *Paradise Lost* sometimes describes the causes of human experience over time in terms of what man is. The very experience of being expelled from Paradise, for example, is, as several critics have pointed out, explained by God to the Son as something that follows by the law of Nature from what man has become as result of his sin (11.48–57).[13] Observing at the outset of his presentation that human experience in general is a function of "supernal Grace contending / With sinfulness of Men" (11.359–60), Michael confirms Sin's view that besides being a kind of action, sin may also be a corrupt and corrupting element residing within man, and indicates that history is essentially a function of divine grace contending with what, as a result of this element, is a depraved human nature. This notion of sin as part of the being or nature of man, besides simply one act performed by him, is again evident when Michael introduces the first vision by telling Adam to behold

> Th'effects which thy original crime hath wrought
> In some to spring from thee, who never touch'd
> Th'excepted Tree, nor with the Snake conspir'd,
> Nor sinn'd thy sin, yet from that sin derive
> Corruption to bring forth more violent deeds.
>
> (11.424–28)

Identifying the sinful act of disobedience as a kind of Urcause of what all humans, no matter what their nation, do and experience, Michael here also identifies the corrupt human being resulting from that act as the immediate cause of the violent deeds that constitute history (see also 12.90–93; 285–89).

Milton's naturalistic causal analysis of human experience, however, differs from that of the republicans in that his conception of human nature is different from theirs and he grants momentous causal power to a particular act of treason which for them never occurred. More importantly, Milton's account of the causes of human experience grants extensive power to supernatural agents. There is, first of all, Satan, the "cause" that moved Adam and Eve to fall off from their creator (1.28), and Milton describes in great detail the particular way in which Satan manages to affect man in this way. In addition, though Michael does not mention them, the narrator early in the poem claims that the other rebel angels exercise a significant influence over humankind once Satan has done his work, for "wand'ring o'er the Earth," they will induce man to forsake God and "Devils to adore for Deities" (1.365, 373). Moreover, because in the final three books of the poem Milton represents human depravity and death not only as the consequences of a human act of disobedience and something that conforms with the law of nature, but also in terms of the activity of Sin and Death, the entire human experience of disease, suffering, and death is made to appear at least in part as the result of the ongoing machinations of supernatural agents. Finally, there is of course God who throughout the poem is described as affecting human history by directly acting within it and upon the very being of its agents.

III

Over the course of the *Discourses*, Machiavelli provides several broader visions of the particular sequences of causally related events he describes in such detail. First, drawing heavily on Polybius's account of the *anacyclosis*, "the cycle of political revolution, the law of nature according to which constitutions change, are transformed, and finally revert to their original form" (309), he early in the work envisions the history of the world as the experience of particular nations endlessly progressing through the three "good" and the three "bad" forms of government (from monarchy, to tyranny, to aristocracy, to oligarchy, to democracy, to anarchy, and back to monarchy). Any society's progression through these forms may, however, be interrupted by its being conquered by another nation, or, as Machiavelli makes clear immediately following his discussion of the cycles of government, by its establishing a mixed form of government that, because it avoids the defects of each form, can remain stable over long periods of time. Second, Machiavelli sometimes envisions history in terms of political societies (whatever form of government they may have) which begin in a state of order or goodness and then simply disintegrate and die, unless they undergo "renovation." Renovation, Machiavelli explains in the remarkable opening chapter of book 3 of the *Discourses*, is a "reduction" to an institution's "starting-point," a "return to its original principles" (386), that has the effect of reminding its members of those principles, making them respect and live in accordance with them, bringing "men back to the mark" (387). In his discussion of how Rome was renovated by both external events (such as the invasion by the Gauls) and internal events (such as the introduction of various institutions, virtuous individuals, and "drastic actions" [387] performed by some of its citizens), Machiavelli suggests that history is essentially the endless establishment and disintegration of discrete political societies and other institutions "in the process of time" (386), but where that disintegration may be retarded and even reversed by "renovation." Both of these descriptions of history in terms of discrete political societies naturally progressing through various institutional forms or resisting with varying degrees of success natural processes of deterioration through renovation are perhaps consistent with Machiavelli's vision of the world as a kind of homeostatic system within which the amounts of good and evil remain the same but are simply distributed differently as composite bodies are founded and undergo various transformations. He presents this vision when, objecting to men who idealize the past, he asserts that "the world has always been in the same condition, and that in it there has been just as much good as there is evil, but . . . this evil and this good have varied from province to province. This may be seen from the knowledge we have of ancient kingdoms, in which the balance of good and evil changed from one to the other owing to changes in their customs, whereas the world as a whole, remained the same" (266–67). This way of thinking about history is, however, challenged by a vision according to which all people of all nations constitute a single body which starts off in a state of health but becomes increasingly malignant, regardless, it seems, of what forms of government are in place and whether or not they are renovated. The corruption proceeds until this body is "purged," not by means of a supernatural agency, but simply in accordance with nature, and then reconstituted as a healthy body that, though able to "grow better," again becomes more and more malignant over a long period of time until it is once again purged through destruction (289–90). Finally, harping on the theme of the virtue of the ancients and the vice of the moderns, Machiavelli sometimes sees history simply as a long slide from ancient virtue to modern corruption (see 98, 278, 334, 433, 479). In so doing, he brings considerable pressure to bear upon his homeostatic vision of history and conforms with aspects of his vision of the world as a single community that becomes increasingly corrupt over long periods of time and is then purified in a moment of destruction, ad infinitum.

Given that Milton in *Paradise Lost* thinks of human nature and the causes of human experience in a way that differs fundamentally from the way the republicans think of these things, it is not surprising that he also differs from them on the issue of the pattern and shape this experience assumes over the long run. He differs from them, first of all, by representing the entire experience of mankind as one that occurs within a broader experience of supernatural deities residing in the universe at large for eternity. Though the invocation to the poem gives no indication of it, it is in fact within a larger story about God, his Son, angels, Satan, Chaos, Night, Sin, and Death that the story of man is told. Indeed, the poem presents the history of man as a means by which the struggle between the supernatural deities, which preexists the advent of mankind, is waged and brought to an end. There is thus a sense in which Milton's historiography is less anthropocentric than republican historiography that departing from classical epic, tends not to situate human experience within struggles between the immortals taking place on a stage of much broader temporal and spatial dimensions than that occupied by the human players.

Milton's basic conception of human experience as something that unfolds within a universe where supernatural deities interact produces a vision of human history as a relatively brief experience of happiness in Paradise, an extended experience of misery and death outside Paradise, and a final endless experience of happiness in Paradise for some and misery in Hell for others. Those critics who, on the basis of the graphic presentation of suffering in the final books, claim that Milton presents history as having a tragic shape or pattern, are thus mistaken, since they fail to acknowledge this tripartite structure of human experience that Michael insists upon by continually interrupting his description of human suffering with references to the second coming that marks what he calls the "happy end" (12.605).[14] Human history would have had a tragic shape if no one able and willing had volunteered to pay the deadly ransom, and God, demanding as he certainly would have, that justice be served and that that ransom be paid, either simply annihilated Adam and Eve on the spot, or permitted them to have a posterity which, like them, would suffer, die, and then live in eternal misery with Satan and the fallen angels in Hell.

It is on the basis of this three-stage model that human experience as we know it (that is, the middle stage) is conceived, first, as the experience of being *banished*. This is made clear when God tells Michael to "drive out the sinful Pair, / From hallow'd ground th'unholy, and denounce / To them and to thir Progeny from thence / Perpetual banishment" (11.105–8). As Eve recognizes at the end of the poem, Adam is one "Who for my wilful crime art banisht hence" (12.619). But human experience as we know it is also conceived as the experience of being both justly and mercifully punished for an act of treason. As Michael puts it responding to Adam's objection to the suffering mankind must endure, because man failed to reverence God's image in themselves, "so abject is thir punishment" (11.520). And it is clear that the experience of death, which defines human life during this stage, is the payment of a penalty, though there is also an element of release in it. Finally, this middle stage of human history is also conceived as the state of being *tried* during which individuals perform actions the quality of which will determine whether or not they in particular will participate in the final regaining of life in Paradise. As God puts it, human life after the Fall is essentially "Life / Tri'd in sharp tribulation, and refin'd / By Faith and faithful works"(11.62–64).

Although these notions of human experience as essentially the experience of banishment from Paradise, punishment for a crime against God, and trial, upon which not our fame amongst men but the status of our souls in the afterlife depends, are alien to the republicans, it could be said that some of the specific patterns of the second stage of history as Michael represents it resemble in some ways the big picture as Machiavelli and the republicans see it. As Machiavelli sometimes envisions world history in terms of periods of decline terminated by floods, fires, or plagues that purge the world and reconstitute virtue, so Michael describes how mankind after the Fall will become so corrupt that God out of anger will destroy the world and how mankind will then live "With some regard to what is just and right" (12.16) before again becoming corrupt. And as Machiavelli sometimes envisions history as the long slide from ancient virtue to modern corruption, so Michael's narrative is premised upon a state of virtue in the distant past followed by a state of corruption running up to the present. There is also a sense in which Michael's narrative of human experience between the loss and the regaining of Paradise can be said to confirm the Machiavellian view that the amount of goodness and badness in the world remains the same. For though he points to particular virtuous individuals such as Enoch and Noah and other heroes of faith, the overall impression is that the "sinfulness of Men" (11.360) contending with God's grace remains basically the same with the result that the ethical condition of the world remains basically the same as well.

But rather than representing the cataclysmic flood as a natural oc-currence, something that follows naturally from the corruption of hu-mankind, Michael describes it as something that is directly caused by an angry God, and he makes clear that history will not be an endless repetition of such periods of corruption terminated by purgative floods or fires. And whereas for Machiavelli the transition from ancient virtue to modern corruption was a long, slow process caused mainly by changes in education, law, religion, and custom, for Michael the tran-sition from ancient virtue to the corruption we now know was a punc-tual event caused by one bad act. In addition, as Michael makes clear in his discussion of "those days [when] Might only shall be admir'd, / And Valor and Heroic Virtue call'd" (11.689–90), those whom Machiavelli regarded as the virtuous ancients are for Michael simply early instances of "Plagues of men" (11.697). Concentrating on Israel, Michael in no way shares Machiavelli's sense of a progress of virtue from one part of the world to another while the total amount of virtue within it remains the same. Moreover, he has nothing to do with the Polybian/Machi-avellian concept of history as the *anacyclosis* that is sporadically inter-rupted by conquest and the establishment of mixed forms of govern-ment. And while he does attend to some extent to the existence of societies and institutions over time (such as the earliest human society, Israel, and the church) and the way they become corrupt, he does not invest in the Machiavellian notion of renovation. On the contrary, his descriptions of both Enoch and Noah demonstrate the total inefficacy of virtuous individuals who would renovate their societies by preaching and setting good examples for them by getting back to basics. In his ac-count of the corruption of the church (12.502–51), he mentions nei-ther St. Francis nor St. Dominic who for Machiavelli renovated it. Fi-nally, by envisioning postlapsarian human history as an experience that can be broken down into the six-stage sequence described by Augus-tine or a three-stage sequence (Cain and Abel to Noah; Noah to Christ; Christ to now) deriving from Joachim de Fiore and Augus-tine,[15] Michael introduces ways of periodizing human experience as we know it that are totally foreign to classical republican and Machiavel-lian historical vision.

Describing the difference between the republican and the Miltonic vision of history in these ways is still in an important sense inadequate. For it proceeds on the premise that, for all of the differences between them, both visions still agree in thinking of history as a sequence of events that, even if they do recur, can best be imaged as points on a continuous line extending unidirectionally and infinitely through space, and best be described by a sophisticated narrative that presents them in the order in which they occur and that makes clear and intelligible the causal connections between them. But this is not the case, for Michael's vision of history is strongly informed by the typological theory of interpretation and history, according to which events in the life of Israel described by the Old Testament are promises and signs, the fulfilment and meaning of which are events in the life of Christ described by the New Testament and Revelation.[16] As Erich Auerbach and other scholars make clear, this typological vision of history "obviously introduces an entirely new and alien element into the antique conception of history."[17] And observing the way in which Michael explicitly uses the typological vocabulary, reverses the order of events, continually interrupts his narrative with references to the first and second coming, describes some particular events extensively and huge tracts of time in a single line, alludes to earlier passages in the poem, and narrates in a plain syntactical style, several critics have indeed come away with the impression that Michael presents a nonlinear vision of history.[18] Michael's description of earthly relations of space, time, and cause which presupposes a classical linear model of history thus uneasily coexists with his description of the Son as both promise and fulfilment which presupposes a very different model.

IV

For Machiavelli and the ancients, the value of the past derives first from its potential to furnish us with "examples," "cases," and "instances" that "prove," "show," "indicate," "verify," "teach," "illustrate," "bear witness to," and "bear out" various propositions about politics and war. Thus, numerous examples, including that of Coriolanus, show the importance of having "a legal outlet for the anger which the general public has conceived against a particular citizen" (124–25); "numerous examples" from ancient times show that it is difficult for a people accustomed to live under a prince to preserve their liberty should they by some accident acquire it (153); "history shows again and again" that not gold but good soldiers are the sinews of war (303); several ancient and modern instances and examples show that infantry is superior to cavalry (328–33). By properly studying the past, and narratives of the past, as Machiavelli both claims to do and hopes to teach others to do, we can learn these "practical lessons" (99) and "principles" (158). And by coming to know these things about the world, we will be able to *act* more effectively and avoid the "errors," "mistakes," and "blunders" that are inevitably and repeatedly committed by those who do not know these things and that constitute the bulk of those military and political events Machiavelli thinks of as history. The past is also valuable, for both Machiavelli and his precursors, as a storehouse of examples in the sense of models and exemplars of shrewd and noble behavior that can *move* and *inspire* us to imitate them. Thus, in *The Prince*, Machiavelli recommends reading history as an essential element of the "intellectual training" of all princes, in part because this will allow them to "do what eminent men have done before him: taken as their model some historical figure who has been praised and honored; and always kept his deeds and actions before them" (48–49; see also 17–18, 26, 83–84). And throughout the *Discourses*, Machiavelli presents various actions and men as exemplars and models to be "followed," "emulated," and "imitated" (138, 268, 338, 388, 396, 410, 504, 522, 524). Machiavelli thus affirms the value of history mainly on grounds that, regardless of the goals people may have, it provides knowledge and models that can help them achieve those goals.

Like Machiavelli, Milton presents history as something that, at least properly attended to, can provide people with evidence for propositions about themselves and their world, including its political dimension, and he thinks of the knowledge that may be derived from this evidence as something that can help them to avoid the mistakes and errors of others and to act well. Milton thinks this knowledge can benefit humankind in this way because, like the republicans, he thinks of humankind (in its fallen form) and its condition as remaining basically the same over time. In addition, Milton by way of Michael might reasonably be seen to conform with the republican practice of singling out virtuous examples to be imitated. For, as some readers have observed, single men such as Enoch and Noah seem to have set a model that Milton himself followed, and it seems clear that, even if they did fail to reform their societies, Michael is presenting them as figures to be emulated by all.[19] The Son, too, emerges as an example to be followed, for at the end of it all, Adam claims to have been "Taught this by his example whom I now / Acknowledge my Redeemer ever blest" (12.572–73). Some of the particular propositions that Michael urges Adam and the reader to learn from his account of history, moreover, are the same as those the classical Roman historians and Machiavelli urge us to learn from their very different understandings of history. Sallust himself, for example, might well have written that man's woe stems from "Man's effeminate slackness" (11.634). Adam's claim to see "Peace to corrupt no less than War to waste" (784) in light of the giants' profligacy and indulgence in "luxurious wealth" following their "great exploits" (790) may also reasonably be seen to confirm both classical republican and Machiavellian perspectives on the evils of luxury that creep in when a society no longer fears an enemy and lives in peace. And Michael's observations on liberty, reason, and passion have rough precedents in the writings of the classical republicans. Finally, some of the specific ethical lessons Michael draws from history also conform with republican ideas concerning how to behave well: by inferring from history that one is to be temperate, moderate, patient, reasonable, and just, and by presenting history as something that provides rare examples of such behavior that, indeed, inspire Adam to follow them, Michael affirms some of the virtues championed by Cicero, Sallust, and Livy.

This, however, hardly warrants the claim that Michael "specifically bends scriptural material toward the presentation of historical lessons of a significantly meritocratic and republican cast"—not, at least, where this would mean presenting lessons of the kind presented by Polybius, Sallust, Livy, and Machiavelli.[20] For Michael's lessons, including the ones about politics, are essentially Christian lessons which, as such, are fundamentally at odds with those of the republicans. First of all, Michael not only shows no interest in but is openly hostile to a particular kind of wisdom which, for the classical republicans and Machiavelli, was one of the major sources of the value of studying history: wisdom about military affairs. Thus, rather than presenting the battle scenes as opportunities for Adam and us to see, for example, that soldiers are the sinews of war or that one should never rely on mercenaries, he observes that they display "great exploits . . . of true virtue void" (11.790). In so doing, Michael presents scriptural material directly toward the presentation of lessons of a significantly antirepublican cast. Moreover, the wisdom Michael directs Adam and us to derive from his vision of history consists mainly of an awareness of the truths of a religion to which the ancients did not subscribe and of which Machiavelli is highly critical. Michael is clear and explicit about this from the start when he informs Adam that he will "show" (357) Adam what shall come in future days so that he "may'st believe, and be confirm'd" (355) that the loving God is present in the fallen world and provides signs of that presence.

As we have seen, Michael goes on to present human history as the
occasion for knowing a wide range of other propositions, some of
which are less consoling than this concerning the ubiquity of God.
Thus, he displays to Adam "a monstrous crew" of diseases that Adam
"may'st know / What misery th'inabstinence of Eve / Shall bring on
men" (11.474–77), that he may understand that this kind of suffering is
just punishment for the way humankind vilified God's image in themselves (515–25), but that he may also understand that those who live in
accordance with "The rule of not too much" (531) can live to an old
age and "be with ease / Gather'd, not harshly pluckt, for death mature"
(536–37). Besides identifying the particular individuals in the history
he reveals to Adam and explaining the nature of the societies in which
they exist, Michael continues to present history as something that
"shows" other important general propositions about the human condition. Thus, God saves Enoch "to show thee what reward / Awaits the
good," and he proceeds to present the flood as the "punishment" the
rest shall suffer (709–10). This flood, moreover, shall carry away the
Mount of Paradise on which they now stand and turn it into a barren
island haunted by seals, orcs, and sea-mews, "To teach" Adam "that
God attributes to place / No sanctity, if none be thither brought / By
Men who there frequent, or therein dwell" (836–38). The survival of
Noah and the animals and God's covenant with man in the form of a
rainbow assures Adam that "Man shall live / With all the Creatures,
and thir seed preserve" (872–73), and means, as Michael further explains, that the natural world shall hold its course until the end of time
when "fire purge all things new, / Both Heav'n and Earth, wherein the
just shall dwell" (900–901).

Michael's account of Nimrod in book 12 is rightly taken by Adam as
evidence not of the republican understanding of the relation between
man and animals but of the Christian view he already holds on grounds
of personal experience: God gives dominion to man over the animals
but not over men. Michael identifies further general but in some ways
ambivalent propositions about liberty, reason, passion, and tyranny
which may be inferred from this incident. In response to Michael's
narration of the rise of the nation of Israel, Adam comes to see that "all
Nations shall be blest" in the seed of Abraham (12.277), but Michael
also makes this narrative the occasion for informing Adam of the basic
truths of Pauline theology (285–306). In response to Michael's narration of the history of Israel from the entry into Canaan to the birth of
the Messiah, Adam comes to understand "Why our great expectation

should be call'd / The seed of Woman" (378–79), but he still stands in
need of correction when it comes to understanding exactly how the
Messiah will redeem him and defeat Satan, Sin, and Death (386–435).
Michael then concludes his narrative with an account of church corruption and the persecution of Christians from which Adam and we
are to learn not classical republican and Machiavellian views on how
religion is to be used to create and sustain a healthy republic, but the
Protestant theory of limited religious toleration that Milton offers in
Of Civil Power and *On Christian Doctrine*. On the grounds of Michael's
narrative, Adam thus comes finally to know that the Son is, as Michael
says, "thy Saviour and thy Lord" (544). "Greatly instructed" (557)
Adam states what he has learned and shows that he has achieved what
Michael calls "the sum / Of wisdom" (575), but this Christian wisdom
concerning the power of weakness, meekness, and suffering has little in
common with the wisdom about war and politics the ancient pagan republicans derived from their study of history and valued so highly.
This Christian wisdom is, moreover, explicitly repudiated by Machiavelli who felt not only that the worldly strong defeated those who attempted to subvert them through weakness and suffering, but also that
those who preached this ethos, as Milton through Michael here does,
"have made the world weak, and . . . handed it over as a prey to the
wicked" (*D*, 277–78). Though Machiavelli appears to respect figures
such as Christ and St. Francis, one of the lessons of history according
to *The Prince* and the *Discourses* is that the world is a place in which one
overcomes the worldly strong and wise only by being more worldly
strong and wise than they.

It is in part because the propositions about the world Michael derives from history are so different from the ones Machiavelli and the
republicans derive from it that the way of life he recommends to Adam
and to us is also so different: "add / Deeds to thy knowledge answer-
able," he tells Adam, "add Faith, / Add Virtue, Patience, Temperance,
add Love, / By name to come call'd Charity, the soul / Of all the rest"
(12.581–85). Michael here informs Adam that in light of the human
history he has revealed to him, he is not only to know certain things
about himself and the world, but also to commit himself to a particular
way of living and looking at life which follows from this knowledge. In
so urging Adam and Eve to live in a way which accords with what they
have come to know from his revelation of history, Michael follows
through with an intention he announces to Adam at the outset when
he says that from his revelation of history, Adam is to learn not just in

the sense of coming to know, but in the sense of coming to be patient and to feel passions moderately (11.360–66).

Over the course of his observation of history, Adam does indeed take on different attitudes and commits himself to a particular kind of life in addition to achieving the sum of knowledge and wisdom. Thus, in light of his recognition that misery is just punishment but also that some kinds of suffering may be avoided by living temperately, Adam commits himself to patiently attending his dissolution (11.547–52), though he finds it difficult to sustain such an attitude in the face of what Michael later shows him. In light of the knowledge he so rapidly achieves about his posterity and its world, Adam thus also comes to adopt a particular attitude to life and a resolution to live in a way that is consistent with this knowledge and which is exemplified by men such as Enoch and Noah. In so doing, he may reasonably be seen to confirm the general republican notion that the value of history derives from the way it provides both insights into the nature of reality and in-spiring models of behavior that are appropriate to that reality. But the "deeds" to which he and other Christians are to be committed are en-tirely different from the celebrated acts of the Romans that were com-monly referred to by this word. Michael's use of it here to refer to acts of love and kindness is a quiet but aggressive Christian usurpation of the republican vocabulary, one that is also evident in the way Milton uses words such as "noble," "virtue," and "corruption" over the course of the poem. Adam's "deeds" will be different because the world as it is envisioned by Polybius, Livy, Cicero, Sallust, and Machiavelli is dif-ferent from the world as it is envisioned by Milton's second divine historian.

V

In *Paradise Lost*, then, Milton differs sharply from both classical and Renaissance republicans when it comes to the importance of Roman political, social, and military history, the importance of the history of Israel, the nature of the human subject that experiences history, the causes of this experience, the overall shape of this experience, and its meaning and value. This fact has significant consequences for the way in which Milton's poem is related to republicanism, at least where re-publicanism is understood as a tradition of thinking about politics run-ning from Aristotle to Machiavelli. For, as we have seen, most of the major texts of this tradition are either historical narratives or commentaries on them, and it may therefore reasonably be argued, as it has been by several scholars, that rather than being a tradition of political thought, republicanism is essentially a tradition of historiography. But even if we continue to think of republicanism as a coherent tradition of political thought, it seems clear that a comprehensive definition of it must include an account of the way its principal figures think about history. In light of such a definition of republicanism and the way in which Milton represents history in *Paradise Lost*, it is clear that in this poem Milton not only departs from but openly repudiates a major dimension of republican political thought.

As we observed earlier, an understanding of history is just one of several elements that have been taken to define the thinking of major figures in republican tradition. Besides a way of thinking about history, propositions about liberty, forms of government, virtue, citizenship, empire, eloquence (and how they are related to each other) have been proposed by various scholars to constitute the core of the tradition. That Milton differs from the republicans on history thus means that he differs from them on one important issue and leaves open the possibility that he conforms with them on others. But because the way in which the republicans think about history is profoundly interrelated with how they think about these other issues, those who differ from them on history must differ from them to an important extent on other issues as well. This is clearly borne out by our discussion here. We have seen in passing, for example, that though there are some similarities between them, the essentially Pauline definition of virtue in terms of patience, religious faith, temperance, hope, obedience, and love that Adam and we are to derive from the spectacle of history is in crucial ways different from classical and Machiavellian definitions of it in terms of qualities needed to be a good citizen and statesman. And though many of the observations presented here support Armitage's claim that Milton is a poet against empire, they do not support his contention that Sallust and Machiavelli, too, are opposed to empire, and that Milton's views on empire in the poem therefore confirm him as a classical republican. On the contrary, it would seem to be more reasonable to think that, as a poet against militaristic imperialism, Milton is a poet against classical republicanism. Moreover, while Milton in this poem conforms in some ways with the republicans on the issue of the forms of government, he says nothing of the mixed form of government, the affirmation of which is at the heart of the entire tradition.

Thus, while the main argument presented here is aimed at displaying how Milton differs from republican thinking about history, it also indicates that he differs from their thinking about other crucial subjects as well.

This argument does not, however, discredit the argument that the epic poet is a republican in the sense that his poetic imagination is deeply informed by mid-seventeenth-century Protestant English "republican culture," which was extremely variegated and which was influenced by a wide range of authors. Though in *Paradise Lost* Milton does not take on board the major tenets of the republican tradition of political thought, the poem is still *topical* in many ways and has considerable "political resonance" as some critics put it. But if, as Worden claims, the English republicans generally shared Machiavelli's "approach to history," and if, as Smith claims, "the preference for analytical history with associated moral and strategic comment (as in Machiavelli's *Discorsi*)" is "a hallmark of English republican thought," then it is important to see that, reflecting its "republican milieu," Milton's epic displays considerable indifference and even hostility toward it as well.[21]

Notes

1. See Mary Anne Radzinowicz, "The Politics of *Paradise Lost*," in *Politics of Discourse*, ed. Kevin Sharpe and Steven Zwicker (Berkeley: University of California Press, 1987), 204–29; Perez Zagorin, *Milton Aristocrat and Rebel: The Poet and his Politics* (Rochester: D. S. Brewer, 1992); Nigel Smith, *Literature and Revolution in England 1640–1660* (New Haven, CT: Yale University Press, 1994); Martin Dzelzainis, "Milton's Classical Republicanism," in *Milton and Republicanism*, ed. Quentin Skinner, Armand Himy, and David Armitage (Cambridge: Cambridge University Press, 1995), 3–24; David Armitage, "John Milton: Poet against Empire," in *Milton and Republicanism*, ed. Skinner, Himy, and Armitage, 206–25; Quentin Skinner, "Milton and the Politics of Slavery," in *Milton and the Terms of Liberty*, ed. Graham Parry and Joad Raymond (Cambridge: D. S. Brewer, 2002), 1–22; Peter Lindenbaum, "John Milton and the Republican Mode of Literary Production," in *Critical Essays on John Milton*, ed. Christopher Kendrick (New York: G. K. Hall, 1995), 149–64; Barbara Riebling, "Milton on Machiavelli: Representations of the State in *Paradise Lost*," *Renaissance Quarterly* 49 (1996): 573–97; John Creaser, "Prosody and Liberty in Milton and Marvell," in *Milton and the Terms of Liberty*, ed. Parry and Raymond, 37–55; David Norbrook, *Writing the English Republic: Poetry, Rhetoric and Politics, 1627–1660* (Cambridge: Cambridge University Press, 1999); Barbara Lewalski, "*Paradise Lost* and Milton's Politics," *Milton Studies* 38 (2000): 141–68; Martin Dzelzainis, "Republicanism," in *A Companion to Milton*, ed. Thomas Corns (Oxford: Blackwell, 2001), 294–308.

2. Norbrook, *Writing the English Republic*, 437.

3. Jonathan Scott, "Classical Republicanism in Seventeenth-Century England and the Netherlands," in *Republicanism: A Shared European Heritage*, ed. Martin van Gelderen and Quentin Skinner, vol. 1 (Cambridge: Cambridge University Press, 2002), 61; see also Thomas Corns, "Milton and the Characteristics of a Free Commonwealth," in *Milton and Republicanism*, ed. Skinner, Himy, and Armitage, 26–27; Paul Stevens, "Milton's 'Renunciation' of Cromwell: The Problem of Raleigh's *Cabinet-Council*," *Modern Philology* 98 (2001): 363–92; Laura Lunger Knoppers, "Late Political Prose," in *A Companion to Milton*, ed. Corns, 320; Jonathan Scott, *England's Troubles* (Cambridge: Cambridge University Press, 2000), 324–41; Gary Remer, "James Harrington's New Deliberative Rhetoric: Reflections of an Anticlassical Republicanism," *History of Political Thought* 16 (1995): 532–57; Glenn Burgess, "Repacifying the Polity: The Responses of Hobbes and Harrington to the 'Crisis of the Common Law,'" in *Soldiers, Writers and Statesmen of the English Revolution*, ed. Ian Gentles, John Morrill, and Blair Worden (Cambridge: Cambridge University Press, 1998), 202–28; Kevin Sharpe, "'An Image Doting Rabble': The Failure of Republican Culture in Seventeenth-Century England," in *Refiguring Revolutions*, ed. Kevin Sharpe and Steven Zwicker (Berkeley: University of California Press, 1998), 25–56; Paul Rahe, *Republics Ancient and Modern*, 3 vols. (1992; repr., Chapel Hill: University of North Carolina Press, 1994), and "Antiquity Surpassed: The Repudiation of Classical Republicanism," in *Republicanism, Liberty, and Commercial Society, 1649–1776*, 233–69; Paul Rahe, "The Classical Republicanism of Milton," *History of Political Thought* 25 (2004): 243–75.

4. Blair Worden, "English Republicanism," in *The Cambridge History of Political Thought 1450–1700*, ed. J. H. Burns with Mark Goldie (Cambridge: Cambridge University Press, 1991), 445–46.

5. J. G. A. Pocock, *The Machiavellian Moment* (Princeton, NJ: Princeton University Press, 1975), 3, 56, 88. See also Bruce Smith, *Politics and Remembrance* (Princeton, NJ: Princeton University Press, 1985).

6. Niccolò Machiavelli, *The Discourses*, ed. Bernard Crick, trans. Leslie J. Walker; revised by Brian Richardson (1970; repr., New York: Penguin, 1988), 98. All references to the *Discourses* (*D*) are to this edition and are cited parenthetically in the text. All references to *The Prince* (*P*) are to George Bull's translation (1961; repr., New York: Penguin, 1999), and are cited parenthetically in the text.

7. See, for example, Polybius, *The Rise of the Roman Empire*, trans. Ian Scott-Kilvert (New York: Penguin, 1979), 42, 44, 178, 302, 540–41; Lucan, *Civil War*, trans. Susan H. Braund (Oxford: Oxford University Press, 1992), 1.1–7, 67–69, 160; Cicero, *The Republic*, trans. Niall Rudd (Oxford: Oxford University Press, 1998), 38.

8. John Milton, *Paradise Lost*, in *John Milton: Complete Poems and Major Prose*, ed. Merritt Y. Hughes (New York: Odyssey, 1957). All references to *Paradise Lost* are to this edition and are cited parenthetically in the text.

9. See Nicholas von Maltzahn, *Milton's "History of Britain": Republican Historiography in the English Revolution* (Oxford: Clarendon, 1991). For the importance of patriotism in republican tradition, see Maurizio Viroli, *Machiavelli* (Oxford: Oxford University Press, 1998), 148–74. On Milton's renunciation of the national, patriotic epic he had earlier considered, see Christopher Hill, *Milton and the English Revolution* (1977; repr., New York: Penguin, 1979), 360–65; Andrew Barnaby, "'Another Rome

in the West?': Milton and the Imperial Republic, 1654–1670," *Milton Studies* 30 (1993): 67–84; Anne-Julia Zwierlein, "Pandemonic Panoramas: Surveying Milton's 'vain empires' in the Long Eighteenth Century," in *Milton and the Terms of Liberty*, ed. Parry and Raymond, 191–214.

10. On Milton's move away from his early alliance with classical notions of what was worthy of record, see Irene Samuel, "Milton and the Ancients on the Writing of History," *Milton Studies* 2 (1964): 131–48.

11. See Polybius, *The Rise of the Roman Empire*, 302–11; Cicero, *The Republic*, books 1 and 2. Though, in the preface to *The War With Catiline*, Sallust claims that "Fortune is supreme in all human affairs," and though in his later *The War With Jugurtha*, he has Sulla remark that "human destinies are controlled for the most part by Fortune" (139), this historian generally emphasizes the natural causes of the events he narrates. See *Sallust*, trans. J. C. Rolfe (1921; repr., Cambridge, MA: Harvard University Press, 2000).

12. See Felix Gilbert, *Machiavelli and Guicciardini: Politics and History in Sixteenth-Century Florence* (Princeton, NJ: Princeton University Press, 1965), 218; Peter Bondanella, *Machiavelli and the Art of Renaissance History* (Detroit, MI: Wayne State University Press, 1973), 22–24; Janet Coleman, "Machiavelli's *via moderna*: Medieval and Renaissance Attitudes to History," in *Niccolò Machiavelli's "The Prince,"* ed. Martin Coyle (Manchester: Manchester University Press, 1995), 40–64.

13. See John Rogers who, citing earlier critics, forcefully makes this point in *The Matter of Revolution: Science, Poetry, and Politics in the Age of Milton* (Ithaca, NY: Cornell University Press, 1996), 147–61.

14. For history as tragedy, see Norbrook, *Writing the English Republic*, 465–66; Lewalski, "*Paradise Lost* and Milton's Politics," 163; David Loewenstein, *Milton and the Drama of History* (Cambridge: Cambridge University Press, 1990), 92–125. For further argumentation against this view, see Marshall Grossman, *Authors to Themselves: Milton and the Revelation of History* (Cambridge: Cambridge University Press, 1987), 165.

15. See H. R. MacCallum, "Milton and Sacred History: Books XI and XII of *Paradise Lost*," in *Essays in English Literature from the Renaissance to the Victorian Age*, ed. Millar MacLure and F. W. Watt (Toronto: University of Toronto Press, 1964), 149–68; Edward W. Tayler, *Milton's Poetry: Its Development in Time* (Pittsburgh, PA: Duquesne University Press, 1979), 71; Loewenstein, *Milton and the Drama of History*, 96.

16. See Stanley Fish, "Transmuting the Lump: *Paradise Lost*, 1942–1979," in *Doing What Comes Naturally* (Durham, NC: Duke University Press, 1989), 247–93; Regina Schwartz, "From Shadowy Types to Shadowy Types: The Unendings of *Paradise Lost*," *Milton Studies* 24 (1988): 123–39; William Walker, "Typology and *Paradise Lost*, Books XI and XII," *Milton Studies* 25 (1989): 245–64; Loewenstein, *Milton and the Drama of History*, 120–25.

17. Erich Auerbach, *Mimesis*, trans. Willard Trask (1953; repr., New York: Anchor, 1957), 64–65.

18. See Isabel McCaffrey, *"Paradise Lost" as "Myth"* (Cambridge, MA: Harvard University Press, 1959), 61; H. R. MacCallum, "Milton and Sacred History," 167–68; Stanley Fish, *Surprised by Sin* (1967; repr., London: MacMillan, 1997), 310, 322.

19. See, for example, Steven Zwicker, "Lines of Authority: Politics and Literary Culture in the Restoration," in *Politics of Discourse*, ed. Sharpe and Zwicker, 256–59.

20. Mary Anne Radzinowicz, "The Politics of *Paradise Lost*," 213.

21.Worden, "English Republicanism," in *Cambridge History*, ed. Burns, 464; Smith, *Literature and Revolution in England*, 339.

The "Legend of Holinesse" and the Fall of Man: Spenser's *Faerie Queene* 1 as Milton's Original for *Paradise Lost* 9 and 10

Christopher Bond

IN *THE REASON OF CHURCH GOVERNMENT*, MILTON RECALLED HIS YOUTHFUL musings over the nature of his projected epic, and in particular the question of "what K[ing] or Knight before the conquest might be chosen in whom to lay the pattern of a Christian Heroe" (1:813).[1] Of course, when *Paradise Lost* came to be written, his plans turned out rather differently. An obvious candidate for this heroic role—Prince Arthur, Christian and patriot—had already been used by Edmund Spenser, and Milton openly eschewed "fabled knights / In battles feigned," not to mention kings (9.30–31).[2] In his poetic maturity, Milton seemed at pains to distance himself from the old-fashioned, aristocratic milieu of his great precursor: the "Knights and Ladies gentle deeds" and "Fierce warres and faithfull loves" of Spenser's song (1 Proem 1.5, 9).[3] But this reconsideration of Miltonic heroism returns to *The Faerie Queene* to explore the importance for Milton of the poem's didactic purpose and its use of heroic exemplarity. The depiction of "the pattern of a Christian Heroe" and Spenser's earlier version of it were still crucial to Milton's poetic design.

Notwithstanding Milton's desire to cast off the antiquated trappings and belligerent heroism of *The Faerie Queene*, the strength of his literary relationship to Spenser has scarcely been in doubt.[4] In *Areopagitica*, Milton himself declared "our sage and serious poet Spencer" to be "a better teacher than Scotus or Aquinas" (2:516), and Dryden claimed that "Milton had acknowledged to me, that Spenser was his original."[5] More recently Harold Bloom has stated that Spenser's "actual influence on *Paradise Lost* is deeper, subtler and more extensive than scholarship has so far recognized."[6] But the copious body of Spenser-and-Milton criticism has tended to concentrate on general discussions of Milton's use of Spenserian language, or of the reworking of individual Spenserian scenes and images.[7] Critics have paid comparatively little attention to questions of character and structure, and in one sense it is easy to see why. While the plot of *The Faerie Queene* is episodic, that of *Paradise Lost* is linear, and while Spenser introduces a large number of characters over the course of his sprawling masterpiece, Milton's cast is kept small—a feature that attests to his original conception of the epic as a tragic drama.[8] This essay will, however, suggest a broader conceptual debt to Spenser in the structure and characterization of *Paradise Lost* and in particular demonstrate the importance of book 1 of *The Faerie Queene*—"The Legend of the Knight of the Red Crosse, or of Holinesse"—to a reading of the later books of *Paradise Lost*.

Spenser's project was "to fashion a gentleman or noble person in vertuous and gentle discipline": that is, to present a model of Christian heroism through the action and characterization of his epic ("Letter to Raleigh," *Faerie Queene*, 714). (Again, one might say "the pattern of a Christian Heroe.") In order to analyze and define this notion of perfect heroism, Spenser took a number of minor heroes and described the faltering and painful progress of each one toward the acquisition of a particular quality. These figures—Red Crosse, Guyon, Artegall—undergo a sequence of adventures designed to develop and test that virtue. Each book has its own knight and its own moral ideal, and the action of the book is essentially the action of the knight. We as readers identify with their human fallibility, and we learn with them as we watch their errors and successes. These characters are instructive by their very imperfections, and it is these imperfections that engage our interest.

At some stage of their quests, however, each of these knights encounters the very different figure of Arthur. According to Spenser's "Letter to Raleigh," Arthur represents "magnificence in particular," the Aristotelan virtue that "is the perfection of all the rest, and conteineth in it them all" (*Faerie Queene*, 716). The Prince is not perfect, but he still seems to have attained in large part the qualities that the lesser heroes struggle so hard to learn.[9] This less fallible hero is also a composite hero. He appears in each book and displays a number of different virtues: he thereby serves as an integrating factor in Spenser's episodic design. In this sense he could be said to dominate the poem, but he still comes across as an oddly shadowy, removed, and rather inhuman figure. His appearances are often fleeting and are mostly limited to apocalyptic victories, such as that over Maleger in book 2, or to providential interventions to solve the mistakes of the other, lesser heroes. He does not generate plot in the way that each knight does with his individual quest, nor does he demonstrate their weaknesses. In short, there is a certain lack of human interest: an Aristotelean moral concept is an odd hero for a poem.

So there are in *The Faerie Queene* two levels of heroism: one fallible, human, engaged and supplicant, and the other more perfect, less human, detached and interventionist.[10] Strong elements of this broad structure of characterization persist in *Paradise Lost* in the persons of Adam and the Son. Adam may be "the goodliest man of men since born / His sons" (4.323–24), but the entire plot of the epic is dependent on his all-too-human fallibility. We see much of Adam, and we are told much about his weaknesses. His flawed actions provoke the crucial event of the poem and place him in a situation in which he is unable to act independently.

Adam's fall necessitates the intervention of the Son, who, like Arthur, remains in the background for much of the poem and appears only at such moments of crisis as a representative of God's judgment and forgiving grace. Just as Arthur's quest for the Faerie Queene serves as the organizing principle of Spenser's poem, so the career of the Son forms the wider story that lies behind the action of *Paradise Lost*. His own creation, the War in Heaven, his creation of the world, his descent to Eden, and his anticipated Incarnation all extend the scope of the poem beyond the events in the Garden, but the Son's direct involvement in the plot nonetheless feels curiously small compared to Adam's. Like Spenser's Arthur, he fails to engage our interest in the way that the more flawed heroes do.[11] Having outlined these two heroic types, we may look in more detail at the ways in which Milton borrowed and reshaped these basic Spenserian models, concentrating on book 1 of *The Faerie Queene*, where biblical influence—particularly of the Book of Genesis—is strongest, and on books 9 and 10 of *Paradise Lost*, where the human characters most firmly command our attention.

As James C. Nohrnberg has shown, in creating Red Crosse Spenser looked back to the medieval tradition of the Holy Fool, a saintly but

simple Christian Everyman, a tradition that included the biblical Adam.[12]
In canto 10 of book 1, Red Crosse meets Contemplation, a character
who reveals to him his true identity and describes his childhood history. After he was stolen from his parents by an elf, he is told:

> Thence she thee brought into this Faery lond,
>   And in an heaped furrow did thee hyde,
>   Where thee a Ploughman all unweeting fond,
> As he his toylesome teme that way did guyde,
> And brought thee up in ploughmans state to byde,
> Whereof Georgos he thee gave to name.
>
> (1.10.66.1–6)

By identifying the Knight in this way, Spenser is, of course, nominat-
ing him as George, the national saint of England. But Contemplation
has previously addressed the Knight as "thou man of earth" (1.10.52.2),
and he is here also identifying him with the Greek word *georgos* ("a
tiller of earth") and its root *ge* (simply, "earth") and associating him
with a mysterious ploughman. The accepted etymology of "Adam" was
from the Hebrew word for "red"—the color of the clay from which he
was formed. The derivation of mankind from the soil is supported by
two biblical references: "The Lord God also made the man of the dust
of the grounde" (Gen. 2:7) and "The first man *is* of the earth, earthlie"
(1 Cor. 15:47).[13]

The association with the ploughman reinforces this characterization: Adam was, of course, the first tiller of the soil. But it also alludes
to the English work that stood behind Spenser as he wrote his own religious epic: Langland's *Piers Plowman*. We thus also see a connection
between George and the Dreamer, Will, of the earlier poem.[14] They
are both examples of the well-meaning but at times bewildered and
erring figure of the Christian Everyman, who takes many wrong turns
on his journey toward truth and salvation and who tends to ignore or
misinterpret the guidance of others—for example, Red Crosse's liaison
with Duessa after his warning from Fraudubio in canto 2. Spenser's
"Letter to Raleigh" reinforces this identification. George is described
as "a tall clownishe younge man," a figure of rather foolish and rustic
aspect (*Faerie Queene*, 717). But his first appearance, "Y cladd in
mightie armes and silver shield" bearing "on his brest a bloodie
Crosse" is explicitly defined as "the armour of a Christian man speci-
fied by Saint Paul v. Ephes" (1.1.1.2, 2.1, "Letter to Raleigh," *Faerie
Queene*, 717).[15] The Knight is thus at once holy man and fool, hero and

saint—an amalgam of which the biblical Adam was taken as the paradigm.

Milton's Adam is a character firmly in this tradition. His innate
goodness is scarcely in doubt, but his judgment is flawed, his reasoning, at least after Eve's fall, often deeply confused, and his inability to
accept advice or admonition a major cause of his predicament. Without imagining that Milton in any way simplistically based his character
on Spenser's, we can see Red Crosse and, at a greater distance, Langland's Dreamer standing behind the human hero of *Paradise Lost*.[16] The
corresponding analogy between Piers and Arthur should also be noted.
Both function as exemplary figures who operate in a space between the
human and the divine and whose contact with Will and Red Crosse,
though fleeting and enigmatic, is crucial to the plot and to the development of these flawed, aspirant characters.[17]

The extent to which Milton used elements of the Knight as a prototype for Adam is perhaps most apparent in the extraordinary emotional
range displayed by both characters in the course of their degradation
and redemption. Spenser's initial description of Red Crosse alerts us to
how difficult it will be for the Knight to control his passions:

> Yet armes till that time did he never wield:
> His angry steede did chide his foming bitt,
> As much disdayning to the curbe to yield.
>   (1.1.1.5–7)

His impressive martial gear only emphasizes the inexperience and
naiveté of the wearer, and his inability to manage his steed anticipates
the wildness of the emotions he will go on to display. Soon enough, he
and Una are lost in a "shadie grove," in which they "wander too and fro
in waies unknowne" (1.1.7.2, 10.5). After his encounter with the monster Error—the prototype for Milton's Sin, that is "Halfe like a serpent
horribly displaide, / But th'other halfe did womans shape retaine"—he
rarely seems to escape this state of moral confusion (1.1.14.7–8).
Spenser represents his various and violent emotions over the course of
the book by describing his encounters with different allegorical figures
that typify the negative sides of his character—the wrathful Sansloy,
Orgoglio, the embodiment of pride, or the representative of the opposite extreme, the "man of hell, that calls himselfe Despayre" (1.9.28.5).
In canto 9, only the entreaties of Una prevent his suicide, and even
after the providential intervention of Arthur, Red Crosse is acutely vulnerable.

The psychological pattern that Spenser's hero displays—naiveté, error, wild emotion, pride, self-blame, despair, the contemplation of suicide—is remarkably close to that displayed by Milton's Adam. Just like Red Crosse, he becomes divided against himself, appearing in the depth of his misery "estranged in look and altered style" (9.1132). After the Fall, his own encounter with an error that is both serpentine and female, Adam appears with Eve in a condition of great emotional volatility and distress. Milton lists their "high passions" as "anger, hate, / Mistrust, suspicion, discord," that "shook sore / Their inward state of mind" (9.1123–25). A similar catalogue describes the pair as they appear before the Son at 10.111–14. Of these passions, the anger of Sansloy is powerful, but for Adam, despair takes a stronger hold.

He desires to cut himself off from the opportunity of salvation by hiding from "those heavenly shapes" who will "dazzle now this earthly, with their blaze / Insufferably bright" (9.1082–84) and seeks refuge in a darkened wood, Milton's version of Error's home in Spenser.[18] When the passages are placed side by side we may see the closeness of the parallel. Spenser writes of Red Crosse and Una:

> A shadie grove not farr away they spide,
> That promist ayde the tempest to withstand:
> Whose loftie trees yclad with sommers pride,
> Did spred so broad, that heavens light did hide,
> Not perceable with power of any starr.
>
> (1.1.7.2–6)

Milton's description of Adam's desired hiding place repeats all the key details: the shade, the height and breadth of the trees, and the lack of star-light:

> some glade
> Obscured, where highest woods impenetrable
> To star or sunlight, spread their umbrage broad
> And brown as evening.
>
> (9.1085–88)[19]

In the next book we hear Adam's self-denunciation and longing for death. Just as Arthur's appearance could not prevent Red Crosse's susceptibility to Despayre, Adam, even after the intervention of the Son, indulges in the Knight's excessive consciousness of his own errors. By berating himself as "To Satan only like both crime and doom" (10.841), he takes as his model the definitive "man of Hell."

Having seen how Milton follows the psychological pattern of Spenser's Red Crosse in his characterization of Adam, we should next compare Milton's Eve with the composite Una/Duessa figure of *The Faerie Queene*. It is crucial to consider this pair as two halves of a whole, or as positive and negative types of femininity. Una is wholly good and Duessa wholly evil, and they are types rather than a more developed and ambiguous creation like Eve. But elements of the two types are deliberately present in Milton's heroine, and just as we should recognize Red Crosse behind Adam, so too should we understand Una and Duessa as aspects of the character of his wife. This comparison is strengthened by Spenser's association of his heroine with the biblical Eve, an association that corresponds with his identification of Red Crosse with the biblical Adam. Broadly put, before her fall, Eve is mostly like Una.[20] After the Fall, and before her reconciliation with Adam, she is mostly like Duessa.[21] Early in book 9, Adam emphasizes her one-ness and their indivisibility by addressing her as "Sole Eve, associate sole" (9.227). Una—the "One" of *The Faerie Queene*—first appears as the Knight's associate, but trust soon breaks down between both couples and two disastrous separations result.

Once Archimago has gulled Red Crosse into thinking Una unchaste by showing her false image copulating with another sprite, the Knight's faith in her is broken, and he abandons her. In her place, the whore Duessa appears, seduces the Knight, and precipitates his lapse into the pride that ends in despair. A comparison of the relationship between Adam and Eve with this story shows Milton placing a similar importance on the dangers of division. Archimago, after he has driven Red Crosse away from Una, delights in seeing "his guests . . . divided into double parts," and when Eve proposes that they divide their labors, Adam expresses a justifiable fear of an enemy "somewhere nigh at hand" who "Watches, no doubt, with greedy hope to find / His wish and best advantage, us asunder" (1.2.9.1–2; 9.256–58). Just as Red Crosse is most vulnerable when apart from Una, so Satan's opportunity comes when Eve "from her husband's hand her hand / Soft she withdrew" (9.385–86).

Once Eve goes her own way, she submits to a verbal seduction by Satan that parallels the supposed sexual seduction of the false Una by the sprite. The successful temptation of Eve by Satan is also meant to be read in sexual terms, as the two meet in the fashion of characters from a *pastourelle*, a lustful knight, and a willing maiden (9.445–54).

She then herself seduces Adam first verbally—he is "fondly overcome with female charm" (9.999)—and then sexually. The first response of the couple to the Fall is violent sexual arousal, but after they make love, Adam is quick to denounce his wife, whose apparent goodness he claims that he "understood not all was but a show / Rather than solid virtue" (10.883–84). Unfair as this charge may be, it is still true enough that the Eve he parted from so unwillingly was not the same Eve who returned after her fall. Milton thus makes Adam reminiscent of Red Crosse, who is genuinely deceived by the substitution of Una by a debased version to whom virtue is indeed nothing and show everything. The Una/Duessa dichotomy and the Knight's confusion are residual in the profound change that Eve suffers after she is "deflowered" (9.901) —Adam's word—by Satan and in her husband's bewildered response to two contrasting sides of femininity.

A comparison of the two seduction scenes that mark the hero's fall into error shows the importance of Spenser for Milton's depiction of Adam's relations with the fallen Eve. Duessa appears to Red Crosse with a fair greeting, but then upbraids him "with reproch of carelesnes unkind . . . for leaving her in place unmeet, / With fowle words tempring faire, soure gall with hony sweet" (1.7.3.6–9). Eve approaches Adam with the same combination of sulky resentment and flirtatious devotion:

> To him she hasted, in her face excuse
> Came prologue, and apology to prompt,
> Which with bland words at will she thus addressed.
>   Hast thou not wondered, Adam, at my stay?
> Thee I have missed, and thought it long, deprived
> Thy presence.
>
> (9.853–58)

The two couples retire to make love in similarly shaded and flower-strewn locations. In Spenser, Red Crosse and Duessa:

> bathe in pleasaunce of the ioyous shade,
> Which shielded them against the boyling heat,
> And with greene boughes decking a gloomy glade,
> About the fountaine like a girlond made.
>
> (1.7.4.2–5)

Milton has Adam take Eve by the hand:

and to a shady bank,
Thick overhead with verdant roof embowered
He led her nothing loth; flowers were the couch.
(9.1037–39)

Compared to love making before the Fall, postlapsarian sex is enervating and causes a kind of unsatisfied hangover. Adam and Eve burn in lust (9.1015) and what begins with mere "Carnal desire" (1013) ends with the oppressiveness of a "grosser sleep / Bred of unkindly fumes" (1049–50). The physically debilitating and morally degenerative effects of sex correspond to those suffered by Red Crosse after intercourse with Duessa: "both carelesse of his health, and of his fame," the Knight lies with her, "pourd out in looseness on the grassy grownd," as "his manly forces gan to fayle, / And mightie strong was turnd to feeble frayle" (1.7.7.3, 2, 6.4–5).

In both *The Faerie Queene* and in *Paradise Lost*, these sexual lapses by flawed Everyman figures prompt the intervention of the poems' more perfect, elevated heroes, and the interventions of Arthur and the Son serve to emphasize the fallibility of the more human characters. As Spenser's Knight is like the biblical Adam, and his Una like the biblical Eve, so his Arthur is at times deliberately Christlike. He first appears in canto 7 in response to the Knight's fall, and the anticipation at stanza 36 that his virtue will live on for his people even after his death at once identifies him with Christ. His rescue of the Knight from Orgoglio's dungeon in canto 8 is analogous to Christ's Harrowing of Hell, and in the first stanza he is associated with "heavenly grace" and "deliverance" (1.8.3, 9), an association that is repeated in the opening stanza of canto 9, shortly before his departure from book 1.

After the Fall, Milton's God the Father sends the Son to the Garden, in his role as "Man's friend, his mediator, his designed / Both ransom and redeemer voluntary" (10.60–62). There he delivers the inevitable punishment, but tempers the sentence by aid and mercy and "intercession sweet" (228):

So judged he man, both judge and saviour sent,
And the instant stroke of death denounced that day
Removed far off.

(209–11)

Milton anticipates the Incarnation as Christ's appearance as a man among men, stresses his restorative function, and shows the Son break-

ing a spiritual impasse in the career of the lesser hero. Like Arthur in
The Faerie Queene, his role in the action is brief but crucial, and it provides the reader with a direct comparison of the two heroic types used
by both poets. We see side by side the human example, who instructs us
by his error, and the divine or quasi-divine model, who instructs us by
his perfection. Just as the aspirant knight, Red Crosse, meets in Arthur
"the image of a brave knight, perfected in the twelve private morall
vertues," so too the first man, Adam, meets in this scene the "greater
man," who will "Restore us, and regain the blissful seat" ("Letter to
Raleigh," *Faerie Queene*, 715; *Paradise Lost*, 1.4–5).[22]

A comparison of these episodes demonstrates the theological distinctions that Milton drew between himself and his precursor in terms
of the kinds of mercy and grace represented by Arthur and the Son, and
of the models of Christian redemption and education represented by
Red Crosse and Adam. The rescues of the lesser by the greater heroes
are the crucial moments at which we see, in theological terms, the extension of divine grace to man, and in terms of the didactic technique
of these poems, the exemplar and the novice side by side, each measur-
able by the other (*Faerie Queene*, 1.8.2–45; *Paradise Lost*, 10.1–223).

For Spenser, the grace represented by Arthur may be understood in
Calvinist terms as a violent, irresistible moment of change. Grace over-
whelms the sinner with a force that he neither seeks nor is able to engage with, as Arthur rends the iron door of Orgoglio's dungeon and enters "with furious force, and indignation fell" (1.8.39.5–6). For the
Arminian Milton, grace comes in the form of a conversation with God:
a process of warning, instruction, and encouragement, which is prayed
for and which allows change through education and self-healing (10.1–
223, 10.1010-11.71).[23] Subsequently, Red Crosse's journey to the belief
that God does care for him—via his restorative sojourn in the House of
Holinesse and his refreshment by the Well of Life and the Tree of
Life—is longer, more painful, and, most importantly, less independent
than Adam's. We overhear Adam learning—from the Son, from Eve,
and from himself—and hence we learn with him as witnesses to the
process by which "To better hopes his more attentive mind / Labour-
ing had raised" (10.1011–12). Spenser allows Red Crosse no such interiority, and Arthur's symbolic embodiment of grace shows us only the
broader outlines of his redemptive scheme.

The role of pride in the falls of Red Crosse and Adam is a second
principal point of difference between Spenser's and Milton's treatments
of the secondary hero. Red Crosse's infatuation with Duessa leads to

his imprisonment by Orgoglio, representative of his own pride, and in the opening stanza of canto 8, Spenser explicitly blames the "foolish pride" of Red Crosse for his fall into "sinfull bands" that requires him to be saved by the "heavenly grace" and "stedfast truth" brought by Arthur (1.7.8–15, 1.8.1). Adam's infatuation with Eve reveals in contrast his apparent lack of self-esteem; it is Eve's pride and his dependency that cause their fall. As she eats the fruit, we are told that "nor was godhead from her thought" (9.790), and when she reports her crime, Adam concludes that he has no choice but to follow his wife, since "to lose thee were to lose my self" (959).[24] Arthur's intervention to save Red Crosse from his own pride tips him over into despair, from which Una must rescue him in turn; likewise, Eve's love for Adam pulls him out of his postlapsarian despair (1.9.52–53; 10.909–46).[25]

But Milton emphasizes Adam's ability, once he has received grace, to piece together with Eve the meaning of the Son's oracle and hence to understand that God does love his creation, however flawed. His speech to her at 10.1013–96 is punctuated throughout by the diction of careful and rational thought: "doubt not but God / Hath wiselier . . . let us seek / Some safer resolution, which methinks / I have in view, calling to mind with heed . . . whom I conjecture . . . What better can we do."[26] This Arminian notion that all humans are offered sufficient grace to make their own way toward holiness led Milton to depart at this crucial juncture from the structural pattern he had largely followed. He thus stresses his doctrinal difference from Spenser, who begins the "redemptive" canto 8 with an apparent affirmation of the Calvinist conception of mankind as being unable to work toward its own salvation, and as an otherwise entirely helpless beneficiary of divine intervention.

This deliberate modification in *Paradise Lost* of the theology of the "Legend of Holinesse" nicely encapsulates the vexed relationship between Milton and his poetic and religious teacher. Harold Bloom has written of Milton's attempt to subsume his literary forebears within his own epic and to establish its primacy over the work of his chronological predecessors. The biblical influence on *The Faerie Queene* is probably strongest in book 1, and, as we have seen, Spenser's Red Crosse is already a figure for the biblical Adam, as Una is for the biblical Eve. By going back to Genesis and directly rewriting these figures according to his own conception, Milton does indeed assert his own primacy. He makes Spenser seem derivative and himself original.[27]

By incorporating Red Crosse into his Adam, however, Milton achieves far more than just a suppression of anxiety over his own belatedness. Although we admire the exemplary figures of Arthur and the Son, we identify with the more fallible characters of the Knight and Adam. We are sympathetic to Red Crosse's confusion and emotional volatility, and by having Adam repeat much of this behavior, Milton adds greater human interest to his own hero. Milton's conception of heroism—that it must include the error and humiliation that instruct the hero in Christian virtue—is remarkably close to Spenser's notion of a Knight who, in order to educate the reader in a particular virtue, must show us how hard that virtue is to attain.

Critics have sometimes disqualified Adam from heroism on the grounds of his supposed "failure" and have regarded *Paradise Lost* as a "negative" work, because Satan achieves his object and man is expelled from Paradise.[28] But by making Adam like Red Crosse and the Son like Arthur, Milton reinforces the "positive" nature of his poem by anticipating the inevitable triumph of God and man over evil. Just as Milton constantly reminds the reader of the eventual victory of Christ, so Spenser reminds us of the coming kingship of Arthur, and ends book 1 on a high note, as the spiritually and physically healed Red Crosse defeats the dragon and liberates Una's parents. His vision of the New Jerusalem from Mount Contemplation, "Wherein eternall peace and happinesse doth dwell," is, of course, the ancestor of Adam's vision that concludes in "joy and eternal bliss" (1.10.55.9; 12.551). Both poets use the redemption of mankind through Christ and the sacraments of his church as the necessary counterbalance to the misfortunes and despair of their heroes. Adam's speech to Michael (12.561–73) acknowledges that he has learned the lessons for the individual from the archangel's description of Christian history. *Paradise Lost* is thus an account of Adam's progress towards becoming a true Christian just as "The Legend of Holinesse" is an account of the Knight's difficult, but ultimately successful, struggle to acquire that essential virtue.[29] Because Spenser shows us this redemption so explicitly at the end of book 1, Milton is able to use the optimistic conclusion to the story of Red Crosse as a redeeming backdrop both to the career of his own Christian hero and to his poem as a whole.

NOTES

I am grateful to Professors David Quint and John Rogers of Yale University for their help in the preparation of this essay.

1. John Milton, *The Reason of Church Government*, in *Complete Prose Works*, 8 vols., ed. Don M. Wolfe et al. (New Haven, CT: Yale University Press, 1953–82). All references to Milton's prose are to this edition and are cited parenthetically in the text.

2. John Milton, *Paradise Lost*, ed. Alastair Fowler, 2nd ed. (New York: Longman, 1998). All references to *Paradise Lost* are to this edition and are cited parenthetically in the text.

3. Edmund Spenser, *The Faerie Queene*, ed. A.C. Hamilton, 2nd ed. (New York: Longman, 2001). All references to *The Faerie Queene* are to this edition and are cited parenthetically in the text.

4. For a dissenting voice, see Annabel Patterson, "Couples, Canons, and the Uncouth: Spenser-and-Milton in Educational Theory," *Critical Inquiry* 16 (1990): 773–93.

5. John Dryden, "Preface to *Fables, Ancient and Modern*," in *Essays*, vol. 2, ed. W. P. Ker (Oxford: Clarendon, 1900), 247.

6. Harold Bloom, *A Map of Misreading* (Oxford: Oxford University Press, 1975), 125. One scholar who has attempted to look further is Sung-Kyun Yim, " 'Redcross' and 'Adam': Christian Humanism in Spenser and Milton," *Journal of English Language and Literature* 48 (2002): 149–68. Unfortunately for the present writer, this article is only available in Korean. I have, however, read an English abstract, from which it is plain that Yim's project—"to compare the two heroes, or more appropriately the two protagonists . . . portrayed in the two representative epics of the English Renaissance" (168)—partially anticipates my own.

7. Perhaps the most common such approach is to relate the temptation narratives of both *Paradise Lost* and *Paradise Regained* to the episode in which Spenser's Guyon visits the House of Mammon. See Maureen Quilligan, *Milton's Spenser: The Politics of Reading* (Ithaca, NY: Cornell University Press, 1985), 46–78; Patrick Cullen, *Infernal Triad: The Flesh, the World, and the Devil in Spenser and Milton* (Princeton, NJ: Princeton University Press, 1974), 174–81; and A. Kent Hieatt, *Chaucer, Spenser, Milton: Mythopoeic Continuities and Transformations* (McGill: Queen's University Press, 1975), 215–45.

8. See Quilligan, *Milton's Spenser*, 44: the later work has a "plot of Vergilian sinuosity" with its " 'single' action," while "utterly opposite to the shape of *The Faerie Queene* are the formal proportions of *Paradise Lost*. Set next to Spenser's poem, Milton's epic does have the slender clarity of classical sculpture, which by contrast makes *The Faerie Queene* look authentically gothic."

9. Arthur's principal weakness is his lovesickness for the Faerie Queene. His admission of hopelessness at 1.9.8–16 is quickly followed by a warning against the ultimate danger of such a disposition to despair in the story of the lovelorn and suicidal Sir Terwin (1.9.27–30). The wounds Arthur receives from the lustful Cymochles in the *psychomachia* of 2.8.31–39 further indicate his own trait of concupiscence, as does his thoughtless pursuit of Florimell at 3.1.18–19.

10. The most important modern study of dual heroism, Thomas M. Greene, *The Descent from Heaven: A Study in Epic Continuity* (New Haven, CT: Yale University Press, 1963), bases its analysis of the primary, "deliberative" hero (like Agamemnon or Goffredo) and the secondary, "executive" hero (like Achilles or Rinaldo) on Tasso's preface to the *Gerusalemme liberata*, "The Allegory of the Poem." Greene also considers Milton's God and Adam to fit into the Agamemnon/Achilles pattern (19). This paradigm has shown me how the secondary hero learns from the example of the

primary hero, but this essay, in contrast to Greene's work, will focus principally on the actions of the more removed heroes and on the contemplative nature of the more involved heroes: on the direct interventions in the plot by Arthur and the Son that provide the turning points of *The Faerie Queene* and *Paradise Lost* and on the moral and psychological development of Red Crosse and Adam that provide the reader with lively and instructive examples of human error.

11. The existence of two heroes in *Paradise Lost* who are different in kind, not merely in degree, has, of course, given considerable mileage to the question of who, if anyone, is the hero of the poem. This matter is discussed at length in John M. Steadman, *Milton and the Paradoxes of Renaissance Heroism* (Baton Rouge: Louisiana State University Press, 1987), 19–41. He quotes Addison's famous judgment that in *Paradise Lost* "it is certainly the Messiah who is the hero, both in the principal action, and in the chief episodes" (26), but contradicts it with his own opinion that "the central action is man's own action, and the epic person or principal hero is man himself—Adam as progenitor and type of the human race. Satan and the Son, on the other hand, are essentially machining persons, and in the strictest sense neither of them can be regarded as a hero" (29). It is striking that these comments could be as easily made of Arthur, who while being crucial to both individual incidents and to the overall structure of the poem, certainly feels like a "machining person," and of Red Crosse, whose numerous imperfections make him in a certain sense less heroic, but unquestionably more human.

12. See James C. Nohrnberg, *The Analogy of "The Faerie Queene"* (Princeton, NJ: Princeton University Press, 1976), 261–62: "It is not uncommonly asserted that Redcrosse is an everyman, and indeed his links to Adam have been shown . . . his naiveté, his susceptibility to deception, his stumbling and humiliation, all suggest his type . . . the high fool, or saintly *simplicissimus*, is a character on whom much depends, who nevertheless does not know well what he is about or who he is. . . . There is a sense in which Adam is the prototype for such a high fool, for he is in this world, but not of it, and he has failed to ask the questions upon which all has depended."

13. I refer to the Geneva Bible of 1560. See John Hankins, *Source and Meaning in Spenser's Allegory: A Study of "The Faerie Queene"* (Oxford: Clarendon Press, 1971), 116.

14. See Leslie-Anne Crowley, *The Quest for Holiness: Spenser's Debt to Langland* (Milan: Arcipelago Edizioni, 1992). Crowley correctly observes that the reader learns with the Dreamer and Red Crosse as they develop, but fails to note that, just as the Dreamer develops by aspiring to become like Piers, so Red Crosse develops by aspiring to the example of Arthur. The functions of example (Piers) and intermediary (Will) are not collapsed by Spenser into the single figure of Red Crosse, as she suggests, but are rather kept distinct in the persons of Arthur and Red Crosse (49–51).

15. For a discussion of the representation in these opening stanzas of the duality of mankind, see Cullen, *Infernal Triad*, 22–24.

16. The comparison with Red Crosse is suggested, but not developed, by John M. Steadman, *Moral Fiction in Milton and Spenser* (Columbia: University of Missouri Press, 1995), 143. For evidence that Milton knew Langland's poem, see Jackson Campbell Boswell, *Milton's Library: A Catalogue of the Remains of John Milton's Library and An Annotated Reconstruction of Milton's Library and Ancillary Readings* (New York: Garland, 1975), 152.

17. See Judith H. Anderson, *The Growth of a Personal Voice: "Piers Plowman" and "The Faerie Queene"* (New Haven, CT: Yale University Press, 1976), 159: Arthur, like Piers, is an "important, evolving figure . . . a complex symbol with theological dimensions" who is at times Christlike. Anderson's discussion of this analogy is largely focused, however, on books 5 and 6 of *The Faerie Queene*.

18. The contrast again reminds the reader of Paul's words of 1 Corinthians 15:47.

19. The parallel is noted in *Spenser Allusions in the Sixteenth and Seventeenth Centuries*, ed. William Wells et al. (Chapel Hill: University of North Carolina Press, 1972), 259.

20. But see also Eve's apparent vanity as she sees herself reflected in the pool at 4.449–67.

21. See Nohrnberg, *Analogy*, 228–39, for the similarity between Duessa and Lilith, Adam's legendary first wife and a demonic, deceiving "false Eve."

22. Ibid., 36. Nohrnberg describes each knight's encounter with Arthur as "a kind of 'golden intersection' of each protagonist with his greater self," a phrase not inappropriate to the meeting of Adam and the Son. He also relates Arthur and his twelve knights to Christ and his twelve apostles (39).

23. The precise nature of Spenser's doctrinal convictions is obscure and controversial. More thorough investigation lies outside the scope of the present essay, but valuable discussions of recent decades include Daniel W. Doerksen, " 'All the Good is God's': Predestination in Spenser's *Faerie Queene*, Book I," *Christianity and Literature* 32 (1983): 11–18; James Schiavoni, "Predestination and Free Will: The Crux of Canto Ten," *Spenser Studies* 10 (1992): 175–95; Darryl J. Gless, *Interpretation and Theology in Spenser* (Cambridge: Cambridge University Press, 1994); and Carol V. Kaske, *Spenser and Biblical Poetics* (Ithaca, NY: Cornell University Press, 1999). Critical opinion likewise differs over the question of whether Adam's desire to reform is prompted by the "Prevenient grace" of God (11.3), or whether it precedes and hence invites it. For the former view, see Jackson Campbell Boswell, "Milton and Prevenient Grace," *Studies in English Literature* 7 (1967): 83–94; for the latter, see Dick Taylor, "Grace as a Means of Poetry: Milton's Pattern for Salvation," *Tulane Studies in English* 4 (1954): 57–90.

24. But see also Adam's admission of his vain pleasure at seeing "my self / Before me" in the face of the newly created Eve (8.495–96).

25. For the importance of Eve's conversation with Adam in his "discovery of self," see Jun Harada, "The Mechanism of Human Reconciliation in *Paradise Lost*," *Philological Quarterly* 50 (1971): 552: "though two divided characters participate in the process, their action achieves a new and perfect wholeness."

26. See Gerald J. Schiffhorst, "Patience and the Education of Adam in *Paradise Lost*," *South Atlantic Review* 49 (1984): 60: "Adam's intellectual, moral and emotional fulfillment—and the reader's share in his fulfillment—is made possible by Adam's free, positive response to adversity and by the supernatural strength of Christ's perfect patience which makes that response possible."

27. See Bloom, *A Map of Misreading*, 131, 142: "Milton's aim is to make his own belatedness into an earliness, and his tradition's priority over him a lateness. . . . The precursors return in Milton, but only at his will, and they return to be corrected."

28. See John Dryden, "Dedication to the *Aeneis*," in *Essays*, vol. 2, ed. Ker, 165: Milton's poem would have ranked with those of Homer, Virgil, and Tasso, "if the Devil had not been his hero, instead of Adam; if the giant had not foiled the knight,

and driven him out of his stronghold, to wander through the world with his lady errant." It is interesting to note Dryden's treatment of *Paradise Lost* as if it were a
chivalric romance, and his implicit connection between the end of Milton's poem
and the opening of *The Faerie Queene*. Steadman, *Paradoxes*, 29–30, points out the
common pattern in epic of fall, followed by redemption, and cites the career of Red
Crosse. His argument, however, that Adam cannot be said to have succeeded at the
end of *Paradise Lost* should not obscure the crucial point that, although he will himself have to leave Paradise, mankind, of whom he is a representative, ultimately will
regain it through Christ.

29. See Nohrnberg, *Analogy*, 178: "Spenser's legend extends from the paradise lost
by Adam to the paradise regained by the Messiah, who is a second Adam." Peter E.
Medine believes, however, that Milton ironizes Adam's confidence that he has been
properly educated; see "Adam's 'Sum of Wisdom': *Paradise Lost* 12.553–87," in *Reassembling Truth: Twenty-first-Century Milton*, ed. Charles W. Durham and Kristin A.
Pruitt (Selinsgrove, PA: Susquehanna University Press, 2003), 95–114.

Losing Paradise in Dryden's
State of Innocence

Anthony Welch

WHY DID DRYDEN SET OUT IN THE EARLY 1670S TO WRITE AN OPERA based on *Paradise Lost*? When *The State of Innocence* was registered with the Stationers Company in the spring of 1674, sales of *Paradise Lost* had been steady, but Milton's poem had not yet created much of a critical stir.[1] By comparison, *The State of Innocence* flew off the bookstands; it reached eleven editions by 1703.[2] Dryden's opera remained unperformed in his lifetime, and we do not know if he even meant it for the stage. Perhaps he wrote the piece to inaugurate the new Drury Lane Theatre, but there is no hard evidence for this.[3] Or he may have expected the opera to form part of the festivities for the marriage of the Duke of York to Mary of Modena, the opera's dedicatee.[4] The larger puzzle is that *The State of Innocence* calls for stage machinery so elaborate that the opera would probably have been impossible to produce at any theater in London. The opera's very unperformability, though, may offer a clue to why Dryden chose this medium to confront *Paradise Lost* in the early 1670s, and why he felt that the poem needed to be confronted. It has been suggested that Dryden's opera aimed to make Milton's neglected poem more accessible to the Restoration reading public.[5] I wish to follow up this suggestion, but from a more skeptical point of view. Far from encouraging readers to embrace *Paradise Lost* on its own terms, Dryden's goal was to prevent the poem from being read in the way that Milton intended. *The State of Innocence* was an early intervention in the reception history of *Paradise Lost*, a preemptive act of interpretation designed, predictably, to correct the poem's politics, but also to rethink its relationship with the epic tradition.

Milton continued to suffer under a political stigma in the late 1660s, and enemies of the Interregnum regime were quick to seek subversive

222

political motives in his late poetry. Toland, his biographer, reports that the licensers quibbled with a number of passages in *Paradise Lost* and threatened to scuttle its publication on the grounds of "imaginary trea- son."[6] The wording is suggestive: it was not only the alleged topical al- lusions, but also the imaginative claims of Milton's poem that carried troubling political subtexts. In Milton's aggressive rhetoric of divine in- spiration, many readers saw suspicious similarities to the language of religious (and therefore political) dissent in Restoration England. *Par- adise Lost* had raised the worrisome possibility that the epic genre could be co-opted for religious radicalism. Several critics have described *The State of Innocence* as an effort to strip Milton's epic of its distasteful reli- gious politics—and, in Marcie Frank's terms, to "create a 'literary' Mil- ton whose aesthetic value is available separately from his political or theological commitments."[7] That strategy is central to Dryden's opera, but it is intimately related to another motive that has not lately received as much attention: Dryden's own epic ambitions, spurred in part by his appointment as poet laureate in 1668. *The State of Innocence* set about changing the way that Milton's poem was being read by his contempo- raries because Dryden was concerned about the direction in which epic poetry might move if *Paradise Lost* were read as Milton intended. In *The State of Innocence*, I suggest, he transforms *Paradise Lost* from an imaginatively subversive religious epic into a chivalric drama under- pinned by Italian epic romance. This drastic rewriting of *Paradise Lost* was meant to smooth out its political unorthodoxies, but Dryden was also trying, in the wake of Milton's poem, to recover the epic form for the Restoration—to lay the aesthetic groundwork for the great nation- alist heroic poem which, in the event, he would never write.

"WHAT MAD PROFUSION ON THIS CLOD-BORN BIRTH"

P. S. Havens has argued that *The State of Innocence* represents, stylisti- cally at least, a "workshop piece" for a future epic of Dryden's own.[8] Looking both backward and forward, it struggles to bring the geneal- ogy of epic poetry, pushed off track by Milton's poem, back into align- ment. Dryden admits to a qualified admiration of Milton in his prose criticism, but he shrinks from granting Milton full status as an epic poet.[9] Dryden finds several excuses for setting Milton apart: *Paradise Lost* lacks a "prosperous" ending; it has too many machining charac- ters; it uses harsh and antiquated words.[10] But his objections finally come down to the fact that Dryden's paradigm for epic writing lies elsewhere: not in visionary hexameral poetry but in the Continental epic romance. When Dryden discusses *Paradise Lost*, he makes it plain that he is holding the poem up to a chivalric romance template—and finding it wanting. Milton's might have been a great epic, Dryden muses, "if the Devil had not been his Heroe instead of *Adam*, if the Gyant had not foil'd the Knight, and driven him out of his strong hold, to wander through the World with his Lady Errant."[11] This is the vocabulary of epic romance.

The same tradition stands behind Dryden's rhymed heroic plays, which he described in retrospect as "an imitation, in little of an Heroick Poem"; Dryden's well-known story that it was Ariosto who had led him to his new dramatic form—while pondering Davenant's operatic *Siege of Rhodes*, he had chanced upon the opening lines of the *Orlando furioso* and the idea of heroic drama suddenly fell into place—amounts to a miniature myth of origins, grafting English drama onto the Continental epic canon.[12] Although he would wait until the 1690s to declare that "*Milton* was the Poetical Son of *Spencer*,"[13] Dryden was already deeply interested in Spenser's Cinquecento Italian literary models, especially Tasso's *Gerusalemme liberata*. In the early 1670s, he described Tasso as "the most excellent of modern Poets," whom he "reverence[d] next to *Virgil*."[14] He cited Tasso's hero Rinaldo as one of his models for *The Conquest of Granada*'s Almanzor, and in the dedication to *Tyrannick Love* he suggested writing a heroic poem for the Duke of Monmouth in the manner of Homer or Tasso.[15] Dryden's own future epic, he later speculated, would tell the story of "King Arthur, Conquering the Saxons" or "the Black Prince . . . subduing Spain," two subjects that neatly fit the Continental epic tradition of Ariosto and Tasso, as filtered through French neoclassicism.[16] Dryden's writings throughout this period show his attraction to contemporary European epics built upon the same literary models, including Marino's *Adone* (1623), William Davenant's *Gondibert* (1651), Georges de Scudéry's *Alaric* (1654), Jean Chapelain's *La Pucelle* (1656), Abraham Cowley's *Davideis* (1656), and Pierre le Moyne's *Saint Louis* (1658). Opera was apparently to take the place of the heroic play for Dryden as a generic middle term, an intermediate stage between the sixteenth-century romance epics and the neoclassical epic of English nationhood that Dryden may already have had *in ovo*.

Milton's foray into the early chapters of Genesis had derailed that agenda. Epic revisionism, biblical poetics, prophetic interiority—these were hardly promising foundations for Dryden's Arthuriad. Dryden would later argue that "an Heroique Poem requires, to its necessary Design, and as its last Perfection, some great Action of War . . . and, in short, as much, or more of the Active Virtue, than the Suffering."[17] We can imagine his reaction to *Paradise Regained*. Dryden would have had good reason, like E. M. Forster's Aunt Harriet at the opera, to ask what had become of Walter Scott. *The State of Innocence* fights back by reclaiming the epic continuities that Milton had threatened to break down. Dryden pushes Milton's readers to approach *Paradise Lost* as he did: as just another link in a genealogy of heroic romance that would continue with Dryden's own epic-to-be.

The opera begins rectifying matters at once. Dryden's dedicatory epistle to Mary of Modena, the bride of the Duke of York, has rightly been viewed as a bold political appropriation of *Paradise Lost*. In Steven Zwicker's words, "having taken [Milton's] theologically dense argument of Protestant radicalism, this poetic statement of republican utopianism, and having eradicated both its politics and its theology, Dryden then proceeded to lay his opera at the feet of . . . the most famous and the most feared Roman Catholic in England."[18] A different kind of charge was also being lobbed. Maria Beatrice d'Este was descended from the Estensi dukes Alfonso I and II of Ferrara, patrons of Ariosto and Tasso respectively.[19] By choosing her as his dedicatee, Dryden implicitly groups himself with the Italian poets. His dedication carefully notes the Este family's connections to Ariosto and Tasso, and allows us to read his version of *Paradise Lost* as a lineal successor to the *Furioso* and the *Liberata*.[20] Not only here, but throughout his opera, Dryden daringly rewrites *Paradise Lost* with Italianate epic romance as his guide.

Dryden long admired the magical forests and pleasure gardens that he found in Ariosto, Tasso, and Spenser. In "Of Heroique Playes," he doubts that "the Enchanted wood in Tasso, and the Bower of bliss in Spencer (which he borrows from that admirable Italian) could have been omitted without taking from their works some of the greatest beauties in them."[21] Readers have often observed that Dryden's Adam and Eve seem fallen before the Fall; this is partly because Dryden has reworked Milton's Eden to draw out its resemblance to Spenser's Bower and the Italians' earthly gardens.[22] Even the layout of Dryden's Paradise, with its prominent "Fountain in the midst" (2.3.1 s.d.), seems to recall Spenser's Bower, where "in the midst of all, a fountaine stood" (2.12.60.1).[23] While Milton takes pains to distance his Paradise from the "Hesperian Fables" of his epic forebears (4.250),[24] Dryden insists on the luxuriant secularity of his own garden, "Where golden Apples, on green branches shine, / And purple grapes dissolve into immortal wine" (2.1.77-78).

Dryden's garden is also alarmingly overgrown. As D. W. Jefferson has quipped, Adam and Eve "simply can't move for vegetation."[25] Adam soon begins to worry about the encroaching vines "Whose too luxuriant growth our Alleys stop, / And choak the paths" (3.1.85–86). This Ariostan excess makes Eve's case for working apart take on real urgency. She complains that "Nature, not bounteous now, but lavish growes; / . . . With pain we lift up our intangled feet, / While cross our walks the shooting branches meet" (4.1.125–28). Dryden's wildly profligate nature not only evokes the lavish overgrowth of Spenser's Bower (2.12.54–55), but also cultivates an atmosphere of sexual excess. On the pair's wedding night, as Eve later reports, the roses above the bower "Flew from their Stalks," and the fish "leapt above the streams" to watch their lovemaking (3.1.36–38). Eve's account of that ecstatic night shocks even the eavesdropping Lucifer, who shakes his head in wonder at all this excess: "What mad profusion on this clod-born Birth," he muses (48).

The prodigal bounty of Dryden's Paradise plays a supporting role in his program of tying Milton's Eden to the sexualized gardens of epic romance. But Dryden does not stop there. A. Bartlett Giamatti has suggested that at least one aspect of Milton's Adam and Eve—their clearly established gender hierarchy—echoes and inverts Tasso's story of Rinaldo and Armida in love.[26] Dryden, however, unleashes the full force of the analogy. The Tasso passage that Giamatti cites, where Rinaldo yields his sovereignty to Armida, points directly to Dryden's Adam, who lays "the whole Creation" at Eve's feet and chooses to obey rather than command her (2.3.47). Dryden takes special relish in the thought of Eve as a Circean temptress—a correspondence only gently floated in *Paradise Lost*, 9.518–22. When Adam woos Eve in act 2, he tells her that if he should fail to win her love, he would "resign" his empire, "And change, with my dumb slaves, my nobler mind; / Who, void of reason, more of pleasure find" (2.3.61–63). Adam's threat to degrade himself into one of the animals of Paradise recalls the stubborn choice of Spenser's Grille, and evokes the power of the romance enchantresses to turn men into beasts.[27] After Eve's fall, Dryden strengthens the relationship between her and these literary temptresses when his Lucifer gloats, "My work is done . . . / She's now the tempter, to ensnare [Adam's] heart" (4.2.144–45). The fall of Adam becomes a straightforward case of sexual temptation, a defeat of chivalric honor by "that soft seducer, love" (147). Throughout the opera, Dryden entangles Adam and Eve in a romance bower of bliss, and elides the fallen with the unfallen world. Under his ministrations, *Paradise Lost* begins to look like one more link in a tradition of epic romance leading to Dryden's projected Arthuriad.

"THE ANARCHIE OF THOUGHT AND CHAOS OF THE MIND"

Dryden's aesthetic motives in taking on Milton's epic were also, of course, political ones. The two categories meet in the question of the literary imagination. Both the early praise and the early criticism of *Paradise Lost* dwell on the poem's sweeping imaginative scale. Joseph Addison, writing some years before his groundbreaking essays on Milton in the *Spectator*, could only marvel at the "hallow'd rage" of the inspired bard; like many of Milton's early readers, Addison found the war in Heaven especially compelling.[28] Another admirer, Charles Gildon, links Milton's divine insight with the poet's blindness. " 'Tis not out of doubt whether [Milton] had ever been able to Sing of Unrevealed Heavenly Mysteries," Gildon reflects, "had he not been altogether depriv'd of his Outward Sight, and thereby made capable of such continued Strenuous Inward Speculations . . . to sing of Matchless Beings, Matchless Things, before unknown to, and even unthought of, by the whole Race of Men."[29] Milton's reputation as a self-proclaimed prophet, professing privileged access to divine mysteries, had already established itself soon after his epic's publication.

This view of Milton struck some of his readers with alarm. In the early years of the Restoration, the claims of the prophetic *vates* sounded disconcertingly like those of the Nonconformist divines. Even before *Paradise Lost*, William Davenant was being applauded for grounding his epic *Gondibert* on rational ethics, sidelining any enthusiastic mysticism that might "increase the melancholy mistakes of the people."[30] Thomas Hobbes praised Davenant for dispensing with an epic invocation: "why a Christian should thinke it an ornament to his Poeme; either to profane the true God, or invoke a false one, I can imagine no cause, but a reasonlesse imitation of custome . . . by which a man enabled to speake wisely from the principles of nature, and his owne meditation, loves rather to be thought to speake by inspiration, like a Bagpipe."[31] The Cambridge Platonist Henry More warned against the exercise of imagination in all of its forms; merely enthusiasm by another name, a "high flown and forward fancy" must be curbed by "the known Faculties of the Soul, which are either the *Common notions* that all men in their wits agree upon, or the *Evidence of outward Sense*, or else a *cleer and distinct Deduction from these*. What ever is not agreeable to those three, is *Fancy*, which testifies nothing of the *Truth* or *Existence* of any thing, and therefore ought not, nor cannot be assented to by any but mad men or fools."[32] Opponents in other respects, Hobbes and More spoke for a broad and growing coalition of conservative social forces that were anxious to stigmatize the language of personal inspiration and to blame it for the worst excesses of the Puritan revolution. This attitude toward poetic inspiration likewise stands behind Samuel Butler's mock invocation in *Hudibras*—to a muse of "Ale, or viler Liquors," in a clear enough indication of where the Puritan poets got their *furor poeticus*.[33]

In this climate, if some readers were prepared to celebrate Milton among the prophets, others grumbled about his claims to personal inspiration. The Earl of Roscommon spoke for many when he urged poets to rein in their divine frenzy: "tho we must obey when heaven Commands, / And man in vain the Sacred Call withstands, / Beware what Spirit rages in your breast; / For ten inspir'd ten thousand are Possest."[34] And the author of *The Transproser Rehears'd* gleefully read Milton's invocation to light in book 3 as the wild fantasy of a Puritan ranter: "No doubt," he titters, "but the thoughts of this Vital Lamp lighted a Christmas Candle in his brain."[35]

Sharon Achinstein has persuasively argued that *Paradise Lost* became a site for poets like Dryden and Marvell to wrestle with "the problem of direct individual inspiration," in a literary debate that stood for a wider political problem: how to respond to religious dissent in Restoration England.[36] In Achinstein's reading, Dryden's rejection of blank verse in *The State of Innocence* signals a turn away from Milton's dangerous insistence on liberty, both literary and religious, and toward a politically charged poetics of restraint. In an environment where unlicensed fancy was linked with the excesses of the Puritan political experiment, Nathaniel Lee's dedicatory verses to the opera take on a decidedly partisan character. According to Lee, Milton's poem "roughly drew . . . / A Chaos, for no perfect World was found," until Dryden intervened to "refine" Milton's primordial materials. When "your Sense his mystic reason clear'd," Lee gushes,

"The melancholy Scene all gay appear'd"; in favoring Dryden's poetic judgment over Milton's moonstruck madness, Lee also cheers the triumph of a gay new political order over the melancholy legacy of the Good Old Cause.[37]

The State of Innocence reworks *Paradise Lost* with this problem of imaginative license in mind. Achinstein concentrates on the politics of rhyme, but Dryden's opera has still more at stake. Dryden often insists that epics have a special right to indulge in flights of fancy. His theory of heroic drama draws on epic poetry precisely because he wants to give his plays "freer scope for imagination."[38] But his defenses of imagination in this period are aggressively secular; reaching toward a modern sense of aesthetic autonomy, they begin to enclose literary writing in a space of gamesome fiction. Dryden's early discussions of the literary imagination are stubbornly Hobbist, rooted in a mechanistic faculty psychology that sees a luxuriant fancy creating mimetic pictures under the stern oversight of aesthetic judgment. In the early 1670s, though, Dryden's "imagination" suddenly expands into something at once more and less ambitious. The essay "Of Heroique Plays" finds Dryden imagining an idealistic, shaping fancy, not just a mimetic one, and with no recourse at all to a restraining judgment. "The heroic poet is not tied to a bare representation of what is true, or exceeding probable," Dryden argues (without any of the usual neoclassical discomfort); the poet is free to "let himself loose to visionary objects," ranging and gamboling outside the bounds of received knowledge.[39]

But although Dryden in these years opens a startlingly wide space for imaginative license, it is smaller than it first appears. For in tracing this magic circle for the literary imagination to range in, Dryden is also marking off his autonomous bubble of fancy from the *public* form of imagination that his contemporaries called "inspiration." Early neoclassicists had generally lumped the two together, and this is why they were just as suspicious of Ariostan romance as of theological disputation.[40] But the Dryden of the 1670s has replaced this ethically engaged and politically efficacious kind of imagination—one that includes the prophetic enthusiasm of the Dissenters—with a private zone of literary fiction. The *Religio Laici* and other writings from this period make it clear that Dryden saw no room for imaginative license in interpreting holy writ; that way lay the proliferation of sects, the profligate assertion of lay authority, and the radical truth claims of *Paradise Lost*. In Dryden's view, Milton's theological epic had dragged the heroic poem out of its safe enclave of fiction-making. The task of

The State of Innocence was to push *Paradise Lost* back toward fictional autonomy—away, that is, from the claims of the prophetic *vates* and toward chivalric romance.

"POOR STATE OF BLISS, WHERE SO MUCH CARE IS SHOWN"

Readers of *The State of Innocence* often lampoon Dryden's Adam and Eve. Adam is a precocious and argumentative child. Eve is "a lady from the Restoration court,"[41] a Shamela to Milton's Pamela.[42] In their crass fallenness, they embody the opera's "skeptical and worldly perspective on the Fall,"[43] as Dryden mischievously "exposes the weaknesses and contradictions inherent in the story."[44] Even Nathaniel Lee's dedicatory poem praises Dryden's "gay" Paradise. But Lee hardly seems to read the opera as satirical comedy, as do some modern readers. For Dryden's Paradise is haunted by fear and desire. An atmosphere of untimely loss pervades the drama, as Dryden insists on finding analogies between Satan's despairing homelessness and the unfulfilled longings of Adam and Eve. They are all restless, as we shall see, because Dryden refuses to grant them—or us—an inspired vision of a prelapsarian world that is categorically irrecoverable. Not only does he never offer a glimpse of Milton's Heaven, but he everywhere refashions Milton's eyewitness diary of prelapsarian life into a story about the impossibility of imagining Paradise.

If Milton's Eve obeys through love, Dryden's Eve obeys through fear. "Forbidd to eat, not daring to repine" (4.2.73), she is held taut between an urge to transgress and a shrinking fear of punishment. Her wary furtiveness contributes to a feeling of claustrophobia and menace in Paradise. Surveillance, indeed, is a key element of life in Dryden's garden. Melissa Cowansage has noticed some of the opera's references to watching, guarding, and boundary-setting, a sinister complement to the angels' penchant for gossip that has amused other critics.[45] When the devil Asmoday worries that some "Etherial Parasite may come / To spie our ills" (1.1.192), he prepares us for Lucifer's mission, to spy with "envious eyes" (2.2.61) on events in Paradise. Milton's Eve, fresh from her fall, worries about God's omniscient gaze, but Dryden's Eve cannot stop thinking about being watched. Even in her first moments of life, she notices that the animals "with up-cast eyes, forsake their shade, / And gaze" on her (2.3.12–13). Adam, too, puzzles over those entranced stares and reads them as a sign of support for his love-suit: "Methinks, for me they beg," he tells Eve; "each, silently, / Demands thy Grace, and seems to watch thy Eye" (2.3.64–65). After the Fall, in an addition to Milton, Dryden's Adam wants to be hidden from all gazes, including his own—to be "Unknown to Heav'n, and to my self unseen"—but Eve despairs of avoiding God's angry eyes: "what hope to shun his piercing sight / Who, from dark Chaos, stroke the sparks of light?" (5.4.15–17).

Their unease at being watched points to the drama's surprising indictment of spectatorship. We would expect Dryden to have some sort of metadramatic fun with themes of seeing and being seen as he turns a narrative poem into a stage play, but he strikes an antitheatrical tone. Although the play abounds with masquelike episodes, most of them have a dark moral coloring: the devils' diversions in Hell, Eve's dream (later re-enacted by Lucifer in the temptation scene), and the grim view of futurity that Dryden's Raphael inflicts on both Adam and Eve at the end of the opera. Dryden's devils, too, appear camera shy. To Milton's account of the building of Pandaemonium Dryden adds a new motive: Beelzebub warns, " 'tis not fit / Our dark Divan in publick view should sit," where "Th' Ignoble Crowd of Vulgar Devils" might hear the leaders' plotting (1.1.77–80). Dryden's Lucifer, justifying his journey to Earth, adds that "Kings are not made . . . for Pageant-show" (1.1.177). Where Milton sometimes implicates his readers as voyeurs—most famously when we first see Adam and Eve through Satan's eyes—Dryden will not let us forget that our view of Paradise comes mediated through the eyes of a fallen poet whose imaginings are less beatific than voyeuristic.

The problem of watching is one of many pressures that make Dryden's Paradise a place of "care." The word appears often in the opera. Raphael explains to Adam, for example, that Eve will take his mind off his worries: "Thou shalt secure her helpless sex from harms; / And she thy cares shall sweeten, with her charms" (2.1.68–69). Raphael does not explain what "harms" threaten Eve before the Fall, or what "cares" have been burdening Adam. It quickly becomes clear, though, that Eve serves more as a source of worry than a respite from it, a creature of "frailty" who needs Adam's "timely care" (4.1.16). She must be frail indeed, since Dryden's choice of words has dragged the "timely care" of Milton's God for the fallen Adam and Eve back into the unfallen world.[46] "Who always fears, at ease can never be," Eve complains in the separation scene. "Poor state of bliss, where so much care is shown / As not to dare to trust our selves alone!" (4.1.171–72). Eve's "care"—char-

ANTHONY WELCH

acteristically hovering somewhere between "attention, regard" (*OED* 3.a.) and "anxiety, mental perturbation" (*OED* 2)—reflects the burden of Adam's and God's tight circumscription of her movements, and, here as elsewhere, it functions as a term of oppression rather than of loving regard.

Adam's own careworn state extends to his whole moral and intellectual position before the Fall. Much of act 4 famously wrestles with the problem of free will. Adam debates a team of angels on the question, and, to the angels' growing frustration, they find Adam determined to be a determinist. "Hard state of life!" Adam mutters after the angels leave. "Since Heav'n fore-knows my will, / Why am I not ty'd up from doing ill?" (4.1.113–14). Bruce King has shown that Dryden's Adam deploys practically every argument available by the mid-1670s in defense of Hobbesian determinism.[47] He does so because, as K. W. Grandsen puts it, Adam "regard[s] his new awareness of free will as a curse rather than a blessing."[48] Transgression seems much more vaguely defined in Dryden's Paradise than in Milton's and leaves Adam especially fearful of sinning in ignorance. In his first question to Raphael after his creation, Adam wants to know how he is to obey Heaven's laws, "unknowing when I err" (2.1.28). Nor can we take much comfort from the angels' reaction to Adam's discomfort with his own free agency. When Adam seems close to blaming God for the sins of his creatures, the angels respond with such vitriol that Adam is left to cry, "Far, far from me be banish'd such a thought" (4.1.77): an echo of the Son's plea to the Father not to destroy humanity in *Paradise Lost* (3.153–54).

For our purposes, Adam's worries about free will are less important in themselves than as a critique of Milton for jumping with both feet into these theological mysteries. When one of Lucifer's devils alerts him to "some new Race, call'd Man," Lucifer sets forth at once the crucial contrast between humans and angels: "We see what is: to Man Truth must be brought / By Sence, and drawn by a long Chain of thought" (1.1.141, 150–51)—that is, by discursive reason. Adam unwittingly echoes Lucifer's reference to a "chain" of discourse in act 4, when he reasons that, even if necessity operates only by remote causes, he still has no free choice: "The force unseen, and distant I confess; / But the long chain makes not the bondage less" (4.1.65–66). When Lucifer and Adam mark the boundaries of human agency, both start with the importance of discursive reason—as Milton's Raphael does— and both find it locked within strictly enforced confines. Far from objecting to these limits on his imagination, Adam clings to them. Not all readers agree with Grandsen that Adam wins his argument with the angels "hands down,"[49] but Adam clearly chafes under the terms of imaginative liberty that they offer him.

Adam's qualms about imaginative license prepare us for Eve's fall, which Dryden blames unequivocally on her overreaching imagination. This emphasis is clearest when Lucifer plots Eve's dream in act 3. Milton had blamed Satan for misjoining Eve's fancies (*PL*, 4.801–9), but Dryden implies that her thoughts, as well as Adam's, had already swirled in moral chaos before Lucifer's appearance. Lucifer observes that their fancy has overcome their sleeping reason, and "wild Idea's takes / From words and things, ill sorted, and misjoyn'd; / The Anarchie of thought and Chaos of the mind" (3.3.6–8). Tellingly, Dryden's description takes up the same terms as Nathaniel Lee's dedicatory poem, which had contrasted the primordial chaos of Milton's imaginings with the controlled judgment of Dryden's adaptation. From early in Dryden's criticism, poetic judgment carries a strong political inflection. In the preface to *The Rival Ladies* (1664), he warns that "Imagination in a Poet is a faculty so Wild and Lawless, that, like an High-ranging Spaniel it must have Cloggs tied to it, least it out-run the Judgment."[50] A version of the spaniel image had been used by Hobbes in his *Leviathan*, and Dryden's redeployment of it suggests a link between the misrule of poetic fancy and threats to the political establishment.[51] Hobbes had written in his *Answer* to Davenant that "Judgment begets the strength and structure, and Fancy begets the ornaments of a Poem."[52] Dryden implies that Milton, like Eve, has toppled that hierarchy, and that *The State of Innocence* is needed to tie Milton up from doing ill. In evoking Hobbesian determinism, Dryden finds a way to derail Adam's prelapsarian bliss, but also to censure Milton for trying to cut through the "long Chain of thought" that fetters the fallen imagination.

"LOST E'R 'TIS HELD; WHEN NEAREST, FAR AWAY"

For Milton, the imaginative recreation of Paradise in his poem offers a reprieve from the tragedy of life after the Fall. The reprieve is fleeting and fragile, and cross-hatched with proleptic warning signs of its coming end, but still a glimpse of Paradise found. His epic links this glimmer of imaginative consolation with his own poetic autobiography, in telling how he has nightly visited the haunts of the Muses, "Smit with the love of sacred Song" (3.29). In Dryden's view, however, the only glimpse of Paradise that we can obtain is of a Paradise slipping out of our hands. As we reach into the mystery of life before the Fall, the fetters of the fallen mind clamp down at once upon us, and the vision disintegrates into fiction. Dryden's real achievement in *The State of Innocence* is to stage this collapse of inspiration into imagination: to create an unfallen world that is already, everywhere, in the process of being imaginatively lost. Eden appears both fallen and unfallen at the same time, not because Dryden lacks consistency, but because he wants to show Genesis collapsing into Ariosto before our eyes. The true Paradise is ripped from us precisely when—and because—we are trying to get it back.

Milton's Satan yearns to forget his pain, but Dryden's Lucifer feels still more intensely haunted by his past. He and the devils longingly imagine a return to their original brightness, and they fantasize about cleansing themselves in the purer air of Paradise. "We'll scour our spots, and . . . all the remnants of th' unlucky War," Lucifer promises (1.1.187–88). He later tells Gabriel and Ithuriel that he intends to "bleach me in the wind" of Eden (3.3.92). And unlike Milton's Satan, who can for a moment become "Stupidly good" (9.465), Dryden's Lucifer tries in vain to "forget, / A while, I am a Devil" (2.2.12–13). Milton equivocates over whether God created humans to fill the place of the fallen angels, but Dryden leaves no doubt of it. Not only Lucifer, but Raphael too, acknowledges that humanity "must supply / The place of those who, falling, lost the Sky" (2.1.21–22).[53] Dryden places this void left by the fallen angels at the center of his play. Perhaps this is why Lucifer describes Eden as an "Abyss of joyes, as if Heav'n meant to shew / What, in base matters, such a hand could do" (3.1.49–50)— as if God had clumsily tried to seal the void by placing Paradise atop it. Adam and Eve reopen the abyss for themselves by eating the fruit, and Adam promptly invites Eve to join him for a nihilistic bout of lust in terms that strongly resemble Lucifer's: "let him [the Father] seize us when our pleasure's past. / . . . death shall find / We have drain'd life, and left a void behind" (5.1.88–90). Even at its most blissful, Dryden's Paradise derives its existence from, serves as a lingering memorial to, and finally re-enacts an earlier traumatic loss that can never be repaired.

The void in Paradise also makes itself felt in Adam's and Eve's incommensurate longings, intense desires with no objective correlative.

Dryden's version of Eve's creation is characteristic. Milton's Eve ponders her reflection "with vain desire" (4.466); Dryden's Eve actually tries to embrace hers:

> And now a Face peeps up, and now draws near,
> With smiling looks, as pleas'd to see me here.
> As I advance, so that advances too,
> And seems to imitate what e're I do:
> When I begin to speak, the lips it moves;
> Streams drown the voice, or it would say it loves.
> Yet when I would embrace, it will not stay:
> Lost e'r 'tis held; when nearest, far away.
> Ah, fair, yet false; ah Being, form'd to cheat,
> By seeming kindness, mixt with deep deceit.
>
> (2.3.18–27)

Dryden's marginal stage direction reads, "*Stoops down to embrace.*" Dryden confirms his Eve's vanity, but he also drives home the feeling that something is missing in Paradise. In one sense, the two Eves before and after the Fall have suddenly come face to face. In scolding her reflection as a "false . . . Being, form'd to cheat," Eve proleptically condemns herself; Adam will castigate her in almost the same terms after he has eaten the fruit. But the secondary target is Milton, since, from Dryden's perspective, Milton's Adam and Eve are both false images, no more within reach than Eve's watery reflection. In Ovid's *Metamorphoses*, as translated by one of Dryden's less artful contemporaries, the narrator chides Narcissus: "*Vain Youth*, why do you, what avoids you, Love? / That Form's destroy'd, if you but hence remove."[54] Dryden offers something more disturbing: "Lost e'r 'tis held; when nearest, far away" suggests a reflection that somehow recedes at Eve's approach rather than at her withdrawal. Dryden's fragile simulacrum of Eden tempts belief, but wavers with our approach, and vanishes at the touch.

Dryden was fascinated by Eve's scene at the pool (in this case, a fountain); he returns to it fifteen years later, for example, in his opera *King Arthur*. And he is not yet finished with the episode here. When Adam arrives, Eve thinks that he must have risen out of the waters: "Art thou the Form my longing eyes did see, / Loos'd from thy Fountain, and come out to me?" (38–39). The surface irony is that Eve was formed in Adam's image and not he in hers. Yet Eve's question incriminates Adam as, like her, an insubstantial "Form," a poetic shadow. And the answer to her question—that the form in the fountain will never share her embrace—signals something that Eve has only begun to understand: there will never be enough love for her in Dryden's Paradise. In a harsh revision of Milton, Eve looks Adam over, and, recognizing some resemblance to herself, nervously remarks that "Thou look'st more sternly . . . / And more of awe thou bear'st, *and less of love*" (42–43; emphasis mine). Something of this nervousness lurks, too, in Adam's description of marital bliss with Eve, "still desiring, what I still possess" (3.1.26).

Hints like these gather into a vision of Adam and Eve that is held in suspension between Milton's biblical bliss and the coarser sexuality of literary romance. The play's erotic language teases us with our own prurient interest in prelapsarian sexuality and pointedly deflects it into secular literary terms. As Eve approaches Adam with the fruit, for example, he tells her that nature has been mourning her absence: while she was gone, "Eden was no more" (5.1.18). Now if Adam seriously means that he has been bewailing Eve's absence that morning, then Dryden has cheated us, offering pain and desire in Paradise when we expected perfect bliss. But if Adam is simply teasing Eve with the hyperbolic language of courtly love, then Dryden has offered us no Paradise at all, just a cynical parody of Restoration libertinage. As we stand at the brink of Adam's fall, Dryden kicks our feet out from under us and reminds us that he never gave us a Paradise to fall *from*.

Dryden's boldest gambit, in filling Paradise with desire and loss, is to link Adam with Satan. This sustained pairing often sees Adam borrowing lines from Milton's Satan, and Lucifer from Milton's Adam. Lucifer's characteristic sentiment, that Paradise "augments my pain, / Gazing to wish, yet hopeless to obtain" (3.3.117), echoes the complaint of Milton's Adam that life has become "a long day's dying to augment our pain" (10.964). Conversely, the uxorious language of Dryden's Adam when he woos the newly-created Eve (2.3.28–35) recalls the fawning compliments of Milton's Satan when he tempts Eve at the Tree (9.538, 546–48). Dryden makes further structural adjustments to enable parallels between his Adam and his Lucifer. By making Adam debate, for instance, with not one but two angels in act 4, Dryden restages Lucifer's altercation with Gabriel and Ithuriel two scenes earlier. But it is Eve herself who draws the most provocative connection between Lucifer and Adam. When Dryden's serpent eats of the Tree of Knowledge, slinks away, and reappears as Lucifer himself, Eve chillingly asks him, "Art thou some other Adam . . . ?" (4.2.46).[55] This follows upon Dryden's most devastating hit, which came a moment earlier: when the serpent first slithers offstage with its stolen fruit, Eve is surprised that "The vent'rous victor march'd unpunish'd hence, / And seem'd to boast his fortunate offence" (4.2.34–35). The serpent's "fortunate offence" can only represent an attack on Adam's famous claim of *felix culpa* in *Paradise Lost*, and on Milton's presumptuousness in letting Adam's conclusion stand. Dryden associates the idea here with other Satanic temptations.[56]

Dryden would later complain of *Paradise Lost* that Milton's "Design is the Losing of our Happiness."[57] After the Fall, his Adam and Eve leave no doubt that they resent having to witness the scope of their loss. Dryden's vision of futurity dispenses with Milton's long historical sequence and focuses instead on two tableaux, one depicting forms of violence and misery and the other a triumphant Heaven of rest. Adam and Eve react to the first with dismay, not only at death itself, but at the fact that Raphael has obliged them to witness it. Eve in particular resists the angel's effort at providential closure.[58] "Who would the miseries of man foreknow?" she protests. "Now, we the fate of future Ages bear; / And, ere their birth, behold our dead appear" (5.4.200–204). This image of a happy birth snuffed out when just on the verge of being glimpsed strikes precisely the tone that Dryden has been building throughout the drama. When Eve sums up the tragedy of postlapsarian life, she could equally be describing Dryden's method of teasing the reader with an inaccessible Paradise: "Unknowing, he receives it, and, when known, / He thinks it his, and values it, 'tis gone" (185–86). After the vision has ended, Adam echoes Eve's protest, refusing to look back at the garden that they must leave behind: "To lose the thought, is to remove the pain" (246).

Ironically, Dryden himself would later be blamed for the imaginative excesses of his operas—"What then," Jeremy Collier demanded of *King Arthur*, "is the Fall of the Angels a Romance?"—and some readers would appeal to Milton's precedent in Dryden's defense.[59] But Dryden wrote his first opera in the nervous climate of the early 1670s, when the Test Act and King Charles's Indemnity Bill had left the English people in real confusion over how religious and political dissidents, including Milton, should be dealt with. Dryden absorbs Milton's theological vision into the idiom of Continental epic romance partly to cultivate his readers' taste for the epic model most congenial to himself, but also to deactivate Milton's "imaginary treason" by folding it up in fiction. *The State of Innocence* ends with Adam and Eve resolving never to look back at their lost homeland. For Dryden, "Paradise

within" consists in a refusal to look back, to succumb to the temptations of chronic retrospection and reenactment. But with that loss
comes a turn to the more humble consolations of imaginative fiction.
Ending her valedictory lament, Eve accepts that, "disposesst, / Farthest
from what I once enjoy'd, is best" (5.4.258–59)—in a final, admonitory
echo of Milton's Satan.[60]

NOTES

1. William Riley Parker, *Milton: A Biography*, 2nd ed., ed. Gordon Campbell, 2
vols. (Oxford: Clarendon, 1996), 1:602–5.
2. Dustin Griffin, *Regaining Paradise: Milton and the Eighteenth Century* (Cambridge: Cambridge University Press, 1986), 147. For more on early editions and
manuscripts of the opera, see Morris Freedman, "The 'Tagging' of *Paradise Lost*:
Rhyme in Dryden's *The State of Innocence*," *Milton Quarterly* 5 (1971): 18–19 and
notes.
3. See Griffin, *Regaining Paradise*, 275. James Anderson Winn, *John Dryden and
His World* (New Haven: Yale University Press, 1987), 262, suggests the opera was
written to compete with the Dryden-Davenant *Tempest*, which had just been revived
at Dorset Garden.
4. The marriage hypothesis is the one usually advanced; for a full summary, see
Francis Harris Fletcher, ed., *John Milton's Complete Poetical Works Reproduced in Pho-
tographic Facsimile*, 4 vols. (Urbana: University of Illinois Press, 1943–48), 3:10–13.
But M. Manuel, *The Seventeenth Century Critics and Biographers of Milton* (Trivan-
drum: University of Kerala Press, 1962), 69–70, has objected that Adam's vicious
postlapsarian abuse of wives would hardly have suited the occasion.
5. See Bernard Harris, "'That Soft Seducer, Love': Dryden's *The State of Innocence and Fall of Man*," in *Approaches to "Paradise Lost": The York Tercentenary Lectures*,
ed. C. A. Patrides (London: Edward Arnold, 1968), 119–36.
6. Cited in Parker, *Milton*, 1:600–601.
7. Marcie Frank, *Gender, Theatre, and the Origins of Criticism from Dryden to Manley* (Cambridge: Cambridge University Press, 2003), 54. Frank explores Milton's
place in Dryden's emerging canon of English 'classics,' on which see more generally
Cedric C. Reverand II, "Dryden and the Canon: Absorbing and Rejecting the Burden of the Past," in *Enchanted Ground: Reimagining John Dryden*, ed. Jayne Lewis and
Maximillian E. Novak (Toronto: University of Toronto Press, 2004), 203–25, and
Joseph M. Levine, *Between the Ancients and the Moderns* (New Haven: Yale University
Press, 1999), 53–109.
8. P. S. Havens, "Dryden's 'Tagged' Version of 'Paradise Lost,'" in *Essays in Dramatic Literature: The Parrott Presentation Volume*, ed. Hardin Craig (Princeton:
Princeton University Press, 1935), 392–93. The view of Dryden's opera as a "workshop piece" is also taken in George McFadden, "Dryden's 'Most Barren Period'—
and Milton," *Huntington Library Quarterly* 24 (1961): 283–96. For the opera's critique of *Paradise Lost* as a heroic poem, compare Griffin, *Regaining Paradise*, 144–46,
and Hugh MacCallum, "The State of Innocence: Epic to Opera," *Milton Studies* 31
(1994): 109–31.

9. Only the epigram attributed to Dryden in the 1688 edition of *Paradise Lost* ranks Milton unequivocally with Homer and Virgil. In the "Dedication of the Aeneis," Dryden makes it clear that only the two ancients and Tasso meet all of his epic criteria. See *The Works of John Dryden*, gen. ed. H. T. Swedenborg Jr., 20 vols. (Berkeley: University of California Press, 1956–89), 5:275. Subsequent references to Dryden's works are from this edition, cited hereafter as *Works*; references to *The State of Innocence* are cited parenthetically in the text.

10. Dryden, "Discourse of Satire," in *Works*, 4:14–15; preface to *Sylvae*, in *Works*, 3:17.

11. Dryden, *Works*, 5:276.

12. Dryden, "Of Heroique Playes," in *Works*, 11:9–10.

13. Dryden, preface to *Fables* (1700), in *Works*, 7:25.

14. Dryden, preface to *An Evening's Love* (1671), in *Works*, 10:211.

15. *Works*, 11:14; 10:107. On the importance of Tasso to Dryden's epic criticism, see John C. Sherwood, "Dryden and the Critical Theories of Tasso," *Comparative Literature* 18 (1966): 351–59, and S. Bernard Chandler, "La Fortuna del Tasso Epico in Inghilterra 1650–1800," *Studi Tassiani* 5 (1955): 73–76.

16. Dryden, *Works*, 3:22.

17. "Discourse of Satire," in *Works*, 4:16.

18. Steven N. Zwicker, "Milton, Dryden, and the Politics of Literary Controversy," in *Culture and Society in the Stuart Restoration: Literature, Drama, History*, ed. Gerald MacLean (Cambridge: Cambridge University Press, 1995), 154.

19. See Dryden, *Works*, 12:344, and compare the dedication of *The Conquest of Granada*, in *Works*, 11:3. Hugh MacCallum notes that by evoking Estensi patronage, Dryden pointedly reverses Milton's turn "away from courtly patronage to his 'celestial' patroness, the Muse"; vatic enthusiasm is rejected for a poetry of patriotic service and panegyric. See MacCallum, "State of Innocence," 112–13.

20. If those hints were not enough, Dryden includes an extended and gratuitous quotation of the *Furioso* in comparing Mary's eyes to the magic shield of Atlante (*Works*, 12:84).

21. Dryden, *Works*, 11:12.

22. In his description of the landscape, Dryden prefers to echo details in *Paradise Lost* that Milton had himself derived from earlier romance epics. For example, Dryden presents his Paradise as a garden "full of Ornament," in Adam's words (2.1.9), with the same indications of strife between nature and art that characterize the Bower of Bliss and its precursors.

23. Edmund Spenser, *The Faerie Queene*, ed. A. C. Hamilton (London: Longman, 1977), 292. Dryden's fountain, where Eve will later see her reflection, is a more clearly architectural feature than Milton's irriguous rill in *Paradise Lost*, 4:227–30.

24. John Milton, *Complete Poems and Major Prose*, ed. Merritt Y. Hughes (New York: Odyssey, 1957), 284. All references to *Paradise Lost* are from this edition and are cited parenthetically in the text.

25. D. W. Jefferson, "Dryden's Style in *The State of Innocence*," *Essays in Criticism* 32 (1982): 366.

26. A. Bartlett Giamatti, *The Earthly Paradise and the Renaissance Epic* (Princeton: Princeton University Press, 1966), 314. Giamatti compares *Paradise Lost*, 4.297–99, with *Gerusalemme liberata*, 16.21.1–2. On gender relations in Dryden's Paradise, see Jean Gagen, "Anomalies in Eden: Adam and Eve in Dryden's *The State of Innocence*,"

in *Milton's Legacy in the Arts*, ed. Albert C. Labriola and Edward Sichi Jr. (University Park: University of Pennsylvania State University Press, 1988), 135–50.

27. See Spenser, *The Faerie Queene*, 2.12.86–87. Eve's masquelike dream in act 3 seems to allude to the same theme. A crew of deformed spirits dances about her; after eating the fruit, they "put off their deform'd shapes, and appear Angels" (3.3.12, 28 s.d.). Their pantomime cunningly maps their release from the bondage of obedience onto the myth of Circe's beasts made men. Lucifer reprises their performance when, instead of tempting Eve as a talking serpent, he convinces her that the fruit has transformed him from a snake into a human being.

28. Addison marvels as Milton "shakes heav'n's eternal throne with dire alarms, / And sets th' Almighty thunderer in arms." See Joseph Addison, *An Account of the Greatest English Poets* (1690), in *Miscellaneous Works in Verse and Prose of . . . Joseph Addison*, 3 vols. (London, 1726), 1:37. Manuel, *Seventeenth Century Critics*, 71, notes the initial popularity of the War in Heaven.

29. Charles Gildon, *A Vindication of Paradise Lost* (1694), in *Critical Essays of the Seventeenth Century*, ed. J. E. Spingarn, 3 vols. (Oxford: Clarendon, 1908–9), 3:200.

30. Sir William Davenant, preface to *Gondibert*, in *Sir William Davenant's Gondibert*, ed. David Gladish (Oxford: Clarendon, 1971), 6. A dedicatory poem by Abraham Cowley makes no secret of the political stakes involved: *"By fatall hands whilst present Empires fall, / Thine from the grave past Monarchies recall. / So much more thanks from human kinde does merit / The Poets Fury, then the Zelots Spirit."* ("TO Sir WILLIAM D'AVENANT, Upon his two first Books of *GONDIBERT*, Finish'd before his Voyage to *America*," in Gladish, 270).

31. Thomas Hobbes, *The Answer of Mr. Hobbes to Sir Will. D'Avenant's Preface before Gondibert*, in Gladish, 49.

32. Henry More, *Enthusiasmus Triumphatus* (London, 1656), 53–54.

33. Samuel Butler, *Hudibras*, ed. John Wilders (Oxford: Clarendon, 1967), 20.

34. Wentworth Dillon, Earl of Roscommon, *An Essay on Translated Verse* (London, 1684), in Spingarn, 2:306.

35. [Richard Leigh], *The Transproser Rehears'd: or the Fifth Act of Mr. Bayes's Play* (Oxford, 1673), 42.

36. Sharon Achinstein, "Milton's Spectre in the Restoration: Marvell, Dryden, and Literary Enthusiasm," *Huntington Library Quarterly* 59 (1997): 8. On the neoclassical aesthetics of restraint and the politics of enthusiasm, see also George Williamson's influential essay, "The Restoration Revolt against Enthusiasm," *Studies in Philology* 32 (1935): 553–79.

37. "To Mr. Dryden, on his Poem of Paradice," in Dryden, *Works*, 12:537. For a similar reading of Lee's poem, see Nicholas von Maltzahn, "Dryden's Milton and the Theatre of Imagination," in *John Dryden: Tercentenary Essays*, ed. Paul Hammond and David Hopkins (Oxford: Clarendon, 2000), 51–52.

38. "Of Heroique Playes," in Dryden, *Works*, 11:9.

39. Ibid. Judgment reasserts itself in Dryden's writing by the late 1670s, and the defense of "Poetique Licence" that prefaces *The State of Innocence* is only a diminished afterglow of the 1672 essay on heroic plays. For Dryden's changing attitudes toward "imagination," see John M. Aden, "Dryden and the Imagination: The First Phase," *PMLA* 74 (1959): 28–40; Robert D. Hume, "Dryden on Creation: 'Imagination' in the Later Criticism," *Review of English Studies* 21 (1970): 295–314; and von Maltzahn, "Dryden's Milton," 32–56.

40. Davenant, for example, is typical in his distaste for Tasso's "Councell assembled in Heaven, his Witches Expeditions through the Aire, and enchanted Woods inhabited with Ghosts" (Gladish, 6), which he associates with pagan superstition and (by implication) with Catholic priestcraft. By contrast, Dryden's criticism was closer to that of later Restoration theorists, who came to view the imagination in two distinct senses: as a (healthy, desirable) impulse in literary writing and as a (wayward, destructive) concept in religious or philosophical writing; see Donald F. Bond, "'Distrust' of the Imagination in English Neo-Classicism," *Philological Quarterly* 14 (1935): 54–69. My approach here is also influenced by Joad Raymond, "Dryden's Fall," paper presented at Yale University, 26 February 2004, which is similarly interested in Dryden's use of Milton in *The State of Innocence* to explore the category of literary fiction.

41. Havens, "Dryden's 'Tagged' Version," 394.

42. Dryden, *Works*, 12:326.

43. Griffin, *Regaining Paradise*, 146, and see Jefferson, "Dryden's Style," 361–68.

44. K. W. Grandsen, "Milton, Dryden, and the Comedy of the Fall," *Essays in Criticism* 26 (1976): 125.

45. Melissa Cowansage, "The Libertarian-Libertine Dichotomy in Dryden's *The State of Innocence*," *English Language Notes* 21(1984): 42.

46. Milton, *Paradise Lost*, 10.1057. Similarly, when Dryden's Eve bids farewell to Paradise, she refers to her flowers not as her "early visitation" (as in *Paradise Lost*, 11.275), but as her "early care" (5.4.250)—an echo of Milton's Eve as she promises to tend the Tree of Knowledge in her first giddy moments after eating the fruit (9.799).

47. Bruce King, *Dryden's Major Plays* (Edinburgh: Oliver and Boyd, 1966), 95–115.

48. Grandsen, "Milton, Dryden, and the Comedy of the Fall," 132.

49. Ibid., 130.

50. Dryden, *Works*, 8:101.

51. See Hobbes, *Leviathan*, 1.3, and Dryden, *Works*, 1:53, 8:273, 12:335.

52. Gladish, 49.

53. Lucifer states the same idea at 2.2.11 and 3.1.52. Compare *Paradise Lost*, 2.834–35, 7.150–56, 9.148–49.

54. *Ovid's Metamorphosis. Translated by Several Hands* (London, 1697), 137. The Narcissus story was translated by "Mr. [William?] Pittis" and "Mr. [Benjamin?] Bridgwater."

55. Eve has just asked Lucifer, "What art thou, or from whence?" (4.2.44)—a close echo of Adam's first words following his creation: "What am I? or from whence?" (2.1.1).

56. Dryden does give his Eve (not his Adam) a muted statement of the *felix culpa* (5.4.235–36), but its optimism is swallowed up in her long valedictory lament a few lines later. Compare MacCallum, "State of Innocence," 127–28.

57. Dryden, "Discourse of Satire," in *Works*, 4:15.

58. Louis Martz, "Dryden's Poem of Paradise: *The State of Innocence, and Fall of Man*," in *John Dryden (1631–1700): His Politics, His Plays, and His Poets*, ed. Claude Rawson and Aaron Santesso (Newark: University of Delaware Press, 2004), 193–95, likewise notes that Dryden's Eve is never fully reconciled to the Fall, and that her exile lament, the most powerful speech in the opera, speaks for a final sense of loss and irresolution in the drama as a whole.

59. Collier continues, "Has it no basis of Truth, nothing to support it, but strength of Fancy, and Poetick Invention? After He had mention'd Hell, Devils, &c. and given us a sort of Bible description of these formidable Things . . . I am surprized to hear him call it a Fairy kind of Writing." (*A Short View of the Immorality, and Pro-faneness of the English Stage* [London, 1698], 189). Elkanah Settle stepped in to defend *King Arthur* on the grounds that Dryden's "betters have done it before him, and Mr. Dryden thinks it no scorn to follow his elder Brother Gamaliel Mr. Milton in his *Paradise Lost*" (*A Defence of Dramatick Poetry* [London, 1698], 99–100).

60. Milton, *Paradise Lost*, 1.247: Satan in Hell is congratulating himself on his distance from God. Dryden turns Satan's presumptuousness back on Milton by *affirm-ing* imaginative distance from God as the orthodox stance.

Through Eve's Looking-Glass

Elisabeth Liebert

Dᴇsᴄʀɪʙɪɴɢ Eᴠᴇ ɪɴ ᴄᴏʟʟᴏǫᴜʏ ᴡɪᴛʜ Rᴀᴘʜᴀᴇʟ ᴛᴏᴡᴀʀᴅ ᴛʜᴇ ᴇɴᴅ ᴏғ ʙᴏᴏᴋ 8 of *Paradise Lost*, Adam characterizes what he had earlier termed "Heaven's last best gift" (5.19) as possessed of an independent volition exercised in speech and action. Although what Eve "wills to do or say" (8.549) contributes in conjunction with her beauty to the difficulties Adam experiences in correctly evaluating his own God-given attributes, the archangel does not challenge his attribution of volition to Eve but rather his response to it, and when Adam redefines and defends his praise of Eve he does so by once again reasserting her autonomy: the "thousand decencies that daily flow / From all her words and actions" (8.601–2) are Eve's voluntary contribution to their paradisal marriage.[1] In Eden, Adam and Eve are "authors to themselves in all / Both what they judge and what they choose" (3.122–23), and Eve clearly exercises choice throughout the epic. Anne Torday Gulden has pointed to the significance of Eve's choice of dinner fruits in book 5 as she selects and prepares a meal that offers "Taste after taste upheld with kindliest change" (5.336).[2] Later, Eve chooses to tend her garden and reserve the pleasure of studious discourse until she is alone with her husband (8.48–54). The sharing of such "high dispute" (55) properly belongs, in Eve's mind, to marital conversation as the broader definition of that word is inclusive of philosophical debate as well as conjugal caresses.

Nevertheless, Eve's exercise of volition in her first speech in book 4 remains largely unexplored, at times denied. To those who read this speech as evidence of her subordination to the wishes of a dominant patriarchy, her fascination with her image in the pool represents a precarious moment of integrity before the "colonization" of the female voice by patriarchal order.[3] Others, desirous of decolonizing Eve, have pointed to a reciprocity in Eden that effectively reinstates her dignity. Eve brings to the marital relationship attributes Adam lacks, and he

learns from her not only to question the workings of the heavenly bodies but more importantly to assimilate qualities generally associated
with the feminine, until the debate over separation "turns on a variant
of the standard gender-linked values" and Adam, falling, "responds to
temptation . . . more emotionally than Eve."[4] She is essential to Adam's
developing self, for in *Paradise Lost*, as Shullenberger tell us, "identity
. . . can only be discovered in relationship."[5] This recognition of the
importance of reciprocity has in turn encouraged readings of Eve's enchantment with her reflection in the pool as a crucial stage in her emotional or psychological development, her identification of an other in
the watery mirror preparing her to be receptive to Adam.[6] But even
this important realization does not address the underlying question of
motivation. Why does Eve choose to recount the story of her nativity
for Adam in this way, at this time? Proposing exactly this question,
Mary Nyquist suggests that, "Set in juxtaposition to the rather bar-
renly disputational speech of Adam's which immediately precedes it in
Book IV, Eve's narrative creates a space that is strongly if only implicitly gendered, a space that is dilatory, erotic, and significantly, almost
quintessentially, 'private.' "[7] The impetus for this creation of a *locus ar-
canus* lies in its contribution to structure and character delineation:
Eve's narrative in book 4 demonstrates a subjectivity that renders her a
fit partner for the Adam who in book 8 will admit to loneliness. It
demonstrates an essential likeness, an equivalent need. But more than
simply "emphasizing her voluntary submission both to the paternal
voice and to her 'author' and bridegroom, Adam," as Nyquist concludes, Eve's first speech in *Paradise Lost* is illustrative of a volition that
remains autonomous: Eve is exercising her will to say.[8] The dual contexts of romance convention and the marital ideal developed by Milton
in the divorce tracts elucidate the nature of her choices in structuring
this speech. Transforming the mirror imagery of romance, she offers
Adam a glass in which to see himself and his need for the "attractive
society of conjugal love," encouraging him toward the celebration of
their union through its reenactment. Drawing attention to their mutual dependence while affirming hierarchy, she voluntarily contributes
to the Miltonic marital ideal with its "prime end" of "a conversing solace and peaceful society," in which, however, the joy of sex would soon
prove cloying and despicable, were it not "cherished and reincited with
a pleasing conversation" (*Tetrachordon*, 2:740).

    In order to illustrate this conscious transformation of an apparently
introspective trope into one that reflects instead upon the mutuality

necessary in relationships, I wish to travel forward two centuries and across Europe, avoiding, if possible, any lurch of alienation in the Miltonic reader, to a work written in Hungary in 1860. It would be satisfying to be able to introduce Imre Madách's dramatic poem *Az ember tragédiája* as indubitably influenced by Milton's epic. Károly Horváth's identification of thematic parallels presupposes Madách's familiarity with *Paradise Lost*, available to him in French or German or in Sándor Bessenyei's Hungarian prose translation of 1796 (reprinted 1817), but in the final analysis such familiarity cannot be conclusively proved.[9] However, even in the absence of incontrovertible evidence of direct influence, the opening scenes of *Az ember tragédiája* briefly rework the story of the Fall in a way that provides an interesting counterpoint to Milton's epic.[10] Scene 1 begins with angelic praise for the completed work of creation, interrupted by Lucifer's criticism of a world in which the creature lacks free will and self-determination. Scene 2 introduces Adam and Eve imparadised in one another's arms. The intrusion of Lucifer with his mocking rationality brings disharmony, driving an ideological wedge between the couple; their haven of shared love momentarily shaken, they succumb to temptation and fall.[11] Conversation with Lucifer continues outside Paradise; the temptation of knowledge is compounded and Lucifer conducts Adam and Eve into the future through a series of dream visions in which they participate as historical characters.

Although overlooked by Horváth, the similarities between Eve's speech at lines 182–90 and her speech in *Paradise Lost* 4.440–91 surely comprise one of the most fascinating instances of parallelism between the two works. Madách's Eve speaks of her nativity and an awareness of her dependence upon Adam, evoking echoes of the Narcissus myth:

> If that glory above us dims, I find it
> down here in your eyes, Adam.
> where else could I hope to find it but in you?
> It was your warm desire that summoned me to life,
> like when the regal sun in streams of light,
> so that it won't be lonesome in the universe,
> paints itself upon the surface of the water
> and dallies with the image, glad to have a mate,
> indulgently forgetting that she is but
> the glimmered likeness of his own fire
> and will fade to nothing when he dims.
>
> (180–90)[12]

This speech focuses more narrowly upon the Narcissus motif than Eve's first speech in *Paradise Lost*, which uses the narcissistic moment more obviously as a point of departure. Additionally, it is now Adam—or the sun—who plays the role of Narcissus, while Eve takes the part of Narcissus's image, as if that image had unexpectedly found a tongue and were to address the enamored boy from beneath the surface of the water. Also worth noting is the fact that, unlike her counterpart in *Paradise Lost*, Eve here reflects nothing but her own voice and her own values. She does not reproduce the remembered speeches of God or Adam, and no voice instructs her in the creation of imagery or the alignment of her loyalties. Rather, she articulates her own feelings of interdependence in imagery drawn from her observation of the natural world.

A closer examination of the speech reveals something surprising. While the image builds toward an expression of the reflection's reliance upon the sun to sustain it (the reflection will fade to nothing when the sun dims), the focus of the passage is not the condition of the reflection but the condition of the sun itself, compelled by loneliness to create and rejoicing in a creation that involves a considerable measure of self-indulgence and self-deception: the sun is glad to have a "mate" and overlooks her ephemeral insubstantiality.[13] Six lines deal with the sun and its need for the reflection, while only two lines—that which introduces the simile and the final line—explore the reflection's need for the sun. Thus what appears at first glance a simple simile is in fact a complex and challenging word-picture that suggests that the act of creation is not only narcissistic but an attempt to compensate for a sense of incompleteness in the individual. The sun creates a reflection on the water not incidentally, as does Eve in *Paradise Lost*, but with deliberate intent, attempting to resolve a lack within itself that precludes happiness. The physical frailty of the reflection reflects and is reflected in the emotional frailty of the sun, in the loneliness that drives it to seek its image on the water.

Madách's Adam responds to Eve's verbal picture by acknowledging the importance of Eve-as-image to his understanding of himself:

> What would I be, if in you my existence did not unfurl—
> as in the echo, as in the flower—to lovelier life,
> in which I can love my own self?
>
> (194–96)[14]

Here, in Eden before the Fall, he recognizes that Eve's existence offers him a mirror of his own, that in her his life finds a new and more beau-

tiful expression, and that in loving her he also loves himself. His reliance on Eve for a sense of completion is actively demonstrated in the
action of the dream sequence that follows the Fall, where his gradual
maturation is, in part at least, prompted and enabled by Eve.[15] Like
Milton's Adam, he discovers that "Eve's beauty *moves* him, makes him
feel."[16] Scene 4 is set in ancient Egypt, with Adam, courtesy of Lucifer,
cast as Pharaoh. Elevated on his throne above the suffering people, he
feels nothing in his heart but "a void, an inexpressible void" (590). Eve's
appearance as a slave woman mourning her dead husband immediately
negates that void and replaces it with feeling. As Adam's first sight of
Eve in *Paradise Lost* "infused / Sweetness into my heart, unfelt before"
(8.474–75), Madách's Pharaoh-Adam, seeing Eve for the first time, asks
in surprise "what unaccustomed feeling enters into my heart?" (608).
He invites her to sit beside him on his throne, where her continued
sensitivity to the collective agony of the Egyptian slaves exposes him to
the world beyond the self. He hears, feels, and experiences through
her: "Through your heart," he tells her, "that wail of woe, like a bolt of
lightning, strikes into my head" (672–73). But his prelapsarian awareness of their mutual dependence has been eroded by the Fall, and although he learns to respond to a world of feeling through Eve, he fails
to recognize the extent of her influence. Renouncing his throne at the
end of scene 4 in response to the awakening she has effected, he identifies not her dynamic influence as evidenced by his own abdication but
only her "female weakness" that "strength might love" (756), seeing
her as "a flower, useless, but pretty" (772–73). Nevertheless, despite
Adam's postlapsarian chauvinism, Eve's first long speech in the drama
establishes the centrality of mirroring to their relationship, ostensibly
identifying the dependence of the image on the creative sun only to
draw attention to the reliance of the sun on its reflection: the portrait
of the self undergoes a metamorphosis to become, through self-mir-
roring, a portrait of the other and of a shared romance.

   While a direct link between Milton and Madách cannot be absolutely maintained, a common source exists in the genre of romance
epic and specifically in Tasso's *Jerusalem Delivered*; Madách owned a
copy of Tasso's epic, and the hero Tancred plays a leading role in scene
7 of his own poem. Eve's reflections in both *Paradise Lost* and *Az ember
tragédiája* owe a debt to the romance trope of mirroring as that effects
a refinement of self-knowledge or an identification of the beloved or,
occasionally, both. In *Jerusalem Delivered*, Rinaldo is recalled to himself
by glancing into the shield belonging to the Wise Man of Ascalon "in

which is mirrored for him what manner of man he is become" (16.30–31).[17] In *Orlando Furioso*, the jeweled walls of Logistilla's palace enable a man "on looking at them . . . [to] see right into his own soul [and] see there reflected his vices and virtues" (10.59).[18] Such mirrors are otherworldly and allegorical, reflections themselves of the glass in which fallen man can glimpse darkly spiritual reality: the jewels of Logistilla's palace "are never spoken of here below" and exist nowhere else, except perhaps, Ariosto's narrator suggests, in Paradise.[19] Such magical mirrors allow perception of an internal state of being otherwise inaccessible; the hero proceeds, strengthened, on his quest. But the mirror can also contribute to a developing relationship with another as, in an archetypal Lacanian progression, refinement of self-knowledge enables the heroine to identify her beloved. Thus, Richard DuRocher draws attention to the role played by mirroring in Britomart's initiation into love in Spenser's *Faerie Queene*.[20] When Britomart first glances into the looking glass fashioned by Merlin to reveal "What ever thing was in the world contaynd . . . So that it to the looker appertaynd," she sees only her own external self:

> Where when she had espyde that mirrhour fayre,
> Her selfe awhile therein she vewd in vaine
> Tho her auizing of the vertues rare,
> Which thereof spoken were, she gan againe
> Her to bethinke of, that mote to her selfe pertaine.
> (3.2.22.5–9)[21]

Significantly, it is through self-contemplation ("she gan againe / Her to bethinke of") that Britomart "*learn[s] to imagine* the possibility of a fitting marriage partner."[22] Although Glauce and Arthur dismiss her fears of incipient narcissism, the congruency between her projected desire and the reality of Artegall suggest that her help meet is, to some extent, created in her image, no external likeness but the artifice of "fancie." Indulging in "selfe-pleasing thoughts," she "fashions" an ideal "as fittest she for loue could find, / Wise, warlike, personable, courteous, and kind" (3.4.5.7–9), and when, a book and a half later, the knight *Salvagesse sans finesse* lifts his helmet, she promptly recognizes his face as "the same which in her fathers hall / Long since in that enchaunted glasse she saw" (4.6.26.5–6).

In *Jerusalem Delivered*, the twin potentialities of the romance mirror to reflect the inner self and the objectified desire of the heart are disassociated and set in antipathy. One mirror contributes to Rinaldo's returning self-awareness and consequent liberation from the enchantments of love, another to his enslavement to Armida. For, before recognizing himself in the Wise Man's shield, Rinaldo is already reflector and reflected in a complex exchange involving various media. While holding up a real mirror for Armida to study herself, he "makes himself mirrors of her limpid eyes"; but these, like the mirror which he holds for her, show not himself but her, so that the two lovers "in varying objects gaze on one object only" (16.20). Rinaldo's enchanted existence, indeed the created world itself, becomes Armida's mirror:

> My flames are the true portrait of your beauties; their shape, their marvelous qualities my breast sets forth in full, more than your mirror. Ah, since you ignore me, you should at least be able to see your own countenance, how beautiful it is: for your sight, that elsewhere is not gratified, would live in joyous happiness, turned upon itself. So sweet an image mirror cannot copy, nor in a little glass a paradise be comprised: the heavens are the mirror worthy of you, and in the stars you can see your lovely semblance. (16. 21–22)

This speech as effectively frames a portrait of the effeminized hero as does the Wise Man's shield, but at this moment, conscious only of himself as reflector, Rinaldo is unaware that in the act of mirroring Armida he might glimpse his own attenuated image, the outlines of a self that glimmer darkly, unobserved, across the surface of his speech. Seeing only her, he is blind to the mirrored contours of himself. Not until the shield dazzles his sight does he see clearly what he has become.

Even more than Britomart's discovery of Artegall in Merlin's looking-glass, Rinaldo's mirroring of Armida illustrates how the beloved in essence and in speech reflects the lover. But it also involves a dangerous lack of self-awareness, as well as the undesirable subordination of masculine to feminine charms. The *otium* of the romance garden unmans the heroic masculine: in the Wise Man's shield Rinaldo sees "his sword, (not to mention other things) made effeminate by his side" (16.30). This temporary subordination of genders and genres as male succumbs to female and epic to romance is embodied in the physical dominance of the woman during lovemaking: Rinaldo lies in Armida's lap. In the *Faerie Queene*, Verdant's "sleepie head" is couched on Acrasia's lap, and Adonis, from whom Venus is wont to "reape sweet pleasure," lies "Lapped in flowers and pretious spycery," while the goddess's sexual domination becomes almost predatory: "But she her selfe, when euer that she will, / Possesseth him, and of his sweetnesse takes her fill" (2.12.76.9, 3.6.46.3, 5–9). The positioning of Madách's Adam and Eve in Paradise also enacts this romance iconography of male sub-ordination: Eve bids Adam "lean on my breast" (174). Significantly, in Milton's Edenic seduction scene the position is reversed. At the end of her speech, Eve leans on Adam, her breast beneath her hair meeting his, while he smiles on her with "superior love" (4.499), a delightful Latinate pun allowing for physical elevation and temporal precedence: Adam's love smiles down at her, is older than hers, as well as being (feminist critics may demur) of greater excellence.

Eve's utilization of the mirror motif in book 4 of *Paradise Lost* to af-firm rather than subvert hierarchy, besides inverting the romance motif, resonates with the role of mirroring in Milton's divorce tracts as spiritual and intellectual congruency that guarantees satisfaction of (primarily) masculine expectations. Again, Milton is working with an established trope. Contemporary writings on marriage can, of course, be cited to prove both Milton's essentially patriarchal position (Mary Nyquist) and his dignified elevation of women (Anne Ferry), depend-ing on one's choice of texts. Nevertheless, it is instructive to consider some examples of the motif, both restricting and mediating female au-tonomy, in sermons and marriage manuals. In his *Directions for Love and Marriage*, published in English translation in 1677 and thus closely contemporary to *Paradise Lost*, Francisco Barbaro wonderingly reports the custom of the Cretenses, who, recognizing that similarity breeds affection, allowed their daughters "as in the loving of Friends, in Hus-bands . . . judiciously [to] chuse the resemblance of their own minds."[23] But such enlightened acknowledgement of the female self as the origi-nal to be reflected in her chosen mate was rare: more commonly the wife was expected to fashion herself to resemble her husband's mind. This is, in fact, the position endorsed by Barbaro: it is the duty of wives, not that of husbands, "so [to] live with their Husbands, that in a manner they might be of one mind and . . . the two should become one."[24] An earlier and more explicit instance of the deployment of the mirror motif to encourage likeness at the expense of independence is found in Robert Dod and John Cleaver's advice on household manage-ment:

> There is a certain discretion and desire required of women to please the nature, inclinations and manners of their husbands, so long as the same importeth no wickedness. For as the looking-glass, howsoever fair and beautifully adorned, is worth nothing if it show that counte-

nance sad which is pleasant; or the same pleasant that is sad: so the woman deserveth no commendation that, (as it were) contrarying her husband when he is merry, showeth herself sad, or in sadness uttereth her mirth. For as men should obey the laws of their cities, so women the manners of their husbands.[25]

Similarly, it seems, in Erasmus's colloquy "Marriage," Eulalia advises the wife of her role as conjugal reflector: "As a mirror, if it's a good one, always gives back the image of the person looking at it, so should a wife reflect her husband's moods." Yet while this definition of a wife's role ostensibly robs her of emotional autonomy, Eulalia qualifies the implied subordination by allowing that the wife might gradually mould her husband for better (or for worse) by reflecting his moods and characteristics, by compliancy and consideration: "What sort of men husbands are," she explains, "depends not a little on their wives."[26]

Milton's divorce tracts present a marital ideal in which mirroring is essential; not physical mirroring as in romance epic, nor yet the studied conjugal mimesis narrowly prescribed by Dod and Cleaver or more liberally by Erasmus, but an intellectual and spiritual congruity discovered (hopes the gentle soul) in marriage, yet not demanded of either partner at the expense of autonomy. Milton does not instruct the wife to conform to her husband's disposition to the extent of suppressing her own nature. The attempt to force disparate minds toward unity is deplored: "what can be a fouler incongruity, a greater violence to the reverend secret of nature, then to force a mixture of minds that cannot unite, & to sowe the furrow of mans nativity with seed of two incoherent and uncombining dispositions" (2:270). In such instances, when instead of likeness "disproportion, contrariety, or numbness of mind" characterizes the marital relationship, divorce is preferable. Milton's imagery often suggests architectural disparity: in unequal marriages, the "mind hangs off in an unclosing disproportion" like a badly hinged door. But if mirror imagery is not explicit, the concept of similarity nevertheless underlies his marital ideal. If wedlock is to be more than "the empty husk of an outside matrimony," the lover must, like Eros seeking Anteros, learn to penetrate the "trim disguises" of physical attractiveness and discover in his partner the "reflection of a coequal & homogeneal fire" (2:255). This reflection is not the "indefinite likeness of womanhood" but a specific, individual similarity characterized by a "unity of mind and heart" that supplies the need of the "wanting soul" (2:273, 252). The Adam of *Paradise Lost*, created in his maker's image and understanding the need for essential similarity, requests and re-

ceives "Thy likeness, thy fit help, thy other self, / Thy wish, exactly to
thy heart's desire " (8.450–51). Like Britomart, he has imagined her
"such, as fittest [he] for loue could find" and instantly recognizes the
newly created Eve as "my self / Before me" (8.495–96).

Characteristic of this ideal of inner likeness is the ability to participate in discourse. The meet help Milton depicts in the divorce tracts
and Adam seeks in *Paradise Lost* is possessed of "all the faculties of the
understanding" as a "fit conversing soul"; she is "an intimate and
speaking help, a ready and reviving associate in marriage" (2:251).
Against a trend of marriage tracts and sermons that enjoin female silence in wedlock, identifying as a woman's best ornaments "temperance
of her mind, silence in her tongue, and bashfulness in her counte-
nance," this description of a fit help emphatically privileges conjugal
discourse.[27] While Francesco Barbaro urges women to "adorn themselves with the famous ornament of silence," and Thomas Becon asserts that "there is nothing that so garnisheth a woman as silence . . .
even as nothing doth more discommend a woman more than the mul-
titude of words," Milton, speaking no doubt from personal experience,
warns that the "bashfull mutenes" fostered in maidens by precisely
such injunctions "may oft-times hide all the unlivelines & naturall sloth
which is really unfit for conversation" (2:249).[28] The man who finds
himself shackled to such a "mute and spiritles mate" after expecting to
discover a speaking help suffers greater loneliness than before (2:251).

But Adam is not disappointed: his Eve *is* a speaking help who, in her
first speech in *Paradise Lost*, conscious of the importance to relationships of mirroring and conversation, offers him a verbal portrait of
herself in which he is also reflected, redeeming the romance motif by
infusing it with the doctrine of marriage espoused in the divorce tracts
and wisely seducing him toward legitimate enjoyment of wedded love.
Although Milton explicitly rejects the subject matter of romance epic
in the prologue to book 9 and relocates the "constant lamp" (4.764) of
Cupid in married love, the conventions of court amours are not altogether expunged from his epic but are rather translated in his portrait
of paradisal love. The detailed description of Eve in book 4 recalls descriptions of romance temptresses, not only the seductive disarray of
Armida, Acrasia, and Alcina, but also the coy charms of the maidens at
play in the pool on Armida's island and outside the Bower of Bliss:

> With that, the other likewise vp arose,
> And her faire lockes, which formerly were bownd

Vp in one knott, she low adown did lose:
Which flowing long and thick, her cloth'd arownd,
And th'yuorie in golden mantle gownd:
So that faire spectale from him was reft,
Yet that, which reft it, no lesse farie was fownd:
So hidd in lockes and waues from lookers theft,
Nought but her louely face she for his looking left.

(2.12.67)

Like the nymphs' hair, like Acrasia's "vele of silke and siluer thin / That hid no whit her alabaster skin / But rather shewd more white, if more might bee" (2.12.77.4–6), Eve wears her "unadorned golden tresses" as a veil that falls to her waist but does not hide her "mysterious parts" (4.305, 312). Her hair conceals and reveals the exquisite pleasures of her body, as does the raiment of the romance seductress, silk or water. But in her innocent beauty she redeems the seeming naiveté of the seductress. Whereas the nymphs blush and laugh, aware of the "secret signes of kindled lust" their wonton play arouses, Eve's "sweet attractive grace" (4.298) is directed exclusively toward her husband, so that when, naked, she serves the visiting Raphael at table, "no thought infirm / Altered her cheek" (5.384–85). In Eden and in Eve's embrace, the dangerous *otium* of romance, symbolized not only in the seclusion of the garden but also in the tantalizing "lockes and waves" that, hiding as much as they reveal, perplex and prolong attainment of the goal, becomes that "sweet reluctant amorous delay" (4.311) that forges more strongly the link of nuptial league.[29] Adam may legitimately enjoy the delights at once concealed and revealed by Eve's wanton ringlets.

In a further inversion of romance convention, in Milton's epic it is the lady of the lake rather than the questing hero who must forgo dalliance with the water, turning from temptation to true love. The pool with its female figures offering sympathy and love must be rejected by the hero seeking the garden's center and its central romance. Eve, entering Eden and existence, lacks a Wise Man or a Palmer to warn her against delight in charming appearance. That role is played by the voice of God:

What thou seest,
What there thou seest fair creature is thyself,
With thee it came and goes: but follow me,
And I will bring thee where no shadow stays
Thy coming, and thy soft embraces, he

> Whose image thou art, him thou shall enjoy
> Inseparably thine, to him shalt bear
> Multitudes like thyself, and thence be called
> Mother of human race.
>
> (4.467–75)

Spenser's Palmer, seeing Guyon gazing on the nymphs, "much rebukt those wandring eyes of his, / And counseld well, him forward thence did draw" (2.12.69.2–3). Although a warning, the words Eve hears hardly constitute rebuke. Unlike the redirective advice given Guyon, or that given Ubaldo and Charles, couched in implicitly pejorative language that becomes explicitly pejorative as the moment of rejection is narrated (15.65), God's speech acknowledges and affirms as the basis of Eve's attraction to her reflection its beauty and reciprocity: her fair reflection came and goes *with* her. Her desire for relationship is noted, encouraged, redirected, but not repressed.

Eve's reflection of this voice is sometimes read as evidence of her colonization by a patriarchal hierarchy, but to read it thus is to ignore the freedom of choice "in all things else" (4.434) that maintains in Milton's Eden. Adam's first speech, recalling God's generosity and their duty to praise him, honoring his one easy prohibition, comprises the "mutuall help to piety" that Milton endorses as among the ends of wedlock identified by the "whole consent of our Divines . . . that in matrimony there must be first a mutuall help to piety, next to civill fellowship of love and amity, then to generation" (2:599). But while Milton summons this opinion to his defense in *Tetrachordon*, his own discussion of wedded love insistently privileges as its prime end the "conversing solace and peaceful society" it generates and sustains. Echoing her author's revaluation of the ends of marriage, Eve frames her response to Adam with an acknowledgment of God's goodness, an assurance that she appreciates this "mutuall help," before reflecting upon Adam's final five words ("yet with thee were sweet" [4.439]) and the love and amity possible in married life. She aims, she asserts, to illustrate her superior happiness in her enjoyment of Adam but—like the word-picture painted by Madách's Eve, like the mirror of Rinaldo's speech in which he reflects and is unwittingly reflected—her narration goes beyond this goal.

Possessed in Eden of choice unlimited, Eve selects and arranges her subject matter, establishing first the desirability of the mutual enjoyment of a responsive other. Unlike the noonday sun in *Az ember tragédiája*, Eve finds the watery image quite incidentally, but having found it, "unexperienc 'd thought" (4.457) leads her to the realization that it offers something attractive. It is not simply the reflection's beauty that appeals to her but its "answering looks / Of sympathy and love" (464–65). The delights of reciprocity essential to wedded love are discovered initially in the simple fact of physical mirroring: "I started back, / It started back, but pleased I soon returned, / Pleased it returned as soon" (462–64). This responsive dance of reflective surfaces comprises conversation of a sort, not yet the union with a "fit conversing soul" that is essential to Miltonic marriage but a discourse limited to glances only. Yet Eve makes it clear that these delights outweigh all others: in order to continue enjoying these "answering looks," she would have lain on the bank indefinitely. Although the image, lacking "Substantial life" (485), is ultimately ineffectual to answer her need for completion in another, her story serves to establish the desirability of and the compulsion toward identification of a mutually satisfying other.[30]

It is important to note that her discovery of the delights of reciprocity precedes God's intervention and is her own. As already noted, God's words serve to affirm the understanding that Eve has already reached. Comparing the response of Milton's God to that of Ovid's narrator, Heather James notes that he does not address Eve as "credule," and although he directs her away from her image to Adam, he does not bid her "alter the kind of attachment she has discovered through purely visual self-reflection."[31] The image *is* important, the divine voice agrees, but Eve is to consider herself reflector rather than reflected and, in so doing, will be enabled to "bear / Multitudes like [her]self," finding a new and infinitely more productive form of mirroring than casting shadows on the surface of the water. Eve characterizes the divine interruption as one of warning but in terms of the composition of her own speech, God's words, with their explanation of her role as Adam's image and his promise of further mirroring in her offspring, also act as a transition between her initial identification of the individual's need for an image and Adam's identification in her of the image he needs. God directs her toward Adam physically and metaphorically by explaining that she is Adam's image as the picture in the pool was hers. If the image in the water offered Eve "answering looks / Of sympathy and love," implicit is the suggestion that, as Adam's image, she is able to offer him that same desirable reciprocity.

God's words effect the reinforcement of the proposition Eve has just outlined, that discovery of the self in the image is a thing to be desired. In the case of Adam's words, she chooses between two possibilities. It is clear from his account in book 8 that after the creation of Eve and before her acceptance of him he speaks twice. Eve overhears his thanks to God for her creation—"She heard me thus," Adam explains (8.500)—and then he addresses to her his "pleaded reason" (510). Exercising choice and selection of his own in his construction of narrative, Adam does not elaborate upon this "pleaded reason" while talking to Raphael; only his earlier speech is fully documented. But this earlier speech, overheard by Eve, does not entirely tally with what she recollects in book 4. The content is similar: in his thanks to God, Adam describes Eve as "Bone of my bone, flesh of my flesh, my self / Before me" and anticipates man and woman becoming "one flesh, one heart, one soul" (8.495–96, 499). But the speech Eve recalls in book 4 is more specific, more expressive of interdependence, more passionately argued, and identifies more precisely a sense that she is necessary to his completion:

> Return fair Eve,
> Whom fli'st thou? Whom thou fli'st, of him thou art,
> His flesh, his bone; to give thee being I lent
> Out of my side to thee, nearest my heart
> Substantial life, to have thee by my side
> Henceforth an individual solace dear;
> Part of my Soul I seek thee, and thee claim
> My other half.
>
> (4.481–88)

Eve's reproduction of this second speech with its more telling exposition of Adam's need for her as the image who completes him seems to stand at odds with her avowed intention to demonstrate that she is the happier of the two, enjoying Adam while he is unable to find "Like consort to [him]self" (448). But the apparent discrepancy turns the reflective glance of her speech on Adam, allowing him to see, in a mirror authorized by God and confirmed by his own pleaded reason, his mutual dependence upon her for happiness. Eulalia, advocating mirroring in marriage, asserts that "What sort of men husbands are depends not a little on their wives." Although what sort of man Adam is depends upon his continued obedience to God, his wife's influence in not insignificant, as will be tragically proven in the Fall. Yet Eve's speech in book 4 is innocent of any postlapsarian intent. Here ambiguity, the possibility of interaction between consciously articulated intention (to assert her greater happiness) and subliminal intention (to remind Adam that his happiness also depends on her), counterbalances an affirmation of hierarchy with an assertion of mutual dependence that underscores the need for reciprocity in marriage. It suggests the play of amorous delay as Eve rekindles in Adam that sweetness unfelt before, recounting their first nuptials as an invitation to renew the experience. And like Madách's Eve, like the wife who heeds Eulalia's advice, Eve is able to influence her husband: Adam is moved to smiles of love and "kisses pure" (502).

Persuading Adam toward a legitimate enjoyment of conjugal love by representing to him his need of her for happiness, Milton's Eve effectively fuses the romance motif of mirroring with the practice of marriage idealized in the divorce tracts. Of itself the narcissistic moment by the pool establishes her awareness of the desirability of interaction with an other, prepares her, as does Britomart's glance into Merlin's mirror, for relationship. It is, as DuRocher maintains, "an innocent form of narcissism . . . perfectly appropriate to her newly created state."[32] But her reflection of that reflection in her first speech in *Paradise Lost* bespeaks an understanding of marriage distilled from her experience of lovemaking since her first waking. Like Milton, Adam needs his "speaking help" and Eve knows it. Mirroring God's words, mirroring Adam's, she frames a looking glass that shows her husband to himself in the context of their relationship and serves to cherish and reincite with pleasing conversation the "amiable and attractive society of conjugal love" temporarily suspended while Adam outlined their responsibilities toward their Creator.

NOTES

1. John Milton, *Paradise Lost*, ed. Alastair Fowler, 2nd ed. (London: Longman, 1998). All references to *Paradise Lost* are to this edition and are cited parenthetically in the text. Like Adam, elevating the spiritual and intellectual contribution to wedded love above "the sense of touch whereby mankind / Is propogated" (8.579–80), Milton calls such acts of peace and love, flowing from the mind, "a far more precious mixture than the quintessence of an excrement" (*The Doctrine and Discipline of Divorce*, in *Complete Prose Works of John Milton*, 8 vols., ed. Don M. Wolfe et al. [New Haven, CT: Yale University Press, 1953–82], 2:248). All references to Milton's prose are to this edition and are cited parenthetically in the text.

2. Ann Torday Gulden, "Milton's Eve and Wisdom: The 'Dinner-Party' Scene in *Paradise Lost*," *Milton Quarterly* 32 (1998): 137–42.

3. Christine Froula sees Eve's "imagination [as] so successfully colonized by patriarchal authority that she literally becomes its voice. As her narrative shows, she has

internalised the voices and values of her mentors: her speech reproduces the words
of the 'voice' and of Adam and concludes with an assurance that she has indeed been
successfully taught to 'see' for herself the superiority of Adam's virtues to her own"
("When Eve Reads Milton: Undoing the Canonical Economy," *Critical Inquiry* 10
[1983]: 329).

   4. Kay Gilliland Stevenson, "Eve's Place in *Paradise Lost*," *Milton Quarterly* 22
(1988): 127. Anne Ferry points to the "gracious reciprocity [and] . . . dignified choice"
implied in the balanced phrasing of "by her yielded, by him best receiv'd" and draws
attention to the fact that this reciprocity and Eve's persuasiveness are "divinely endowed" ("Milton's Creation of Eve," *SEL* 28 [1988]: 113–32, 117, 130). Other valuable studies of reciprocity in Eden include Diane McColley's *Milton's Eve* (Urbana:
University of Illinois Press, 1983); William Shullenberger's "Wrestling with the
Angel: *Paradise Lost* and Feminist Criticism," *Milton Quarterly* 20 (1986): 69–85; and
Kristin Pruitt's *Gender and the Power of Relationship: "United as one individual Soul" in
"Paradise Lost"* (Pittsburgh, PA: Duquesne University Press, 2003).

   5. Shullenberger, "Wrestling with the Angel," 80.

   6. Thus Donald M. Friedman describes Eve's fascination with her reflection as
part of "the developing moral experience of Eve as she comes to understand,
through choice and action, both what she is and what she is meant to be" ("The Lady
in the Garden: On the Literary Genetics of Milton's Eve," *Milton Studies* 35 [1997]:
126). Mary Jo Kietzman makes the similarly sensible observation that "Eve's interest
in the reflection does not have to be read simply as evidence of distorted desire that
must be chastened; it could be read as a first step toward self-understanding that
should be free to go further" ("The Fall into Conversation with Eve: Discursive Difference in *Paradise Lost*," *Criticism* 39 [1997]: 55–88). In "Self-Knowledge in *Paradise
Lost*: Conscience and Contemplation" (*Milton Studies* 3 [1971]: 103–18), Lee Jacobus
suggests a comparison between Eve's discovery of her image in the pool and the disembodied soul's self-contemplation in the river of Paradise in Peter Sterry's 1675 *A
Discourse on the Freedom of the Will*.

   7. Mary Nyquist, "The Genesis of Gendered Subjectivity in the Divorce Tracts
and in *Paradise Lost*," *Milton Quarterly* 22 (1988): 119.

   8. Ibid., 123.

   9. Károly Horváth, "Ádám alakjának világirodalmi előzményeihez," *Irodalomtör-
téntei közlemények* 88 (1984): 52–57. Horváth notes that in *Paradise Lost* 4.194–98
Satan perches on the Tree of Life as a cormorant "devising death" and suggests that
this detail may have influenced Madách's allocation of both the Tree of Life and the
Tree of Knowledge to Lucifer. Exploring literary precursors for Madách's Adam, he
concludes that among the various versions of the fall story available to the Hungarian poet "he was in all likelihood familiar only with Milton's *Paradise Lost*" [Közülük
csak Milton *Elveszett Paradicsomát* ismerte minden bizonnyal] (52).

   10. The title is consistently translated as *The Tragedy of Man*, although "man "
should be understood in an old-fashioned and inclusive sense; the Hungarian for
man in a gendered sense is *férfi*. Similarities between Madách's life and that of Milton are coincidental but interesting. Before the 1848 War of Independence against
the Hapsburgs, Madách had filled various public offices in the Nógrád County in
Hungary, but after being imprisoned in 1852 for sheltering the secretary of defeated
revolutionary leader, János Kossuth, he withdrew from public life and turned his attention to writing. Dramas on biblical and historical themes were his great interest,

but he also explored various stories from Genesis in shorter lyric poems, including "A nőteremtése" ("The Creation of Woman") and "Az elsőhalott" ("The First Man Dead—the Story of Cain and Abel"). Married across the denominational divide (Madách was Catholic, his wife Erzsébet Fráter a Protestant), he discovered too late that his estranged wife's nature was very different from his own; after three children, they eventually divorced in 1854.

11. Like Milton's Satan, Madách's Lucifer cannot bear the sight of Adam and Eve in each other's arms and turns away to avoid the pangs of envy. Encouraging himself, he turns back to his self-appointed task, but falls into doubt whether desire for knowledge could be effective against two "between whom stands, like a haven, guarding their hearts from faintness, raising the one that falls: love" [kik közt, mint menhely áll, / Mely lankadástól óvja szívöket, / Emelve a bukót: az érzelem] (Imre Madách, *Az ember tragédiája* [Budapest: Raabe Klett Kiadó, 1998], 212–14). All references to *Az ember tragédiája* are to this text. Unless otherwise indicated, all translations from Hungarian are my own.

12. "Én még, ha ott fenn a dics elborúl, / Itt lenn találom azt szemedben, Ádám. / Hol is lelhetném másutt kívüled, / Kit létre is csak hővágyad hozott, / Mint –fényár-jában a fejdelmi nap – / A mindenségben árván hogy ne álljon – / A víz szinére festi önmagát / S enyelg vele, örül, hogy társa van, / Nagylelküen felejtvén, hogy csupán / Saját tüzének halvány mása az, / Mely véle együtt semmivé borulna" (180–90).

13. Significantly, Eve describes the sun's image as its "társa," using the same word that God employs in Genesis for the companion he plans to create for Adam, although there the noun is qualified by the adjective "segítő" [helping]. Thus in Gáspár Károlyi's 1590 Hungarian translation, "És monda az Úr Isten: Nem jó az embernek egyedül lenni; szerzék néki segítő társat, hozzá illőt" [And the Lord God said: It is not good for the man to be alone; I will make him a helping mate suitable for him], and "az embernek hozzá illő segítő társat nem talált vala" [a helping mate suitable for the man was not found] (Genesis 2:18, 20).

14. "Mi volnék én, ha mint visszhang- s virágban, / Benned szebb létre nem feselne létem, / Melyben saját magam szerethetem?"

15. Although overlooking the mirror imagery and slow to attribute to Eve a key role in Adam's development, critics have generally recognized Eve's otherness as representative of the energies of the natural or emotive world. In "A Filozófia alapproblémája 'Az ember tragédiájá '-ban," *Athenaeum* (1944): 142–65, Lajos Lengyel argues that at one level Madách's poem comprises "the projection of the contradictions of human nature into a symbolic plot" [az emberi alkat . . . ellenmondásának szimbolikus cselekménybe vetítődése], and identifies in Eve "the projection of [one facet] of the individual's inner being . . . the embodiment of instinctual life" [az ember szellemiséget rejtőalkatának a kivetítődése...az ösztöni élet megtestesítője] (149, 162). István Sőter also sees Eve as the representative of the natural sphere in "A szembesített Madách," *Irodalomtörténeti Közlemények* 78 (1974): 179–85, and, following Sőter, Dieter P. Lotze claims that Eve "is more inclined toward enjoyment of life than Adam. . . . [H]er ties to nature are closer than his; she is emotional and is not given to abstract reflection" (*Imre Madách* [New York: Twayne, 1981], 67).

16. Pruitt, *Gender and the Power of Relationship*, 52.

17. Torquato Tasso, *Jerusalem Delivered*, trans. Ralph Nash (Detroit, MI: Wayne State University Press, 1987). All references to *Jerusalem Delivered* are to this edition and are cited parenthetically in the text.

18. Ludovico Ariosto, *Orlando Furioso*, trans. Guido Waldman (Oxford: Oxford World's Classics, 1998). All references to *Orlando Furioso* are to this edition and are cited parenthetically in the text.

19. Tasso does not explain the allegory of the Wise Man's shield, but by extension of his explanation of the allegory of Rinaldo (the irascible faculty of the soul), Armida (temptation of the appetitive faculty), and the Wise Man (human wisdom converted from its pagan origins by the Hermit as representative of supernatural understanding), the shield, with its ability to free Rinaldo from Armida's thrall and return him to active heroism, recalls that other New Testament mirror, the "perfect law of liberty" of St. James that blesses "in his deed" the man who looks steadfastly into it (James 1:25).

20. Richard J. DuRocher, "Guiding the Glance: Spenser, Milton, and 'Venus looking glas,' " *Journal of English and Germanic Philology* 92 (1993): 325–41.

21. Edmund Spenser, *The Faerie Queene*, ed. A. C. Hamilton (Harlow: Longman, 2001). All references to *The Faerie Queene* are to this edition and are cited parenthetically in the text.

22. DuRocher, "Guiding the Glance," 331

23. Francisco Barbaro, *Directions for Love and Marriage*, trans. anon. (London, 1677), 71.

24. Ibid., 70.

25. Robert Dod and John Cleaver, *A godly form of household government*, in *Renaissance Woman: Constructions of Femininity in England*, ed. Kate Aughterson (London: Routledge, 1995), 81.

26. Erasmus, *The Colloquies of Erasmus*, trans. Craig R. Thompson (Chicago: University of Chicago Press, 1965), 88, 119. In her advice to the unhappy Xanthippe, Eulalia draws on a tradition that goes back to classical antiquity. Plutarch, among others, uses the mirror trope when he recommends that the wife make "her life and character resemble and harmonize with her husband's" as if hers were a mirror of his, and he reminds her of her responsibility "to cultivate the art of handling her husband by charms of character and daily life, training him in good ways with pleasure" (*Plutarch's Advice to the Bride and Groom and A Consolation to His Wife*, trans. and ed. Sarah B. Pomeroy [New York: Oxford University Press, 1999], 7, 9).

27. Barbaro, *Directions*, 86; Barnabe Rich, *My lady's looking glass*, in *Renaissance Women*, ed. Aughterson, 96. Instructions for conduct before and in marriage collected by Aughterson include excerpts from Henry Smith, William Gouge, Samuel Rolands, and William Vaughan, all of whom to one degree or another decree women's silence. While Milton's divorce tracts do argue primarily and perhaps inevitably from the viewpoint of the disappointed male, his insistence on verbal discourse as a constitutive element of marital conversation and his emphasis on mutuality suggest to this reader at least a significant respect for women. Perhaps, as Gregory Chaplin suggests in " 'One Flesh, One Heart, One Soul': Renaissance Friendship and Miltonic Marriage" (*Modern Philology* 99 [2001]: 266–92), Milton's friendship with Diodati shaped his expectations of marriage. In the final analysis Milton, simply and reasonably, wanted a spouse he could talk not only to but with.

28. Barbaro, *Directions*, 86; Thomas Becon, *The book of matrimony* (1564), in *Renaissance Women*, ed. Aughterson, 112.

29. On techniques of delay in Renaissance love poetry to ensure "the renewability, the unending fascination, of sexual love," see William Kerrigan and Gordon

Braden, "Milton's Coy Eve: *Paradise Lost* and Renaissance Love Poetry," *ELH* 53 (1986): 27–51.

30. Shullenberger, "Wrestling with the Angels," goes further to attribute to the image an essentially creative role: "To become an image of an other is to give that other visible, palpable significant presence in the world, to provide symbolic form to the other's self. Eve thus stands in the same identifying relation to Adam as the Son stands in relation to the Father" (80).

31. Heather James, "Milton's Eve, the Romance Genre, and Ovid," *Comparative Literature* 45 (1993): 133.

32. DuRocher, "Guiding the Glance," 330.

Dramatic Silences:
Interpretive Pauses in
Paradise Regained

Tim Moylan

Mɪʟᴛᴏɴ ʟᴀᴄᴇs *Pᴀʀᴀᴅɪsᴇ Rᴇɢᴀɪɴᴇᴅ* ᴡɪᴛʜ sɪʟᴇɴᴄᴇs: ᴍᴏᴍᴇɴᴛs ᴏꜰ sɪɢɴɪꜰ-
icant hesitation, some overtly identified, others easily overlooked and
seemingly inexplicable. Interpretation of these silences depends heavily on textual cues, contextual familiarity, and ultimately on assumptions about the purpose of the poem as a whole. Milton employs two
treatments of silence. The first he identifies and narrates; the second
he implies. Both may be grouped according to the mental operation
taking place during the silence. I identify four kinds: silences of realization, diminution, recovery, and acceptance. Although these categories are not absolute, in each specific moment one mental and emotional action dominates. Attention to the presence of these silences and
to what transpires within them offers greater insight into the thematic
underpinnings of the work.

An overtly identified silence occurs when Satan first hears the voice
of God identifying Jesus at his baptism. The voice abruptly catches
Satan's attention, and the significance of the moment hangs over him
in an identified pause:

> That heard the Adversary, who roving still
> About the world, at that assembly famed
> Would not be last, and with the voice divine
> Nigh thunder-struck, th' exalted man, to whom
> Such high attest was giv'n, *a while surveyed*
> *With wonder.*
>
> (1.33–38; emphasis mine)[1]

We imagine Satan milling with the crowd around the Jordan, only dimly attentive to John's declamations as he "Pretends to wash off sin" (1.73). On hearing the divine voice he twists around to stare intently at Jesus emerging from the water. Milton provides clear textual and contextual cues, so we have enough information to make a good guess at what Satan is thinking. We see in the description of his puzzled wonder his surprise pass into envy, then into rage. We sense also a rising vapor of premonition. The narrated moment of silence clearly dramatizes the character. This strategy typifies all such moments involving static characters in the poem, primarily Satan and his infernal crew, but also God and the angelic host.

An unidentified silence takes place in book 2 and involves the apostles Andrew and Simon. They have been searching for the Messiah they heard dramatically announced at the river. They have covered a good deal of ground, but haven't found him, and they are frustrated. That energy layers onto their deeper cultural yearning for relief from Roman oppression. They vent their emotion in a "choral" lament, which, inflamed with zeal, rises into a prayer, even a demand on God:

> God of Israel,
> Send thy Messiah forth, the time has come;
> Behold the kings of the earth how they oppress
> Thy chosen, to what heighth their power unjust
> They have exalted, and behind them cast
> All fear of thee; arise and vindicate
> Thy glory, free thy people from their yoke.
> (2.42–48)

The line that follows, "But let us wait" (2.49), abruptly reverses the direction of this energy. The apostles lack apparent motivation for the abrupt change of mood. To make sense of the shift we must search in and then beyond the immediate context for an explanation.

Stanley Fish, in "Inaction and Silence: The Reader in *Paradise Regained*," sees in this instance and in the poem as a whole a calculated use of the decision not to act. He posits that this deliberate inaction reinforces the central message of the poem that the proper response to the very human, and hence suggestively satanic, prompting to act of one's own volition is simply not to act. The human will, the self, must "disappear," replaced by the will of the divine.[2] The apostles here, and Mary later, do as Jesus does throughout the poem. They choose inaction as the best response to the provocation of the moment. Although perhaps satisfying from a doctrinal point of view, the choice is very difficult poetically. Fish justifies Milton's forcing this discomfort on the reader by arguing that it demands an active alteration of reader expectation and, by so doing, reinforces the doctrinal lesson. This insight provides a rationale for the inexplicable, even automaton-like, behavior of the apostles, Mary, and Jesus. They act in ways that contrast with very normal and very human responses seemingly without motivation.

If Fish is right and their decision to wait prefigures and so reinforces what Jesus does, what evidence indicates this choice originates within them? Or is it the external, contrived manipulation of the poet? Before answering these questions, we must consider the impact of reading *Paradise Regained* as performance art. The poem is not a play. It lacks the necessary dramatic apparatus and has a narrative simplicity and thematic complexity that make a stage performance difficult. It should, however, be read or at least conceptualized as an oral performance. The poem is episodic, almost scenelike, and dialogue makes up much of the text. Most significantly for my argument, Milton makes effective use of dramatic pause. As actors know very well, silence communicates. As readers/audience we may imbue silences with meaning by drawing on what we already know or believe about the character and the context. Certainly, Milton was familiar with live theater. His Latin poem to Charles Diodati (*Elegia Prima*) suggests he frequented the theater as a young man, and *Comus* and *Samson Agonistes* are either actual stage productions or were conceptualized as theater.

We may apply Fish's insight in accounting for the apostles' and Mary's odd behavior by creating space and time for the emergence of motivation. We may do this in performance by prolonging the normal end of line pause immediately after "arise and vindicate / Thy glory, free thy people from their yoke." If it is held longer than is comfortable, the delay cues the listener/reader to expect some shift in the apostles' frame of mind. When vocalized, the apostles' complaint rings out in the cottage, then dies away into its own echo. Silence follows; a lack of an answer, a response of nonresponse. On the edge of hearing in the contrasting quiet murmurs is the almost inaudible sound of "winds with reeds, and osiers whisp'ring" (2.26). This line contrasts powerfully with the accumulated frustration of the search. The pause dissipates the enthusiasm of the apostles' appeal. The hesitation cautions us to consider the thoughts of Andrew and Simon. We know where they begin, and we know where they end. What we do not know is how they got from one point to the other. A pause, a silence, accents the need for reflection on the oddity of their choice. A parallel to "Sonnet 16, On His Blindness" is striking here. The word "yoke" in *Paradise Regained* refers to the Roman occupation. "[P]atience" (8) in the sonnet uses it to refer to the trials borne in any life by the individual Christian and reminds the complaining voice in the sonnet, presumably Milton, that "who best / Bear his mild yoke, they serve him best" (10–11). This act of "bearing" answers the question of what is to be done. The apostles as well as Milton must simply "stand and wait" (14).

Once alerted to the use of these silences, we can locate them throughout the poem. Their prevalence and variety invite a closer look. Of four categories, the first, a silence of realization, occurs when a recognition and understanding of a larger truth dominates an emotional moment. This occurs typically when a character or group realizes the significance of an event. One example of this kind of silence takes place when the angelic host first grasps the sublimity of Jesus's mission, as God reveals it to them. This takes place in an identified moment of hesitation:

> So spake the Eternal Father, and all Heaven
> *Admiring stood a space*, then into hymns
> Burst forth, and in celestial measures moved,
> Circling the throne and singing, while the hand
> Sung with the voice, and this the argument.
> (1.168–72; emphasis mine)

Milton narrates the angels' moment of silence. The imagery here is almost comic. The angels cluster around God as he explains his plan to Gabriel. They look mutely at one another in dumbfounded appreciation of its sublimity, then suddenly burst into song and flight. Interpreting this moment requires little nontextual information, though traditional angel iconography adds a touch of visual humor Milton may or may not have intended.

A second example of a silence of realization occurs during Mary's meditation. Milton does not clearly identify this pause in the text. We must infer it from Mary's abrupt emotional change of direction. Jesus has not come home and Mary is worried:

> Within her breast, though calm; her breast though pure,
> Motherly cares and fears got head, and raised
> Some troubled thoughts, which she in sighs thus clad.
> (2.63–65)

She reflects on her past and on Jesus's life with her, and in particular on the prophecy of pain appointed to her. She ends her reflection admirably in a resigned acceptance: "Afflicted I may be, it seems, and blest; / I will not argue that, nor will repine" (93–94). Nevertheless, her humanity overcomes her discipline and she asks, "But where delays he now?" (95). Her consolatory answer follows immediately, "some great intent / Conceals him" (95–96). Even for Mary, the Mother of God, the change here is too quick to be satisfactory. The emotional sense demands some hesitation. It begs a dramatic pause long enough for the wheels of her heart and her head to revolve to the proper answer. Although Mary afterward justifies her complacency by remembering the last time Jesus was missing, the initial rapidity with which she consoles herself becomes more acceptable and powerful if we pause to imagine her thought process. It might run something like this: "Why didn't he call to say he was going to be late? He is probably lying dead in a ditch somewhere. Well, maybe not. But if not, he's going to hear about it when he gets home. What could be keeping him if not an accident? It had better be important. It's not like him just to take off like this. The last time he pulled this was with that business at the temple, all that arguing with the scribes. Of course, if this is anything like that, it probably is important, especially after what happened at the river. It must be something like that. It is. I'm sure of it, or I would have heard from him." "[S]ome great intent / Conceals him" (95–96). If we pause in the reading, we give Mary a moment to process all this, a moment to realize that Jesus's disappearance marks a pivotal moment in the divine plan. A full stop intensifies the significance, and it calls attention to the bitterness of the moment. She has not been unmindful of her own prophecy of pain. Nevertheless, she concludes that she must wait, with "patience . . . inured" (102), for whatever will come. Her choice is less simple and automatic than the syntax initially suggests.

The whole poem drives toward its most significant realization, Jesus's full recognition of his divinity. For Jesus this realization confirms both his identity and his mission. For Satan it confirms Jesus as the Christ. The epic climaxes in a single line and the act of standing up. What follows should be a moment of suspenseful silence. Instead, Milton charges on into somewhat anticlimactic comparison of Satan's fall with "Earth's son Antaeus" (4.563) and "that Theban monster" (572). The lack of narrative attention to Jesus's act understates its significance, not in doctrinal, but in human terms. The moment is climactic, but it passes without attention to the suspense it contains. This suggests Jesus's action entailed no risk. The implication is that he *knew* he would not fall. He might simply be standing up to finally get rid of Satan whose persistence had become tiresome. Inserting a silence immediately after the climactic line, however, emphasizes a different interpretation. A dramatic pause implies the outcome of his action is not a given. Jesus does not *know*. His stepping up, then, becomes a complete act of faith, a final sacrifice of the self, without surety. The silence begins in suspense and concludes in confirmation. In it, Jesus's balance is established and his divinity confirmed; his offering of self is accepted, and Satan's eyes and mind are opened to the full realization of what until this point he has willfully doubted. Then Satan should fall. Inserting a silence here highlights and intensifies the moment in which these realizations dawn.

A second category of silences, those of diminution, involve moments in which the accumulated energy or emotion from the preceding rhetoric drains away. One example of these is Satan's request of Jesus for his permission to visit. Satan represents Jesus's granting his request as a bestowing of gentle grace on an undeserving reprobate. Satan's particularly sly twist here involves wrapping the temptation in an outward form of good manners. Jesus's direct refusal grates on the moral ear in its violation of the custom of hospitality. Additionally, Satan's silky tone exerts an undeniable emotional pull. Inserting a pause just before the narrative transition to Jesus's dialogue provides a moment in which this emotional power may evaporate. After Satan finishes his request, "disdain not such access to me" (1.492), Jesus should wait and allow Satan's smirking "humility" to become self-conscious. After a long, progressively more uncomfortable hesitation, we can imagine Satan breaking the tension first with an exasperated "What?" before:

> our Saviour with unaltered brow [says]
> Thy coming hither, though I know thy scope,
> I bid not or forbid; do as thou find'st
> Permission from above; thou canst not more.
> (493–96)

Prolonging the pause gives the machinery of the diabolical time to show through the fabric cover, the bones to show through the thin skin. Jesus's quiet, noncommittal, and apt response then contrasts less with Satan's appeal since the emotional energy has drained from it.

The following moment just before Satan's magician-like dissimulation also benefits from an inserted silence. We can imagine a long mo-

ment of eye contact as the two opponents conclude the first day's ten-
tative conflict. They stare at each other for a long, intense silence; then
Satan with mock dignity snaps forward at the waist and dissolves like
the validity of his arguments into a gray mist. This imaginative, dramatic rendering interprets and intensifies the subtext, the doctrinal
message tucked into Jesus's enigmatic responses. It must be God, not
Satan, who frames the argument.

A second appeal in which silences effectively inform the action is
the temptation of the feast. Satan's spread of meat and drink, proffered
by the fair and beautiful, accompanies his evocative appeal:

> All these are Spirits of air, and woods, and springs,
> Thy gentle ministers, who come to pay
> Thee homage, and acknowledge thee their Lord:
> What doubt'st thou Son of God? Sit down and eat.
>   (2.374–77)

In addition to the sensual imagery playing on the awakening of physical hunger in Jesus, Satan employs his voice with its mellifluous, compelling, and companionable tone urging acceptance of his invitation.
Milton describes Jesus's reply as temperate (378), but that sense of
temperance becomes more effective if it does not follow immediately.
A silence inserted just after "sit down and eat" and held just long
enough to be uncomfortable reduces the pull of Satan's appeal. The
sense of expectation begins to ebb when the appeal fails to produce the
expected rush of acquiescence. Satan here plays the role of affectionate
host urging a guest to stay for a meal. A reluctance to impose or to
change plans restrains the guest, but the host insists, and so he wavers.
Then, he assents, and the polite tension disperses in a rush of warm
cordiality. In this instance, however, the hospitality is specious. Jesus
observes this and ignores the pressure. More significantly, he neither
accepts nor directly refuses the offer as Satan represents it. Instead, he
exposes the fallacy behind the offer. It is tempting to imagine him lift-
ing one of the silver serving covers and asking Satan, "Isn't this the
chicken and pickles that were in *my* refrigerator?" Inserting a silence
just after "sit down and eat" accents the incongruity of the expectation
and alerts us to look hard at our initial acceptance of the way Satan
packages his appeal.

The third form of silence, the silence of recovery, belongs entirely
to Satan. Milton clearly identifies when one of these occurs in the text,
typically following Satan's confutation and rebuke. They take the form

of suspended dialogue during which Satan, at first stunned by a failure, reformulates his pitch and responds. They follow from the fact that Satan's efforts, however subtle and devious, are always extemporaneous. In the beginning, he tells his diabolical council:

> His first-begot we know, and sore have felt,
> When his fierce thunder drove us to the deep;
> Who this is we must learn, for man he seems
> In all his lineaments, though in his face
> The glimpses of his Father's glory shine.
>   (1.89–93)

He does not yet know his opponent, so he cannot fully prepare a means of attack. After his first exploratory attempt, he tells his minions, "[I] [h]ave found him, viewed him, tasted him" (2.131). He has taken the measure of his opponent and come away impressed. He admits to his infernal crew that he is unsure of success. Jesus will require, he says, "Far other labour to be undergone / Than when I dealt with Adam first of men" (132–33), and this labor will involve operating from a shifting base. This approach intensifies the moments that follow each failure. Satan's reaction, usually identified with a spare adjective, is followed by a described hesitation before he renews the assault. Unlike the implied hesitations I call attention to when interpreting the acts of Jesus, the apostles, and Mary, Milton narrates these pauses. After the appeal to wealth at the end of the second book, Satan experiences a significant setback. The third book begins with his silence of reaction and recovery:

> So spake the Son of God, and Satan stood
> A while as mute, confounded what to say,
> What to reply, confuted and convinced
> Of his weak arguing, and fallacious drift.
>   (3.1–4)

It is only after a long moment that he, "At length collecting all his Serpent wiles" (5), renews the attempt. Milton identifies this waiting period and gives it substantial textual reinforcement. Satan gets six full lines to catch his breath. A longer recovery period follows the rebuff at the end of book 3. At the beginning of book 4, Satan spends twenty-four lines in "shameful silence" (22), as the narrator comments on the futility of his persistence. Then, instead of speaking, he acts. He abruptly spirits Jesus off to the mountainside. Milton relays another nineteen lines of description before Satan gets his voice back. These silences require little imaginative speculation because they reinforce rather than contradict reader expectation. Satan's frustrated silences do not bewilder us. In fact, in his behavior we see a disturbingly familiar reflection. Satan does what we would do. He constructs compelling pleas that subtly misrepresent the truth or misplace the point in order to fulfill a deeply personal desire. In each case, Jesus exposes Satan's distortions and reorients his misplaced priorities. We find Satan's moments of silence understandable because they resemble our own. After Jesus rejects the pursuit of glory for himself, saying "I seek not mine, but his / Who sent me, and thereby witness whence I am" (3.106–7), Satan responds in a telling murmur, "Think not so slight of glory" (109). Milton's use of the word "murmuring" here conveys not only the sense of speaking softly, but also that of complaint. For Satan this temptation is personal. In this way it resembles the "murmur" (9) in "Sonnet 16." Both complaints spring from a deeply personal desire. Milton reinforces the personal quality of this temptation for Satan when Jesus finishes his dismissal of the appeal:

> Satan had not to answer, but stood struck
> With guilt of his own sin, for he himself
> Insatiable of glory had lost all.
>   (3.146–48)

Satan's sin, the aggrandizement of self, is of a kind with Eve's. His murmur might be ours, and his regret resonates with our own. We need not strain our imagination much when looking in the mirror.

Jesus has a different relationship to silence when it involves only him, and his moments of silence suggest a more dynamic character than earlier critics generally recognize. Admittedly Jesus's demeanor is not particularly engaging. Milton indicates his taciturn emotions with spare adjectives tucked into the introductions to his responses. Generally, Jesus is "unmoved," "calm," or "stern," although in one moment of unrestrained enthusiasm, he becomes "fervent." These barren descriptors suggest a Jesus simply going through the motions, confident of himself and of his ultimate success. A closer look at books 1 and 2, however, reveals several suggestively human impulses disturbing his divine self-control. As Mary and the apostles did before him, Jesus experiences silences of realization and acceptance.

The first such silence occurs during his initial investigation into his identity. In fact, his whole trip into the wilderness cultivates a silence within which to discover who and what he is as well as the direction of his mission. It is not, however, as quiet as it appears. An internal noise besets him:

> O what a multitude of thoughts at once
> Awakened in me swarm, while I consider
> What from within I feel myself, and hear
> What from without comes often to my ears
> Ill sorting with my present state compared.
>   (1.196–200)

He reviews what he has been told, has read, and how he has responded to the promptings of his heart. He recalls a time when zeal for his people "flamed in [h]is heart" (216) and how that energy passed from a compulsion to act with force to a decision to rely instead on persuasion as the "more humane, the more Heavenly" means (221). His thought here is clearly grounded in an earthly and historical frame of reference. His choice is not inexplicable. Certainly the human as well as the divine may value persuasion over violence. Yet the decision seems almost arbitrary. It lacks evident emotional justification. A hesitation inserted after "Till truth were freed, and equity restored" and before "Yet held" highlights the moment in which his emotional zeal cools and his reason or divine insight asserts itself (1.220–21). Jesus speaks in retrospect here, and the dramatic sense appropriate to a reflection differs from that of more immediate narration. Still, hesitating emphasizes the human quality of the moment. Jesus feels the tug of competing desires and the need to make a choice. Though subtle, this quiet, minor crisis humanizes Jesus. Inserting the silence calls attention to a moment easily missed, especially in a silent reading.

Jesus then recalls his mother's words and what he found in looking to the Scriptures for guidance. Another pause for dramatic effect powerfully reinforces his discovery. Jesus has looked himself up in the library. We can imagine him peering intently into a sacred scroll then looking up suddenly. He has "found of whom they spake / I am" (262–63). Lingering a moment before "I am" adds weight to the line. It draws attention to Jesus's comprehension that he is the one prophesied. For the temporal, human Jesus, this is an epiphany. The natural rhythm of reading pushes past this moment at nearly the same rate as any other, but an attentive reader may, even should, hesitate, pacing the lead-in line so the vocal (even if read silently) punch intensifies the biblical echo "I am."

A third silence of realization in this sequence follows the line, "whose sins / Full weight must be transferred upon my head. / Yet neither thus disheartened or dismayed, the time prefixed I waited" (266–68). The enormity of the first line, that upon his head must fall the weight of all earthly sin, makes his comment in the next line seem either offhand or surreal. At the very least, he should first swallow hard. If not, we lose the sense of his humanity and our affinity with him in a divine but inaccessible radiance. A hesitation here, the taking of a breath, a sigh of mute resignation, serves to keep him close, keep him human enough to make it possible to imitate him as well as admire him. Jesus loses something when he rises preternaturally above human response. In a hesitation, we can empathize with the human struggle behind his acceptance.

Another silence of realization occurs when his reminiscences move forward to the present, to his journey into the wilderness:

> And now by some strong motion I am led
> Into this wilderness, to what intent
> I learn not yet, perhaps I need not know.
>   (290–92)

Inserting a strong hesitation between "yet" and "perhaps" expands the normal weight of the comma and calls attention to the following line, "For what concerns my knowledge God reveals" (294), which identifies the key to Jesus's orientation to the Father. Jesus grounds all his counterarguments to Satan's appeals in this acceptance on faith of the unseen Father's will. He accepts that a divine intent exists, but remains hidden. He recognizes his initial desire to know and understand originates in self-will. The hesitation here highlights his realization that this human desire exists independent of the need dictated by the Father. He then accepts the uncomfortable position he occupies, in doing so modeling a kind of ultimate negative capability.

A similar acceptance occurs in book 2. Jesus's humanity again asserts itself in a moment when he makes a choice, a moment readily intensified by a silence. The forty days have passed, and Jesus feels hunger for the first time.[3] More significantly, he has found no further direction or explanation. In mild exasperation he asks himself, "Where will this end?" (245). The complex syntax of the following lines obscures somewhat the consequence this fast has for him. Clearly, though,

the pangs of human hunger give him pause and require some reconciliation with his faith:

> But now I feel I hunger, which declares,
> Nature hath need of what she asks; yet God
> Can satisfy that need some other way,
> Though hunger still remain: so it remain
> Without this body's wasting, I content me,
> And from the sting of famine fear no harm.
>
> (252–57)

A pause just after "she asks" and before "yet" emphasizes his intellectual and spiritual assessment of, "Now what do I do? I'm starving."
The human response is "I am hungry, and I want to eat." The divine
response is "Though I am hungry, my body does not waste away. The
hunger for the will of God must take precedence. Since God is providing against the natural consequences of hunger, I will wait—even if I
am still really, really hungry." A silence here calls attention to his brief
struggle in accepting the will of the Father. We expect Jesus to come
to this conclusion. He is, after all, Jesus. However, for the reader his
act of acceptance becomes more compelling if even he has to think
about it.

In the end his "thinking about it" informs my argument for the se-
lective insertion and dramatic interpretation of silences into the text.
The silences themselves do not explain the apparent discontinuities in
the narrative. Silence as an interpretive device depends on assumptions
about the poem, and we use our guesses at Milton's intentions and
broader contextual and thematic understandings to fill the empty
space. Emotional discontinuities prompt questions, and the pursuit of
their answers ultimately resolves into the larger question that the
poem asks: how may Paradise be regained? This, in turn, links to how
it was lost in the first place and how that might be reversed. Eve's taking of the apple at the prompting of the serpent was ultimately an act
of selfishness, a choice of self over God. It recapitulates Satan's great
sin. Satan's famous declaration from book 1 of *Paradise Lost*, "To reign
is worth ambition though in Hell; / Better to reign in hell, than serve
in Heav'n" (262–63), elevates the will of the self over that of the Father. For Satan, the prince of deceit, this act constitutes the original
self-deception. His rejection of the primacy of God for the primacy of
self inverts the proper relationship of created to creator. He fails to
trust, fails to believe that acceptance of the will of God will provide ful-

fillment of self rather than the loss of it. Satan fears that by making the divine preeminent, the self will be subsumed. Jesus demonstrates that, paradoxically, the relinquishing of the self does not result in the disappearance of individual personhood.

In making this claim, I disagree with Fish who sees the individual Jesus disappearing in the climactic and ambiguous line, "To whom thus Jesus: also it is written, / Tempt not the Lord thy God, he said and stood" (4.560–61). According to Fish, the "he" of the human and individuated Jesus vanishes into the "He" of the divine through a complete abandonment of the individual self.[4] I suggest rather that this act constitutes a fulfillment of self, a radiation or an amplification of the original human self now fully imbued with or infused by the divine. This commingling and intensifying of the self's potential only becomes possible in a willing displacement of the self from the center, from the locus of control. This requires a human leap of faith, a leap made by a coherent human self acting without surety. As Lewalski points out, Satan's first temptation, to turn stones into bread, is not one of hunger but one of distrust.[5] In the end, so is the final temptation. In casting himself down, Jesus would have presumed upon, tested, the divine, and any test is rooted not in faith but in doubt. Such an act insists on a demonstration of divine power as justification for faith. Jesus refuses this final temptation as he did the first. In stepping up, Jesus trusts. In the pause that follows, the Father confirms that trust by accepting Jesus's gift of self. Satan realizes not only the divinity of Jesus, but also the failure of his own strategy. In clutching the self, Satan loses it. In surrendering the self, Jesus possesses it in abundance.

To regain Paradise, Milton's Jesus must reestablish the proper order of priorities. This task underlies all the major and minor conflicts in the poem. In each case, the principal characters stand and wait rather than assert their will independent of divine direction. Silences of realization, diminution, and acceptance help to counter the natural rhythm of the silently read text and provide for a dramatic interpretation that emphasizes the human struggle these choices involve. Criticism of the poem's static characters and their lack of energy may be offset somewhat by a sensitive reading that makes effective use of intentional hesitations and of meaningful silences. An interpretive understanding of the doctrinal issues that Milton addresses in the poem, and the application of those understandings to the literal oral "reading" of the work, can use the device of silence, of hesitation, of significant pause, to tease out the implications, the meaning of the work.

NOTES

I am indebted to Dr. Sara van den Berg, Beth Human, and other members of the Milton seminar at St. Louis University, Fall 2003, for their editorial assistance and for the suggestion that Satan's mode of argument is essentially extemporaneous.

1. John Milton, *Paradise Regained*, in *John Milton: The Complete Poems*, ed. John Leonard (London: Penguin, 1998). All references to Milton's poetry are to this edition and are cited parenthetically in the text. Silence as a facet of literary interpretation has drawn the attention of a number of critics, notably Bruce R. Smith with *The Acoustic World of Early Modern England: Attending to the O-Factor* (Chicago: University of Chicago Press, 1999), whose central focus is on sound, but who necessarily notes the significance of refraining from making it; Philip C. McGuire, *Speechless Dialect: Shakespeare's Open Silences* (Berkeley: University of California Press, 1985); and Wolfgang Iser and Sanford Budick, eds., *Languages of the Unsayable: The Play of Negativity in Literature and Literary Theory* (New York: Columbia University Press, 1989). McGuire emphasizes close textual and contextual analysis, but especially notes the significance of drama as an act of sound and of performance, one that necessarily and directly engages the participation of the audience (122–23 ff.). His focus is on theatrical performance, but I believe the cooperative quality of actor and audience interpretation he argues for may readily be applied to other genres, particularly Milton's poetry. Also, I was recently referred to a review of Christina Luckyj's book, *"A Moving Rhetoricke": Gender and Silence in Early Modern England* (Cambridge: Cambridge University Press, 1998), which notes how she makes an interesting distinction between acoustic and symbolic silences. Lastly, Milton's association with the theater and the fact that he was likely blind at the time of his composition of *Paradise Regained* and so dictated the work both suggest that dramatic pause of the kind I describe may have been a component of his creative process.

2. Stanley E. Fish, "Inaction and Silence: The Reader in *Paradise Regained*," in *Calm of Mind: Tercentenary Essays on "Paradise Regained" and "Samson Agonistes" in Honor of John S. Diekhoff*, ed. Joseph Anthony Wittreich Jr. (Cleveland, OH: Case Western Reserve University Press, 1971), 25–47.

3. Barbara Lewalski, *Milton's Brief Epic: The Genre, Meaning, and Art of "Paradise Regained"* (Providence, RI: Brown University Press, 1966), 202.

4. Fish, "Inaction," 43.

5. Lewalski, *Milton's Brief Epic*, 202.

Samson and the Chorus of Dissent

Christopher N. Warren

> The sun to me is dark
> And silent as the moon
> *Samson Agonistes* (86–87)

Philology was, for Milton, a place to access the divine. Milton found in places where we might say words and languages come together—where Thomas Pynchon has said we experience "the flinders of luminescent gods"—semantic events that seemed to carry vestiges of the pre-Babel unity of languages.[1] I want to begin with the possibility of a philological pun in Milton's title for *Samson Agonistes* that has so far gone unnoticed by critics, but which has implications for a number of debates with which Milton criticism has more often been concerned—namely, the role of toleration in Milton's late poetry, the role of the chorus in Milton's dramatic poem, and in a less direct way, Milton's ultimate intention with *Samson Agonistes*. Most studies of *Samson* treat the topic of Samson's epithet "agonistes" briefly, if they treat it at all, usually calling casual attention to it on the way to illuminating one or more of Samson's *agones* with Dalila, Harapha, the Philistines in general or excessive self-reproach. Yet there is an element of the title that may demand readers pay less attention to those physical and metaphysical subjects against which Samson is seen to struggle and more attention to who is, or should be, doing the struggling.

As critics have long observed, the name Samson derives from *shemesh*, the Hebrew for "sun," and Milton employs this etymology as early as line 3's "choice of sun or shade," thereafter extending it to inform the themes of corporeal and spiritual blindness.[2] "Agonistes" means "Champion," "contestant in the games," or, alternatively, "one who struggles." On its face, there is little to suggest that the two words of the title do more than that to mark Milton's drama in what he calls "the Greek manner." At once articulating this view and indicating the extent to which it is taken for granted among readers of the drama, John Leonard notes that the title signals "which episode in the hero's life the drama will present" and adds, parenthetically even, "(in the manner of such Greek titles as *Prometheus Bound* or *Oedipus at Colonus*)."[3]

First, I wish to complicate this assumption a bit. In Aristotle's *Poetics*, which Milton cites in his prologue to the drama, having already quoted it in Greek on the title page, the philosopher enjoins: "The chorus also should be thought of as one of the actors; it should be a part of the whole and contribute its share to success in the competitive effort."[4] In Greek, the verb he uses to say "contribute its share to success" is συναγωνίζεσθαι ι (sunagônizomai), which might also be translated as "to champion *with*." My reason for questioning the face value reading of Milton's title is a simple, linguistic syllogism: if Samson, in English, means "sun," joined with "agonistes," the resulting noun "sunagonistes"—"one who shares with another in a contest, a fellow-combatant, coadjutor"—is a word with potentially deep applications for the ensuing drama.[5]

It must be acknowledged that a supposition such as this one is nearly impossible to prove, which is why proving it here is not my intention. Remembering, however, that etymological puns are "by far the most frequent kind of pun," in Milton's poetry, as Edward Le Comte has observed, and that, as John Hale has recently demonstrated, *Samson* is characterized by a "mingling, or meeting, and at times fusing, of [Milton's] two least related languages, Greek and Hebrew," the possibility does open into some important questions about the drama.[6] Nevertheless, whether Milton was offering a learned pun in his title will have to depend on what such a possibility means for the drama itself. By thinking with Milton about what it might mean for the Chorus to "strive with" Samson, this essay claims that the model of charitable, doctrinal debate Milton dramatizes between Samson and the Chorus is meant to contrast sharply with the model of "force" exercised by the Philistines. Although critics have often searched for doctrinal errors in Milton's chorus, this essay argues that such heresy hunting is beside the point. Instead, the divergent processes by which the Chorus and the Philistines deal with doctrinal disagreement—arguing and preaching, on the one hand, and threats and force on the other—are what Milton most wishes to emphasize in his drama. For

Milton, I will argue, the one, "striving with," leads to godly redemption while the other, forced submission, ultimately impels violent destruction.

Sunagônizomai appears only once in the Bible, in a source enormously important to Milton, Paul's letter to the Romans, which Milton references countless times in *De Doctrina Christiana* and no fewer than seven times in a work to which I will return later, *A Treatise of Civil Power in Ecclesiastical Causes* (1659). At Romans 15:30, the Geneva Bible translates *sunagônizomai* to say "strive with." Paul tells the Romans: "brethren, I beseech you for our Lord Jesus Christ's sake, and for the love of the spirit, that ye would strive with me by prayers to God for me, That I may be delivered from them which are disobedient in Judea, & that my service which I have to do at Jerusalem, may be accepted of the Saints." In the passage's image of pious, collective struggle—striving with—Milton could find a description of Christian zeal with which he might join the pagan *Poetics* according to the combinatorial logic of Christian humanism. Since Aristotle uses *sunagônizomai* to prescribe the proper role of the Chorus, however, it is the Chorus that will be the focus of this essay. Milton is clearly hard-pressed to account for his Chorus. In comments that occupy about a fifth of the "epistolary" prologue, Milton writes, "the chorus is here introduced after the Greek manner, not ancient only but modern, and still in use among the Italians."[7] Aristotle's requirement that the chorus "contribute its share to success in the competitive effort" provides the main criterion against which we might examine *Samson*'s Chorus. What may be the title's philological pun prods us to ask if Samson's Chorus acts, in fact, as a fellow combatant against the Philistines.

Building upon N. H. Keeble's and Sharon Achinstein's recent discussions of *Samson Agonistes* as both constructing and participating in 1660s debates on toleration, nonconformity, and dissent, this essay intends to hold the familiar Miltonic source of Aristotle's *Poetics* within this newly proposed Restoration context of conformity and dissent by reading the term *sunagonistes* with an essentially political accent.[8] As distinct from *agonistes*, *sunagonistes* places new emphases on the drama. Onto the unflinchingly martial and combative *agonistes*, the term *sunagonistes*, while still undeniably including those soldierly notions, also maps a landscape of slightly dissonant terms, such as cooperation, assistance, fellowship, and commonality, terms that focus on interaction, dialogue, and coalition, undertaken though they may be in the shadow of a common antagonist. If "agonistes" is the language of the autonomous, liberal hero in uneasy relationship with other men, if not inevitable conflict with them, "sunagonistes," by contrast, is the language of godly—even republican—fellowship.⁹ These terms of godly, republican cooperation, the terms invoked by *sunagonistes*, appear fairly infrequently in scholarship dedicated to Milton's poetry, despite the fact that they are the notions that underlie and in many ways motivate his protolerationist prose project, *Of Civil Power* and *Of True Religion*. Readers familiar with these prose works will recall scores of passages like the following (taken from the latter) that pointedly place discourse and Protestant community before conflict:

> [T]he hottest disputes among Protestants calmly and charitably en-quire'd into, will be found less than such. . . . It cannot be deny'd that the Authors or late Revivers of all these [Protestant] Sects or Opinions, were Learned, Worthy, Zealous, and Religious Men, as appears by their lives written, and the same of their many Eminent and Learned followers, perfect and powerful in the Scriptures, holy and unblamable in their lives: and it cannot be imagined that God would desert such painful and zealous labourers in his Church, and ofttimes great suffer-ers for their Conscience, to damnable Errors & a Reprobate sense, who had so often implor'd the assistance of his Spirit; but rather, having made no man Infallible, that he hath pardoned their errors and accepts their Pious endeavors, sincerely searching all things according to the rule of Scripture, with such guidance and direction as they can obtain of God by Prayer. (8:424–26)¹⁰

If such words are characteristic of Milton's vision of a Protestant com-munity of calm and charitable enquiry, the following are typical of Mil-ton's arguments for toleration: "It is a humane frailty to err, and no man is infallible here on earth. But so long as all these progress to set the Word of God only before them as the Rule of faith and obedience; and use all diligence and sincerity of heart, by reading, by learning, by study, by prayer for Illumination of the holy Spirit, to understand the Rule and obey it, they have done what man can do: God will pardon them, as he did the friends of Job, good and pious men, though much mistaken, as there it appears, in some Points of Doctrin" (8:423–24). Although whatever unity there may be is "achieved" against the hover-ing specter of "popery," the extent to which Protestant "Sects and Opinions" are united in a common Christian project is so self-evident in Milton's later prose as to eliminate the need for further examples. Many discussions of *Samson*, however, fail to import Milton's sense of common Protestant struggle into the drama. The *sun-* in discussions of *Samson* has largely been "dark / And silent as the moon" (86–87).

Here vocalizing the *sun-*, I propose to read the Chorus in terms of the extent to which it fights *with* Samson—that is, on his side—even in disagreement with him. To do so is to emerge from the aural eclipse Milton himself creates. William Riley Parker points the way with the observation that Milton gives his Chorus more long speeches than any of his ancient Greek predecessors have given theirs.[11] Gretchen Ludke Finney calculates that the Chorus provides 27 percent of the dialogue.[12] (Samson by comparison speaks about 39 percent of the lines.) There can be no question that Milton desires to give the Chorus prominence and attach it to Samson in various ways. Eschewing the option of listing merely "Chorus," Milton instead pointedly introduces the "Chorus of Danites," which he calls Samson's "friends and neighbors not unknown" (180). Seeing his "friends" of the Chorus prompts Samson to contrast them with "counterfeit . . . friends [who] / . . . in prosperous days / . . . swarm, but in adverse withdraw their head" (189–92).

Though some commentators see Samson's distinction here between the friends of the Chorus and "counterfeit . . . friends" as an ironic introduction to what will eventually be Milton's unmasking of the Chorus's doctrinal fallacies and pernicious advice, I wish to argue that the Chorus persists in doing just what it needs to do, "strive with" Samson. To make such an argument is to resist a pervasive strain running through the critical tradition of judging the Chorus as either right or wrong, parts of whose legacy we might glimpse in Georgia Christopher's conception of the Chorus as "weak-minded"; Louis Martz's description of the Chorus as "completely lacking in insight"; John Huntley's castigation of the Chorus for "lov[ing] bondage more than liberty"; and Northrop Frye's characteristically memorable, if overly critical, description of the Chorus "standing around uttering timid complacencies in teeth-loosening doggerel."[13] While a more historically alert argument might make use of the antidemocratic strain enmeshed in the fabric of Milton's Restoration republicanism—a perspective through which Milton might denounce "the fickle masses" in the character of the Chorus—none of these seems entirely convincing.

In the face of these negative claims about the Chorus—often made more on the basis of the critical tradition than on fresh reflection—it is worth remembering that the Chorus gives voice to the drama's only rebuke of atheism, and the oft-quoted lines "Just are the ways of God, /

And justifiable to men," echoing *Paradise Lost*, could easily serve as the drama's thesis (293–94). Jon S. Lawry, Anthony Low, and Mary Ann Radzinowicz understand the Chorus in this (recalling *Of True Religion*) more charitable light.[14] But whatever the precise relationship between Milton's views and the Chorus's, I wish to emphasize the chasm that stands between the notions of "striving with" Samson, on the one hand, and always being right, on the other. Insofar as readers attempt to determine the Chorus's moral and doctrinal virtue, it is a chasm that too often goes unnoticed. The Chorus, in my reading, is an invaluable sounding board for Samson's thoughts, throes, and theories and acts as a critical agent in the process that many critics have called Samson's regeneration, though, prompted by Barbara Lewalksi, and for reasons I hope to enumerate, I prefer to think of that process as Samson's acquisition of "true [political] experience."[15] And fallible though it may be, Samson's Chorus inherits what Samson's violent act bequeaths it: a world free of civil laws in ecclesiastical matters, which is also free, incidentally, of an ascertainable divine will that had once adjudicated among the various claims to doctrinal truth.

Having briefly explored the republican and tolerationist implications of the term *sunagonistes* and having looked momentarily at the critical tradition surrounding Milton's Chorus, we can now focus our attention on Milton's drama per se. Practically, the Chorus sees for both Samson and the reader, a function for which the blind Milton must have had considerable regard. At first, Samson is distraught that he is "Blind among enemies" (68), but it is when he is greeted by his coadjutors that Samson becomes grateful for his friends' eyes and sympathy, inviting them to "*see*, O friends, / How many evils have enclosed [him] round" (193–94; emphasis mine). The Chorus further provides the initial memorable and, it must be said, ultimately correct descriptions of Manoa's "locks white as down," Dalila's "Sails filled, and streamers waving," and Harapha, whose "look / [is as] Haughty . . . as his pile [is] high-built and proud" (327, 718, 1068–69).

True, the Chorus's eyes are an imperfect replacement for God's "guiding hand" (1), yet Milton makes clear the practical contribution the Chorus makes. And just as the Chorus strives with Samson on the functional level by serving as his eyes, so too does it help to propel Samson to his commingled spiritual and political regenerations. To reiterate, I do not mean to say the Chorus is always right—far from it. Joan Bennett points to its "self-absorbing [Mosaic] legalism," which, she notes compellingly, Milton felt had been abrogated by Christ's redemption.[16] In the following passage quoting *Paradise Lost* book 7, line 290, she understands Milton to be engaged in an antinomian inquiry into the limits of Hebraic law. Bennett reads Milton as lauding Samson's ability to surpass the Chorus's elementary insistence on the Law: "As the first function of the law is to 'discover sin, but not remove,' so its second function is to lead its truest followers to transcend its own limits by the grace of a God who makes fallen man's efforts to keep a perfect law acceptable 'works of faith.' . . . [The Chorus] are servants under bondage, not yet fully aware of the sin in themselves which the law discovers but cannot remove; pious followers of the Lord, but incapable of faith. Samson, however, reaches the limit of the old law and hence is able to transcend and fill it."[17] This image of the Law that Bennett finds functioning in *Samson Agonistes*, as something to be transcended rather than followed, is suggestive enough. But Bennett mistakenly takes it to mean that readers should therefore distrust the Chorus's "blind interpretation and obedience of the literal law."[18] *Pace* Bennett, the Chorus's so-called mistakes should not impel us to censure the Chorus outright. For one thing, Milton is far more accepting of alternative theological views than Bennett allows, and for another, Milton does not gainsay Hebraic law *generally*. Rather, he considers it from God's perspective as a means to an end. Indeed, Bennett seems to take the same mistaken view of the Law that Adam does in book 12 of *Paradise Lost*. Michael allows that the Law "appears imperfect" to Adam but instructs him that it was "giv'n / With purpose to resign [humanity] in full time / Up to a better cov'nant" (300–302). Bennett, like Adam, works from the law's *appearance* of imperfection without understanding its godly purpose. It is true that legalism is a stop on a teleological progression toward a "better cov'nant," as Bennett points out, but it is not a bad stop as such. From God's perspective, indeed, the Mosaic law is necessary. As Jason Rosenblatt has noted in an important revaluation of the Chorus in *Samson Agonistes*, Samson "experiences [the Mosaic law] not as a restraint but a path."[19]

It is significant that even in the midst of an argument criticizing the Chorus's preoccupation with the Mosaic law's strictures, Bennett does allow that Samson's "own people have shown him the negative limits of that law whose servant they are."[20] Her verb "shown" is precisely the point I wish to make: the Chorus does in fact show Samson the way toward his regeneration. This argument arises not from the deconstructionist stance whereby good relies for its existence on evil or right for its existence on wrong. It arises rather from Milton's protolerationist later prose, wherein he articulates a profound hope in doctrinal debate. In *Of True Religion*, after cataloguing the so-called heresies of his day, he writes, "If it be askt how far they should be tolerated? I answer doubtless equally, as being all Protestants; that is on all occasions to give account of their Faith, either by Arguing, Preaching in their several Assemblies, Public writing, and the freedom of Printing" (8:426). The Chorus's consistent rejoinders to Samson's musings, if not always doctrinally in line with Milton's own thoughts, are always, well, there —prodding Samson to an anti-Erastian, Christian worldview. Bennett speaks of Samson's "growing superiority over the Chorus." While this may be true from a certain limited perspective, the Chorus is not inert. What she calls the "growing superiority" happens only through the Chorus's role as Socratic interlocutor: the Chorus's replies and musings are a necessary and constituent element for anything that might be called Samson's regeneration—a shining example, that is, of the value of doctrinal conversation.

The Chorus's influence is particularly evident in the much-discussed exchange of lines 1368–73, where Samson and the Chorus discuss Samson's obligations to the Philistines. It is here that the main interpretive problem with which this essay is concerned can best be glimpsed:

> Chorus. Where the heart joins not, outward acts defile not.
> Samson. Where outward force constrains, the sentence holds;
>   But who constrains me to the Temple of Dagon,
>   Not dragging? the Philistian Lords command.
>   Commands are no constraints.

Is this is an antagonistic relationship, wherein Samson's reply is preceded by an imagined "No!"? Or is it a more convivial one, wherein it is preceded by an imaginative, "True, but it seems to me more complicated"? A critical tradition to the contrary notwithstanding, a number of reasons suggests that it is the latter. For one, with Samson perplexed by the dilemma of whether to violate the Hebraic laws, the Chorus's counsel ("outward acts defile not") echoes sentiments similar to those that Milton expresses as early as *Comus* ("Thou canst not touch the freedom of my minde" [663]) and later in *Of Civil Power*, where he expatiates on the disjunction between the outward action and the faithful soul (7:255).[21] In the latter tract, legislated religious codes compel only the "outward acts" while the "faculties of the inward man" remain "free and unconstrainable of themselves by nature" (7:256). For this

reason, to imagine Samson rejecting the Chorus outright is to have
Samson reject the important distinction between the act and the conscience that Milton himself shares. Samson's comment that "the sentence holds" further illuminates this more complicated relationship.
"The sentence holds" means (at least) two things, referring both to
that legal sentence which might constrain a moral actor (like Samson
himself) and also to that grammatical sentence previously issued by the
Chorus. Insofar as Samson thinks "the [grammatical] sentence holds,"
the Chorus has got it right, at least in cases "where outward force con-
strains." The thrust of the Chorus's "sentence" is therefore much more
than a "plea for passive obedience," and Samson's response is far from
an out-and-out rejection of the Chorus's argument.[22] Rather, "the sentence" is a precept lying in wait for the facts, inviting inquiry with a
sort of come-hither sententiousness. Samson's reply is careful, respect-
ful, and nuanced—indeed, the very model of the charitable intercourse
Milton propounds. One might even imagine it coming after a lengthy
pause for consideration.

When Samson does respond, he patiently delineates the limits of
the Chorus's precept by interjecting the facts of his own case. He is not
currently present at the Dagonalia, he is sure to point out, and certainly not constrained there. As Samson acknowledges, it is true that if
he had been *constrained* at the festival for the false god, the Chorus
would be correct that the "outward act" of being present at an "idolatrous rite" would not be defiling, for the reason that Samson's body
may have been present at the event but that his heart would have ab-
stained. In the present circumstances, however, whatever the precept,
Samson the voluntary actor would perform the idolatry "freely; ven-
turing to displease / God for the fear of Man" (1373–74). And this is
precisely his conundrum: he is not constrained at the Dagonalia and so
therefore would be choosing to attend the event. Samson the riddler is
ironically confounded by his oppressor's own riddle.[23] Importantly, for
the purposes of this essay, it is the Chorus that helps him discover his
bind.

Just as the Chorus helps to unfold for Samson the terms of the
Philistines' riddle, so too does it help to engender that riddle's answer,
Samson's destruction of the theater. Taken and evaluated, the germ of
the Chorus's precept becomes the fruit of Samson's later action when
Samson realizes the scope of his conundrum. And such an evolution, a
movement toward an answer, happens only as Samson introduces to
the Chorus's inward-outward theoretical dichotomy a practical con-

cern with the physical locus of coercion, a concern born of his present material condition, his own "true [political] experience" (1756). The important work Samson does to delineate the applicability of the Chorus's "sentence" is wholly dependent on the issuance of that sentence itself. The "answer," in other words, is the natural result of "Arguing, Preaching . . . , Public writing, and the freedom of Printing," the constituent elements of charitable debate.

Stanley Fish says about the exchange between Samson and the Chorus under discussion here that it "could go on forever and still be inconclusive."[24] In this assessment, he is both right and wrong. He is right that it could go on forever after Samson's deliverance (and in fact the drama's conclusion implies that something like it does); here, however, it is expressly teleological: the Law is still engaged in "stirring up / Sin," as Michael says in book 12 of *Paradise Lost* (288-89). When the exchange does conclude, then, it is because Samson has arrived at something of an answer, however determined and imperfect that answer might be.

Indeed, in contrast with the Philistine Officer's threats of force against Samson's corporeal body, the Chorus and its perhaps overly broad arguments do profitable work on Samson's "inward man." When the Chorus offers its farewell prayer to Samson, telling him, "Go, and the Holy One / Of Israel be thy guide" (1427–28), the drama is, in fact, significant. The contest to be decided is not necessarily as much between "Israel's God" (1150) and Dagon, as Samson had said earlier, as it is between the unregulated debate that brought Samson to this point and the State "forcers of conscience" who seek an outward performance of Samson's obedience (*A Treatise of Civil Power*, 7:253). Will the State's force compel Samson to prostrate himself before Dagon, or did the Chorus's "apt words have power to swage" (184)? Can debate and liberty make a difference? If, as Sharon Achinstein has written, Samson's interview with the Public Officer permits Milton to theorize the dilemma of a dissenter compelled to pledge obedience outwardly, then the Chorus's doctrinal declarations permit him to think through the avenues by which the same dissenter can transcend servitude to the State and its laws inwardly.[25] Critically, whereas State force yields Samson's violent destruction, "Arguing and Preaching" yields the faithful, regenerate man. "Christ has a government of his own," Milton writes, that "governs not by outward force, and that for two reasons. First because it deals only with the inward man and his actions, which are all spiritual and to outward force not lyable: secondly to shew us the divine excellence of his spiritual kingdom, able without worldly force to subdue all the powers and kingdoms of this world" (*A Treatise of Civil Power*, 7:255). Juxtaposed against the Philistines' State coercion, the free and charitable debate between Samson and the Chorus is demonstrated to be a prime apparatus of Christ's government.

The doctrinal exchange Milton both dramatizes and valorizes between Samson and the Chorus contrasts too with the Philistines' cloistered mechanics of power. Similar in a sense to the way power operates in *Paradise Lost*'s Hell, with Satan convincing Beelzebub off-page and out of readers' view to introduce to the assembly the option of a colonial trip to Eden ("For whence, / But from the author of all ill could spring / So deep a malice, to confound the race / Of mankind in one root" [2.380–83]), the Philistines' apparatus of power is evident, but the hands governing it are not. Readers can only gather contingent inferences about Philistine authority from the Public Officer, who may or may not be a metonym for Philistine power. The Officer's suggestions, for instance, that "This answer . . . will not content them" (1322) and "This will offend them highly" (1333) imply various characteristics about the Philistines (obstinacy and arrogance, perhaps), but in truth Milton denies readers any access to the mind of Philistine power, providing nothing like the internal view he gives of Samson and the Chorus. The Officer tells Samson, "My message was imposed on me with speed," but we as readers get little direct sense of the method of imposition or the will or identity of the imposer. This is not to suggest that Milton bears the responsibility to dramatize every imagined encounter among his characters or that he may make no distinctions between major and minor characters. But it is to note the sharp difference between the worldly forces acting upon Samson. The reconstruction of Samson as a godly actor that occurs among the Danites through visible debate and vigorous discourse stands out against (what Milton at least suggests is) the closeted and imperious Philistine hierarchy.

I use the term "closeted" purposefully to link my vocabulary with that of the genre (a closet drama after all) and, somewhat more suggestively, to link it with a vocabulary available to dissenters of the Restoration period of an abidingly republican mindset. One of the chiefly desirable characteristics of republican government, according to many of its advocates in debates throughout the 1640s and 1650s, was the way power might operate in public transparently rather than behind closed doors, the latter being a prime characteristic of tyranny.[26] Charles's fall, according to an introduction to the Parliamentarian Bulstrode White-locke's memoirs, meant that "the State cabinet was laid open" and that a republic "where Counsels are all publicly canvassed and debated" might soon emerge.[27] The Restoration publisher used a republican vo-cabulary dating at least as far back as *The Kings cabinet opened: or, certain packets of secret letters & papers, written with the Kings own hand, and taken in his cabinet at Nasby-Field* (1645), where the authors successfully mapped onto kingship the characteristic of a "closed" mode of state-craft and onto Parliament the virtues of openness and opening. Such a juxtaposition of modes of statecraft would seem to be at work in *Sam-son Agonistes* as well, only now in the 1660s concerned with both "regal tyranie over the state" and "state-tyranie over the church," an updating that reflects the Restoration's new demands for religious loyalty and is inflected not with the shrill tones of rebellion that marked the 1640s but with a more rhetorical anguish that violence must be the dissenter's only satisfactory answer to the State's nearly paralyzing riddle (*A Trea-tise of Civil Power*, 7:252).

"How much bloodshed have the forcers of conscience to answer for[?]" Milton asks, for example, in *A Treatise of Civil Power*, holding the State responsible for whatever suffering stems from enforced loy-alty (7:253). Samson's destruction both asks and answers that very question.[28] In *Civil Power*, Milton warns an increasingly interventionist and Erastian Parliament against forcing public displays of religious loyalty, "least by compelling [dissenters] to do what wherof they can-not be persuaded . . . he force them to do evil" (7:266). "Force"—an example of which in *Samson* is the Officer's menacing threat of "en-gines to assail / And hamper" (1396–97) the hero— "is no honest confutation" (7:261). Positing two methods of bringing a subject into Christ's flock, then—sturdy debate, which risks only error, and legal force, which risks, if not compels, widespread destruction—the drama in effect demands State tolerance. Dalila's comically self-justifying argument that "liberty / Would draw [Samson] forth to perilous en-terprises" (803–4) is made to look even more absurd by the drama's conclusion, where it is State force, not liberty, that provokes the con-cluding peril.

The drama's final scene, I think, models that tolerationist State. Freed of the Philistines' slavery, freed of their enforced religious obe-dience, the Chorus is also, significantly, freed of Samson. Fish is not al-together wrong when he calls Samson's death "the best of all possible things."[29] No longer does the Chorus have among themselves an elect figure divinely endowed with the capacity to apprehend God's will, inordinately sensitive to God's particularistic wishes.

Now, rather, freed by Samson from Samson, the Chorus lives in a world in which God deems faith, "diligence and sincerity of heart" sufficient—and State force and retributive violence unwarranted (*Of True Religion*, 8:423). Violence may have been the regenerate man's faithful response to codified and enforced spiritual obedience, but the Chorus now inhabits a tolerationist, and therefore postforce, world.

The logic I am suggesting is at work in *Samson Agonistes*—by Samson from Samson, by Law from Law—is the same homeopathic logic with which Milton inaugurates his epistle, where he reminds his readers that Aristotle thought tragedy to be powerful "by raising pity and fear, or terror, to purge the mind of those and such like passions" (463).[30] But Milton is not content simply to cite Aristotle. He then invokes "nature," where "things of melancholic hue and quality are used against melancholy, sour against sour, salt to remove salt humours" (463). Milton makes clear that he considers tragedy to be the genre by which he may most effectively "temper and reduce" the unwanted, the outmoded, the terrible—that which we do not want or need—paradoxically, by providing it. It is through the homeopathic logic of tragedy that Law abrogates Law, and Samson abrogates Samson.

Milton's post-Samson, post-Erastian world, then, reveals a new sort of liberty attended by uncertainty. The formerly united Chorus is now divided into Semichoruses that provide differing spins on the day's events, attempting to corral its meaning into intelligibility. Like *Areopagitica*'s "sad friends of Truth" tracking her dismembered limbs, the two Semichoruses differ in the meaning they make of the destruction of the temple. The first Semichorus believes the Philistines caused their own tragedy. They call attention to "our living Dread" (1673) who "urged [the Philistines] on with mad desire / To call in haste their own destroyer" (1677–78) and "invite[d]" "their own ruin on themselves" (1684). "They brought it on themselves," the first Semichorus seems to say, calling to mind the "forcers of conscience" culpability. But the second sees a volitional actor in that "it." Samson, to them, is the classic autonomous subject, one of Carlyle's "men of history" who, "With inward eyes illuminated," acted willingly upon the Philistines with "fiery virtue" (1689–90). Manoa's admiration for Samson, meanwhile, borders on the idolatrous. He promises to

> build him
> A monument, and plant it round with shade
> Of laurel ever green, and branching palm,
> With all his trophies hung, and acts enrolled
> In copious legend.
>
> (1733–37)

Though they may differ with respect to such important theological questions as free will and the proper role of ceremony, each of these perspectives is unquestionably motivated by faith. And that, for Milton in the post-Samson world, is the prime concern.

As Parliament's fear of religious liberty had led to the mounting Clarendon Code of the 1660s, the following two points were, to Milton, worth making: one, liberty helps, not hurts; two, force was a thing of the Old Testament world. Just as the Philistines' force bred Samson's force, so too would tolerance, in a world whose Old Testament strictures were abrogated by Christ's redemption, breed tolerance. We live in a world *after* Samson, Milton says—postviolence, postforce, postimmediate access to divine Truth. Divine ordination is a relic of the past. So too are laws and titles (like King) that claim to be based on it. "The happiness of a nation," Milton writes, "must needs be firmest and certainest in a full and free Councel . . . *where no single person, but reason only swais*" (*Ready and Easy Way*, 7:427; emphasis mine). He repeats the notion again: The nation is "safer and more thriving in the joint providence and counsel of many industrious equals" (7:427). Why? Because "no man or body of men *in these times* can be the infallible judges or determiners in matters of religion to any other mens consciences but their own" (*A Treatise of Civil Power*, 7:242–43; emphasis mine).

Ultimately, I have suggested we read *Samson Agonistes* as a sort of gloss on the weighty phrase "in these times." On the whole, the drama *in*cludes an episode of immediate revelation, but it *con*cludes with a portrait of the new paradigm: fallible men talking among themselves. "Schisms will be while men are fallible," Milton writes in *Of True Religion* (8:436), and Milton's divided Semichoruses illustrate such a schism. The concluding scene, for Milton, is the anti-Erastian, tolerationist agon in which an individual can and should be less an agonist, striving *against* others, than a *sunagonist*, striving *with*, struggling *with*, contesting *with*, in advancement toward God. Milton attempts to end what he calls "the long hot Contest [of] whether Protestants ought to tolerate one another" and replace it with the contest of tolerant protestants

fighting together against error (*Of True Religion*, 8:429). It is a world of
striving and struggling that, unlike its predecessor, need not be tragic.
In the end the members of Milton's Chorus are coadjutors, fighting together, striving, arguing, preaching in faith. In this new paradigm,
State enforced loyalty and uniformity codes are, as we might say in a
more contemporary parlance, so last covenant.

NOTES

1. Thomas Pynchon, *The Crying of Lot 49* (New York: Harper Collins, 1965), 102.

2. John Milton, *Samson Agonistes*, in *John Milton:The Complete Poems*, ed. John Leonard (London: Penguin, 1998). All references to Milton's poetry are to this edition and are cited parenthetically in the text.

3. John Leonard, ed., *John Milton: The Complete Poems*, 917.

4. Aristotle, *Poetics*, trans. Gerald Else (Ann Arbor: University of Michigan Press, 1967), 51, 1456a.

5. Henry George Liddell and Robert Scott, *A Greek-English Lexicon* (Oxford: Clarendon, 1940).

6. Edward Le Comte, *A Dictionary of Puns in Milton's English Poetry* (New York: Columbia University Press, 1981), ix; and John K. Hale, *Milton's Languages: The Impact of Multilingualism on Style* (Cambridge: Cambridge University Press, 1997), 180.

7. Milton, *John Milton: The Complete Poems*, ed. Leonard, 464.

8. See N. H. Keeble, *The Literary Culture of Nonconformity in Later Seventeenth-Century England* (Leicester: Leicester University Press, 1987); and Sharon Achinstein, *Literature and Dissent in Milton's England* (Cambridge: Cambridge University Press, 2003).

9. Quentin Skinner, *Liberty Before Liberalism* (Cambridge: Cambridge University Press, 1998); Philip Pettit, *Republicanism: A Theory of Freedom and Government* (Oxford: Oxford University Press, 1997); Richard Tuck, *The Rights of War and Peace: Political Thought and the International Order from Grotius to Kant* (Oxford: Oxford University Press, 1999), 8–9; David Norbrook, "*Areopagitica*, Censorship, and the Early Modern Public Sphere," in *The Administration of Aesthetics: Censorship, Political Criticism, and the Public Sphere*, ed. Richard Burt (Minneapolis: University of Minnesota Press, 1994), 3–33.

10. John Milton, *Of True Religion*, in *Complete Prose Works of John Milton*, 8 vols., ed. Don M. Wolfe et al. (New Haven, CT: Yale University Press, 1953–82). All references to Milton's prose are to this edition and are cited parenthetically in the text.

11. William Riley Parker, *Milton's Debt to Greek Tragedy in "Samson Agonistes"* (New York: Barnes & Noble, 1968), 140–41.

12. Gretchen Ludke Finney, "Chorus in *Samson Agonistes*," *PMLA* 58 (1943): 649–64, 656.

13. See Georgia Christopher, "Homeopathic Physic and Natural Renovation in *Samson Agonistes*," *ELH* 37 (1970): 364; Louis Martz, "Chorus and Character in *Samson Agonistes*," *Milton Studies* 1 (1969): 133; John Huntley, "A Revaluation of the Chorus' Role in Milton's *Samson Agonistes*," *Modern Philology* 64 (1966): 139; and

Northrop Frye, *The Return of Eden: Five Essays on Milton's Epics* (Toronto: University of Toronto Press, 1965), 108.

14. See Jon S. Lawry, *The Shadow of Heaven: Matter, and Stance in Milton's Poetry* (Ithaca, NY: Cornell University Press, 1968), 359–62; Anthony Low, *The Blaze of Noon: A Reading of "Samson Agonistes"* (New York: Columbia University Press, 1974), 118–35; and Mary Ann Radzinowicz, *Toward "Samson Agonistes": The Growth of Milton's Mind* (Princeton, NJ: Princeton University Press, 1978), 62.

15. Barbara Kiefer Lewalski, "Milton's Samson and the 'New Acquist of True [Political] Experience,' " *Milton Studies* 24 (1988): 233–51.

16. Joan S. Bennett, "Liberty Under the Law: The Chorus and the Meaning of *Samson Agonistes*," *Milton Studies* 12 (1978): 145.

17. Ibid.

18. Ibid., 151.

19. Jason Rosenblatt, *Renaissance England's Chief Rabbi: John Selden* (Oxford: Oxford University Press, 2006), 108. Rosenblatt further notes Milton's remarkable "sympathy for Judaic self-understanding" in the drama, which, he suggests, Milton had derived largely from John Selden's 1640 *De Jure Naturali et Gentium juxta Disciplinam Ebraeorum* (102).

20. Bennett, "Liberty Under the Law," 154.

21. See Achinstein, *Literature and Dissent in Milton's England*, 143.

22. Ibid.

23. For a discussion of Samson as riddler, see John Rogers, "The Secret of *Samson Agonistes*," *Milton Studies* 33 (1997): 111–32.

24. Stanley Fish, *How Milton Works* (Cambridge, MA: Harvard University Press, 2001), 415.

25. Sharon Achinstein, "*Samson Agonistes* and the Drama of Dissent," *Milton Studies* 33 (1997): 133–58.

26. David Norbrook, "The English Revolution and English Historiography," in *The Cambridge Companion to Writing of the English Revolution*, ed. N. H. Keeble (Cambridge: Cambridge University Press, 2001), 235.

27. "The Publisher to the Reader," in Bulstrode Whitelocke, *Memorials of the English Affairs* (London: Nathaniel Ponder, 1682), sig. A2V, qtd. in Norbrook, "The English Revolution," 235.

28. I elaborate on this point in Christopher Warren, "When Self-Preservation Bids: Approaching Milton, Hobbes, and Dissent," *English Literary Renaissance* 37 (2007), 118–50.

29. Stanley Fish, "Spectacle and Evidence in *Samson Agonistes*," *Critical Inquiry* 15 (1989): 556.

30. I am grateful to James Fleming for this point.

"Intimate Impulses," "Rousing Motions," and the Written Law: Internal and External Scripture in *Samson Agonistes*

David V. Urban

An intriguing issue in *Samson Agonistes* is the problem of immediate spiritual revelation from God and whether Samson discerns accurately God's "promptings." Milton raises this question by portraying Samson's direct spiritual revelation as potentially delusional, but also as a legitimate means of divine communication that, when correctly understood, can lead to redemption. In this sense, *Samson Agonistes* depicts a Hebrew God whose leadings may finally be known by the genuine servant of God who has first demonstrated obedience to the divine commands codified in the written Scripture. Throughout the drama, the matter of immediate revelation is addressed in conjunction with the question of whether a specific revelation can be trusted if it goes against the explicit teachings of the written Scripture. Milton's Samson considers himself to be the recipient of divine inspiration, for he believes God has led him to marry his two Philistine wives, the woman of Timna and Dalila, even though marrying a Canaanite woman goes against Mosaic Law. Indeed, Samson's violation of a clear scriptural command accomplishes God's broader commandment in written Scripture, for he obeys the larger sense of the Law. But in his discernment of God's "leadings" in his two marriages, Samson proves himself to be both a successful and an unsuccessful interpreter of special revelation: he properly recognizes God's true will in his first marriage, but because he has been deluded by his own lusts and presumption, he mistakes his unlawful desire for Dalila as God again leading him to marry a Philistine woman. By the end of the drama, however, we see Samson restored to his position as a useful servant of God. He has come to demonstrate an unswerving fidelity to the written Law, and Samson is once again able to discern divine promptings that lead him to obey God in a way that transcends the letter of the Law even as it fulfills the Law's greater purpose.

Samson's role as a wise recipient of immediate revelation is predicated on the supreme freedom of God himself, who, in special circumstances, inspires his servants to act against his written Law in order to accomplish a higher purpose. Just after Samson tells how God inspired him to seek marriage with the woman at Timna, the Chorus celebrates God's prerogative to act over and against his written Law in order to accomplish his will; in doing so they also reprove those who would call God unjust for his ostensibly contradictory commands:

> Yet more there be who doubt his ways not just,
> As to his own edicts, found contradicting . . .
> . . . .
> As if they [the doubters] would confine th' interminable,
> And tie him to his own prescript,
> Who made our Laws to bind us, not himself,
> And who hath full right to exempt
> Whom so it pleases him by choice
> From National obstriction,without taint
> Of sin, or legal debt;
> For with his own Laws he can best dispense.
> He would not else who never wanted means,
> Nor in respect of th'enemy just cause
> To set his people free,
> Have prompted this Heroic Nazarite,
> Against his vow of strictest purity,
> To seek in marriage that fallacious Bride.
> (300–301, 307–20)[1]

The Chorus's representation of God's approach to his own written Law here resembles Milton's discussion in *De Doctrina Christiana* of the superiority of the internal scripture over the external, written Scripture. In his chapter "Of the Holy Scripture," Milton writes that "[t]he pre-eminent and supreme authority [over the Scripture of the Bible] . . . is the authority of the Spirit, which is internal" (6:587).[2] If Milton considers this to be the case for individual persons, how much more so for God himself. Although Milton's teachings concerning the identity of the Holy Spirit are certainly heterodox, he does affirm the

Holy Spirit to be "a minister of God . . . produced, from the substance of God" (6:298). Thus, if the Holy Spirit within the believer is prompting him to act against the written Scripture, the believer is not acting on his own, but has been prompted by God himself. In his supreme freeness, God chooses to work in a way that ostensibly violates his written word, yet in doing so the overall spirit and integrity of the written text is affirmed, not disregarded. Certainly this is the case with Milton's Samson.

At this point, we should ask how such action by God can be reconciled with Milton's cautious and strategic pronouncement that he "do[es] not teach anything new" in *De Doctrina* (6:127). Furthermore, how can God's seemingly unscriptural promptings in Samson be reconciled with Dayton Haskin's insightful comment that Milton's heterodoxies are, in effect, his attempt to uphold "the Bible only"?[3] Such questions may seem unanswerable at first—until we realize that the Chorus's above lines are, in fact, an apologia for the book of Judges itself. Judges 14:4 asserts that Samson's demand to marry the woman of Timna "was of the Lord, that he sought an occasion against the Philistines; for at that time the Philistines had dominion over Israel."[4] This verse ought to strike us as odd, because we may recognize Samson's reportedly God-given desire to be in contradiction with Deuteronomy 7:3, where the Israelites are commanded not to intermarry with the foreigners among them, as such unions would lead to idolatry. This prohibition is reinforced in Judges 3:5–7, which links intermarriage and idolatry. Why then, we ask, would God use such a seemingly contradictory method later in Judges to accomplish his purpose? Milton's orthodox contemporary, Matthew Poole, writes in his commentary on Judges that "this action of Samson's, though against common rules, seems to be warranted . . . principally by the instinct and direction of God." A bit later, addressing Samson's violation, Poole writes that such "pollution" was a "necessary dut[y] . . . being contracted by Divine instinct and direction, and in order to God's honour, and therefore dispensed with by the author of that law, and required by him for his service."[5] Poole explains that God at times freely inspires his servants to act in ways contrary to the written Law in order to accomplish his higher purpose.

Milton's explanation of this subject is similar to Poole's. For him, God has perfect freedom to go above such a prohibition because, in the Chorus's words, he "made our Laws to bind us, not himself" (309). Furthermore, the Chorus suggests that, in the end, such action on

God's part is not truly contradicting his law; rather, it is another dimension of his employing of it. The Chorus affirms, "For with his own Laws he can best dispense" (314). The meaning of the word "dispense" here (a word also used by Poole), as Roy Flannagan notes, is to "administer justice," not, as we might easily misconstrue, "get rid of."[6] In other words, somehow, in his infinite wisdom, God, in going above his Law, is actually administering it perfectly.[7] Although Milton's text is not specific, we may surmise that God's seeming transgression of his own Law is in fact a fulfillment of his overall intention behind that specific prohibition. If we go back to Deuteronomy 7, we see that the chapter begins as follows: "When the Lord thy God shall bring thee into the land whither thou goest to possess it, and hath cast out many nations before thee, the Hittites, and the Girgashites, and the Amorites, and the Canaanites, and the Perizzites, and the Hivites, and the Jebusites, seven nations greater and mightier than thou; and when the Lord thy God shall deliver them before thee, thou shalt smite them, and utterly destroy them; thou shalt make no convenant with them, nor show mercy unto them" (7:1–2). These verses are immediately followed by the prohibitions against intermarriage and idolatry in 7:3–4. Thus, we can see that the command that God seemingly has violated with respect to Samson and the woman of Timna is actually something that is predicated upon both his commandment to destroy these same nations and his promise to enable the Israelites to do so. Since the prohibition against intermarriage with these nations is subordinate to the command to destroy them, it seems likely that Milton reasoned that the external Scripture was in no way violated by God's free act in this situation.

Having established the theological framework for Samson's own inspirations, let us examine his own discussion of such divine promptings. Early on, Samson tells the Chorus about the supernaturally ordained circumstances of his first marriage:

> The first I saw at Timna, and she pleas'd
> Mee, not my Parents, that I sought to wed,
> The daughter of an Infidel: they knew not
> That what I motion'd was of God; I knew
> From intimate impulse, and therefore urg'd
> The marriage on; that by occasion hence
> I might begin Israel's Deliverance,
> The work to which I was divinely call'd.
> (219–26)

Samson's description of his divine "impulse" to marry the woman is, as we might expect, consistent with both the Chorus's statement about God's freedom to work "above" his Law and Milton's discussion of the superior "internal scripture" of the Spirit in *De Doctrina*. Although Samson's parents, knowing only the external Scripture of the Law, are concerned about his choice, Samson's perception of the internal scripture of God's Spirit overrides this prohibition and enables him to act toward God's ultimate goal to bring about "Israel's Deliverance" from the Philistines. The fact that Samson was indeed obeying God's Spirit when following this "intimate impulse" is demonstrated by the Spirit's repeated empowerment of the Hebrew champion in his decisive victories over the Philistines in Judges 14 and 15. In marrying the woman of Timna, Samson recognizes and follows a genuine "motion" from God, and we see that this new revelation of the internal scripture brings about the more encompassing command of written Scripture, the destruction of the Canaanites. Because he walks in obedience to God's Spirit in this first marriage decision, Samson here does not violate the Law but acts as a vessel through which God sovereignly "dispenses" with his Law. Samson is guiltless "[o]f sin" (313).[8]

Even though Samson acts obediently in his first marriage, we soon see that such rare divine promptings do not give the recipient unfettered freedom to override the Law. Samson's description of his allegiance to the "internal scripture" of the Spirit is immediately followed by an admission that reinforces Milton's commitment to "the Bible only." Telling of his ill-fated marriage to Dalila, Samson contrasts his former "promptings" with his recent transgressions:

> I thought it lawful from my former act,
> And the same end; still watching to oppress
> Israel's oppressors: of what now I suffer
> She was not the prime cause, but I myself.
>   (231–34)

We see here that Samson condemns himself for his own presumption in violating the written Law. We learn later from his father Manoa that with Dalila Samson also "didst plead / Divine impulsion prompting how [he] might'st / Find some occasion to infest [Israel's] foes" (421–23). By the time he speaks the above lines, however, Samson recognizes that, in the case of Dalila, he "had rationalized a 'motion' from self and . . . symbolically violated the trust of God."[9] With his first wife, Samson had received a special prompting from God that did in fact "exempt" him from the "National obstriction" against marrying a Canaanite, thus leaving Samson "without taint / Of sin" (312–13). In the case of Dalila, however, Samson used this earlier prompting as pretext to marry a second Philistine. In his arrogant presumption, he "thought lawful" that which was clearly unlawful in the written Scripture. Simply put, Samson, in his pride and self-indulgence, mistook the promptings of his libido for those of the Spirit, and Samson, still basking in the military success that followed his previous marriage, no doubt further justified his decision with the belief that marriage to Dalila would bring about further conquest in the name of the Lord.[10] But in his self-reflection and contrition, Samson displays an altogether different attitude. Here, he upholds the written Scripture fully, recognizing that he may diverge from it only when God's own Spirit clearly overrides, for a specific occasion, a specific portion of the written Law, to bring about a greater principle within it.

Samson's suffering for his miscalculations with Dalila makes him cautious against any further violations of God's Law. He displays his new devotion even as God prepares him once again to go against the written Scripture. After the Philistine Officer relays his lords' command for Samson to entertain at Dagon's feast, Samson replies that he cannot, for "Our Law forbids at thir Religious Rites / My presence" (1320–21). Here, Samson is likely alluding to Exodus 23:24, "Thou shalt not bow down to their gods, nor serve them."[11] As his discussion with the Chorus upon the Officer's departure reveals, Samson guards against transgression. He refuses to go to Dagon's feast even though the Chorus makes three logical arguments in favor of his attendance: (1) The Philistine lords might respond violently to his obstinacy (1348–53); (2) Samson is already serving the "Idolatrous" Philistines in his current labor (1363–64); (3) Samson's service at Dagon's feast would not really be idol worship, for "Where the heart joins not, outward acts defile not" (1368). However, Samson is as steadfast in his resistance to them as he was to the Officer, returning their arguments with noticeably pious rebuttals. Now a man of patience, Samson is not being egotistically obstinate. His resistance reflects his renewed commitment to the external Law of Israel's God, a devotion that qualifies him again to be a conduit for the internal scripture of the Spirit.[12]

Samson, having just stood his ground against the Chorus's arguments, now suddenly reveals that God could still use him—or any of them—at the feast of Dagon:

> Yet that he may dispense with me or thee
> Present in Temples at Idolatous Rites
> For some important cause, thou needst not doubt.
>
> (1377–79)

Milton's use of the word "dispense" here again attracts our attention. Hughes notes that the term "dispense with" here means "to arrange to remit a penalty for a person so that he may do a forbidden act."[13] Thus, God may choose now to "dispense" his Law in a way which will "dispense with" Samson—even though Samson ostensibly breaks God's Law—in order to accomplish God's higher purpose of destroying the Philistines. Here we see what Leonard Mustazza recognizes in Samson's taunting of the giant Harapha: that Samson's adroit use of language "turns out to be the prelude to direct heroic action,"[14] an action which, to quote John M. Steadman, is "the logical culmination of a spiritual process rather than . . . the effect of purely external causes."[15] At this point, we trust that Samson will be able to recognize properly God's promptings: in his matured state he has gained an unswerving commitment to God's external Scripture; as a result, he now has the wisdom to discern and follow the internal scripture of the Spirit. Here, argues Robert Fallon, Samson "stands ready, empty of self, to receive the divine command, which comes as 'rousing motions.' "[16]

Samson's report to the Chorus of this divine command displays his recovered spiritual assurance:

> Be of good courage, I begin to feel
> Some rousing motions in me which dispose
> To something extraordinary my thoughts.
> I with this Messenger will go along,
> Nothing to do, be sure, that may dishonor
> Our Law, or stain my vow of Nazarite.
>
> (1381–86)

As he receives these "rousing motions"—strikingly reminiscent of the "some strong motion" that prompts Milton's Son in *Paradise Regained* to go into the wilderness to be tempted by Satan (1.290; and we should note that all three gospel accounts of Jesus's temptation state that the Spirit "led" or "driveth" him into the wilderness[17]), Samson shows himself a matured servant of God. Far from the reckless man who used a "leading" as pretense to break the Mosaic Law, Samson here describes his obedience to the internal scripture of the Spirit as fundamentally

consistent with that of the external Law.[18] He repeats his resolve to
keep the written Scripture twice more before his departure (1408–9,
1423–25). In light of Samson's clear progress with regards to the external Scripture, we can answer Stanley Fish's following caveat: "the
reader who remembers the history of Samson's 'rousing motions' may
be wary of labeling these new motions 'of God.' " We may label them
as such because Samson, in his transformed fidelity to the external
Scripture, now properly recognizes the signs of the internal scripture
of God's Spirit upon him. From this perspective, I take issue with Fish's
earlier idea that the "rousing motions" play a part in "Samson's breaking free of the Law's bondage."[19] Indeed, it is the Law itself that gives
Samson guidance to restrain his carnal "motions" and, from a perspective of such restraint, to discern the "rousing motions" as being from
God. In this sense, Mary Ann Radzinowicz is only partly correct when
she states that Samson here "announc[es] his resolution to answer
nothing but the inner authority of his own sense of God."[20] Samson's
"inner authority" is submitted to the whole of the external Law of God,
and because of this, he is able to discern when this "inner authority"—
prompted by God himself—may command him to transgress, ostensibly, some aspect of that external Law.[21] Here again a comparison to the
Son of *Paradise Regained* is instructive. Although his situation does not
exactly parallel that of the repentant Samson, we may note that Milton's Spirit-led Son also demonstrates the ability to disregard a portion
of the Hebrew Scripture in favor of a larger truth therein; indeed, his
final defeat of Satan occurs when he successfully thwarts the tempter's
misuse of the letter of the external Scripture by his own superior obedience to the truth of that same external Scripture (4.551–71).[22]

When the Messenger comes to report Samson's final actions to
Manoa, we hear neither that Samson prostrated himself before the
Philistine god, nor that he maintained his purity by assiduously avoiding any action that could be perceived as spiritually defiling. Rather, we
are told that, before his last act of heroic destruction, Samson "perfor-
m'd" (1626) for the Philistines' entertainment. Significantly, such a
performance is exactly what the Officer initially commanded of Samson, a command Samson refused, as we noted, because of his loyalty to
the Mosaic Law. Samson's "performance," however, is sanctified because it is done in obedience to the leading of God's Spirit that begins
with the "rousing motions" Samson describes before he departs.

We see further indications that, to the end, Samson is being guided
by the Spirit-given internal scripture that enables him to transcend

certain isolated details of the written Scripture in order to obey the
overall message of that same Scripture. The Messenger tells us that,
while leaning against the temple pillars, Samson with "eyes fast fixt he
stood, as one who pray'd / Or some great matter in his mind revolv'd"
(1637–38); Samson then makes the following declaration, which immediately precedes his destruction of Dagon's temple:

> Hitherto, Lords, what your commands impos'd
> I have perform'd, as reason was, obeying,
> Not without wonder or delight beheld.
> Now of my own accord such other trial
> I mean to show you of my strength, yet greater;
> As with amaze shall strike all who behold.
>
> (1640–45)

The degree to which Samson, at this point, is in step with the Spirit of
God has been observed by a number of critics. John Spencer Hill
writes that Samson's destruction of the temple "is an act of responsive
choice, a free action in which the will of the instrument co-operates
with, and is submerged in, the will of God."[23] Similarly, Albert R. Cirillo sees this point as a critical juncture in Samson's "movement . . .
from darkness to light." "At this moment," Cirillo comments regarding Samson's silent prayer, "Samson achieves his closest communion
with God, as the actual intense light of noon becomes the inner light
which displaces the darkness of his despair."[24] More recently, in an
essay that portrays Samson as the violent champion of Israel's terrifying God—a God whom the Semichorus calls "our living Dread"
(1673)—Michael Lieb contends that here Samson "implement[s] the
full force of God's awesome power. . . . He is 'our living Dread' incarnate."[25] As Lieb's essay makes clear, the God with whom Samson identifies so closely is deeply disturbing to the modern mindset. Such disturbance, however, should not prevent readers from recognizing the
profound identification Samson here achieves with the God who em-
powers his final act.[26]

Lieb's argument for Samson's intimate identification with God is
based on the assertion that in his declaration to the Philistines, Samson
employs "the discourse . . . of God," specifically in announcing that his
final display of strength would be done "of my own accord" (1643).
Connecting Samson's "of my own accord" with God's own oath formula—*biy nishbati* (by myself [or "of my own accord"] I have sworn)—
in the Hebrew Scriptures, Lieb writes that "the Miltonic Samson in ef-

fect subsumes within himself the divine role implied by the phrase biy nishbati."[27]

While Lieb's argument uses Samson's "of my own accord" to highlight his intense connection with God, this same phrase has been used by Joseph Wittreich, both in *Interpreting "Samson Agonistes,"* and very recently and much more extensively in *Shifting Contexts*, to portray an unregenerate Samson who here acts on his own, apart from divine directive.[28] For scriptural evidence he cites John 11:49–52, where the high priest Caiaphas tells the council, in response to their statements about Jesus, "Ye know nothing at all, Nor consider that it is expedient for us, that one man should die for the people, and that the whole nation perish not." Wittreich notes that John comments that Caiaphas here speaks "not of his own accord" [The King James Version reads, "this spake he not *of himself*" (emphasis mine; Gr. *aph autou*)]; that is, he acts after divine intervention, under the influence of divine inspiration . . . *of his own accord* denies the agency of God which NOT of his own accord credits him."[29] This reductive assessment of the Greek prepositional phrase that Wittreich and the Revised Standard Version render as "of his own accord," however, is not consonant with the New Testament itself. Jesus in John 10:18 demonstrates this most clearly. There, he tells his listeners "No man taketh it [my life] from me, but I lay it down *of myself* (*ap ematou*). I have power to lay it down, and I have power to take it again. *This commandment have I received of my Father*" (emphasis mine). Here, Jesus uses the same Greek phrase (altered only for the first person) to indicate a decision Jesus was making "of myself" (or "of my own accord" in the RSV) that is clearly being done in response to his Father's command. This verse is especially important to our understanding of Milton's Samson (and his phrase "of my own accord") because Samson was routinely seen as a type of Christ by commentators contemporary to Milton.

We should also note that in the only two New Testament verses where the King James Version actually uses the phrase "of his own accord," both instances use it in ways that clearly portray such action as resulting from divine impulsion. In Acts 12:10, the gate leading to the city opens for Peter "of his own accord" (New International Version, "by itself"); here, Peter is being led from jail to safety by "the angel of the Lord" (12:7; cf. 12:7-11). The other instance is in 2 Corinthians 8:16-17, where Paul reports the following: "But thanks be to *God, which put the same earnest care into the heart of Titus* for you. For indeed he accepted the exhortation; but being more forward, *of his own accord* he went unto you" (emphasis mine). Here again, the agent who acts "of his own accord" is inspired by God himself. In light of these examples, the argument that Samson acting "of my own accord" necessitates him acting apart from divine direction is hardly persuasive. Rather, Samson's use of this phrase provides us with compelling evidence to believe that the "rousing motions" Samson speaks of are indeed from God.[30]

The Semichorus also declares that Samson, though physically blind, acted "With inward eyes illuminated / His fiery virtue rous'd / From under ashes into sudden flame" (1689–91). These lines, particularly the notion that the "illuminated" Samson's "virtue" was "rous'd," recall Samson's previous reference to the "rousing motions" that originally had led him to follow the Philistine Officer to the temple festival. Indeed, Samson's decisions to follow the Officer, to perform at the festival, and to pull down the temple pillars, are all motivated by the same overarching leading of God's Spirit—the "internal scripture" of which the *De Doctrina* speaks. In his "obedience unto death," Samson allows the new revelation of the internal scripture to guide him to a more perfect adherence to the external Law of God. Samson's obedience also demonstrates his resignation to the sovereign will of God, a resignation so unlike his earlier self-indulgence. This obedient resignation enables Samson to be used, once again, as God's instrument of judgment upon the Philistines; it also permits the Chorus to call— rightly so—the once-faithless Samson God's "faithful Champion" (1751).

Notes

This essay incorporates a portion of a previously published essay entitled " 'Rousing Motions' and the Silence of God: Scripture and Immediate Revelation in *Samson Agonistes* and *Clarel*," *Leviathan: A Journal of Melville Studies* 4 (2002) that is also forthcoming in a book-length study by Duquesne University Press. I wish to thank the editors of *Leviathan* and Duquesne University Press for permission to print.

1. John Milton, *Samson Agonistes*, in *John Milton: Compete Poems and Major Prose*, ed. Merritt Y. Hughes (New York: Odyssey, 1957). All references to Milton's poetry are to this edition and are cited parenthetically in the text.

2. John Milton, *Complete Prose Works of John Milton*, 8 vols., ed. Don M. Wolfe et al. (New Haven, CT: Yale University Press, 1953–82). All references to Milton's prose are to this edition and are cited parenthetically in the text.

3. Dayton Haskin, *Milton's Burden of Interpretation* (Philadelphia: University of Pennsylvania Press, 1994), 35.

4. All biblical quotations are from the King James Version, unless otherwise noted, and are cited parenthetically in the text.

5. Matthew Poole, *A Commentary on the Holy Bible*, 3 vols. (1685; repr., London: Banner of Truth, 1963), 1:488–89.

6. Roy C. Flannagan, ed., *The Riverside Milton* (New York: Houghton Mifflin, 1998), 810. Another germane such use of "dispense" is found in the words of Thomas More's Vincent, who states "god may dispence wher he will & whan he will, & may commanund [of his emissaries] . . . to do the contrary . . . as sampson had by inspiracion of god, commaundment to kill him selfe . . . pulling down the howse vppon his own hed at the fest of the phelisties," "A Dialogue of Comfort Against Tribulation" (1553), in *The Complete Works of St. Thomas More*, 15 vols., ed. Louis L. Martz and Frank Manley (New Haven, CT: Yale University Press, 1963–86), 12:140–41, qtd. in Joseph Wittreich, *Shifting Contexts: Reinterpreting "Samson Agonistes"* (Pittsburgh, PA: Duquesne University Press, 2002), 209. See also *The Oxford English Dictionary Online*, 2nd ed. (Oxford: Oxford University Press, 1999), "dispense," entries 9–13, "dispense with," especially entry 10: "To deal administratively with (a law or rule, ecclesiastical or civil) so as to relax or remit its penalty or obligation in a special case; to give special exemption or relief from." Examples listed include the following quotation from Francis Bacon from *The Elements of the Common Laws of England*, published in 1636: "Necessity dispenseth with the direct letter of a statute law."

7. For an altogether different interpretation of Milton's views on this matter, see Joan S. Bennet, *Reviving Liberty: Radical Christian Humanism in Milton's Great Poems* (Cambridge, MA: Harvard University Press, 1989), 129–32. Operating on the assumption that "Milton believed God's eternal laws to bind first of all God himself" (129), Bennet also holds a low estimation of the Chorus's perspective (120), a critical assumption of recent decades (begun by John F. Huntley, "A Revaluation of the Chorus' Role in Milton's *Samson Agonistes*," *Modern Philology* 64 [1966]: 132–45) with which I generally do not concur. It seems, however, that the meaning of "dispense" mitigates against Bennet's interpretation of God's relationship to his laws.

8. The notion that God prompted Samson to take the Woman of Timna but not Dalila is supported by E. M. W. Tillyard, *Milton* (1930; repr., London: Chatto & Windus, 1949), 338; and Arnold Stein, *Heroic Knowledge: An Interpretation of "Paradise Regained" and "Samson Agonistes"* (Minneapolis: University of Minnesota Press, 1957), 172. Recently, John T. Shawcross in *The Uncertain World of "Samson Agonistes"* (Cambridge: D. S. Brewer, 2001), 7–8, attributes both marriages to Samson's "carnal desires," although he does not address Judges 14:4, which states that Samson's attraction "was of the LORD, that he sought an occasion against the Philistines." For Harold Skulsky in *Justice in the Dock: Milton's Experimental Tragedy* (Newark: University of Delaware Press, 1995), 56–57, Judges 14:4 "confirms" the view that Samson's first marriage was indeed divinely initiated. Stanley Fish, in *How Milton Works* (Cambridge, MA: Harvard University Press, 2001), rightly asks who we ought to believe concerning who *really* inspired Samson's taking of his wives. Fish notes that Samson sees, in hindsight, his first marriage as "of God" and his second as not; the Chorus sees "in both [marriages] manifestations of God's inscrutable will"; Manoa sees both marriages as "violation[s] of tribal law" (401). However, I believe that we justly can believe Samson's report and recognize that here Fish unnecessarily confuses the matter by claiming that the Chorus in 300–21 is referring, very likely, to either or both of Samson's marriages when it seems clear enough that the Chorus is referring to his first. (See Flannagan, 811; compare also the similarity between 315–17 in *Samson Agonistes* and Judges 14:4.)

9. Stein, *Heroic Knowledge*, 172.

10. An intriguing (albeit, I believe, incorrect) interpretation of the "divine impulse" that Samson feels and that leads him to his marriages to his wives is given by Albert C. Labriola in "Divine Urgency as a Motive for Conduct in *Samson Agonistes*," *Philological Quarterly* 50 (1971): 99–107. Labriola argues, using a portion of *De Doctrina Christiana* for support, that in both instances God himself was in fact prompting Samson, but that these promptings were examples of "evil temptation, in which God 'presents occasions of sin' or 'blinds the understanding' of the sinner" (100). Labriola's argument places Milton's thought in *Samson Agonistes* more in line with traditional Calvinistic understanding of God's prompting of sinful action in wicked figures to accomplish his purpose. But Labriola's argument does not address the Chorus's explicit statement that God's prompting of Samson to marry the Woman of Timna does in fact leave Samson "without taint / Of sin."

11. Merritt Y. Hughes, ed., *John Milton: Complete Poetry and Major Prose*, 583 n. 1320.

12. Anthony Low's observations on this passage, in *The Blaze of Noon: A Reading of "Samson Agonistes"* (New York: Columbia University Press, 1974) are worthy of citation: "Although Samson now knows that he need not obey the Mosaic law simply for its own sake, and recognizes how easily God can set it aside for some good cause, he also knows that he cannot dispense with the law himself, on his own judgment, and that no state has the authority to dispense him from it. He will not go to the temple because, unless he is inspired to the contrary, the law represents God's will in the matter, and God's will must come before man's" (200).

13. Hughes, ed., *John Milton: Complete Poetry and Major Prose*, 584 n.1377.

14. Leonard Mustazza, "The Verbal Plot in *Samson Agonistes*," *Milton Studies* 23 (1987): 254.

15. John M. Steadman, " 'Faithful Champion': The Theological Basis of Milton's Hero of Faith," in *Milton: Modern Essays in Criticism*, ed. Arthur E. Barker (New York: Oxford University Press, 1965), 480.

16. Robert Thomas Fallon, *Captain or Colonel: The Soldier in Milton's Life and Art* (Columbia: University of Missouri Press, 1984), 246.

17. See Matthew 4:1, Mark 1:12, and Luke 4:1. For a discussion positively comparing Samson's and the Son's leadings, see Don Cameron Allen, *The Harmonious Vision: Studies in Milton's Poetry* (Baltimore: Johns Hopkins University Press, 1954), 94. For a view that sees a significant difference between the Son's spiritual leadings and Samson's, see Wittreich, *Shifting Contexts*, 220.

18. As Skulsky observes in *Justice in the Dock*, here "the overriding purpose of the law [is] better served by going" to Dagon's temple "than by staying away" (66).

19. Fish, *How Milton Works*, 419, 418.

20. Mary Ann Radzinowicz, *Toward "Samson Agonistes": The Growth of Milton's Mind* (Princeton, NJ: Princeton University Press, 1978), 345.

21. For a skeptical discussion of Samson's relationship to the Law, see Wittreich, *Shifting Contexts*, 227–32. For a comparatively sympathetic discussion, see Shawcross, *The Uncertain World of "Samson Agonistes*," 140–42.

22. The matter of whether Samson's "rousing motions" are indeed a prompting of God's Spirit has been a matter of vigorous critical debate, and it is arguably the defining issue regarding whether Milton's Samson is read as ultimately regenerate or unregenerate. Additional studies that explicitly question these motions' divine origin

include Irene Samuel, "*Samson Agonistes* as Tragedy," in *Calm of Mind: Tercentenary Essays on "Paradise Regained" and "Samson Agonistes" in Honor of John S. Diekhoff*, ed. Joseph Anthony Wittreich Jr. (Cleveland, OH: Case Western Reserve Press, 1971), 255; Derek N. C. Wood, *"Exiled From Light": Divine Law, Morality, and Violence in "Samson Agonistes"* (Toronto: University of Toronto Press, 2001), 129–39; Wittreich, *Shifting Contexts*, 230; Abraham Stoll, "Milton Stages Cherbury: Revelation and Polytheism in *Samson Agonistes*," in *Altering Eyes: New Perspectives on "Samson Agonistes*," ed. Mark R. Kelley and Joseph Wittreich (Newark: University of Delaware Press, 2002), 281–306. Much of the most effective recent material defending the divine origin of Samson's final "motions" come from authors who discuss forthrightly the unsettling degree of violence in Samson and his God. These include David Loewenstein, *Milton and the Drama of History: Historical Vision, Iconoclasm, and the Literary Imagination* (Cambridge: Cambridge University Press, 1990), 126–51, and "The Revenge of the Saint: Radical Religion and Politics in *Samson Agonistes*," in *The Miltonic Samson*, *Milton Studies* 33 (1996): 159–80; Skulsky, *Justice in the Dock*; Michael Lieb, "The God of *Samson Agonistes*," in *The Miltonic Samson*, 3–25. Significantly, both Loewenstein and Lieb reaffirmed their positions in their March 12, 2004, addresses to The International Milton Congress at Duquesne University during a plenary session on "Milton and Terrorism." Another recent study that affirms the divine origin of the "rousing motions" is Shawcross, *The Uncertain World of "Samson Agonistes*," 132–33.

23. John Spencer Hill, *John Milton Poet, Priest and Prophet: A Study of Divine Vocation in Milton's Poetry and Prose* (London: Macmillan, 1979), 172.

24. Albert R. Cirillo, "Time, Light, and the Phoenix: The Design of *Samson Agonistes*," in *Calm of Mind*, ed. Wittreich, 219, 225. We may note that the very notion that Samson is actually praying has come under scrutiny. Stanley Fish in *How Milton Works* states that "the moment is radically indeterminate. 'As one who pray'd' says neither that he is or is not praying" (447). But to seriously entertain the notion that Samson was not praying here implies that Milton is not simply offering a variation on Samson's prayer in Judges 16:28 but even a denial of the biblical account altogether.

25. Lieb, "The God of *Samson Agonistes*," 14, 16.

26. For a perspective that argues that, because of Samson's final vengeful act of violence, the drama's "subject cannot be Samson restored to divine favor" (239), see Samuel, "*Samson Agonistes* as Tragedy," 235–57. For fuller studies questioning the premise that *Samson Agonistes* shows Samson in a divinely regenerative role, see Wittreich, *Interpreting "Samson Agonistes"* (Princeton, NJ: Princeton University Press, 1986), and *Shifting Contexts*; and Derek N. C. Wood, *"Exiled From Light."* As mentioned in note 22, aforementioned works by Lieb, Loewenstein, and Skulsky all present regenerative readings that directly address the disturbing degree of violence in Samson and his God. So too does John P. Rumrich, "Samson and the Excluded Middle," in *Altering Eyes*, ed. Kelley and Wittreich, 307–32. A regenerative reading that addresses matters of violence in a more sympathetic manner is offered by Elizabeth Oldman, "Milton, Grotius, and the Law of War: A Reading of *Paradise Regained* and *Samson Agonistes*," presented March 12, 2004, Duquesne University, at The International Milton Congress.

27. Lieb, "The God of *Samson Agonistes*," 15, 16. Lieb cites Jeremiah 22:5 and 19:13, as well as Genesis 22:16 and Hebrews 6:13, both of which Milton cites in *De Doctrina Christiana* (6:85).

28. Wittreich, *Interpreting "Samson Agonistes,"* 111–12; *Shifting Contexts*, 220–26.

29. Wittreich, *Shifting Contexts*, 224–25. The influence of this reading is seen explicitly in Karen Weiser, " 'House' and 'Home': Illuminating Redemption in *Samson Agonistes* and *Paradise Regained*," a paper presented at the 2003 Conference on John Milton, Murfreesboro, TN, October 24, 2003.

30. Skulsky, *God in the Dock*, 75, also directly links Samson's acting "of my own accord" with the God-sent "rousing motions" of line 1382.

Samson Regained:
A Play in Perpetual World Premiere

Bill Goldstein

> The year is 1955. Most members of the group are con-
> nected with the university's theater, and their repartee is
> clever. Says the aging former director: "One does not
> stage 'Samson Agonistes' for profit." Responds the new
> young hotshot director: "One does not stage 'Samson
> Agonistes' at all if he has any sense.' "

THE EXTENSIVE PERFORMANCE HISTORY OF *SAMSON AGONISTES* IN THE
twentieth century has remained largely unexamined until recently.[1]
This essay documents aspects of this largely unknown performance
history and explores the eighteenth- and nineteenth-century commentary on *Samson Agonistes* that in first imagining it as a stage-worthy dramatic poem established the critical foundation that made the long-delayed performances of Milton's supposed closet drama inevitable.[2] A
quotation from Virginia Woolf provides an illuminating context for
understanding the theatricality of *Samson Agonistes*.

Writing in her diary on November 7, 1928, Woolf talked about her
work in progress, a novel provisionally titled "The Moths" but later
published in 1931 as *The Waves*. She envisioned it, she said, as "an abstract mystical eyeless book: a playpoem."[3] Though Woolf was reflecting on her own work, her comment distills the myriad beauties of
Milton's 1671 *Samson Agonistes*—a biblical tragedy at its foundation attempting to rescue from mysticism into history two religious exemplars (paired as it was upon first publication with *Paradise Regained*) and
a work as abstracted from its form—written as a play but not, if we
read Milton's epistle literally, meant to be performed—as Woolf intended her own novel. Eyeless is itself a literal, all the more potent if

unconscious, echo of Samson's bitter self-denunciation, that "Design'd for great exploits," he is now rendered "Lower than bondslave," that once the "great Deliverer," he is now to be found "Eyeless in Gaza at the Mill with slaves" (32, 38, 40, 41).[4]

Woolf's friend Vita Sackville-West would soon write a novel, *All Passion Spent*, which took its title from the final line of Milton's poem and was published by Hogarth Press in 1932. *Eyeless in Gaza* would become the title of a popular novel by Aldous Huxley, published, with the appropriate lines from *Samson Agonistes* as an epigraph, soon after in 1936. Woolf's allusion to Samson and the titling of these two novels suggest the centrality of Milton's Samson to the literary and political currents of the 1920s and 1930s, when performances of *Samson Agonistes* became relatively frequent in England and were reviewed and discussed, in particular, in *The Times* of London.

As literary criticism would have to wait until 1928 for Woolf to coin the term appropriate to Milton's final published work, so would history have to wait until the dawn of the twentieth century for the "play-poem" *Samson Agonistes*, and not some adaptation of it, to establish a presence on the stage.

Samson Agonistes has a significant past as a play—but this is virtually hidden even from those Milton scholars most intimately familiar with it as a poem. It is also a past virtually unknown to those who today, and over the last century, have performed *Samson Agonistes* on the stage. Milton's tragedy, which seems to have been first performed in public in 1900, is a play with a performance history, but without the performance tradition, or development of stage conventions, that would be crucial for its continuing life in the theater. Its performances are novelties, or appear to be so, leaving little or no legacy of textual editing or other theatrical guidelines (or shortcuts) of use to subsequent producers and directors. The record of performances is largely buried in school or museum archives, traceable mainly through newspaper reviews of some performances and stray references to other planned or remembered performances.[5] This collection of references forms an almost anecdotal history, and is thus a kind of samizdat literature, which is perhaps appropriate given the revolutionary political content of the work. A significant number of the performances since 1900 appear to have been reviewed, most of them in *The Times* of London, though none, after a presentation at the Milton tercentenary in 1908, took place in London. Similarly, virtually none of the many performances in the United States, the first of which seems to have taken place at

Princeton University in 1921, was given in New York (no performance in America has been reviewed in a major newspaper or magazine). Except for one performance in 2003 at New York's 92nd Street Y, which featured Claire Bloom as Dalila, and a very small handful elsewhere that I have been able to trace, those that have been produced in the U.S. have been presented by schools, in churches, or at academic conferences (the production at the 92nd Street Y, itself an institution with a religious affiliation, was given a second time at Bryn Mawr College).[6] The performances of the last one hundred years have taken place in isolation and have not built upon one another. No performances of Samson or Dalila are touchstones for a generation; no filmed performances, like Olivier's Hamlet, define the part for decades. Those who stage the play are—pun intended—flying blind.

Audiences, too, whether the general public or more specialized academic or church groups, know little of what to expect in terms of staging or declamatory style, and thus how to judge the individual presentation. One hindrance has been the popularity and influence of Handel's adaptation of *Samson Agonistes*, an oratorio first presented in 1743, which has given the work continuous theatrical currency, albeit in a truncated and distorted form (with libretto by Newburgh Hamilton), but which has had a counterproductive effect on the range of dramatic interpretations seemingly available to those who have since that time performed the original work. Many performing Milton's dramatic poem appear to believe they must adhere to the ideal of the oratorio, which the American Heritage dictionary defines as "A composition for voices and orchestra, telling a sacred story without costumes, scenery, or dramatic action."[7]

John K. Hale, who organized a performance of *Samson Agonistes* at the University of Otago, New Zealand, in May 2002, directed by a local director with ten actors from an amateur company, was only dimly aware of previous productions, he reported: "I knew of a performance (acted reading), which is described in *Milton Quarterly*, I think, some early volume of it, possibly at an early International Milton Symposium or other conference. It had a professional actor playing Samson, in dark glasses,"[8] Hale wrote. That performance, part of the second annual Le Moyne Forum, took place at Le Moyne College in Syracuse, New York, in May 1979, and is probably the performance most Milton scholars are familiar with; the October 1979 *Milton Quarterly* account by William P. Shaw is the fullest we have so far had of a staging of the play. But that performance was unduly limited by an ad-

herence to the conventions of oratorio, as Shaw's detailed description
of the preparations for the May 4, 1979, performance reveals. Shaw indicates of the presentation that "The actors met on stage as four professionals used to playing off and against each other but now within the
severe constrictions of Milton's play—very little movement or physical
action, no touching one another, no choreography, just the power of
the human voice, facial expression, and a few hand gestures."[9]

Nowhere does Shaw explain why these severe constrictions are
within Milton's play, for if one is going to override or ignore Milton's
apparent proscription of performances on the stage ("to which this
work was never intended")[10] and present it at all, there is certainly
nothing within the text that proscribes any particular conception of
movement, gesture, or characterization. It is almost as if Shaw and his
cast, conscious of countermanding Milton's apparently expressed wish
that the play not be performed, attempted to eliminate from the presentation as much of the actual physical manifestations of display as
possible. Creating a performance focused mainly on the sound of the
poetry, Shaw nullified the potential theatrical impact of its being performed. As Lawrence Hyman commented to Shaw, "You all realized
that it was not 'intended' for the stage, and concentrated not on movement or on the interaction of the characters, but on the language
which gives the inner drama" (72). Shaw himself felt, he wrote, that a
"full-scale 'representational' production of *SA* might draw unnecessary
attention to the play's theatrical limitations (by modern standards)
whereas the stylization of this modified reader's theatre format may actually be closer to the kind of stylization Milton would have wanted,
similar to the kind he would have found in Greek tragedy where the
actors would have sung and/or recited their lines while doing ritualized
dancing" (72).

The legacy of this unnecessary sense of constriction underlies why
most performances have occurred at churches, or schools, or academic
conferences. Actors and directors, producers and set designers don't
come of age seeing *Samson Agonistes*, making its absence from the
boards a self-perpetuating conundrum. Too often, only those with an
educational or spiritual interest in the work undertake to present it.
While we must be grateful to those who in the twentieth century were
dedicated enough to perform the work in the first place, the entomb-
ing of *Samson Agonistes* as a spoken-word oratorio, performed with
only rudimentary movement, or by seated performers who interact
with one another not at all, as it was performed in spring 2003 at the

92nd Street Y and by a separate group, The Lark Ascending, at New York's German Evangelical Church,[11] is a dissatisfying turn away from the true potential of the "playpoem." This "oratorio effect" was on stultifying display at the 92nd Street Y performance, for example, where the actors were seated for the entire performance and also during the Lark Ascending performances, when the characters did not for the most part look at one another. That the actors had, however, to look at their scripts is understandable if dramatically unwelcome—particularly for the blind Samson—given the one-off nature of the performances, including the 1979 performance at Le Moyne.

Contrarily, at the University of Otago, the "actors' visual representation of Dalila's effect on Samson," was particularly effective: "Dalila, absorbed in her supplications to her husband, leaned towards Samson, and Samson, fearful of his wife's seductive influence of him, leaned backwards and away from her, so the space between the two actors seemed filled with the energy of the opposing ends of two magnets."[12] At the Lark Ascending performances, Dalila, unfortunately not gaily bedecked as the chorus exclaims at her entrance but clad all in black, was behind Samson, who for no discernible reason faced away from her and toward the audience.

I

Critics in the eighteenth and nineteenth centuries, including Thomas De Quincey and Samuel Coleridge, intuitively understood what *Samson Agonistes* could be. Byron and Shelley imitated *Samson Agonistes* in their own plays, and together with Blake, took inspiration from the dramatic and theatrical elements of *Samson Agonistes* in collectively charting the way for mental theater—a mental theater rather different in substance from the "inner drama" that the Le Moyne performance conjured for Lawrence Hyman and others in that audience of specialists.

Ideas of Milton's *Samson Agonistes* from the roughly 150 years before the first performance of *Samson Agonistes* in London in 1900 provide a historical context for understanding the recent and contemporary performance history of the dramatic poem. The Bishop of Atterbury, Alexander Pope, Coleridge, and De Quincey all grasped the work's theatrical possibilities.

Critical works, as well as editions of *Samson Agonistes* from the late nineteenth century regularly cite the anecdote that Bishop Atterbury wanted Alexander Pope to divide *Samson Agonistes* into acts and scenes for a performance at Westminister.[13] On June 15, 1722, Atterbury wrote to Pope, referring to a shared journey of the previous evening:

> I hope you won't forget what pass'd in the Coach about *Sampson* [sic] *Agonistes*. I shan't press you as to time: but sometime or other, I wish you would review, and polish that Piece, if upon a new Perusal of it (which I desire you to make) you think as I do, that it is written in the very Spirit of the Ancients, it deserves your care and is capable of being improv'd, with little trouble, into a perfect Model and Standard of Tragic Poetry, always allowing for its being a story taken out of the Bible which is an Objection that at this time of day, I know is not to be got over.[14]

Despite traditional interpretations of the passage, the letter to Pope does not explicitly state that a performance of the play was Atterbury's goal, and Verity, in his influential 1892 edition of *Samson Agonistes*, cites Thomas Newton's 1812 *Life* of Milton (part of his monumental edition of Milton's poetry) as his source,[15] adding, "What authority Newton had for this statement I have been unable to discover."[16] Verity, quoting the letter, notes that the date "tallies therefore with Newton's explanation that the scheme fell through because of Atterbury's commitment to the Tower, which took place in August of that year" (lxvi).

Twenty years later, in March 1742, almost a full year before Handel's *Samson* was first presented at Covent Garden on February 18, 1743, a stage version of *Samson Agonistes* came close to being produced in Dublin—the failure of which bears out the Shakespearean warning to beware the Ides of March, the date for which this Aungier Street Company production was announced (after being delayed earlier in the year). Playbills were printed, but on March 6, 1742, the Dublin *Mercury* announced that "The Company finding it impossible to get up the Tragedy of *Sampson* [sic] *Agonistes* [in] the Time propos'd, as it requires the most extraordinary Application in Study, as well as in Musical Parts, both Vocal and Instrumental, have prevail'd on the Author, to a longer day," a day which never came. This version of *Samson*, "originally by the Sublime Milton," according to an announcement advertisement, was one of the director's, Mr. Dixon's, own, and it was replaced by his "new Comedy," *Nature*, "since finished for that purpose."[17] ("Tickets delivered for *Samson Agonistes* will be taken the first night, and every other, during its Performance," the newspaper announced [307].) The presentation of Milton's *Samson* by Dixon, a painter and linen copperplate printer, was undone, it was reported, by "a dispute among the proprietors of the Theatre" arising from the fact that Dixon "introduced so great a number of characters, that every performer of consequence in the theatre, whether actor, singer, or dancer, had a part allotted to him for the illustration of the piece" (307), suggesting that the theater was crushed beneath the weight of Dixon's ambitions as surely as the theater in the play itself is crushed by Samson's strength. As Baker later wrote in *Biographia Dramatica*, "I remember to have seen in the possession of a gentleman in Dublin (one Mr. Dixon) an alteration of this poem, said by himself to be his own, so as to render it fit for the stage: and the same gentleman also shewed me a bill for the intended performance."[18]

More than a century afterward, De Quincey, in his 1852 essay "The Antigone of Sophocles," stated, "Probably the best exemplification of a Grecian tragedy that ever *will* be given to a modern reader is found in the *Samson Agonistes* of Milton," proceeding briefly to argue his point (a view shared by Goethe and Coleridge). But most interesting is his comment that "I am satisfied that Milton meant him [Samson] to *dance*."[19] The remark is a severe rebuke, or at least a genial refutation, of the philosophy of staging that has governed the performances of *Samson Agonistes* so far described and represents one Romantic's instinctual grasp of the inherent theatricality of Milton's dramatic poem.

Further to this point is the work of an anonymous critic, writing in "Have at You All: Or The Drury Lane Journal," of February 20, 1752, who reviewed a performance of Francis's *Eugenia* at Covent Garden. His incidental reference to *Samson Agonistes* is significant: "Mr. Francis has successfully avoided the common fault of buskin'd expression. . . . In this he has judiciously imitated the simplicity of the ancients, and of our Milton's '*Samson Agonistes*,' as he has also done in the contrivance of the fable, by preserving the unities."[20]

The comparison of a staged play to Milton's poem indicates that by the mid-eighteenth century *Samson Agonistes* was read, and envisioned, as a theatrical work (perhaps the critic might have even seen it performed—a performance we as yet know nothing about). It would be otherwise unusual to compare a staged play to a written work. In any case, Samuel Coleridge also frequently spoke of *Samson Agonistes* in comparison with stage works, as the record of his conversations in his *Table Talk* demonstrates. There are numerous variations there on his comment from February 17, 1833, that "The styles of Massinger's plays and the Sampson [*sic*] Agonistes are the two extremes of the arc within which the dialogue of dramatic poetry may oscillate. Shakespeare in his great plays is the midpoint." In *Samson*, Coleridge says, "colloquial language is left at the greatest distance, yet something of it is preserved, to render the dialogue probable."[21] Coleridge echoes the anonymous critic's reference to the avoidance of "buskin'd expression," and he shares the sense of that critic, writing eighty years before, that the words of *Samson Agonistes* were dialogue—and that he heard them, if only in his mind, as dialogue spoken aloud, or acted out.

Critics' intuition apart, it is surprising, simply for commercial reasons, that *Samson Agonistes* was not presented on the stage in the late eighteenth century: stage versions of Milton's *A Masque* were astoundingly popular. Hogan's history of the London stage records that the work was presented 215 times between 1776 and 1800, making *Comus*, as it was called, by far the most popular afterpiece of the period (and the only noncontemporary work among the most often given, including *Peeping Tom* and *Who's the Dupe?*).[22] "No work of Milton enjoyed more favor upon the stage than *Comus*, and perhaps no great poem was ever so buffeted by the vicissitudes of time and theatrical expediency," writes Alwin Thaler.[23] Though comedy was as always more popular than tragedy, as Hogan notes, it seems a lucrative missed opportunity that London audiences were denied a second theatrical offering from the author of one of the most frequently presented plays of the era. *A Masque*, which was written for performance at Ludlow Castle, but was itself not really intended for the "stage," was given more often than *Hamlet* and *Macbeth*, which were performed 150 times, indicating a contemporary taste for drama that might have made an inviting climate for *Samson Agonistes*.[24]

This appreciation of Milton's dramatic poem as theater[25] comes despite Milton's own comment, in his preface, that he omitted division into scenes and acts because they refer "chiefly to the stage (to which this work was never intended)." But there is ambiguity in Milton's intention. Did he mark the scenes and acts for his own purposes but omit them from the printed text? The possibility of this reading is amplified by the apparently contradictory statement that follows Milton's famous declaration. "It suffices," he adds, "if the whole drama be found not produced beyond the fifth act" (464), an instruction that raises the suspicion that though *Samson Agonistes* was never "intended" for the stage, Milton understands it may eventually be produced—or even wishes that it might be. That the statement is made in the past tense—*Samson Agonistes was* never intended for the stage—is defiantly ambiguous about the dramatic poem's future as a play, for Milton might have as easily written, to which this work *is* never intended and settled the business. Milton, the poet of prophecy, here leaves teasingly, or prophetically, open the disposition of the piece. In this spirit, Milton's epistle, his "explanation . . . in behalf of this tragedy, coming forth after the ancient manner, much different from what among us passes for best," may be read not only as a "self-defence" explaining the structure of the poem for readers, but as an elaborately cloaked stage direction, accounting for the "modelling therefore of this poem," and the "measure of verse used in the chorus" (464), of particular value for those producing the play—or those performing it at a time when "the ancient manner" is once again more highly valued on the stage than in Milton's own day.

II

The first recorded public performances of *Samson Agonistes* occurred in London in April 1900, presented by the Elizabethan Stage Society under the direction of William Poel, who would also be responsible for its next performance, at the Tercentenary of Milton's birth, in December 1908, under the auspices of the British Academy. The initial "performance, or to say better, a public recitation"[26] took place on Saturday, April 7, 1900, at the Lecture Theater of the Victoria and Albert Museum, and was repeated on Wednesday, April 11, 1900, at the St. George's Hall, in Langham Place. "Stage annals are silent concerning any public representation of 'Samson Agonistes,' " *The Athenaeum* of April 14, 1900, noted. "It would have been more stimulating had the delivery been better, but was fairly interesting and pleasurable. A work with less dramatic grip than 'Samson Agonistes' is not easily found, but the speeches, apart from their autobiographical revelations, have intensity as well as beauty."[27] The review in *The Academy* was less generous. The performance, the critic wrote,

> was an interesting experiment, but it was hardly more. . . . But "Samson" was never written to be acted, and it is therefore hardly fair to judge it as a stage play. It is a magnificent poem, but it is not a great drama. . . . The whole thing is statuesque to the point of woodenness. In a sense "Samson Agonistes" is a faithful copy of Attic tragedy, but it is Attic tragedy seen through Puritan glasses, dour and hard and doctrinaire. . . . But it would be ungrateful to reproach the Society for the

short-comings of Saturday's performance. . . . The acting was undistin-
guished, but it would have needed superb elocutionary power and great
intellectual gifts to give Milton's long rhetorical speeches with effect,
and the argumentative passages would probably have been intolerable
under any circumstances. It was therefore no disgrace for the actors to
fail in so hard a field.[28]

A notable feature of the first presentation, which the program announced was being "Acted for the first time in England,"[29] was music
(by Arnold Dolmetsch)—this despite Milton's remarks in his preface,
the *Athenaeum* critic noted, that music is "not essential to the Poem,
and therefore not material." The *Athenaeum* critic said, "It is perhaps
futile to object to the introduction of music," and though a bit discom-
fited, it seems, that the play was being done at all—indicating that Milton "expressly states" that the poem was never intended for the stage—
he nevertheless takes the producer to task for ignoring those
interpretive remarks that are in the play, quoting Milton on Manoa's
hair, which the poet describes as "white as down" (327). "In this representation Manoa's . . . locks were not only not white as down, but were
scarcely grizzled." The *Academy* critic was particularly displeased with
the music: "the choruses of Milton are not the choruses of Aeschylus.
It was perhaps a little unkind of Mr. Poel to emphasise this fact by the
music to which those choruses were set."[30]

Max Beerbohm, reviewing Poel's 1908 Milton Tercentenary production in *The Saturday Review*, described the scenery as a "tenebrous
array of purple curtains" and said that Dalila's costume included a hoop
skirt and Medici collar "while the rest of the characters wore some sort
of vaguely Phrygian attire."[31] Beerbohm was scathing: "For good
downright boredom, mingled with acute irritation, commend me to
the evening I spent last Tuesday in the theatre of Burlington House.
The Milton Tercentenary has produced a fine crop of dulness and silli-
ness, but nothing quite so silly and dull as this performance." (His article, "Agonising Samson," said the play failed because "the first, the
most important task for a producer of this play is to find an actor who
can be a passable Samson," which one Mr. Ian Maclaren evidently was
not.) Also devastating was the comment in *The Academy*: "Our representative attended the performance given . . . under the auspices of the
President and Council of the British Academy. As, however, he is unable to say anything in its favour, we think it kinder to say nothing
about it."[32]

But most remarkable was the anonymous favorable review, signed "X," in *The Athenaeum*,[33] which praised the performers ("the band of actors deserve praise for an appreciation of the poetry they had to deliver") and remarked, "This is the first time, apparently, that the play has been acted, and the result fully justifies the experiment," despite the fact that the 1900 performance had also been reviewed in the publication. One might have expected editorial memories to be slightly longer. (The review noted as well the performers'—and the audience's—stamina: "Greek plays in modern days have usually been divided into scenes. 'Samson' was acted without a break, and, in view of the fact that it contains an unusual number of long speeches, and runs to 1,758 lines—an amount never reached by Aeschylus, and surpassed only by the 'Phoenissae' and the 'Oedipus Coloneus'—it says much for the actors that at no time did the play become tedious.") In fact, a hallmark of the history of *Samson Agonistes* on the stage is that newspapers as well as producers mistakenly call performances a first-time ever event, as if, as my subtitle indicates, the play is in perpetual world premiere, where to both performers and audience, each performance seems to be a first. A note in the program for the Lark Ascending performances, which for some reason states the performance is "A World Premiere," nevertheless indicates, "We know of only four performances involving professionals in modern times," erroneously citing the 1979 performance at Le Moyne as the most recent until that time.[34]

More understandable than the mistake in *The Athenaeum*, perhaps, is the lapse in *The New York Times* of May 8, 1938, which announced that "Wells College students will introduce the dramatic poem, '*Samson Agonistes*,' by John Milton, to the American stage, when they present the poem . . . as the final feature of the annual May Day program."[35] This Nicholas Nabokov presentation, with a cast "made up principally of seniors," Constance Holladay of Minneapolis playing the part of Samson, and Sybil Bower of Wausau, Wisconsin, playing Dalila, had a text adapted by Nabokov (who wrote music for the choruses) and George Tyler, instructor in classics, according to *The Times*. It was so successful it was repeated the next month at the Wells commencement, which also merited an item in *The Times*,[36] though, alas, the production was not reviewed. ("The sets for the play have been designed in the manner of early Italian painters and will represent a series of interlocking hills which recede into the distance," *The Times* reported.)

The highly unpublicized American premiere appears actually to have taken place in 1921, at Princeton University, given by the recently founded student group, Theatre Intime. The only record of the Intime's *Samson Agonistes*, a version arranged by Professor George McLean Harper, a biographer of Wordsworth, which seems to have been presented twice, is a cast list for the performance; no other material is known to survive. The drama of Samson was apparently of continuing interest for Intime: the prior year, Intime presented *Samson and Delilah, or The Rape of the Lock*, a "grand opera" in two acts cobbled together from music by Massenet, "Assorted Hymn Writers and Others."[37]

As part of this developing performance history, it is worth noting that the first Russian edition, published in St. Petersburg in 1911, includes some stage directions added by the translator, N. A. Brianski. At the beginning of the play, for example, Brianski omits Milton's scene-setting headnote, "The Scene before the Prison in Gaza," and incorporates as a stage direction that "Samson comes out of the prison gate accompanied by a boy," adding, of course, a boy not found in Milton. Midway through Samson's opening monologue, Brianski advises that "the boy leaves."[38] Later in the play, Harapha and Manoa are told when to leave as well.

Interest in *Samson Agonistes* was revived in England during the thirties, the period when Vita Sackville-West, Aldous Huxley, and Virginia Woolf all made the allusions to it already cited. The play was in the air—or at least in the columns of the London *Times*, where those who did not venture to the schools and theaters outside of London for the sporadic productions would at least have been able to read about them. Nevil Coghill, who had worked with William Poel, presented the play in the Fellows' Garden at Exeter College, Oxford, in 1930, a production reviewed in *The Times* on May 23, 1930; the critic noted that in presenting the work Coghill was "piously disobeying Milton's injunction"[39] against performance. The reviewer commented on how rare performances of the play were: "*Samson Agonistes* appears to have been performed publicly only three times within recent memory—once in London before the War [presumably the 1908 production], once in America [perhaps the 1921 Princeton production], and once in an abridged form by the new poet laureate in his theatre on Boar's Hill." (The poet laureate, John Masefield, had a theater built next to his country home, where later in 1930, a group of five girls recited Yeats's poetry as a birthday present to the poet.)

Michael Redgrave, the son of the noted actress Margaret Scudamore (who had, like Coghill, been an associate of Poel's in her heyday), was a schoolmaster at Cranleigh School, when he directed and starred in a production of the play in March 1933, a production favorably reviewed in *The Times*, which printed a dramatic photograph of the players. A second performance, in May 1933, followed upon the favorable review attention, undoubtedly encouraging others to undertake the piece. Coghill presented the play again in 1935 as part of the Tewkesbury Festival, when it was once again reviewed in *The Times*.[40] Additional performances, at Cambridge in 1936 and at the Maddermarket Theatre, Norwich, in 1938, were also reviewed in the paper, on occasion with photographs. This veritable rush of performances in the 1930s arose, I would suggest, from the sense of a developing performance tradition that the several productions, coming on the heels of one another and seen and/or read about by an educated theater-going public centered on and around London, engendered—the disappearance of which, and our recent unfamiliarity with, has impeded continuation of that tradition in America, certainly, and also in England after World War II.

The 1930s were, of course, a time in need of Milton's *Samson Agonistes*, as England in particular attempted to understand what its role ought to be in fighting Fascism. It is no accident that the spate of performances coincided with the rise of Hitler. At a time in which the threat of war, from 1933 to 1938, became more and more palpable, England was forced, in the arts (and also in the political realm in a time of appeasement), to consider what ought to be appropriate response to tyranny and to propose potential scenarios for a subject people.

Since that prewar period, presentations by professional companies have been so rare that critics judge it simply as a historical or literary curiosity or—that frequently repeated word in newspaper accounts—an "experiment."[41]

III

Sir Michael Redgrave has been the most ardent champion of *Samson Agonistes* on the stage. His high-profile 1965 production, three decades after he presented the play at Cranleigh School, inaugurated the Yvonne Arnaud Theatre in Guildford and was performed in repertory with Turgenev's *A Month in the Country*, starring Redgrave and Ingrid Bergman, and a production of the eighteenth-century operetta *Lionel and Clarissa*, by Bickerstaff and Dibdin. The theater (and within that whirlwind Milton's dramatic poem) received an enormous amount of publicity in the British press, partly because of Bergman's return to the British stage; Redgrave's second turn as Samson, consequently, was in all likelihood the most widely reviewed of all productions (there are twenty-two reviews preserved in Redgrave's scrapbooks at the Theatre Museum of the Victoria and Albert, with notices in such varied papers as the *Surrey Advertiser & County Times*, the *Evening Standard*, and *Daily Mail*).[42] The opening of the theater was covered as national news in Britain, akin to the opening of Lincoln Center in New York, and was chronicled as such from the groundbreaking ceremony, which included an appearance by Vanessa Redgrave. *Samson Agonistes* was performed thirteen times from June 14–July 6, 1965, with two previews reserved for Arnaud founders, surely the longest run of performances ever given, and thus was seen by the largest audiences in the play's stage history. *A Month in the Country*, with Bergman and Redgrave, transferred to the West End in the fall of 1965, where it was a hit. Redgrave's *Samson Agonistes* disappeared from the boards—and Milton's play was spottily produced for the next three decades in the United States and the United Kingdom.

The Times of London only wrote about the play again in 1998, when Northern Broadsides, in Yorkshire, produced it (a version noteworthy for its imposing sets by sculptor Sir Anthony Caro, in his first work for the stage). Once every thirty-five years does not a theatrical tradition make, as Jeremy Kingston, the *Times* reviewer in 1998 noted: "Barrie Rutter's [the director and star] convincing achievement for Northern Broadsides makes me feel the work deserves an airing more often than once in a generation."[43]

Before the 1965 Arnaud production, apparently the first by a professional theater company in nearly thirty years, there were scattered performances at schools in Britain and the United States, including one at Oxford during the 1951 Festival of Britain, performed in one of the college gardens with Part 2 of Shakespeare's *Henry IV* (mentioned in a *New York Times* travel roundup of Festival of Britain events)[44] and another by Nevil Coghill, also in 1951, presented, as was becoming all too common, in church, albeit St. Martin-in-the-Fields, in central London, on May 7 of that year.[45] In 1955, the very year of the clever conversation imagined in Frederic Raphael's *The Glittering Prizes* and quoted in this essay's epigraph, the New York University Hall of Fame Players at the Gould Memorial Library presented *Samson Agonistes* in the Bronx. *The New York Times* announced that performance in advance (but did not review it afterward) as an "experimental dramatic reading of John Milton's epic poem,"[46] perhaps confusing the work with *Paradise Lost*. A brief review of a 1960 performance by students at the Harrow County School is reprinted on the Internet.

IV

Despite periodic attempts by professional theater companies to stage the playpoem as a play, and not simply to render it as a poem read aloud by many voices, De Quincey's exhortation that Samson ought to dance is a largely unfulfilled challenge. (I leave aside Martha Graham's choreography of *Samson Agonistes* to music by Robert Starer, which was presented frequently by her company after its 1962 premiere.) The Redgrave and Northern Broadsides performances have not been the progenitors of a robust theatrical tradition, and *Samson Agonistes* remains largely the property of amateurs. In America and Britain, the play continues to be a curiosity as noted previously, presented mostly at schools, churches, and academic conferences. (Even the performance Atterbury envisioned for Westminster was for Westminster School, as Verity, in his 1898 Cambridge edition points out: the "English tragedy," he wrote, "was to take the place of the ordinary Latin Comedy acted in the great dormitory at Christmas" [lxvi].)

In 1978, Frank L. Huntley of the University of Michigan prepared a version of *Samson Agonistes* for "church, synagogue, college and community theater groups"[47] that was performed in celebration of the 150th anniversary of the founding of St. Andrews Episcopal Church in Ann Arbor in May 1978,[48] and later at the Kalamazoo Cathedral. (Huntley's version, which cut the text by one-third, was never published.) *Samson Agonistes* had a run of four performances at the 1999 Fringe Festival in Minnesota, but a brief review by local critic Bryon Gunsch called the performance "disappointing," and said the "performers were strong but not quite strong enough to be heard over the chanting of Samson's personal demons or the clanking of his chains."[49]

In 1985, there were three performances at a Yale Milton conference. In the same year, there was a performance at Eastern Nazarene College, where the play was paired with *Everyman*.[50] Additionally, there is a reference in the entertainment listings of *The New York Times* of May 18, 1985,[51] to a production by The Classic Theater, under the direction of Maurice Edwards, but the performance was not reviewed. More recently, in 2001, there was another performance at a church in Chalfont, Buckinghamshire, a place with Miltonic associations.

Having attended the Lark and Y performances in New York in 2003, I can say that the stage-worthiness of the piece was not convincingly demonstrated. But the presentations were basically readings with limited movement in the LeMoyne/Shaw tradition. The chorus at the 92nd Street Y was divided for two players, the poets John Hollander and Rosanna Warren; annoyingly, John Hollander pronounced "Dalila" as "Delilah" throughout. Additionally, both Samsons, Alvin Epstein at the Y, Richard Edelman at the Lark Ascending, were older actors and slight of frame, and therefore doubly inappropriate as physical manifestations of Samson, just as Ian Maclaren was in Max Beerbohm's day. Even Michael Redgrave, in the Arnaud production, was hideously costumed as a monster of sorts, production photographs reveal. A strapping young Samson, such as the American Shakespearean actor (and movie star) Liev Schreiber could more dramatically convey Samson in his full plenitude and as only temporarily weakened. A younger Samson would not only be more believable as a representation of the Samson of Judges, but it would explain as well Dalila's attraction to him and provide a visual counterpoint to the exploits of strength and daring that Samson recounts in his soliloquies, feats not too distant in his past that in his retelling foreshadow his show of strength that will bring down the theater at the climax. A more youthful Samson might also remind an audience that his hair had been shorn—and his strength in consequence temporarily sapped—by stratagem, increasing the foreboding an imposing physique might impart to the dramatic proceedings. It is a crippling theatrical convention that a part with speeches as long as those Milton gives to Samson require a kind of desexualized King Lear in exile, which is how the Samsons of the New York productions played him.

Casting an older actor as Samson also, if unintentionally, highlights the idea that the role is an autobiographical representation of Milton himself in old age, a theme noted in the reviews of the 1900 and 1908 London performances, where the autobiographical nature of the play was seen as its chief, if not only, reason for presentation. As the *Times* critic noted of the Coghill production in 1930, "If it is ever legitimate to read into a work of art the autobiography of its creator, it must be so here. It is impossible not to feel everywhere the reminiscences of the poet's own experience, his blindness, his unhappy marriage, the defeat of his religious and civil ideas, which give his drama a peculiar depth and poignancy."[52] Poel himself, in a note in the program for the 1900 performance wrote, "As a whole, this tragedy is considered by the late

Sir A. W. Ward to surpass all Milton's work in personal interest. The scene between Samson and Dalila is no doubt reminiscent of the poet's unhappy first marriage."[53]

V

One cannot conclude from the most recent New York performances that *Samson Agonistes* does not meet the requirements of the dramatic stage. (The Lark's performance was complete and ran to three hours with intermission. The Y presented an edited version of about ninety minutes without intermission.) As long as news and reports of performances are often only rumor—there is a lengthy 2001 exchange on the Milton listserv with comments from correspondents about performances they had heard about but never seen—*Samson Agonistes* remains a play apparently without a past. Further to the point, in 1930, a few days after *The Times* reviewed the Coghill production at Exeter College, the poet laureate, John Masefield, wrote a letter to the paper that praised the performance: "To watch and hear it is to be absorbed into a world of great poetry." (Note that even Masefield did not say "great drama"; of course the piece's status as drama was as uncertain as contemporary estimates of the poem and the achievement of Milton himself in Masefield's T. S. Eliot–influenced era.) The poet laureate added, "May I mention yet one other production of the play? Mr. Stuart Vinden produced it in Birmingham some five years ago, in a way which will always be a happy memory."[54] A Tufts performance at an unknown date in the 1960s (cited on the above-mentioned listserv), this Birmingham production at some point in the mid-1920s, the incomplete but apparently authoritative reference to previous performances in the Lark Ascending program, reveal, with other performances no doubt soon to be recalled, an expanding theatrical past for *Samson Agonistes*—a performance history regularly revised and refreshed with new details but persistently and substantively elusive.

Most theater professionals, like most theatergoers, have probably never even read Milton's 1671 tragedy. How much less likely is it that they have ever seen a performance of it? *Hamlet* is not the property of Shakespeare scholars. It has a public that may never have read Shakespeare but exults in the theatricality of presentation and performance, the star turn that Shakespeare's leading roles are—and that the part of Samson could be. By documenting the performance history of *Samson Agonistes*, we restore something of the play's heritage as a stage work, and perhaps point the way to its continuing future as drama, as a theatrical rather than academic affair.

To quote Satan, "United thoughts and counsels, equal hope / And hazard in the glorious enterprise" (*Paradise Lost*, 1.88–89). As he exhorts, "Let us not slip th'occasion" (178).

Notes

1. John J. O'Connor, "TV View: Another Prize from Britain," *The New York Times*, January 15, 1978, D29, quoting an exchange between two characters in "The Glittering Prizes," in his review of the BBC miniseries by Frederic Raphael.

2. Tim Burbery's chronological list of performances, published in *Milton Quarterly* 38 (2004): 35–49, omits many of the performances I cite. Professor Burbery presented a version of his article at the same October 2003 John Milton Conference at Middle Tennessee State University, Murfreesboro, TN, at which I presented an earlier version of this essay.

3. Virginia Woolf, *The Diary of Virginia Woolf, Volume III, 1925–1930* (London: Hogarth Press, 1980), 203. All references to this volume of Woolf's *Diary* are to this edition and are cited parenthetically in the text.

4. John Milton, *Samson Agonistes*, in *The Complete Poems*, ed. John Leonard (New York: Penguin, 1998). All references to Milton's poetry are to this edition and are cited parenthetically in the text.

5. Full-text searches of *The New York Times* and *The Times* of London electronic databases, available on the Web through ProQuest Historical Newspapers, were an invaluable aid to finding not only reviews but also incidental references to performances of *Samson Agonistes*.

6. *Samson Agonistes*, directed by Robert Scanlan, was presented on Monday, April 21, 2003, as part of the Y's series, "The Poet's Theatre." I attended the performance. Samson was played by Alvin Epstein.

7. *The American Heritage Dictionary of the English Language, Third Edition* (Boston, MA: Houghton Mifflin, 1992), 1272.

8. E-mail to author from John K. Hale, June 11, 2003. The production, with actors from the Globe Theatre, was directed by Harry Love, who has directed a series of Greek tragedies for the school's Classics Department. It was the third event in a weekend programme, "Milton-Sequels: The 24 Hour Milton Event," about sequels to *Paradise Lost*. Hale said of the actors, "Two were very talented and experienced, for Samson and Dalila, and the others fitted in around those two. A chorus of three spoke together or singly, in attempts to give some authenticity or at least variety." The play was performed complete. Further details of the performance are available in "Humanities News," May 2002, a departmental newsletter published by the University of Otago.

9. William P. Shaw, "Producing *Samson Agonistes*," in *Milton Quarterly* 13 (1979): 69–79. Shaw says that he "originally intended a full-scale production, but the actors (all non-Miltonists who volunteered for the project) rejected this. In fact, after reading the play they had serious doubts about the wisdom of their decision to do the

play" (70). Shaw defines the production as a "reader's theatre format" and says that there was no attempt at representational costuming or props because that "would have raised audience expectations of a full-scale production or invited comparisons to such a production," but the fact that the performance was rehearsed for two months, involved a text edited specifically for the event and included "lighting effects, stage movement, some few stage props (chairs and platforms), and entrances and exits" (71), indicates that whatever the performers' efforts to lower the audience's expectations—and dramatic temperature—as carefully executed and acted a performance as possible under the conditions was intended. The oratorio-like reading was also a necessary one given the actors' limitations, as their comments to Shaw reveals (70). The performance, with 242 of the play's 1758 lines cut, lasted an hour and forty-five minutes, according to Shaw.

10. John Milton, "Of that sort of dramatic poem which is called tragedy," in *Complete Poems*, ed. Leonard, 464.

11. The Lark Ascending, under the direction of Nancy Bogen, gave two performances of the piece at the German Baptist Church in February 2003, which I describe later in this essay. I attended the second performance. Two further planned performances at New York University were cancelled. The performance was repeated at the North American Society for the Study of Romanticism at Fordham University's Lincoln Center campus on August 2, 2003, which I also attended, and once again at the City University of New York Graduate Center, on April 2, 2004, during the Renaissance Society of America's meeting that year in New York. The performance of the complete text of the play ran about three hours, suggesting that the play was acted more slowly in New York than at Le Moyne.

12. Nicola Learmonth, University of Otago "Humanities News," May 2002.

13. I. P. Fleming, ed., *Milton's Imitation of Greek Tragedy: "Samson Agonistes"* (London, 1876), vi, and the introduction to A. Wilson Verity, *Milton's "Samson Agonistes"* (Cambridge: Cambridge University Press, 1892). I am grateful to Professor Joseph Wittreich for these important citations. Max Beerbohm, reviewing the first performance of *Samson Agonistes* in 1900 for *The Saturday Review* repeats the information about Atterbury. Beerbohm's review is reprinted in *More Theatres, 1898–1903*, with an introduction by Rupert Hart-Davis, foreword by Louis Kronenberger (Taplinger Publishing Company, 1969), 256–59.

14. Alexander Pope, *The Correspondence of Alexander Pope*, 5 vols., ed. George Sherburn (Oxford: Clarendon, 1956), 2:124.

15. Verity cites Thomas Newton's edition of *Paradise Lost* (London, 1749), vol. 1, xliv, in *Samson Agonistes*, with introduction, notes, glossary, and indexes by A. W. Verity (Cambridge: Cambridge University Press, 1892), n. 1, lxiii.

16. Verity, lxiii.

17. *Dublin Mercury*, March 6, 1742, cited in John C. Greene and Gladys L. H. Clark, *The Dublin Stage, 1720–1745: A Calendar of Plays, Entertainments, and Afterpieces* (Bethlehem, PA: Lehigh University Press, 1993), 307.

18. David Erskine Baker, *Biographia Dramatica* (1812), 2: 240. Greene, in citing this quotation, indicates, "The playbill is now in possession of Mrs. William S. Clark" (307).

19. "The Antigone of Sophocles," reprinted in Thomas De Quincey, *The Collected Writings of Thomas de Quincey: New and Enlarged Edition*, ed. David Massen (A. and C. Black, 1889–90), 10: 372.

20. Reprinted in *The London Stage, 1660–1800: A Calendar of Plays, Entertainments & Afterpieces, Together with Casts, Box-Receipts and Contemporary Comment, Compiled from the Playbills, Newspapers and Theatrical Diaries of the Period, part 4, 1747–1776*, ed. G. W. Stone Jr. (Carbondale: Southern Illinois University Press, 1960–68), 1:294.

21. Samuel Coleridge, *Table Talk*, reprinted in *Collected Works*, vol. 14, *Table Talk II* (Princeton, NJ: Princeton University Press, 1990), 201–2.

22. Introduction in *The London Stage*, Part 5, 1776–1800, ed. C. B. Hogan, clxx.

23. Alwin Thaler, *Shakespere's Silences* (Cambridge, MA: Harvard University Press, 1929), 233. Thaler's chapter is entitled "Milton in the Theatre."

24. Several versions of *Comus* succeeded one another on the stage through the eighteenth and nineteenth century. No theater seems to have presented the play complete as Milton wrote it. Thaler notes in *Shakespeare's Silences*:

> From 1738 until the middle of the nineteenth century Comus maintained itself upon the stage not only at Drury Lane and Covent Garden, but also in Dublin, Edinburgh, Bath, and the provinces in general. Great professionals vied with noble amateurs in exploiting the popularity of the piece. Few indeed were the players of any consequence who did not have *Comus* in their repertory, and more than a few won fame in it. The versions they used are extant in a score of editions. At least four separate and distinct adaptations were made in the course of time. (233)

Thaler provides some details of the adaptations and performances (233–56). He makes the point, "Without such observation the popularity of *Comus* with the players and the public is not easily explained. With it, the stage-history of the piece becomes a significant commentary upon the taste of the times, and a striking record of the shifty devices by which the managers capitalized the fame of a great poet" (259, 233). The prevalence of these shifty devices and producers' eagerness to deploy them makes it an even greater surprise that *Samson Agonistes* was not attempted in abbreviated or altered form. *King Lear* was presented in a 1681 adaptation by Nahum Tate, with about eight hundred lines cut, according to Stanley Wells (*The History of King Lear*, Oxford Shakespeare [Oxford: Oxford University Press, 2000], 62). Tate removes "entirely the character of the Fool; he modernizes the language at many points; he adds a love story of his own composition," Wells writes. The Tate version ends happily. As Wells explains, "[A]t the time Tate wrote, Shakespeare was not thought of as an immortal classic, but as a dramatist whose works, however admirable, required adaptation to fit them for the new theatrical and social circumstances of the time, as well as to changes in taste" (63). The Tate version "supplanted Shakespeare's play in every performance given from 1681 to 1838," according to Wells (*Lear*, 63). Milton, unlike Shakespeare in the eighteenth century, may have been "an immortal classic," but that does not seem to have protected *A Masque*.

25. It is important to note an aspect of the publication history of *Samson Agonistes* in the eighteenth century. It appeared in *Bell's British Theatre, Consisting of the Most Esteemed English Plays*, vol. 34 (London, 1797). Bell printed *Comus* in volume nine of the series in 1780. The inclusion of both plays in the series establishes

them as theatrical works by presenting them in the context of performed plays. That the publication by Bell is also the first separate publication of *Samson Agonistes* without Milton's epistle underscores the attempt to position the dramatic poem as a play. The poem is also included in the one-penny series, *Dicks' Standard Plays*, Number 126, published by John Dicks, 313 Strand, London, no date given, and significantly, *Samson Agonistes* was published fairly early in the series, which includes 566 plays in the 1840s printing I own. *Comus* appears later, at number 167, and even plays by Shakespeare, such as *The Taming of the Shrew* (number 197), *All's Well That Ends Well* (number 225), and *King Henry IV, Part 2* (number 231) appear later. The series is advertised as "Free Acting Drama, for representation of which there is no legal charge," and notes, "Each Play is printed from the Original Work of the Author, without Abridgment. . . . To the Theatrical Profession, Amateurs, and others, this edition is invaluable, as full stage directions, costumes, &c., are given." Stage directions, such as "Attendant leading him," at Samson's entrance, are inserted.

26. "Notes of the Foreign Stage," *The New York Times*, April 22, 1900, 18.

27. *The Athenaeum*, No. 3781, April 14, 1900, 475.

28. *The Academy*, April 14, 1900, 317–18.

29. Reprinted in the commemorative volume, *Notes on Some of William Poel's Stage Productions* (London: A. W. Patching, 1933), n.p.

30. Yet music forms a part of many noteworthy subsequent presentations. Composer Nicholas Nabokov, a cousin of writer Vladimir Nabokov and chairman of the music department at Wells College, directed performances in 1938 with his own music—and an all-female cast—at the college, described later in this essay. Robert Simpson composed music for a brass ensemble for performances of *Samson Agonistes*, directed by Basil Ashmore (who also adapted the play), on November 11–14, 1974, as part of the Milton Tercentenary Festival, November 3–24, 1974, "At and around Chalfont, St. Giles, Buckinghamshire." In addition to Simpson's music, compositions by different composers were rotated at each of the four performances, including pieces by Mozart, Bach, Holst, and Beethoven, according to a program, which lists Yehudi Menuhin, Alec Guinness, and John Gielgud among the patrons of the production. Music composed by Dinu Ghezzo, a professor of music at New York University, was also central to The Lark Ascending performances, directed by Nancy Bogen, first presented in New York in February 2003 and repeated at the North American Society for the Study of Romanticism at Fordham in August 2003 and again at the Renaissance Society of America meeting in April 2004 (where Ghezzo's music was replaced).

31. Reprinted in Max Beerbohm, *Around Theatres*, 527.

32. *The Academy*, December 19, 1908, 580.

33. *The Athenaeum*, December 19, 1908, 799–800.

34. Program, "A Dramatic Reading of *Samson Agonistes* by John Milton," Saturday, August 2, 2003, Fordham University, which reprints the notes from the February 2003 performances.

35. "'Samson Agonistes' to Be Staged at Wells; Music is Specially Written for Milton Poem," *The New York Times*, May 8, 1938, 49. The article shared the page with several photographs of May Day queens under the title, "Queens Who Reigned Over Their Subjects for a Day."

36. "Alumnae Meet at Wells: Student Dramatic Group Gives Milton's 'Samson Agonistes,' " *The New York Times*, June 12, 1938, 38. Additionally, *The New York Times* radio listings for November 5, 1938, indicate a Sunday matinee performance of the play at 3:00, on station WBZ, though, unfortunately, no cast or information other than the title is provided: "Today on the Radio: Outstanding Events on All Stations," *The New York Times*, November 5, 1938, 14.

37. Theatre Intime collection, Seeley G. Mudd Manuscript Library, Princeton University, Box 1, folder 1 (*Samson and Delilah*); Box 1, folder 3 (John Milton's "Samson Agonistes"). I am grateful to Professor Susan Wolfson of Princeton, who provided the full name of "Professor Harper" and pointed out his expertise in Wordsworth.

38. I am grateful to Vladimir Lenskiy for translating Brianski's introduction and inserted stage directions. The introduction of stage directions into the text of *Samson Agonistes* by some British and American editors began in the nineteenth century, with the Todd edition of 1801, and is a significant development in the theatricalization of *Samson Agonistes*. I discussed the implications of this practice and views of the theatricality of *Samson Agonistes* in the eighteenth and nineteenth centuries in a paper, "Prelude to Performance: Eighteenth- and Nineteenth-Century Views of the Theatricality of *Samson Agonistes*," presented at the International Milton Congress, March 2004, Duquesne University, Pittsburgh, PA.

39. " 'Samson Agonistes' at Oxford," *The Times*, May 23, 1930, 14. The Dalila of the production was Coghill's wife, Elspeth.

40. *The Times*, July 24, 1935, 12.

41. "The Milton Tercentary: Performance of 'Samson Agonistes,' " *The Times*, December 16, 1908, 14.

42. Redgrave scrapbook, THM 31/1/1/48, Sir Michael Redgrave archive, Theatre Museum, Victoria and Albert Museum.

43. "Good Hair Day," *The Times*, September 18, 1998, reprinted at http://www.northern-broadsides.co.uk/Pages/prev_samson.htm.

44. "England, Scotland, Wales, Northern Island: A Directory of Festival Information," by Oden and Olivia Meeker, *The New York Times*, February 18, 1951, 236. The Oxford Festival of which this was a part took place July 2–16, 1951.

45. "Drama Society's Plans: Plays in Churches," *The Times*, April 21, 1951, 8.

46. "Dramatic Reading of Milton," *The New York Times*, March 23, 1955, 27.

47. Harrow School message posted on http://www.jeffreymaynard.com/Harrow_County/Samson Agonistes_The%20Critic.htm; Milton-list message posted on http://www.urich.edu/~creamer/milton/archives/2001/200109a.txt, September 3, 2001, by Paul Stanwood, University of British Columbia. Stanwood adds, "I'm sure there have been many public readings or performances of *Samson Agonistes*. In the early '60s, Michael Fixler and I took part in one at Tufts University, in the chapel there, which drew a very large and enthusiastic audience."

48. Burbery, *Milton Quarterly*, 38.

49. http://www.mact.net/reviews/samson_agonistes_review.htm.

50. http://www.enc.edu/org/Theater/archives.html. Other plays presented that season were *The Fantasticks* and *Peter Pan*.

51. "Going Out Guide," *The New York Times*, May 18, 1985, 12. An additional listing appeared in the Arts & Entertainment Guide of June 2, 1985, G18. The Cu-

bicolo company, also under the direction of Maurice Edwards, presented several plays by Joyce Carol Oates in the 1970s, according to an Oates Web site, http://www.usfca.edu/fac-staff/southerr/theatre1.html.

52. " 'Samson Agonistes' at Oxford," *The Times*, May 23, 1930, 14.

53. Poel, "Programme," n.p.

54. " 'Samson Agonistes' at Oxford," Letters to the Editor, *The Times*, May 26, 1930, 15.

Contributors

CHRISTOPHER BOND is a Major Scholar of the Inner Temple, London. He received a B.A. in Classics and English from the University of Oxford and a Ph.D. in Renaissance Studies and English from Yale University, where he wrote a dissertation on "Exemplary Heroism and Christian Redemption in the Epic Poetry of Spenser and Milton." He has published an article in *Renaissance Studies* on Lucan and Florentine political thought and one in *English Literary Renaissance* on Spenser, Langland, and the Medieval Mystery Plays.

LARA DODDS is an assistant professor of English at Mississippi State University. She has published essays on Milton and Sir Thomas Browne and is currently working on a book project about Margaret Cavendish and literary history.

CHARLES W. DURHAM, professor emeritus of English at Middle Tennessee State University, is codirector of the biennial Conference on John Milton and coeditor of six collections on John Milton, including *Arenas of Conflict: Milton and the Unfettered Mind* (SUP, 1997) and *Milton's Legacy* (SUP, 2005), winners of the Irene Samuel Memorial Award for the most distinguished collection on Milton. He has also served as president of the Milton Society of America.

JAMIE FERGUSON is visiting assistant professor of Honors and English at the University of Houston. He is currently completing a dissertation on the nexus between biblical translation and literary imitation in sixteenth-century English writing.

BILL GOLDSTEIN is completing his Ph.D. in English at the Graduate Center of the City University of New York. The founding editor of the books site of *The New York Times* on the Web, he writes for *The Times* on books and publishing and frequently moderates panel discussions for "Times Talks," the paper's public speaker series. He also reviews books for *Weekend Today* in New York on NBC. He started his career in journalism at *Publishers Weekly* and was assistant book editor at *Newsday* as well as a senior editor at Scribner. A National Arts Journalism Program fellow at the Columbia School of Journalism in 2003–4, he has taught at Hunter College and New York University. An earlier verion of his essay included here won the Renaissance Society of America's Graduate Student Essay Prize in *Renaissance and Early Modern Studies.*

BRYAN ADAMS HAMPTON is an assistant professor of English at the University of Tennessee at Chattanooga and also serves as the coordinator for the Humanities Program. His work has appeared in *Milton Studies* and *The Age of Milton* (2004), and he has an essay forthcoming in *A Poem in Ten Books: "Paradise Lost," 1667*, edited by John Shawcross and Michael Lieb.

PITT HARDING is an assistant professor of English at Jacksonville State University in Alabama. His essay, "Milton's Serpent and the Birth of Pagan Error," appeared in the winter 2007 issue of *Studies in English Literature 1500–1900.*

ELIZA FISHER LASKOWSKI currently holds a postdoctoral lectureship at the University of North Carolina at Chapel Hill, where she completed her doctoral degree in 2006. Her research interrogates the cultural multiplicity of masques, juxtaposing performance practice and the complex sociopolitical agendas deployed by a broad range of artists and patrons working in the form.

ELIZABETH LIEBERT received her doctorate from the University of Otago, New Zealand, and is currently an assistant professor at Louisiana State University in Shreveport. She has published on Milton in *Milton Quarterly* and *Parergon.*

TIM MOYLAN is completing his dissertation "Pageantry in the Age of Elizabeth I" at St. Louis University. His article, "Advising the Queen: The Theme of Good Governance in Civic Entry Pageantry" won the Agnes Strickland prize from the Queen Elizabeth I Society and will be published in a collection entitled *Elizabeth I and the "Sovereign Arts": Essays in History, Literature, and Culture.*

ANNABEL PATTERSON is Sterling Professor of English Emerita at Yale. Although she has been writing about Milton steadily for thirty years and edited the Longman's *John Milton*, she has never yet written a monograph on him. Perhaps this is because she keeps changing her mind about him.

KRISTIN PRUITT, professor emerita of English at Christian Brothers University, is the author of *Gender and the Power of Relationship: "United as one individual Soul" in "Paradise Lost."* She is codirector of the biennial Conference on John Milton and has coedited six collections on Milton, including *Arenas of Conflict: Milton and the Unfettered Mind* (SUP, 1997) and *Milton's Legacy* (SUP, 2005), winners of the Irene Samuel Memorial Award for the most distinguished collection on Milton. She is president-elect of the Milton Society of America.

WILLIAM SHULLENBERGER is the Joseph Campbell Chair in the Humanities at Sarah Lawrence College. He has published miscellaneous poetry, as well as essays in various collections and journals on Milton, Herbert, Donne, Vaughan, Crashaw, Wordsworth, Keats and Dickinson. From 1992–94, he was a Fulbright Lecturer in American Literature at Makerere University in Kampala, Uganda, and has co-authored with Bonnie Shullenberger *Africa Time: Two Scholars' Seasons in Uganda.*

GLENN SUCICH is currently serving as a visiting assistant professor at Northwestern University, where he teaches courses on Milton, Shakespeare, and the relationship between early modern magic, science, and religion.

DAVID V. URBAN is assistant professor of English at Calvin College. His articles and reviews have appeared in *ANQ, Christianity and Literature, Cithara, Leviathan, Milton Quarterly, Milton Studies, Religion and Literature, Seventeenth-Century News*, and he has chapters in several books. He is completing and editing the late Calvin Huckabay's *John Milton: An Annotated Bibliography, 1989-1999* and is working on a monograph on Milton's use of self-identification with figures from biblical parables. Along with Peter Medine and John T. Shawcross, he is coediting a collection of essays on vision and violence in Milton's writings, a festschrift for Michael Lieb.

WILLIAM WALKER teaches English Literature in the School of English at the University of New South Wales, Sydney, Australia. He has published essays on Milton in *Milton Studies, Modern Philology, History of*

Political Thought, and *Milton Quarterly*. His essay on Milton and Machiavelli in this collection is part of a forthcoming book that describes how *Paradise Lost* is related to the republican tradition of political thought.

CHRISTOPHER N. WARREN, a doctoral student in English at Merton College, Oxford, is interested in poetics, humanist methods of inquiry, and law. His dissertation in progress focuses on literary genres and the law of nations in early modern England.

ANTHONY WELCH is assistant professor of English at the University of Tennessee, Knoxville. He has published essays on Milton and his contemporaries in *Milton Studies* and *Modern Philology*, and he is working on a book about music in the late Renaissance epic.

Index

Shaw, William P., 309–10, 322, 324–25 n. 9
Shawcross, John T., 303 n. 8, 304 n. 21, 305 n. 22
Shelley, Percy Bysshe, 311
Sherwood, John C., 239 n. 15
Shirley, James, 147
Shugar, Deborah, 89 n. 38, 110 n. 11
Shullenberger, William, 15, 17–18, 85 n. 3, 86 n. 12, 244, 258 n. 4, 261 n. 30
Simpson, Robert, 327 n. 30
Singleton, R. H., 85 n. 5
Sirluck, Ernest, 47, 51
Skinner, Quentin, 183, 202 n. 1, 290 n. 9
Skulsky, Harold, 303 n. 8, 304 n. 18, 305 nn. 22 and 26, 306 n. 30
Smith, Bruce, 202–3 n. 5, 275 n. 1
Smith, George William, Jr., 89 n. 36
Smith, Henry, 260 n. 27
Smith, Joseph H., 88 n. 29
Smith, Nigel, 51, 61, 64 n. 20, 202 n. 1
Sõter, István, 259 n. 15
Spenser, Alice (countess dowager of Derby), 69
Spenser, Edmund, 19–20, 70, 83–84, 206–17, 218 n. 8, 220 n. 23, 224–26, 248–50, 254
Sprat, Thomas, 182 n. 35
Stanwood, Paul, 328 n. 47
Starer, Robert, 321
Steadman, John M., 95–96, 143 n. 21, 219 nn. 11 and 16, 221, n. 28, 298
Stein, Arnold, 303 n. 8, 304 n. 9
Sterry, Peter, 258 n. 6
Stevens, Paul, 203 n. 3
Stevenson, Kay Gilliland, 258 n. 4
Stoll, Abraham, 305 n. 22
Strong, Roy, 161 n. 12
Stulting, Claude n. Jr., 66 n. 45
Sucich, Glenn, 14–15, 24 n. 1
Summers, Joseph, 142 n. 19
Svendsen, Kester, 44, 180 n. 11

Taaffe, James, 87 n. 21
Tacitus, 184
Tanner, John S., 180 n. 14, 181 n. 16
Tasso, Torquato, 218 n. 10, 220 n. 28, 224–26, 239 nn. 9 and 15, 241 n. 40, 247–49, 260 n. 19
Tate, Nahum, 326
Tayler, Edward W., 204 n. 15
Taylor, Dick, 220 n. 23
Thaler, Alwin, 314, 326 nn. 23 and 24
Tillyard, E. M. W., 303 n. 8
Toland, John, 223
Toulmin, Stephen, 64 n. 14
Townshend, Aurelian, 71
Trismigestus, Hermes, 54
Tuck, Richard, 290 n. 9
Turgenev, Ivan, 319
Turner, Victor, 85 n. 1
Tuve, Rosamond, 73, 87 n. 14
Tyler, George, 317
Tymme, Thomas, 53, 63 n. 4

Ulreich, John C. Jr., 131, 141 n. 7
Urban, David V., 22–23, 302

van den Berg, Sara, 275
van Helden, Albert, 80 n. 12
van Helmont, Jean Baptiste, 52, 64 n. 19
Vaughan, Henry, 58
Vaughan, Thomas, 58–59
Vaughan, William, 260 n. 27
Verity, A. Wilson, 312, 321, 325 nn. 13 and 15
Vinden, Stuart, 323
Virgil, 77, 121–22, 127–28 n. 32, 186, 220 n. 28, 224, 239 n. 9
Viroli, Maurizio, 203 n. 9
Visiak, E. H., 109 n. 1
von Maltzahn, Nicholas, 203 n. 9, 240 nn. 37 and 39

Waldock, A. J. A., 127 n. 26, 142 n. 20, 144 n. 36
Walker, Julia M., 180 n. 9
Walker, William, 19, 204 n. 16
Walls, Peter, 160 n. 7, 161 n. 11
Ward, A. W., 323
Warren, Christopher, 22, 291 n. 28
Warren, Rosanna, 322
Waswo, Richard, 144 n. 37
Weber, Max, 90 n. 39

Weiser, Karen, 306 n. 29
Wells, Stanley, 326 n. 24
Whalen, Robert, 140–41 n. 4
Whitelocke, Bulstrode, 287
Wilden, Anthony, 88 n. 29
Wilkins, John, 168–71, 179 n. 6, 181 nn. 17 and 18
Williamson, George, 240 n. 36
Wilson, Thomas, 109 n. 1
Winn, James Anderson, 238 n. 3
Wittgenstein, Ludwig, 106, 111–12 n. 41
Wittreich, Joseph, 301, 303 n. 6, 304 nn. 17 and 21, 305 nn. 22 and 26, 325 n. 13
Wolfson, Susan, 328 n. 37
Wood, Derek n. C., 305 nn. 22 and 26

Wood, Thomas, 97, 98
Woodhouse, A.. S. P., 88 n. 28, 162 n. 22
Woolf, Virginia, 307–8, 318
Worden, Blair, 184, 202
Wordsworth, William, 318, 328 n. 37
Wycliffe, John, 48

Yeats, William Butler, 73
Yim, Sung-Kyun, 218 n. 6
Young, Frances, 127 n. 29

Zagorin, Perez, 202 n. 1
Zwicker, Steven, 205 n. 19, 225
Zwierlein, Anne-Julia, 204 n. 9
Zwingli, Huldrych, 132